The Social
Construction
of Europe

Edited by

Thomas Christiansen
Knud Erik Jørgensen
Antje Wiener

SAGE Publications

London • Thousand Oaks • New Delhi

First published 2001

Introduction and Chapters 2, 3, 4, 5, 6, 8, 9, 10, 11 revised and reprinted by permission from the *Journal of European Public Policy* Volume 6 Number 4 pages 528–691 © 1999 Taylor and Francis Limited.

Chapters 7 and 12 revised and reprinted by permission from the *Journal of European Public Policy* Volume 6 Number 5 pages 721–742 and 775–782 © 1999 Taylor & Francis Limited.

Bibliography and Notes for contributors revised and reprinted by permission from the *Journal of European Public Policy* Volume 6 Number 4 pages 692–720 © 1999 Taylor and Francis Limited.

SAGE Publications Ltd
6 Bonhill Street
London EC2A 4PU

SAGE Publications Inc.
2455 Teller Road
Thousand Oaks, California 91320

SAGE Publications India Pvt Ltd
32, M-Block Market
Greater Kailash - I
New Delhi 110 048

British Library Cataloguing in Publication data

A catalogue record for this book is available from the British Library

ISBN 0 7619 7264 1
ISBN 0 7619 7265 X (pbk)

Library of Congress catalog card record available

Typeset by Solidus (Bristol) Ltd, Bristol

Printed in Great Britain by The Cromwell Press, Trowbridge, Wiltshire

Contents

Preface

This book introduces a novel perspective to students of European integration. It offers a concise insight into an emerging debate about the pros and cons of applying constructivist perspectives to European integration. While constructivist thinking has been discussed in different disciplines for some time, constructivist approaches have not been introduced in a thorough and systematic way to the study of European integration. The goal of this book is to provide such a focused perspective on the relevance and applicability of constructivism, as well as to contribute to the development of constructivist theory.

Most of the chapters evolved out of a conference on 'Constructivism and Research on European Integration' sponsored by the Danish Social Science Research Council and organized at Femmøller Strand by the Department of Political Science at the University of Aarhus, Denmark. Other chapters, including those in the debating section, were written later in the process. The volume includes a thoroughly revised and updated introduction, and, demonstrating the broad reach of, as well as an urgency about the debate, an entirely new chapter by Ernst B. Haas.

We are very grateful to the conference participants and to the anonymous referees for constructive comments on the draft chapters, as well as to the research assistants, Ida Sofie Belling and Niels Hovgaard Steffensen, for their assistance during the conference and their support in preparing the outcome for publication. Most contributions first appeared as a special issue of the *Journal of European Public Policy*. Hence, we are extremely grateful for Jeremy Richardson's support as the editor of *JEPP* and for the help of the editorial team at Routledge/Taylor and Francis in facilitating this publication. Finally, we have very much enjoyed working with Lucy Robinson of Sage Publications. Her unfaltering support, enthusiasm for the project and professional management throughout the publication process have been invaluable to this final product. All three editors have been part of the European Commission's *Jean Monnet Project* which has been vital in supporting and encouraging European and transatlantic collaboration in the field of European integration studies. We would like to take this opportunity to express our gratitude to the project.

Thomas Christiansen, Knud Erik Jørgensen and Antje Wiener
Aberystwyth, Aarhus and Belfast

1

Introduction

Thomas Christiansen, Knud Erik Jørgensen and Antje Wiener

INTRODUCTION

There is a certain paradox in that what is often referred to as *la construction européenne* has not received any systematic attention from constructivist scholars.[1] As we witness the rise of a constructivist turn in the social sciences, it is odd that a process so explicitly concerned with the construction of a novel polity has largely escaped the attention of constructivist theorizing. Indeed, the European 'construction' is often regarded as so advanced that many European integration scholars have turned to comparative political analyses. In their view, the European Union (EU) has arrived at a stage where the shape and type of polity are less interesting than explaining variation in policy and politics (Caporaso 1998b: 335; Sandholtz 1998). This evolutionary approach to European integration builds on the observation that after intergovernmental beginnings 'as the EC has developed, the relevance of comparative politics has increased, along with its offshoots in policy analysis, interest group analysis and liberal theories of preference formation' (Caporaso 1998a: 7).

In proposing a constructivist approach to the study of European integration, we seek to go beyond explaining variation within a fixed setting. Instead, in this introduction we draw on recent international relations (IR) theorizing to stress the impact of 'social ontologies' and 'social institutions' on the continuing process of European integration. We argue that finding the tools to analyse the impact of intersubjectivity and social context enhances our capacity to answer why and how European integration arrived at its current stage. Undeniably, variation across policy areas is an important aspect of the integration process. However, neglecting the constructive force of the process itself, i.e. pushing intersubjective phenomena, and social context aside, lays the ground for missing out on a crucial part of the process. If the process is to be explained, it cannot be done within a research context that is closed towards interpretative tools.

How can a philosophical position like constructivism be useful for research on European integration? In contrast to other introductory accounts of constructivism, we do not begin with a presentation of what various IR scholars, comparativists or legal scholars conceive of as being a constructivist stance.[2] In our view, such approaches are likely to reduce potential options to what is already present in the social science literature. We therefore approach constructivism at a philosophical level that in principle is independent of European integration, before turning to integration studies. This enables us to locate philosophically the theoretical origins of differing approaches. In subsequent sections we move down the ladder of abstraction towards constructivist theorizing of European integration.

What makes constructivism particularly well suited for research on European integration? A significant amount of evidence suggests that, as a process, European integration has a *transformative* impact on the European state system and its constituent units. European integration itself has changed over the years, and it is reasonable to assume that in the process agents' identity and subsequently their interests and behaviour have equally changed. While this aspect of change can be theorized within constructivist perspectives, it will remain largely invisible in approaches that neglect processes of identity formation and/or assume interests to be given exogenously.

Proceeding in three steps, this introduction charts a path towards a constructivist research programme for the study of European integration. The *first step* develops a general understanding of the nature of constructivism; the *second step* highlights the debate over constructivist approaches in IR and demonstrates how they have become central to a constructivist research programme; the *third step* highlights the potential of this programme for European integration. By way of conclusion, we argue that a constructivist research programme bears enormous potential for research on European integration and ought to be actively pursued to overcome limitations in the field.

FOUNDATIONAL CO-ORDINATES OF CONSTRUCTIVISM

While definitional exercises are seldom rewarding, they can nevertheless result in heuristically fruitful pointers for subsequent moves. Since this book constitutes a plea for applying constructivist approaches in research on European integration, this introduction needs to define constructivism. John G. Ruggie, who has consistently explored processes of international institutionalization, provides a particularly succinct definition, stating that

At bottom, constructivism concerns the issue of human consciousness: the role it plays in international relations, and the implications for the logic and methods of social inquiry of taking it seriously. Constructivists hold the view that the building blocks of international reality are ideational as well as material; that ideational factors have normative as well as instrumental dimensions; that they express not only individual but also collective intentionality; and that the meaning and significance of ideational factors are not independent of time and place.

(Ruggie 1998: 33)

Ruggie thus specifies a social ontology (human consciousness and ideational factors) and argues that it has particular epistemological ramifications. It follows that at an abstract level of reasoning, constructivists merely claim that there is such a thing as socially constructed reality. To some, this may sound trivial or common-sensical, but it nevertheless runs counter to several research strategies, informed by positivism or materialist philosophies of the social sciences. In our view, the claim has five consequences.

First, it needs to be recognized that social constructivism is a specific position in the philosophy of the social sciences (Guzzini 2000; Jørgensen 2001). It therefore cannot, in itself, serve as a substantive theory of European integration. It would be a mistake to compare *theories* of European integration such as neo-functionalism to constructivism. Furthermore, this is no attempt at developing a constructivist 'grand theory' of European integration. Even though there are connections between key *aspects* of neo-functionalist theorizing – e.g. processes of *socialization*, *learning*, transfers of *loyalty*, *redefinitions* of interest and, in general, the *transformative* perspective – and *aspects* of constructivism (Wendt 1992, 1994; Ruggie 1998: 11), such overlap should not lead to a conflation between one and the other.

Second, constructivism claims that in contrast to material reality social realities exist only by human agreement (Searle 1995: 1–29; Collin 1997). This accounts for social realities being both potentially 'changeable' and 'contestable' as well as durable. Furthermore, social realities tend to have a more 'local' than 'global' presence and are confined to a limited time-frame rather than to the discrete charm of timelessness. All this is most pertinent to the study of the European integration process that has as much, if not more, to do with socially constructed realities as it has with material reality.

Third, constructivism focuses on social ontologies including such diverse phenomena as, for example, intersubjective meanings, norms, rules, institutions, routinized practices, discourse, constitutive and/or deliberative processes, symbolic politics, imagined and/or epistemic communities, communicative action, collective identity formation, and cultures of national security. Even if these features merely constitute a point of departure, they indicate a whole range of social constructivist features that are ready to be employed in research on European integration. By emphasizing that social ontologies constitute a key dimension of constructivism, we distance ourselves from a view that reduces constructivism to primarily an issue of epistemology.

Fourth, at the philosophical level we can identify two basic currents of constructivism, something that complicates matters, but also multiplies our options for developing substantive theories about European integration. The two currents are:

[i] *constructive realism*, according to which the agent has an epistemic but not an ontological influence, that is, knowledge is constructive in nature, but the existence of the world does not depend on the existence of an agent ... [and ii] *constructive idealism*, according to which the agent has both an epistemic and an ontological influence on the known world.

(Ben Ze'ev 1995: 50)[3]

Whichever option is selected evidently has profound consequences for the application of constructivism in European studies. Do Europeanists, by means of their research, effectively contribute to the 'Europe' they study? Indeed, can 'Europe' exist without the huge literature about it? For example, Kaiser (1966) in one of his early writings, was in no doubt that scholars are deeply embedded in the environment in which they work and that, in turn, they somehow contribute to the creation of the object they aim at exploring.

Fifth, constructivism is a social theory that reaches across disciplines which therefore helps us to transcend recurring inter-disciplinary squabbles, be it IR vs. comparative politics or IR vs. European studies. Furthermore, social constructivism has the potential to counter tendencies towards excessive specialization in studies of European integration, tendencies to know more and more about less and less (cf. Kratochwil 2001).

Having thus characterized some of the key defining features of constructivism, we now proceed to delineate where constructivism parts ways with different and, to a certain degree, competing perspectives.

CO-ORDINATES OF CONSTRUCTIVISM IN THE META-THEORETICAL LANDSCAPE

Constructivism can also be characterized *ex negativo*, that is, by reference to what it is not. A starting point is the current tendency to operate with the three meta-theoretical positions of constructivism, rationalism and postmodern approaches.[4] While these positions are often presented on a spectrum, we consider situating them on corners of a triangle as more adequate since, in general, scholars tend to position their work in-between the corners. See Figure 1.

Like constructivism, both rationalism and reflectivism are far from coherent and fixed positions. Both include several currents of thinking and, even if they are useful labels, they tend to have little meaning when attempts at explicit definition are being made. Indeed, when Katzenstein *et al.* (1998: 671) promise a section on rationalism, they deliver merely 'realism and liberalism after the Cold War'. Similarly, when Moravcsik (1998: 19) presents his 'rationalist framework' he avoids defining precisely the term 'rationalism'. However, employing the deductive method on texts written by self-proclaimed rationalists, it seems as if the following key words can help to nail down some substance: the deductive-nomological model of causal explanation, materialism, more or less strong rationality assumptions.

Reflectivism presents an even less coherent position, as readily admitted by most reflectivists. Some attempt to turn this into a virtue: according to Smith 'reflectivist

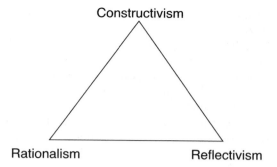

Figure 1 Major contemporary theoretical positions

accounts are united more by what they reject than by what they accept' (1997: 172). He proceeds by listing postmodernism, feminist theory, normative theory, critical theory and historical sociology. However, with the exception of postmodernism, all remaining strands of theories appear to be compatible with constructivism. To give just one example: feminist theory comes in both postmodern and constructivist versions. Therefore, Smith's negative definition appears to be the most succinct and appropriate as reflectivism has an identity as simply the mirror-image or antithesis of rationalism.

In our view, each position has certain advantages and disadvantages. For some the benefits of postmodern approaches are clearly associated with an awareness of the political. As Smith notes, reflectivism has 'much wider notions of politics', has much to say about the 'deeper questions of identity and governance', 'questions of inclusion and exclusion', the 'nature of society–state relations', the 'nature of democracy', 'gendered aspects of the new Europe', and inquiries into the construction of the 'other' (Smith, 2000). Others argue that the prime merit of postmodern approaches is that they 'change the perspective' (Diez 1996, 1998c: 139), or 'that the European Union can best be understood as a post-modern text, and perhaps as a post-modern polity' and emphasize – in a characteristically postmodern fashion – that 'trying to "identify" postmodernism is, of course, the ultimate absurd act' (Ward 1995: 15). Nevertheless, Derrida's contribution (1992) is heralded as an attempt to 'uncover the semiotics of European studies' (1995: 17). In response, constructivists would note that there is not very much reflectivist research on European integration. It therefore remains to be seen whether reflectivist approaches have as much to offer as Smith claims. We suggest that constructivism has much to contribute on precisely the issues raised by Smith. The subsequent section elaborates further on this point. Here it suffices to state that one of the major contributions of constructivist approaches is to include the impact of norms and ideas on the construction of identities and behaviour.

Based on a comparatively narrower conception of European integration, rationalists seek to *normalize* the politics of the EU (Hix 1998; Moravcsik 1998: 4–5). Their interest in phenomena that are conceivable within rationalist assumptions contributes to their theoretical strength as well as their weakness. It is a strength because a reduced number of features can be investigated in a more detailed and parsimonious fashion that is underpinned by a familiar positivist epistemology. It is a weakness because causal explanation is considered the only form of explanation, thus leaving conceptions of social ontologies, i.e. identity, community and collective intentionality, largely aside. This configuration of focal points and delineations has prompted Risse (1999) to claim that the rationalist position can easily be subsumed within a constructivist perspective which, however, can offer much more, since it is based on a deeper and broader ontology. This volume seeks to provide evidence for this claim.

THE CONSTRUCTIVIST TURN IN INTERNATIONAL RELATIONS

With a view to exploring the possible analytical capacity of constructivist thought for research in European integration, this section turns to the constructivist debate in IR.[5] The argument builds on a problem that has been identified in a seminal article by Kratochwil and Ruggie (1986) as the contradiction between epistemology and ontology immanent in regime theory. They argued that, unless the constructed nature of norms were theoretically addressed, regime analysis would continuously face the problem of contradictions between (positivist) epistemology and a social ontology (norms). As they wrote:

> [I]nternational regimes are commonly defined as social institutions around which expectations converge in international issue-areas. The emphasis on convergent expectations as the constitutive basis of regimes gives regimes an inescapable intersubjective quality. It follows that we *know* regimes by their principled and shared understandings of desirable and acceptable forms of social behaviour. Hence, the ontology of regimes rests upon a strong element of intersubjectivity. Now, consider the fact that the prevailing epistemological position in regime analysis is almost entirely positivistic in orientation. Before it does anything else, positivism posits a radical separation of subject and object. It then focuses on the 'objective' forces that move actors in their social interactions. Finally, intersubjective meaning, where it is considered at all, is inferred from behaviour. Here, then, we have the most debilitating problem of all: epistemology fundamentally contradicts ontology!
>
> (Kratochwil and Ruggie 1986: 764; emphasis in original)

Three moves in IR theorizing have contributed to what has come to be dubbed 'the constructivist turn' (Checkel 1998) in the discipline. For our argument it is important to recognize that the sequence of these three moves was not necessarily temporal, but that it is essentially analytical. The first move was epistemological, highlighting the consequences of bringing intersubjectivity into the analysis of regimes. The problem arose on the basis of a lacking match between the concept of 'regime' as entailing converging views on norms, principles, rules and decisions in a specific issue area, on the one hand, and an epistemological framework that assumed actors' interests as given, on the other. As Kratochwil and Ruggie pointed out, the perception of shared norms was conditional on an analytical framework that allowed for an understanding of intersubjectivity. It followed that a conceptual framework that was not fit to conceptualize intersubjectivity could not properly understand how regimes work. Indeed, they found that

> [I]n many . . . puzzling instances, actor *behaviour* has failed adequately to convey intersubjective *meaning*. And intersubjective meaning, in turn, seems to have had considerable influence on actor behaviour. It is precisely this factor that limits the practical utility of the otherwise fascinating insights into the collaborative potential of rational egoists which are derived from laboratory or game-theoretic situations. To put the problem in its simplest terms: in the simulated world, actors cannot communicate and engage in behaviour; they are condemned to communicate through behaviour. In the real world, the situation of course differs fundamentally.
>
> (Kratochwil and Ruggie 1986: 764–5) (emphases in original)

They saw three possible solutions to the problem. The first imaginable solution was to deny it altogether. The second solution was to adopt an intersubjective epistemology that could be claimed to be compatible with a positivist epistemology, and the third solution was to open epistemology to more interpretative strains. While, at the time, the last option appeared most valid (Kratochwil and Ruggie 1986: 765–6), the constructivist turn and the ensuing debate among IR theorists in the 1990s demonstrated that the other solutions were not entirely misplaced either. The tendency to combine a positivist position with an intersubjective ontology, which is common among sociological constructivists in particular, proves the point (Wendt 1992, 1994; Jepperson *et al.* 1996).

The second move was ontological. It suggested that, while global structure was important for state behaviour in international politics, it was not established by the principle of anarchy in itself (Waltz 1979), but resulted from social interaction among states (Wendt 1992, 1999). Subsequently, it stressed the impact of the social interaction of states on the structure of the international system. This approach has most prominently been promoted by Alexander Wendt's suggestion to apply Giddens' structuration theory as a second order or meta-theoretical approach to IR theorizing (Wendt 1987, 1991). Defining the third move, others have more recently contributed to refine sociological constructivism by elaborating on institutional aspects in particular. Setting out to design a research programme based on the importance of shared norms in international politics, they defined the third move. While some constructivists have shown the impact of national norms on international politics (Finnemore 1996a; Klotz 1995; Katzenstein 1996a), others stress the impact of international, as well as European, norms on changes in domestic politics (Forschungsgruppe Menschenrechte 1998; Risse 2000). The three moves have contributed differently to the debate over norms and communication. Indeed, IR theorists developed different ways of approaching the impact of norms on IR, and it is possible to divide constructivists roughly into two camps.

The first group of scholars combined insights from the macro-sociological institutionalism of the Stanford School around John Meyer with Giddens' structuration theory. The coupling of these two sociological approaches founded the *sociological constructivist* perspective in IR, which has promoted constructivism as a research programme (Katzenstein 1996a). The major goal of this programme is to study the impact of norms on actors' identities, interests and behaviour. While symbolic interaction constructs meaning, it is assumed that social reality does exist beyond the theorists' view. Following this logic, sociological constructivism stresses the importance of empirical work in order to approach the world out there. The constructive power of language plays a role in the context of processes of 'arguing' (Risse 1999) or 'persuasion' (Checkel in this volume).

The second group of scholars employs constructivism in a more radical way. It does not assume an objective world out there, but seeks to understand the ways in which the world is constructed. Following Wittgenstein's concept of language games, it is assumed that construction involves more than symbolic action of speechless actors. Instead, *Wittgensteinian constructivists* propose to include language as action. The assumption is that, beyond mere utterances, language constitutes meaning within specific contexts. If successfully performed, speech acts cause a particular meaning that, in turn, leads to rule-following. This version of constructivism seeks to explore the constructive power of language interrelated with rules that are inherent to a specific social context (Hollis and Smith 1990; Onuf 1989; Kratochwil 1989; Fierke 1998; Buzan *et al.* 1998; Zehfuss 2001).

ESTABLISHING THE MIDDLE GROUND

The assumption of mutually constitutive social action as a significant factor towards the construction of identity, and therefore interest and behaviour in global politics, offers a theoretical perspective that challenges both neo-realist and neo-liberal IR theorizing. As such, it is paralleled by constructivist moves in various communities of IR scholars. Debates in Britain, Scandinavia, Germany and Canada on IR all centre around developments in constructivist thinking. The point of this brief detour into IR theorizing is to stress the intersubjective nature of constructivism itself. Theorizing does not develop out of context; instead, the respective political culture and the participants of a debate bear on the way theories, or for that matter research programmes, are shaped too. To situate constructivism in the field of IR theorizing, it is helpful to refer back to the theoretical debates which in the 1970s have come to shape a triangle with the three corners of liberalism, realism and radicalism. In the 1980s, that triangle has taken the shape of a kite stretching towards the extreme of rationalism beyond its head, and towards reflectivism at its tail, respectively (Wæver 1997a: 23) (Figure 2). The difference between the two is epistemological. It is manifested in the assumption of endogenous and exogenous interest formation, a gap that offers little choice for synthesis.

Yet, with the constructivist turn in the 1990s, in between these poles a constructivist interface is emerging. According to most observers this constructivist space is located in the middle ground between rationalist (neo-realist, neo-liberal)

Rise and fall of the inter-paradigm debate

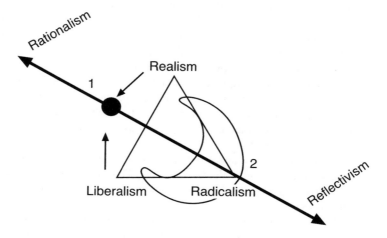

Figure 2 IR debate of the 1980s (Wæver 1997a: 23)

and reflectivist (postmodernist, post-structuralist) positions which are dia-
metrically opposed in their fundamental epistemological assumptions (Keohane
1988). Constructivist approaches are developed from positions between these
incommensurable theoretical standpoints, being able to 'talk' to each. Most
constructivists take great pains in pointing out aspects of commonality with
and distinction from both extreme poles. As Adler has pointed out, constructivists
'juxtapose constructivism with rationalism and poststructuralism' to then 'justify
its claim to the middle ground' (Adler 1997b: 321; see also Risse 1999: 1).

As this volume seeks to demonstrate, however, constructivists do not exactly
'seize' the middle ground as a territory which has become available as the result of an
interparadigm dispute. Instead, constructivist debates are part of a process that is
best identified as *establishing* the middle ground. This process expands according to
a logic of arguing over theoretical positions. Constructivists share the practice of
distancing themselves from the rationalist and the reflectivist poles, respectively.
This shared practice forms a distinguishable starting point of all constructivist
approaches. While constructivists do not share one epistemological position, they
agree on the relevance of ontology over epistemology. Consequently, constructivist
positions do not converge on a third point of the theoretical triangle, but form
a semi-circle over the two incommensurable poles of rationalist and reflectivist
approaches. This semi-circle emerges as each constructivist position is formed
by the distance to each pole on the hypotenuse. This position is defined by three
aspects. First, a preference of ontology over epistemology, second, a distinction
from the incommensurable positions of rationalism and reflectivism, yet the ability
to engage in talk with both, and, third, the variation in preferences for methodological tools (e.g. identity, speech-act, learning, persuasion, discourse). In a word,

all constructivists keep a distance from the poles, they allow for variation amongst themselves, and they share the crucial focus on ontology. The positions on the semi-circle which result from these theoretical preferences do keep with the principle of the theoretical triangle (see Figure 1), however, since their distance to the poles varies, so does their position on the semi-circle. Subsequently, the interface that ultimately results from positioning forms the shared middle ground that is established by and through constructivist debates. The Thales theorem of an angle inscribed in a semi-circle is a right angle, represents this dialogue over theoretical approaches most accurately as one of establishing the middle ground on a semi-circle in which the shared assumptions are represented by the interface of all triangles (see Figure 3).

The new theoretical space provided by this process involves any chosen point on the semi-circle above the hypotenuse. The image of this semi-circle is key to constructivist theorizing because it allows us to assess the process of *situating* positions that emerged from debates within the middle ground. Different from the practice of 'seizing' the middle ground – presumably, a strategic act of territorial conquest – the metaphor of establishing the middle ground thus reflects the process of arguing about differing positions. On the centre stage of IR in the 1990s, this process of theoretical positioning has largely focused on juxtaposing 'constructivist' thinking with the two corner positions on the hypotenuse. What this volume sees emerging not only in IR but increasingly in approaches to European integration, is the establishment of middle ground positions. While these positions differ amongst themselves, they take on the challenge of contradicting epistemological and ontological preferences which was once identified as a major challenge for IR scholars. The constructivist turn in European integration thus evolves from and offers a contribution to further development of key theoretical debates in the field of IR theory.

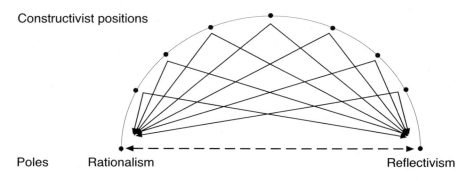

Constructivist positions

Poles   Rationalism   Reflectivism

Figure 3 Establishing the middle ground

INTEGRATION THEORY AND META-THEORY: THE CONSTRUCTION OF THE EURO-POLITY

The previous sections demonstrated the extent to which constructivist approaches have become integral to debates in philosophy and IR over the past decades. So where is the corresponding turn in the study of European integration? It is our contention that a research programme similar to that of constructivism in IR has not been developed, even though both the rationale for, and the building blocks of, such a programme are clearly there. Building on a critique of developments in integration theory, this section substantiates our argument. We demonstrate that constructivist thinking about European integration is seriously underdeveloped, despite the great potential of a number of approaches which have been, or could be, utilized in the analysis of the process.

As we noted at the outset, it is in the 1990s that integration theory has diversified beyond the traditional debate between (liberal) intergovernmentalism and supra-nationalism/neo-functionalism. Approaches inspired by IR theory have been accompanied by comparative politics approaches, on the one hand, and by the treatment of European integration as 'new governance', on the other. These developments leave integration theory as a three-cornered race, with *sui generis*, IR-based and comparative politics approaches providing different models of analysis based on very different assumptions about the nature of the integration process. Where does this leave theoretical choices? By drawing the line between rational and constructivist approaches it has been suggested that the binary debate be continued. For example, in contrast to establishing a middle ground – the way ahead proposed here – Hix stresses the differences between theoretical approaches, thus suggesting positions not *in relation to* the poles but *at* the poles (Hix 1998).

This leaves out the arguably more important question of how the *move* from interstate bargaining to politics within an emerging polity actually happened and where it might lead. Studying integration as *process* would mean concentrating research efforts at the nature of this change, asking to what extent, and in which ways, a new polity is being constituted in Europe (Christiansen 1998). In our view, it is the constructivist project of critically examining transformatory processes of integration rather than the rationalist debate between intergovernmentalists (implicitly assuming that there is no fundamental change) and comparativists (implicitly assuming that fundamental change has already occurred) which will be moving the study of European integration forward.

In order to move beyond binary oppositions and instead establish a constructivist middle ground in European integration, we introduce a number of constructivist approaches. There are three ways in which constructivism can have an impact on studies of European integration:

- development of theories
- construction of frameworks of analysis
- meta-theorizing.

First, development of middle-range theories seems to us to be a fertile and imperative strategy for constructivists. Second, constructivist theories could be combined in different frameworks of analysis in order to develop an understanding of aspects of European integration. Our image of the constructivist turn in research on integration is therefore not a 'grand' constructivist theory of European integration, but rather bringing together various – currently disparate – constructivist approaches within frameworks of analysis. Third, meta-theorizing, e.g. structuration theory, may also be included as a research strategy. It simply *opens* avenues for inquiry where several other theories *reduce* features that can be investigated. This means, for example, that a social constructivist approach would not seek to ignore or invalidate the rationalist search for 'member state preferences', but that it addresses the wider question of how state preferences have come to be socially constructed.

At the outset we argued that constructivist approaches are particularly well suited for the study of European integration. It will be clearer with a view to the study of polity formation as a major challenge for integration studies why we argue this case. Constructivism is of intrinsic value to the social sciences, but it ought to have a special place in the study of what is a process of long-term political and social change in Europe. Therefore, in studying a process in which the social ontologies are subject to change, research failing to problematize these ontologies has severe limitations. By contrast, the constructivist project explicitly raises questions about social ontologies and social institutions, directing research at the origin and reconstruction of identities, the impact of rules and norms, the role of language and of political discourses. Moving from this recognition to developing frameworks of analysis requires the identification of the elements of the process of polity formation, and an indication of the way in which constructivist approaches will help us to understand these. In doing so, we need to return to the generic aspects of constructivism established in the first part of the article.

Above we referred to various social ontologies (norms, institutions, practices, etc.) that concern constructivist research because they offer a plethora of phenomena to be researched. We argue that while these phenomena have been investigated by some scholars, they certainly have not been comprehensively studied. What has been lacking is a coherent framework that would bring together existing approaches and indicate the way ahead for further research. In the following, elements of such a framework will be outlined. In particular, we will look at theories designed to study the juridification and institutionalization of politics through rules and norms; the formation of identities and the construction of political communities; the role of language and discourse. With respect to each of these we will discuss existing work and seek to demonstrate the potential of future applications. These approaches, as elements of a constructivist research programme, facilitate the systematic study of European integration as polity formation. It is a strategy that promises to advance substantially our understanding of transformatory processes in Europe, and thus to achieve the aims we set out at the beginning.

RULES AND NORMS IN EUROPEAN GOVERNANCE

If integration is understood as 'integration through law', as it has been by the substantial community of EU law scholars for decades, rules and norms are of paramount significance. Without rules, and without compliance with these, the EU would not be what it is. Rules and norms in the EU are not just treaties, secondary legislation and the case law of the European Court of Justice (ECJ). Beyond these we also need to consider the often unwritten administrative procedures of the EU policy process, as well as a multitude of common understandings, inter-institutional agreements and informal modes of behaviour which are reproduced every day in the political and administrative practice of the EU.

The study of the formal rules and legal norms of the integration process has been the reserve of legal scholars for most of the post-war period. Despite Weiler's pioneering work on the dynamic relationship between legal and political integration – what he termed the 'dual character of supranationalism' (Weiler 1986) – it has taken integration researchers some time to recognize the significance of rule-making in the EU. During the 1980s and 1990s there has been more interest in various aspects of legal regulation among political scientists, and there is now a growing body of literature on the 'juridification' of the EU (Bulmer 1997; Joerges and Neyer 1997a). Furthermore, studying the legal dynamics of integration has been the means of seeking to transcend the traditional divide between law and political science (Shaw and More 1995; Stone and Sandholtz 1997; Armstrong and Shaw 1998).

One way of bringing the study of rules and norms into a constructivist framework of analysis is the application of Giddens' structuration theory to European integration. Apart from the influence of this approach on IR theory, it has also been utilized in the study of European law (Snyder 1990). There is a need to come to grips with the nature of the European polity as an increasingly rule-bound arena for social interaction. The EU has developed institutional features beyond the original design and certainly beyond the purpose of managing economic interdependence – it is more than simply a 'successful intergovernmental regime' (Moravcsik 1993). As it stands, the EU is not exclusively based on the original set of political and legal organs, but has come to include shared norms, commonly accepted rules and decision-making procedures. As such, it is structured through a saturated regime of legal and institutional norms – the *acquis communautaire* (Wiener 1998b; Jørgensen 1999).

The dynamic interaction between institutional norms and political action is an aspect of the integration process that has made in-roads into both institutional and policy analysis of the EU (Aspinwall and Schneider 2000). With regard to the former, there has been the introduction of a constructivist or sociological variety of neo-institutionalism. The aim of these approaches has been to locate EU institutions at the interface between structural change and political agency rather than to study their formal role (Bulmer 1994; Pierson 1996). The discussion of the rules and norms of integration leads inevitably towards a wider debate about the 'constitutionalization' of Europe which has been of growing interest both to legal scholars and political scientists (Curtin 1993; Dehousse 1995; Weiler 1995, 1997; Nentwich and Weale 1998; Shapiro and Stone 1994; Stein 1981; Christiansen and Jørgensen 1999). This process is closely linked with '"European" citizenship practice' (Wiener 1998a). The relationship between individuals and the emerging polity is an increasingly important focus of research, both in terms of the development of the institution of Union citizenship and in terms of re/constructing identities through the practices of, for example, socialization and symbolic politics.

POLITICAL COMMUNITY AND IDENTITY FORMATION IN THE EURO-POLITY

This close association between the principles of 'citizenship' and 'nationality' in the domestic context leads us to interesting questions about identity, community and inclusion/exclusion that can be addressed through constructivist research. The concept of community played a key role in classic integration theory (Haas 1964; Deutsch *et al.* 1957). Contemporary constructivist research focuses on security communities (Adler and Barnett 1996) and on political identity in Europe (Neumann 1998; Neumann and Welsh 1991; Bakke 1995; Witte 1987; Smith 1993; Laffan 1996; Howe 1995). Despite these examples, it is difficult to claim that systematic efforts are under way to explore community-building processes in European integration. Constructivist research on identity formation exists in three categories. First, research into the nature of a potential 'European identity'; second, research into the reconstruction of national identities under the influence of the integration process; and, third, informed by the results of both the above, there is the question of the plurality of national identities and cultures, and the extent to which a European political identity or political culture can be founded upon such difference. Theories of identity formation are imported to the study of European integration. These approaches – fairly close to the reflectivist end of the semi-circle in Figure 3 – deliberate the likelihood of a non-ethnic, 'postnational' community of citizens, perhaps to stand alongside Shaw's conception of postnational constitutionalism (Shaw, in this volume). The argument that a non-homogenous 'community of Europeans' will form despite the existing diversity of national identities – a claim contested by others (Howe 1997) – demonstrates both the need and the challenges for further research into questions about identity in Europe. A corollary to such questions about the construction of a political community in the EU is research into Europe's international identity (Bretherton and Vogler 1999).

The construction of this 'Europe' has depended on the parallel construction of 'others' (variously located in the East, South, West or in Europe's past) against which a separate European identity is seen as being constructed, created or invented (Neumann and Welsh 1991; Ward 1997; Schmitz and Geserick 1996). This kind of discussion leads to the question of inclusion and exclusion (Neumann 1999) and to research about diverse national and temporal interpretations of what 'Europe' actually constitutes (Wæver 1990; Holm 1993; Jachtenfuchs *et al.* 1998). Indeed, the success of the European project might well depend on the distinctive interpretation each nation can extract from the discourse on 'Europe'.

DISCOURSES, COMMUNICATIVE ACTION AND THE ROLE OF IDEAS

If the study of identity formation is accepted as a key component of constructivist research, the role of language and of discourses becomes crucial. Treaties, directives and communications from and to the European institutions speak a specific and unique language which is often only understood by a limited circle of insiders. However, with the growing importance of EU policies in the 1990s, a lobbying community has produced an entire professional class that shares the language.

Language is also important when considering *Euro-speak*: the purpose-built vocabulary of terms to describe (and shape) the reality of the EU. Asymmetrical integration, opt-outs, flexible integration, the pillar structure of the Treaty, plans for a multi-speed Europe, the 'regatta approach' to enlargement are terms and concepts which have dominated the debate about integration (Schmitter 1991). While actors clash over the meaning of specific issues, the expansion of a unique vocabulary into increasingly common knowledge contributes to bind them together and assists the construction of a European political class. Understood in this way, the development of a particular language of integration occurs both in a broad sense (the European project) and in a narrow sense (within particular policy areas). Discourse on subsidiarity is a prominent example of a discourse which gives meaning and direction to the integration process (Neunreither 1993; Hueglin 1994; Sinnott 1994; Armstrong 1993; Smith 1993; Somsen 1995; Wallace, H. 2000). Discursive constructs such as the 'democratic deficit' or the 'partnership principle' in structural policy are other examples of the abundance of targets for future discourse analysis.

In general, language is operative in every aspect of the EU, and there are numerous starting points for studies of discourse. With their focus on the impact of language in processes of deliberation, bargaining and negotiation, Habermas's theory of communicative action as well as Wittgensteinian speech-act theory offer great potential for integration studies. So far, Habermas's theory has been brought into IR theory debates (Müller 1994, 2000; Risse 1999; Linklater 1998; 119–23) and its relevance for studies of diplomacy and negotiations in the EU has been suggested (Joerges and Neyer 1997a; Lose 2001). Given the specific institutional and social context for élite communication in the EU, the significance of such approaches for a constructivist programme is evident. While rationalists often dismiss 'merely symbolic' discourse, the theory of communicative action enables analysis of these otherwise ignored dimensions of policy-making. Discourse analysis therefore constitutes a fruitful avenue for constructivist research, and indeed there are already quite a few examples of this being employed in European integration studies (Diez 1998a, 1998b; Larsen 1997; Holm 1993; Rosamond, this volume).

Another arena for the constructivist analysis of European integration is the role of ideas (Jachtenfuchs 1995) and of epistemic communities (Haas 1992), which have been important areas for constructivist research elsewhere. In a broad sense, a starting point here is the study of the 'European idea' and the way in which this idea has contributed to the creation of novel forms of governance (Morgan 1980). Given the advanced state of European integration, there have also been applications in more specialized areas of research. The field of monetary integration, in particular, has attracted research into the role of ideas (Marcussen 1998b; Verdun 1996). Such work has emphasized the significance of a common belief in neo-liberal economic and monetary policy for the consensus among decision-makers and central bankers in bringing about the economic and monetary union (EMU) project. Recognizing the importance of common beliefs and values leads to the recognition of epistemic communities as a research agenda, resting on the importance of technical knowledge and scientific expertise for European governance (Joerges 1996), and demonstrating the way in which the role of ideas, knowledge and epistemic communities can be integrated in constructivist EU policy analysis (Radaelli 1995, Surel 2000).

POSITIONING CONSTRUCTIVIST APPROACHES IN THIS VOLUME

The contributions to this volume are positioned on the semi-circle above the imaginary line linking the two extreme poles of rationalism and reflectivism (see Figures 3 and 4). While the exact positions are arguable, to be sure, the positioning that most authors have more or less explicitly carried out in the process of writing their contributions includes two steps: (1) a differentiation from the poles, and (2) the distinction of the author's own position among a larger field of constructivists.[6] The location on the semi-circle as presented in Figure 4 is none the less the product of what the editors have identified as crucial indicators for each contributor's approach. We briefly explain the respective positioning 'clockwise'.

Jeffrey Checkel proposes to include the notion of 'learning' in seeking to go beyond rationalist assumptions that interests are given. To that end, he aims to explain variation in domestic norm changes in response to changes of supranational norms. The variation depends on domestic institutional contexts, as well as actors' capabilities for learning. Checkel endorses a combination of rational choice and

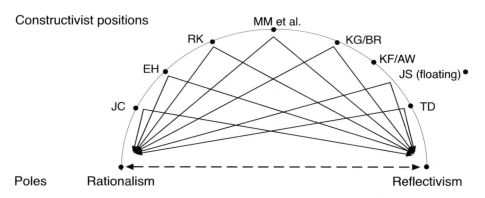

Figure 4 Positioning constructivists

sociological institutionalist approaches, arguing that sociological constructivists in particular, lack a proper account for agency. Ernst B. Haas compares the neo-functionalist theory of European integration (NF) to constructivism. He distinguishes among three different types of constructivism and subsequently makes a convincing argument for family resemblance between neofunctionalism and what he labels 'softly rational' constructivism. In reviewing these different types of constructivism, Haas expresses, however, strong reservations about the usefulness of hermeneutics and post-positivist approaches. Emphasizing the importance of shared ontological assumptions of NF with both, liberal intergovernmentalism (LI) and social constructivism he suggests, however, that NF parts company with LI regarding the epistemological dimension.

Rey Koslowski's contribution argues for a constructivist re-interpretation of the EU's development in terms of federal theory. His chapter demonstrates that, on the basis of such a re-interpretation of existing constitutional rules and norms, the federal elements of the Euro-polity can be identified. Martin Marcussen *et al.* argue that interests, identity and behaviour are dependent on norms. They seek to explain and predict behaviour based on the reconstruction of 'identity-options'. They thus agree with the structural approach of sociological constructivism. However, they add the importance of language for the emergence and change of identity-options in different national contexts. Ben Rosamond and Kenneth Glarbo are both concerned with the modes and effects of discursive constructions in EU policy-making. Rosamond analyses the construction of a discourse about 'globalization'. He argues that it is the social construct of the discourse 'globalization' rather than its material manifestations which drives the agenda of EU policy-making and structures subsequent political action. Glarbo argues for a phenomenologically informed position which is sociological interactionism. His contribution thus has a strong leaning towards interpretative frameworks of analysis including, for example, the element of intersubjective understanding. However, he also shares with the rationalists the ambition for first-order theorizing and parsimonious explanations that have been described by Jepperson *et al.* (1996) as 'normal science' procedures.

The Fierke and Wiener contribution makes a clear distinction from the exclusive reference to material capabilities of actors that is key to rationalist approaches, and suggests that instead, social capabilities play a key role in explaining decisions about the enlargement of international institutions. The reference to the ontology of speech-acts as a political practice which determines institutional identity distinguishes the approach of this chapter from the 'reflective' pole. The preference of a focus on speech-acts as part of a process of mutual constitution over, say, the process of learning, sets the specific position among constructivist positions.

The one contribution from a lawyer's perspective provides no clear positioning. While Jo Shaw avoids explicit reference to either the theoretical positions on the poles or to theorizing among constructivists, the chapter presents a normative position which is probably best characterized as constructive idealism, none the less. We therefore locate the contribution not on the circle, but 'floating by' (possibly in search for constructivist tools on offer on the circle). Finally, Thomas Diez's chapter clearly endorses an interpretative epistemology. He begins with the assumption that discourse lies at the centre of constructing the world. Thus, actors are important insofar as they contribute to the discourse by the act of 'speaking'; discourse structures subsequent action. Diez's approach is epistemologically different from sociological constructivist positions since he emphasizes understanding (as opposed to explaining).

Andrew Moravcsik's and Steve Smith's respective chapters offer critical comments on this volume's chapters from two pole positions of 'rationalism' and 'reflectivism', respectively. Smith argues that it will prove difficult for constructivism to keep an independent position. He takes issue with the middle-ground argument offered by this volume, arguing that, eventually the epistemological divide will take its toll. Moravcsik, in turn, argues that constructivists do not live up to their own aims and ambitions, that is, they do not provide sufficient proof of their hypotheses. According to Moravcsik, constructivists remain too much at the level of meta-theoretical analysis, presenting unfalsifiable claims and not delivering what is to be expected from their theoretical claims, i.e. mid-range substantive theories that would be testable *vis-à-vis* competing theories. Both these critiques are likely to provoke responses from constructivists and hence stimulate further the debate about the merits of social constructivism.

This is demonstrated by Thomas Risse and Antje Wiener who, in their response to the comments by Moravcsik and Smith, reiterate the key aspects of social constructivist approaches as a theoretical perspective on European integration. They stress constructivists' preference for ontology over epistemology, and, subsequently, the key role of intersubjectivity and the impact of the social on decision-making processes. They point out that this ontological focus ultimately allows constructivists to engage in conversations which lead to establishing the middle ground for theorizing European integration, as a process that does not exclude conversations with the poles.

CONCLUSION

In this introduction we have put forward an argument for enlarging the theoretical toolbox of European integration studies. We envisage a 'constructivist turn' in the study of European integration. While meta-theoretical thinking has an impact on theorizing, it has been largely absent from the study of European integration. Constructivism, which has an important place in the social sciences, and which has demonstrated its value in IR, has yet to make as big an impact on European integration theorizing – a state of affairs all the more surprising in view of the traditionally strong link between IR debates and integration theory.

However, this introduction has also shown that many assumptions derived from constructivism are already contained in a number of important contributions to European integration research. It suggests that more are to follow, once a constructivist research programme is established. Beyond the examples provided, the contributions of this book point in a number of promising directions. There is, in our view, tremendous potential for research based on constructivist assumptions.

Acknowledgements

An earlier version of this chapter was presented at the International Studies Association Meetings, Washington, D.C., 16–20 February 1999. Many thanks to the participants of that panel session for their useful comments. We also thank Jeff Checkel, Thomas Diez, Markus Jachtenfuchs, Martin Marcussen and Thomas Risse for concise and helpful comments on earlier drafts. Finally, we would like to acknowledge gratefully the stimulating discussions on these issues with our graduate students in Aarhus, Aberystwyth, Hannover and Belfast.

NOTES

1   For an example of literature on *la construction européenne*, see Fernando M. Dehousse, *La construction européenne* (Paris: Fernando Nathan, 1979).
2   Among eminent books and articles that introduce constructivism, we recommend Searle (1995), Taylor (1978) and Collin (1997).
3   Philosophers John Searle (1995) and Finn Collin (1997) operate with similar distinctions.
4   See, for example, Smith 1997, 2000; Ruggie 1998; Hix 1998; Risse 1999; Adler 1997b; Diez 1996, 1997. Terminology somewhat varies among theorists. Thus Smith (1997, 2000) refers to 'reflectivism' whereas Ruggie (1998: 35) prefers 'postmodern constructivism'. What Ruggie calls 'neo-utilitarianism', Smith dubs 'rationalism', and what Smith calls 'constructivism', Ruggie terms *'neo-classical'* constructivism.
5   For a discussion of recent developments in social constructivist thinking in IR see Fierke and Jørgensen (2001).
6   With the exception of the Shaw article.

Part 1

SOCIAL CONSTRUCTIVISM AND THEORIZING EUROPEAN INTEGRATION

2

Does Constructivism Subsume Neo-functionalism?

Ernst B. Haas

WHY COMPARE NEO-FUNCTIONALISM WITH CONSTRUCTIVISM?

A case can easily be made that the Neo-functionalist approach, developed in order to give the study of European regional integration a theoretical basis, is a precursor of what has lately been called Constructivism. Both clearly reject realism, neo-realism, and world systems theory as useful interpretations of international relations; but both retain affinities to other IR theories such as neo-liberal institutionalism, pluralist liberalism, decision-making schemes and peace theory. Both feature the importance of ideas and values as explanations of behaviour and accept the constraining power of multilateral institutions, even if such constraints were not anticipated by actors at the time such organizations were set up. And both see important continuities between domestic and foreign policy decision-making.

But others object to the notion that the two are ontologically part of the same family. Neo-functionalists accept a kind of soft rational choice ontology which puts them closer to utilitarianism than most constructivists consider acceptable. The core epistemologies which neo-functionalists have featured are more akin to positivism than many constructivists consider legitimate. At least, neo-functionalists do not make positivism a target for the contempt which many constructivists heap upon that view.

It is my intention to sort out these differences and similarities to show that Neo-functionalism is indeed a precursor of a certain type of Constructivism, but not of all the IR studies that currently claim that label. I justify the comparison, in part, because I wish to clarify lines of intellectual descent. But, more important, I wish to demonstrate the need to disaggregate that non-theory called Constructivism in order to rescue a 'softly rational' ontology from its fuzzy embrace. First, I summarize the ontological essence of Neo-functionalism.[1]

Neo-functionalism; Evolving Ontologies

Neo-functionalism (NF) originated as a theory explaining the process of European integration; efforts were made to extend its usefulness to the exploration and – we hoped – the successful explanation of regional integration in general.[2] Finally, I tested the power of NF in a global setting in which no supranational institutions were active and where governments remained the core actors – and found it wanting.[3]

The theory was self-consciously designed to reject the ontological assumptions of realism. NF differs from Marxist theories by holding groups to be the core actors, not classes with fixed interests. It rejects the utopianism of idealist-liberal theories because of its insistence that group interests are rationally determined and defended, and hence not subject to ready change by mere persuasion.

States, instead of struggling for power, are expected to defend their preferences and to co-operate when co-operation was deemed necessary for their realization. State preferences are seen as resulting from changing domestic competitions for influence; there is no fixed and knowable national interest. Preferences of political actors are formulated on the basis of the values held; they, in turn, determine an actor's sense of interest. In short, NF carried the assumptions of democratic pluralism over into policy formulation relating to international matters by dis-aggregating the state into its actor-components.

Regional integration was expected to occur when societal actors, in calculating their interests, decided to rely on the supranational institutions rather than their own governments to realize their demands. These institutions, in turn, would enjoy increasing authority and legitimacy as they become the sources of policies meeting the demands of societal actors. Originally, NF assumed that integration would proceed quasi-automatically as demands for additional central services intensified because the central institutions proved unable to satisfy the demands of their new clients. Thus, activities associated with sectors integrated initially would 'spill over' into neighbouring sectors not yet integrated, but now becoming the focus of demands for more integration.

The ontology is 'soft' rational choice: societal actors, in seeking to realize their value-derived interests, will choose whatever means are made available by the prevailing democratic order. If thwarted they will rethink their values, redefine their interests, and choose new means to realize them. The alleged primordial force of nationalism will be trumped by the utilitarian-instrumental human desire to better oneself in life, materially and in terms of status. It bears repeating that the ontology is *not* materialistic: values shape interests and values include many non-material elements.[4]

The rational component of the original version of NF bears a strong resemblance to what later became known as path-determination. Choices, once made, carried their own internal logic for producing specific eventual outcomes; the rationality imputed to the actors' choices initially made it likely, in later decisions, that branching points consistent with the initial objectives be chosen. This, of course, turned out to be wrong. By 1970 neo-functionalists were amending NF in significant ways.[5] The spill-over became neither automatic nor irreversible; remaining nationalisms were given their due; governments were conceded to retain the preponderance of power over supranational actors; extra-regional practices and institutions in which European countries are embedded were given more causal significance than was true in the original NF. Most important, outcomes other than a federal state were envisaged; the notion of political community was drastically reconceptualized.[6]

Neo-functionalism Revisited

Some commentators on the European *relance* after 1985 conclude that these events bear out the analysis provided by a revised NF.[7] Others do not. Thus, the treatments of European integration that rightly stress the role of law and of legal actors in advancing the process, make generous use of NF ideas in explaining the motives and tactics of litigants, and occasionally even the reasoning of judges. Sandholtz and Zysman mix NF reasoning about actor motives with emphasis on global political economy trends. Pierson's historical institutionalism is easily combined with NF, as is Hix's emphasis on the increasing relevance of concepts derived from comparative politics rather than international relations.[8]

Several authors argue that NF was the most appropriate theory for dealing with the first fifteen years of European integration, but is no longer. They maintain that the name of the game in Europe is 'multi-level governance'. Demands for the improvement of participatory democracy at all levels of governance go hand in hand with controversy over the extent of subsidiarity, or of centralization, thus allowing for a Europe *a plusieurs vitesses*, asymmetrical commitments to central institutions and more decentralized decision-making. Neither NF nor Jean Monnet imagined these refinements.[9]

However, some scholars reject NF altogether. Some do so because they consider that rational choice via formal modelling makes unnecessary the concern with variable actor preferences because it allows a stylized mode of explanation that achieves analytic independence from historical contexts. Others do so because they deny the importance of supranational institutions as shapers of new actor expectations.[10] Committed federalists, of course, persist in rejecting NF because of its instrumentalist ontology and its gradualism.[11]

Given these core characteristics of NF and its lingering appeal to current scholarship, we must now face the question of NF's fit with constructivism.

Dimensions for Comparing Neo-functionalism with Constructivism

Neo-functionalism did not originate as a theory of international relations; its purpose was more modest: to explicate and possibly predict the prospects of political integration, first in Europe, then in other regions, and eventually in a global setting. The name of the game was to understand how human collectivities can move 'beyond the nation-state'. Constructivism, on the other hand, was devised as an explicit theory of general international relations. It was not linked to the attainment of a specific outcome, such as the creation of supranational political community. Despite these different origins and purposes the two theories share many common commitments: they stress the causal role of ideas and values in defining actor preferences (interests) rather than more abstract structural features enshrined as social facts by theorists.

Why does it matter whether NF and Constructivism are close kin or not? Suppose we conclude that NF and Constructivism are not closely related and that NF should not be subsumed by a more general Constructivism. Such a finding would enable us to consider NF a manifestation of a type of theorizing that stresses the disaggregation of the state in the search for explanations, the tradition we might call 'liberal-pluralist'.[12] While getting rid of 'the state' as the core actor, this tradition retains the 'soft rationalist' assumption that actors, whatever their values and interests, act deliberately in pursuing what they want. Their preferences do not result from random choice; their selection of means are the result of calculation; they can and do change their minds, and hence their preferences and thus whatever passes for the 'national interest' of their state. NF would find a home, but not among the constructivists.

But what if NF can be reasonably subsumed by Constructivism? In that case it retains its lease on life by gaining legitimacy within the family of constructivists as the lore that explicates the phenomenon of transnational political integration. NF would become a theory of international relations by virtue of such an affiliation. It would gain generality, lose its specificity.[13]

Before we make a systematic comparison of the two we have to specify the dimensions along which the comparison is to proceed. We want to know whether the two are, or are not, compatible with respect to these ontological issues:

1   How important is the fact that the dependent variables are not the same (even though many of the independent ones are)?
2   How is the agent-structure problem resolved? If structures are held to matter, how are they defined and identified?
3   Is there a level-of-analysis problem to be resolved? If all action is presumed to take place at the level of 'the second image' there is no issue. But what if the respective theorists hold that the first and/or third images matter as well? How can explanation proceed if action takes place by using several images at the same time?
4   How are actors expected to define their preferences? How much choice do actors have in the selection of preferences?
5   Do the two use identical epistemologies? Are they both tied to positivism in some way even though some constructivists explicitly reject it?

Any putative clustering of attributes we might be tempted to undertake at this stage must await a more careful delineation of the universe of Constructivism.

Types of Constructivism

Constructivism, said its originators,

> is a constructive response to the challenge of the 'post' movements. It rejects the 'slash-and-burn' extremism of some post-modern thinkers who leave nothing behind them, nowhere to stand, nothing even for themselves to say. . . . While constructivists join the 'post' movements in calling into question much of the orthodoxy of postwar IR scholarship, they reject neither empirical research nor social science as such. Instead, constructivism maintains that the sociopolitical world is constructed by human practice, and seeks to explain how this construction takes place.[14]

This much all constructivists accept, though some persist in including the 'post' movements in their own typologies, albeit shunted off into the ghetto. However, if we look at the all-important issue of *how actors construct their own interests*, the field breaks down into three quite different schools of thought.

1   The 'systemic school' holds that interests result from the definition of actor identities, which in turn result from the role played by the actor in the global system. State-actors are constituted by that system and take their roles from their perceived positions in it. Leading theorists include Alex Wendt and David Dessler, who, however, acknowledge a kinship to such world-society British theorists as Hedley Bull, Anthony Giddens, and Barry Buzan.[15]
2   The 'norms and culture' school maintains that interests derive from the cultural matrix in which actors live. This setting generates the norms which underlie collective choices. Prominent theorists include John Meyer, Friedrich Kratochwil, Christian Reus-Smit, Keith Krause, and Bill McSweeney. Much empirical work on the role of norms in shaping foreign policy derives from this school. International society is the preferred site for finding embedded norms.[16]
3   The 'soft rationalist' school holds that actors derive their interests from their notions of political causality. Their ontological understanding of what makes 'their' world tick informs their definition of interests. This school subsumes the scholars who look for the origins of interest in consensual knowledge and in epistemic communities of knowledge-purveyors. Soft rationalists find the origin of interests within nation-states, but also look to transnational movements as stimulants. Prominent theorists include Peter Katzenstein, Emanuel Adler, Peter Haas, Harvey Starr and Andrew Farkas.[17]

Why do I prefer this typology to others now being discussed? Hollis and Smith familiarized us with the juxtaposition of two approaches to IR theorizing: 'explanatory' (realist ontology with positivist epistemology) efforts as against attempts at 'understanding' (idealist ontology with a hermeneutic epistemology). Constructivism is the prime exhibit of the hermeneutic approach. This typology is a very dangerous oversimplification because it denies constructivists the right to attempt explanatory and predictive statements. According to Hollis and Smith any effort to use ontologies other than individualistic and interest-maximizing ones precludes the use of methods associated with scientific inquiry.[18] I insist, along with most other constructivists, that we all remain part of social science. Therefore I reject the Hollis-Smith dichotomy.

So do several others. Katzenstein, Keohane and Krasner show that rationalism and constructivism are by no means always incompatible. However, their own typology muddies the waters by including postmodern approaches as one branch of constructivism even though this school strongly identifies with a hermeneutic view about epistemology. In Ruggie's view there are three kinds of constructivists distinguished by their epistemologies: postmoderns who reject social science notions of causality, neo-classicals who espouse Weberian and Durkheimian methods and concepts, and naturalistic scholars who adhere to scientific-realist notions of truth. He identifies with the second (as do I) even though he also believes in the mutual constitution of the world's norms by ideas and structures, a position closer to the naturalistic strand.[19]

Which type of Constructivism resembles Neo-functionalism?

The main characteristics of NF and our three kinds of Constructivism are summarized in Table 1.

NF's characteristics coincide exactly with those of Soft Rationalism three times and partially twice. On the other hand, they do not coincide at all, fully or in part, with systemic constructivism, and only twice, partially, with constructivists of the cultural persuasion. The verdict is clear: NF has a great deal in common with one type of Constructivism only, the type which remains unwilling to break completely with the utilitarian/individualistic tradition and insists on softening the anti-positivism of many constructivists by embracing the pragmatist epistemology.

I highlight the similarities. There is a common commitment to an ontology of 'soft' rational choice. Actors are expected to choose in terms of their perceived interests and to select means deemed most appropriate for realizing them. They are also expected to change interests if and when the ideas and values inspiring them undergo alteration, and to substitute new means for old ones found to be unsatisfactory by the actor. In short, a utilitarian-individualistic mode of behaviour prevails. Actors are conceptualized as actual or potential learners.[20] Ideas inspire interests, or, as Weber might have put it, ideas *are* interests.[21]

Moreover, the epistemologies of the two schools are strikingly similar. They rely heavily on ideal types. These, in turn, are derived mostly by following the mode of abductive reasoning made familiar by American Pragmatist philosophers, though hardly invented by them. NF and Soft-Rationalist Constructivism both reject positivism as the sole road to knowledge and are willing to settle for the less determinative and less magisterial guidance of the pragmatist philosophy of science.[22]

The overlap is not quite as clean when it comes to the issue of whether agency

Table 1 Comparison of Neo-functionalism and three Constructivisms

Dimension	Neo-functionalism (Haas version)	Organizational	Systemic	Norms/Culture
Dependent Variable	political community	international cooperation; value/policy integration	types of anarchy and conflict	international co-operation; value integration
Agent/structure Relationship	agency favoured	structuration; agency favoured	structuration; structure favoured	structuration; agency favoured
Chief Actors	organizations (all kinds)	organizations (all kinds)	states	states, groups governments
Level of analysis	second image favoured	third/second image tension; 2nd image favoured	third image favoured	unresolved tension between 3rd and 2nd images
Derivation of actor interests	values and material needs	collectively-defined values and needs	socially-defined identities	values, norms
Dominant Epistemology	Weberian; pragmatism	Weberian; Durkheimian; pragmatism	scientific realism; Durkheimian	unclear

trumps structure as a source of actor conduct. The emphasis on ideas as sources of perceived interest dictates a concern with actor motivations on the part of both schools, in contrast to the other Constructivisms. Still, my NF has no concern with structures at all, while that of Lindberg and Scheingold, for example, does. 'Soft Rational' Constructivism shows more concern about a possible interaction between structural and agential forces than NF did. Nevertheless, the concern with motivation as cause makes the two quite similar, though a constructivist who takes the principle of structuration very seriously, without bending it in favour of agency as most of us do, will part company with NF.

Similarly, commitment to the second image is not a totally consensual matter. NF is concerned with regional institutions, national governments, political parties and interest groups as the main actors. Soft Rational Choice constructivists are also, especially with these actors as they impinge on multilateral institutions and negotiations. But some are more attuned to the constraining influence of international structures – or what counts as such – than was true of my NF, though not of others'.

The main lack of congruence derives from a disagreement about the dependent variable. There is an overlap, but not an identity of concerns. Constructivists can easily subsume NF's concern with political community formation under their more general interest in processes of international co-operation and value integration. But NF cannot expand its focus to the much more general interest of Constructivism in processes of value integration that are not expected to end up as political communities, either at the regional or the global level. Perhaps I was right after all when, in 1975, I argued that NF was obsolescent because actor concerns have shifted to global interdependence and our disciplinary interests should follow them.

ACKNOWLEDGEMENTS

I am indebted to Chris Ansell, Anne Clunan, Peter Haas, Andrew Moravcsik, and John Ruggie for thoughtful comments. Remaining lapses are my own fault.

NOTES

1   Since I am generally considered the originator of the neo-functionalism used in studies of the European Union (and its predecessors) I shall immodestly use my own work for setting the scene. It should be conceded immediately that *The Uniting of Europe* is quite unaware of epistemological conundra and necessities. Early NF did not profess an articulate epistemology though the work was generally cast in the Weberian tradition. By the time *Beyond the Nation State* was done the epistemological commitment had become Parsonian, a stance abandoned in subsequent work, which came to embrace the pluralism of Charles Peirce.

2   See Haas and Schmitter 1964: 705–37; Haas 1967: 315–43. We predicted successfully that regional integration would not readily occur in Latin America and I explained in the preface of *The Uniting of Europe*, 1958 edition, that the explanatory power of NF in leading to new political communities was confined to settings characterized by industrialized economies, full political mobilization via strong interest groups and political parties, leadership by elites competing for political dominance under rules of

constitutional democracy accepted by leaders and followers. My reasons for limiting the explanatory scope of NF are illustrated with reference to most regional integration efforts then ongoing in 'The Study of Regional Integration', see Lindberg and Scheingold, eds. 1971: 3–44.

3   See Haas 1964. The dependent variable in this study was 'system transformation', not 'political community' as in the original NF. See Saeter (1998) for an extended effort to use this version of NF, found by me not to predict successful integration on the global level, for an amended theory explaining European integration better than the original NF.

4   I chose the label 'soft rational choice' because most of the criteria for the 'hard' variety cannot be satisfied. Green and Shapiro hold that 'rational choice theorists generally agree on an instrumental conception of individual rationality, by reference to which people are thought to *maximize their expected utilities in formally predictable ways. . . . The further assumption [is] that rationality is homogeneous across individuals under study.*' (1994: 16). The italicized words and phrases refer to ideas I do not share. The maximization of utilities is a microeconomic concept of intentionality which excludes values as shapers of preferences; revised NF makes possible retrodiction, not formal prediction of anything more specific than a range of possible outcomes; and if values differ, preferences will vary non-homogeneously. Jon Elster's (1986: 16) criteria of rational choice that considers intentions as causes also cannot be met. It requires optimality in the search for solutions to choices, absence of contradictions among beliefs, and the action must be 'caused' by desires and beliefs, not merely rationalized, and the results must have been intended by the agent. Agents in NF are assumed to be acting consistent with their desires and beliefs but cannot meet the other conditions of rationality.

5   These changes are discussed in the preface to the 1968 edition of *The Uniting of Europe* and in the contributions by Leon Lindberg, Stuart Scheingold, Donald Puchala, Joseph Nye, and Philippe Schmitter in Lindberg and Scheingold (1971). They were elaborated further by Lindberg and Scheingold in *Europe's Would-Be Polity* (1970). For the final self-critique and revision of NF, see Haas (1975).

6   See especially Haas, 1995: 72–85, 1971: 26–32.

7   For such arguments see Ojanen, 1998: ch. 3; Michelmann and Soldatos, eds, 1994, especially the essay by David Mutimer; Keohane and Hoffmann, eds, 1991.

8   The arguments of these authors are all represented in Nelsen and Stubb, eds, 1998.

9   Schmitter 2000: 2–3; Hooghe and Marks 1999; Marks, Hooghe and Blank 1998: 273–93.

10 Examples of rational choice argumentation include Cederman 1997; Mattli 1999. Andrew Moravcsik is the most visible defender of the continuing centrality of the nation-state and its government as the engine of integration. See Moravcsik 1998. For a scathing critique of this argument see Saeter 1998: 49–61. I find it at least very curious that despite great similarities in both ontological and epistemological assumptions my treatment and Moravcsik's turn out to be so different. His ontology is described in detail as 'liberalism' in Moravcsik 1997. Its core assumptions are identical with those of NF and seem quite compatible with certain kinds of constructivism as well. It is difficult to understand why he makes such extraordinary efforts to distinguish his work from these sources.

11 For examples see the pieces by Pinder and Tsoukalis 1998: 189–94, 335–44.

12 The theorists in question all straddle the undemarcated boundary between comparative politics and international relations. All derive from the tradition of political sociology. The most prominent are Gabriel Almond and S.M. Lipset. Others of note include Ole Holsti, I.M. Destler, Louis Kriesberg, James Rosenau and the last work of Quincy Wright.

13 At this point a warning is in order: constructivism is not just any theoretical position which is opposed to 'rational individualism', as some commentators seem to think. First of all, not all constructivists consider 'rational individualism' to be the cardinal sin to be

purged from scholarship. Moreover, to consider anything that questions positions derived from, or consistent with, utilitarianism to be part of Constructivism is to bias the content of that approach unforgivably. For an example of such extreme work, see Jørgensen, ed. 1997. See also the same author's *The Social Construction of the Acquis Communautaire* 1999 for the misuse of an alleged constructivist approach merely to demonstrate that the Commission's claim for a sacrosanct Acquis is socially constructed rather than intrinsic. If Constructivism is to be taken seriously it must be more than a tool for debunking one's antagonists.

14 Kubalkova, Onuf, Kowert 1998: 20. See also pp. 42–3 for material on the historical lineage of this mode of thought.

15 John Ruggie fits into this group as well as the 'soft rationalist' one. He sees socially constructed identities as central, as well as structuration processes mutually constituting agents and structures. However, his notion of structuration favours agents over structures more than does Wendt's. Ruggie does not consider constructivism a theory of IR, but a guide to theorizing. See Ruggie 1998: 32ff.

16 Nicholas Onuf does not consider constructivism a theory of IR, but a general social theory using 'rules' as its core primitives. Structuration is central in his conceptualization. He differs from Wendt and Dessler, with whom he has otherwise much in common, by rejecting scientific realism as the appropriate epistemology. See Onuf 1989: chapter 3, and Gould 1998.

17 I have adapted the typology of constructivism developed by Keith Darden for characterizing all approaches; he subscribes to this school, though he would dispute my choice of label because he calls his approach 'pragmatism'. See Darden 2000: 37–51. I also find very appropriate for present purposes the typology developed by Anne L. Clunan, 'Constructing Concepts of Identity' (2000).

18 Hollis and Smith 1990. The authors find both modes valid for different purposes. Alexander Wendt uses a typology which is consistent with the core distinction drawn by Hollis and Smith. He sees three kinds of constructivism: postmodern, feminist and modernist. The 'modernist' variety includes all the remaining constructivists. All are challenging materialist-individualistic ontologies, even though many of the 'modernists' (including Wendt) are committed to rationalistic epistemologies. See Wendt 1999: ch. 1, especially pp. 29–32. Emanuel Adler's typology also respects the distinction between explaining and understanding. Feminist, postmodern scholars and explicitly antipositivist writers represent the latter. Only 'modernists' retain their faith in the explanatory power of social science. It is unclear to me how this category relates to the rejection of individualistic-utilitarian calculation some constructivists consider the essence of their creed. Adler makes nothing of the fact that all constructivists reject the belief in rank-ordered preferences, but that many accept a softer view of rational choice as guiding actor behaviour and therefore justifying a rational research strategy by scholars. See Adler 1997: 319–52.

19 Katzenstein, Keohane, and Krasner (1998: 680–2). Ruggie (1998: 32ff).

20 The theory of collective learning I developed to work out the changes state policy undergoes in response to interactions within international organizations and negotiations is a direct outgrowth of the ontology of 'soft' rational choice first elaborated in the context of NF and subsequently applied in the larger context of international co-operation which constructivists like to study. See Haas 1980: 357–405, 1990.

21 Those who follow Durkheim's lead rather than Weber's would argue that ideas take shape as norms guiding actors, and thus become social facts. Some constructivists advance such an ontology, notably Ruggie and Adler, while also adhering to the soft rational choice argument about interests I associate uniquely with 'my' school of Constructivism. Hence my concept of 'actor dissatisfaction' – essentially a utilitarian notion – is not congruent with theirs.

22 For descriptions of pragmatism as I use the term here (see Toulmin 1972; Laudan 1996).

3
Understanding the European Union as a Federal Polity
Rey Koslowski

INTRODUCTION

Understanding the European polity in federal terms seems rather matter-of-fact to many European policy-makers and scholars.[1] In contrast, when most American international relations (IR) scholars who were steeped in neo-realism and neo-liberal institutionalism see the word 'federal', in reference to Europe, they are more apt to think of constitutional plans and prescriptive theories that have little to do with 'reality'. Owing to the dominance of the conceptual construct of international anarchy/domestic hierarchy and the state-centric theories it produces, IR scholars have generally tended to view federalism as a feature of domestic political organ-ization in the prototypical mode of the modern federal state or as domestic political structures that are projected to the international level as blueprints for regional or global political integration – a hypothetical federal state writ large. From the stand-point of mainstream IR theory, federalism belongs to the field of comparative politics or to the musings of idealists who dream of European or world federations.

This chapter attempts to bridge the gap between IR scholars who tend to dismiss federalism and the scholars and policy-makers who understand the EU in federal terms, consider mainstream IR useless for their subject matter and, therefore, ignore potentially useful new approaches generated within the IR community. By refocusing attention on political practices, intersubjective meanings and informal norms, constructivism may be useful to developing federal theories for EU analysis that avoid the stereotypical legalism and idealistic prescription that have given feder-alism such a bad reputation among IR scholars. Conversely, the detailed analysis of the EU which has been generated by using federalism as a theoretical prism (see, e.g., Capelletti *et al.* 1986; *Publius* 1996), the rich theoretical tradition of federalism (e.g. Althusius, Puffendorf, Kant, Tocqueville, Proudhon) and policy-makers' common understanding of the EU in federal terms provide IR scholars with a productive medium for gaining a better understanding of the emerging European polity.

With the Treaty on European Union, member states have entered into a type of political relationship that is neither domestic nor international, as conventionally defined. A classic way of understanding a political relationship that is neither domestic nor international is to think of it in federal terms. If one eschews state-centric thinking in one's constructivist approach and focuses instead on the political practices of all actors at all levels without presupposing the primacy of states, it enables analysis of the institutionalization of relationships in political life throughout world politics. By focusing on federal principles evident in political practice, one can utilize federal theory to analyse political relationships to better understand what politics are rather than what they should be, and to better understand what the European Union (EU) is rather than what it may never become.

The argument proceeds in five steps. First, I briefly review EU federalism within IR theory and develop a constructivist approach to using federal theory by drawing on the work of Friedrich Kratochwil and Nicholas Onuf. It is important to note that I propose a constructivist approach to federal theory rather than a constructivist theory of European integration. Just as one may use a rational choice approach to federal theory, which is then used to explain European integration (e.g. McKay 1996), one may employ a constructivist approach to demonstrate the utility of federal theory in comprehending the nature of the European polity as well as understanding the dynamics of its politics. The balance of the chapter demonstrates how political practices have become institutionalized into federal political relationships that cumulatively are beyond those of a confederation but are not those of a federal state. The second section reviews the deliberate efforts to form a federation by treaty that have in many ways fallen short of the mark but have, with the ratification of the Maastricht Treaty, established a form of federal polity. In contrast to intentional federation by treaty, federal political relationships have often inadvertently emerged though legal judgments that have, in effect, 'constitutionalized' the Treaty; through the member states' collective representation of the EU to those states which wish to join it; and through the enforcement of the rights of nationals of one EU member state who are in another. In the third section, I utilize constructivist insights to appraise the import of such federal political relationships by examining the act of bargaining among member states. In this way, the bastion of intergovernmentalism, the Council, can also be understood in federal terms. In the fourth section, I contend that the Union citizenship established by the Maastricht Treaty differentiates the EU from traditional forms of confederation. Although Union citizenship is constitutive of a federal polity, it is unlike any previous federations. The fifth section examines EU member states' adoption of the federal principle of subsidiarity and considers the opening of political spaces that this engenders. The added value of taking an explicitly non-state centric constructivist approach is made clear through an examination of subnational politics and regionalism in the EU as well as forms of consociationalism operating at the European level.

1. A CONSTRUCTIVIST APPROACH TO EU FEDERALISM

IR scholars have spilled enough ink about EU federalism;[2] the problem lies in the way in which it has been conceived. Rooted in *foedus*, the Latin word for treaty, federalism is an idea, a theory, an ideology, etc., that manifests itself in several political forms, the most important being federation[3] and confederation.[4] Modern federalism has three primary sources: the English-speaking world, particularly the experience of the United States; confederations that existed in the Germanic world; and federal unions that had been postulated in Utopian peace plans for Europe beginning in the fifteenth century (Elazar 1993: 190). Federalism played an important role in the early development of IR theory as a foil for realism in the development of the international anarchy/domestic hierarchy dichotomy which both realists and many federalists subsequently incorporated into their worldviews.[5] When one adheres to the hierarchy/anarchy conceptual dichotomy, the EU can be conceived of either as a confederation of sovereign states or a federal state itself.[6] The problem is that Europe has moved beyond confederation, yet the EU may *never* become a federal state, à la 'United States of Europe'.

Unfortunately, many discussions of European federalism in the IR literature are teleological. Discussions of federalism either implicitly or explicitly advocated the transformation of Europe into a federal state[7] or they focused on the process of integration leading to that goal,[8] or they framed their arguments in speculative terms about the unlikeliness of ever achieving a federal state. For example, Stanley Hoffmann argued:

> The success of Federalism would be a tribute to the durability of the nation-state; its failure so far is due to the irrelevance of the model. . . . Between the cooperation of existing nations and the breaking in of a new one there is no stable middle ground. A federation that succeeds becomes a nation; one that fails leads to secession; half-way attempts like supranational functionalism must either snowball or roll back.[9]

In that EU federalism may never fit the prototypical United States model of the federal state, this teleological approach obfuscates analysis of the present.

Given the teleology of many federal theories, federalists often tend to denigrate what European integration has already occurred, often in explicit or implicit comparisons with existing federal states or a postulated European federation (Spinelli 1966; Wistrich 1991). Given the teleology of the realist vision of integration, realists have not taken European unification seriously because, according to their theories, it is not likely to happen. Therefore, realists have had relatively little to say about the contemporary EU (see Ruggie 1993: 140). Because many federalists remained fixated on federation as the only stable political form beyond existing states, their theories, ironically, were often just as state-centric in approach as the realists they criticized.

In contrast to those who could only conceive of EU federalism in a state-centric teleology, several alternative non-state centric conceptualizations of federalism have been offered including a network image drawing on the tradition of 'integral federalism' (Diez 1997), concepts of 'multi-level governance' which are not always explicitly federal in their terminology but often describe similar relationships (Scharpf 1994; Marks *et al.* 1996; Kohler-Koch 1996; Christiansen 1997), and more nuanced forms of federal theory that may begin with constitutional and legal analysis of federations and confederations but also examine a wide variety of federal arrangements and relationships between these two forms that may be more useful in understanding the EU (e.g. Elazar 1987; Sbragia 1992; Forsyth 1996; Schmitter 1996).

Indeed, one can see a certain progression in the definition of federalism in the classic works of federal theory from state-centric approaches that focused on descriptions of institutions, to a focus on political action, to a broader comparative understanding of federalism that more accurately captured the variety of federal polities beyond the American case. Reflecting his view that federalism originated with the US Constitution, Kenneth Wheare defined federal government as 'an association of states so organized that powers are divided between a general government which in certain matters . . . is independent of the governments of the associated states, and, in their turn, independent of the general government' (Wheare 1964: 2). In contrast, William Riker defined federalism in terms of a constitutionalized bargain: 'A constitution is federal if (1) two levels of government rule the same land and people, (2) each level has at least one area of action in which it is autonomous, and (3) there is some guarantee (even though merely a statement in the constitution) of the autonomy of each government in its own sphere' (Riker 1964: 11). Daniel Elazar defines federalism as 'the combination of self-rule and shared rule through constitutionalized powersharing on a non-centralized basis' (Elazar 1993: 190). He notes:

> [U]sing the federal principle does not necessarily mean establishing a federal system in the conventional sense of a modern federal state. The essence of federalism is not to be found in a particular set of institutions but in the institutionalization of particular relationships among the participants in political life. Consequently, federalism is a phenomenon that provides many options for the organization of political authority and power; as long as the proper relations can be developed that are consistent with federal principles.
>
> (Elazar 1987: 12)

Just as anarchy does not mean anomie,[10] and norms may constitute and regulate practices within an anarchical international society (Bull 1977), federal norms may govern political relations in the absence of a federal state. As opposed to decentralization of power within a unitary polity, in which power is delegated to constituent units, non-centralization means that power was not delegated and cannot be arbitrarily recentralized. That is, federalism denotes constitutionalized powersharing among mutually recognized political actors at several levels of governance. Moreover, as the British experience amply demonstrates, constitutionalization need not be the single act of a constitutional convention, but rather the gradual accumulation of rules and customary practices that become accepted as legitimate over time. Constitutionalized powersharing is not limited to the internal governance of states, given that over the past decades the Treaty of Rome has effectively become more than an international treaty through the introduction of legal principles and practices that have made it, together with the corpus of its successor treaties, a *de facto* constitution of the European polity (see Stein 1981; Capelletti *et al.* 1986; Weiler 1991; Mancini 1991).

If one takes a constructivist approach to this concept of federalism and focuses on the political practices of all actors at all levels without presupposing the primacy of states currently recognized by international law, it enables analysis of the institutionalization of relationships in political life throughout world politics. A constructivist approach is useful because constructivist analysis is not wedded to existing legal structures or political organizations as 'units of analysis' *per se*.[11] Rather, constructivism focuses on human practice, the contingency of practice and the mutual relationship between agents and structures.[12] The international system is understood as an interacting collection of human-made institutions including, but not limited to, states.[13] Institutions are settled or routinized practices constituted and regulated by norms (Kratochwil 1989) and states are institutions whose existence is dependent upon the reproduction of particular sets of practices. Not simply a legal entity or a formal organization, the state is an ensemble of normatively constituted practices by which a group of individuals forms a special type of political association. This political association is perpetuated by reproduction of the constituent individuals into successive generations of members of the association as well as by the reproduction of the normatively constituted practices of individual members.

If one understands both the international system and the state in terms of the reproduction of a given set of normatively constituted practices, international and domestic politics are not hermetically sealed within their own spheres. Political practice is divided into these two realms only by the historical fact of the state as the institutional set-up that organizes politics. Therefore, politics need not be understood as only taking place either inside or outside of the state and world politics encompasses more than the interactions between states.

Nicholas Onuf provides a very useful description of the complex institutional landscape of non-state centric constructivist approaches:

> Society is a complex institution within which many other related institutions are to be found. Agents are likely to act as if their society's boundaries are clear and accepted, even if observers, including agents, have a hard time specifying those boundaries to anyone's satisfaction. States are societies that have exceptionally clear boundaries as well as highly developed institutions for conducting relations with other states. The complex institution within which states function as relatively self-contained societies is itself a society. Within international society, states function as primary agents including many other, more or less self-contained institutions. . . . The sum total of institutions and their relations add up to a society of staggering complexity and constant change.
>
> (Onuf 1998b)

In this institutional complexity, present-day states are historical artefacts of the clear delineation of boundaries, the mutual recognition of those boundaries through the conventions of sovereignty and the institutionalization of boundaries through the reproduction of practices of societies constituted as sovereign states whose diplomacy and foreign policy actions are recognized as legitimate 'statecraft' by the rest of international society.

The institutional complexity that Onuf attempts to come to grips with is not historically unique. Indeed, Johannes Althusius provided one of the first attempts to conceive politics between polities with less than clear boundaries and this attempt became recognized as the first theory of federalism (Friedrich 1968: 12). In contrast to Bodin's (1967) absolutist conception of sovereignty (which Bodin developed as a description of, and prescription for, the differentiation of the kingdoms of France, Spain and England as monarchical states emerging from feudalism), Althusius drew on Aristotle to conceptualize the empirical reality of the Germanic polities like the Swiss Confederation and the Holy Roman Empire and to develop a very different concept of politics. 'Politics is the art of associating (*consociandi*) men for the purpose of establishing, cultivating and conserving social life among them . . . [those who live together] pledge themselves each to the other, by explicit or tacit agreement, to mutual communication of whatever is useful and necessary for the harmonious exercise of social life' (Althusius 1964: 12). Althusius viewed each polity as an association composed of smaller associations – the family made up of individuals, the city made up of families, the empire made up of cities and principalities. Hence, Althusius held that all government is in some sense mixed government and sovereignty ultimately rests with 'the people'. By conceiving the empire as a universal association made up of component associations, Althusius offered a conception of politics focusing on the inherently social nature of political life at all levels.

The 'societal federalism' of Althusius (Hüglin 1991) shares a common Aristotelian root with the 'constructivist core' proposition that humans produce and reproduce their world through the practices of social interaction (Kratochwil 1996). Federalism is also linked to constructivism, in the work of Nicholas Onuf, who, after introducing the concept of constructivism into the field of IR, went on to co-author a history of conceptual change that focused on the innovative American federal union and its impact on IR theory via a shift from natural law doctrine to the positive law of states (Onuf and Onuf 1993). In a sense, a constructivist approach to federalism can be viewed in terms of a return to a very old tradition of political thought trained on another instantiation of political organization that is not solely centred on the state – the emerging European polity with its criss-crossing fuzzy boundaries between overlapping functional and territorial authorities. A non-state centric constructivst approach to federal theory leads to the recognition that federal political relations may govern practices that cross state boundaries, such as 'transgovernmental relations' between localities and regions of several states (Keohane and Nye 1974; Duchacek 1986). Similarly, federal political relationships may exist across functional rather than territorial lines, i.e. the art of association need not be limited to states or their territorial components. As the above quote should make clear, Althusius is a common wellspring of modern federalism and consociationalism (*Publius* 1986).

While such a constructivist approach may be promising, there is a risk of a very different kind of constructivism in any attempt at understanding European integration in federal terms. While the societal federalism of Althusius is rooted in the political practice of confederations and federations in German-speaking parts of the world (Gierke 1990; Renzsch 1989), the strain of federal theory most closely associated with contemporary European integration is that of Utopian peace plans for Europe which became increasingly popular during the Enlightenment (Heater 1992). Given a certain theoretical inertia that tends to pull EU federalism in the direction of this tradition of thinking, EU federalism is all too susceptible to examining 'what is' in terms of what 'should be'. If the constructivist approach to IR is mated to the criticism of existing institutions for prescriptive purposes, there is a danger that 'constructivism' becomes a form of what Friedrich Hayek dubbed 'rational constructivism'.

Traced back to Descartes, rational constructivism contends that 'since man has himself created the institutions of society and civilization, he must be able to alter them at will so as to satisfy his desires and wishes' (Hayek 1979: 3). Hayek contrasted rational constructivism with the critique of rationalism offered by David Hume who developed 'a theory of phenomena that are "the result of human action but not of human design"' (Hayek 1979: 5). Although the 'world is of our making', all the institutions that comprise it are not necessarily intentional, a point that Onuf also makes with reference to Hayek (Onuf 1998a: 142). As Hayek noted, social institutions need not have been rationally constructed for the purposes they now serve. Similarly, the institutions of world politics, and more specifically the European polity, may be the outcome of *unintended* as well as intended practices that have become routinized over time.

In sum, a non-state centric constructivist approach to federal theory expands the ambit of European federalism beyond the internal constitutional analysis of states or the projection of a federal state to the European level to include additional dimensions of supranational, subnational, transgovernmental and consociational relations in a broad spectrum of federal arrangements between federation and confederation. It shifts the focus away from prescriptive planning of a federal European future to the analysis of past and present political and legal practices that have become routinized into institutions characterized by federal relationships. All too often the narrative of European integration has been cast in terms of federal failure – of political integration that is non-federal. Although intentional efforts to build a European federation have indeed failed to produce a federal state, it does not mean that political practices that lacked a federal intent have not produced a federal outcome, regardless of what it may be called. That is, even European institutions that are not explicitly named as such (owing to the terminological phobias of particular member states) may still be quite federal in all but name.

2. INTENTIONAL FEDERALISM BY TREATY AND THE UNINTENTIONAL CONSTITUTIONALIZATION OF POWER-SHARING

A European federation was the explicit goal of several of the Community's founders[14] and such federal aspirations were reflected in the mixture of institutions established by the Treaty of Rome. Although the Commission, Court of Justice, and Parliament were components of an incipient institutional framework of a future federation, the European Economic Community (EEC) embodied both supranational and intergovernmental institutions whose future development remained open to bargaining among the member states within the intergovernmental Council of Ministers. Nevertheless, given that EC member states entered into a permanent alliance by integrating the economic resources required to make war upon each other, according to William Wallace, they had, in a sense, entered into a *de facto*, if not *de jure*, confederation (Wallace 1982).

The European Parliament's 1984 *Resolution on the Draft Treaty establishing a European Union* brought federal objectives once again to the fore of European integration (Burgess 1989). Although the Draft Treaty did not contain the word 'federal', its provisions incorporated federal principles and strengthened supranational institutions, and thereby put federalism squarely on to the Community's reform agenda. The subsequent intergovernmental conference (IGC), however, aimed at the lowest common denominator of agreement among member states (Moravcsik 1991) and the resulting Single European Act (SEA) thereby essentially bypassed much of the Draft Treaty's implicit federalist agenda as embodied in the Draft Treaty's proposals for political integration. During the next round of Treaty revision in 1990, member states established an IGC on political union in addition to one dedicated to economic and monetary union. At the conference on political union, representatives of European Community (EC) member states considered an avowedly federal draft treaty put forward by the Dutch (*Agence Europe* 1990: 3). Unable to reach consensus on the Dutch draft treaty, EC member states settled on somewhat less ambitious provisions that, nevertheless, are federal in nature, if not explicitly named as such (Corbett 1992: 277–81). These include relinquishing powers to make their own monetary policy, introducing institutions for common foreign and security policy (CFSP) as well as co-operation in justice and home affairs (JHA), codifying a Union citizenship and adopting the principle of 'subsidarity' (see Pinder 1991; Sbragia 1992; Duff 1993; Duff *et al.* 1994). At the very least, the Maastricht Treaty transformed the *de facto* confederation of the EC into a formal confederation – the EU (Lister 1996; Elazar 1998). Some scholars have gone further by considering the EU as an incipient federation that is, for the most part, being realized with monetary union (McKay 1996).

In most cases, member states intended the Maastricht Treaty to take their political relationship beyond confederation. Indeed, many governments, such as the Dutch and the German, made no bones about depicting their actions as steps toward a federal Europe. In contrast, the British government spared no efforts in insisting that the Union they were entering was in no way a federation. This contrasting behaviour illuminates the role of intersubjective meanings vested in particular words by political actors, and draws attention to the invaluable insights of constructivism regarding speech acts and mutual (mis)understandings. While the Germans tend to view federalism in terms of power-sharing and limited central government, the British tend to associate federalism with the loss of sovereignty to an overbearing Leviathan. Owing to such perceptions, the Major government insisted on keeping all references to federalism out of the Maastricht Treaty. Despite all the psychic rewards this victory in Treaty drafting may have brought to the British, it did not alter the reality of the new federal aspects of the polity that the Treaty constituted. Nomenclature is not necessary for practice, as the absence of the word 'federal' in the United States Constitution amply demonstrates. Moreover, establishing a federation by way of a treaty is not the only way by which federalism can come to inform political practices. Indeed, the unintended development of federal political relationships through the routinization of political practices may have equal, if not greater, impact on the course of political integration.

For example, during the three decades before the signing of the Maastricht Treaty member state judges' case referrals, European Court of Justice (ECJ) rulings, and member state governments' tolerance of growing EC legal prerogatives effectively 'constitutionalized' the Treaty; however, it is far from clear that a European federation was always the intended outcome of all the relevant actors. Joseph Weiler has pointed out that the doctrines of direct effect and supremacy, in combination with the doctrines of implied powers and human rights, 'fixed the relationship between Community law and Member State law and rendered that relationship indistinguishable from analogous legal relationships in constitutional federal states' (Weiler 1991: 2413). Most neo-functionalists and federalists overlooked the process of legal integration as they focused on economic integration leading to political spillover or treaty revisions (Burley and Mattli 1993). Some judges in national courts may have referred cases to the ECJ with the intent of widening the ECJ's jurisdiction with explicit or implicit objectives of seeing a federal Europe some day; however, motivations also included strengthening judicial review within their own states (Shapiro and Stone 1994) and furthering the prospects of the legal profession to which they belonged (Burley and Mattli 1993).

Member state governments also inadvertently contributed to the 'constitutionalization' of the Treaty when they stipulated the conditions of joining the EU in terms of accepting the *acquis communautaire*, which meant a self-definition of 'the accumlated obligations and commitments agreed under the treaties and legislation of the EC over the years' (Wallace and Wallace 1996: 52). As Jørgensen (1998) points out, the *acquis* is a good example of what Kratochwil calls an 'institutional fact' (Kratochwil 1989: 25–8) that emerged from the speech acts of EU officials to others, but has in turn given a very real meaning to the accumulated legal practices within the EU that in total have become constitutive in nature. That is, EU officials' speech acts of representing the EU to prospective members have been used internally by judges and politicians alike to construct (or constitute) the EU's own legal and political identity in terms of an *acquis communautaire*, which goes beyond an international treaty or a set of international treaties.

Moreover, the institutionalization of a federal legal framework through the routinization of practices may involve decisions in cases that may seemingly have little to do with the 'constitutionalization' of the treaty through the enunciation of new doctrines. For example, decisions on individual rights and anti-discrimination may have much broader consequences for federalism than at first is apparent, as it has been for cases involving the treatment of nationals of one state while they are in another. In the 1989 *Cowan* judgment, the ECJ held that a British citizen who had been assaulted after leaving a French metro station should receive compensation for damages entitled to French citizens because he had received a service and, therefore, for France to deny his case standing because he was not a French citizen would violate the non-discrimination provisions of Article 7 of the Treaty.[15] The everyday practicalities of internal movement have facilitated the process of legal integration by creating circumstances leading to legal conflicts between resident aliens and the member states in which they reside. Grievances emerge from these conflicts that enable individuals to evoke EC law for remedy in member state courts. Decisions in cases such as *Cowan* effectively enabled virtually any citizen of a member state to claim rights through a *de facto* expansion of the definition of rights bearers under the Treaty from 'workers' and providers of services to those receiving services as commonplace as purchasing a metro ticket. The circumstances of these cases provide *topoi*, or what Cicero called 'seats of arguments', that 'not only establish "starting points" for (legal) arguments, but locate the issues of debate in a substantive set of common understandings' (Kratochwil 1989: 214, 219). Moreover, the selection of *topoi* is a means of characterizing an act (e.g. riding the metro is receiving a service). Such characterizations in large measure determine which set of rules (e.g. Article 7 of the Treaty) should be applied to the case at hand (Kratochwil 1989: 212–48). Essentially, the social and economic interaction of citizens of one member state who are in another member state produces concrete cases. According to one justice, decisions rendered by the Court regarding the status and rights of citizens of one EU member state who are in another have proved pivotal in using the Treaty of Rome's provisions for free movement to constitutionalize the Treaty (Mancini 1991: 186). As students of US federalism may quickly recognize, the United States Supreme Court utilized the US Constitution's interstate commerce clause in a similar manner to enforce civil rights and strengthened the federal government relative to the states in the process (Lenaerts 1992).[16]

3. THE MEANING OF BARGAINING AND CONFLICT IN A FEDERAL CONTEXT

By focusing on the intersubjective meanings of particular acts, constructivism enables alternative and illuminating interpretations of what practices actually mean in a given context. For example, even the practices among member states within the seemingly conflictual intergovernmental processes of the Council, which are generally characterized as being the antithesis of federalism, can be understood in federal (or 'confederal') terms (Forsyth 1996: 40; Bulmer 1996).

The combination of the EU's federal legal structure, its incomplete federal institutions, federal principles and federal constitutional provisions provides a set of norms that both constitute and regulate political practices, even within the intergovernmental processes of the Council. Weiler (1991) noted that the constitutionalization of the treaty coincided with the strengthening of inter-governmentalism in decision-making. He went on to explain this apparently paradoxical divergence between political and legal trends using Albert Hirschman's (1970) analysis of exit, voice and loyalty. Weiler argued that institutionalization of the legal structure closed off the option of selective exit; that is, not leaving the Community altogether, but rather the avoidance of treaty obligations. Hence, the formulation of Community regulations became much more important because the direct effect and supremacy of Community law made member states respect their obligations as determined by the ECJ.[17] This prompted the member states to closely control integration by expanding the role of the intergovernmental Council of Ministers and European Council at the expense of the Commission.

If intergovernmental bargaining in the EU takes place under the shadow of a federal legal context, it significantly differs from interstate bargaining within international organizations. That is, for example, an EU agreement signed by a member state may have different consequences from an International Tele-communications Union, International Monetary Fund or UN agreement owing to the routine application and enforcement of EC law in the member state's legal system. As the stakes therefore became much higher, bargaining between the Commission and the member states, as well as among the member states themselves, became more prone to increased conflict and deadlock. While increasing conflict can be interpreted as evidence of 'anarchy' and persistent member state 'sovereignty', increasing conflict in bargaining can also be indicative of increasing shared rule, that is of a federal political relationship. As member states accept the federal legal structure by not exiting, they bargain even more aggressively to protect their interests within these legal constraints and in the process confirm a federal relationship in the given policy area.[18]

Of course, the institutionalization of a federal Community legal order varies across issue areas, as does the authority of the EU *vis-à-vis* member states. For example, by adopting the pillar structure of the Maastricht Treaty, member states opted to keep CFSP and co-operation in JHA outside of the Community legal order. This act, in and of itself, however, is a testament of the degree to which leaders of member states recognized the gradual process of legal integration and the trans-formation of member state sovereignty that the emerging federal legal order wrought.

4. POLITICAL AND ECONOMIC PRACTICES CONSTITUTING FEDERAL INSTITUTIONS: UNION CITIZENSHIP

Dual state/suprastate citizenship is a quintessential institution of federation because it fundamentally differentiates federations from confederations. In a federation, 'general and regional governments both operate directly upon the people; each citizen is subject to both governments' (Wheare 1964: 2). Drawing on Wheare's definition, Richard Nathan (1991) viewed European citizenship as a primary reason to consider the EU a federation. Although Union citizenship was established by the Maastricht Treaty, it was not an invention of IGC negotiators with federalist agendas. Rather, the Maastricht Treaty merely codified a set of norms that governed state practices regarding free movement of 'workers' and then 'persons', which had gradually evolved over the preceding decades. European citizenship was initially based on Treaty of Rome provisions and EC directives ensuring the free movement of labour, the piecemeal expansion of the redefinition of 'workers' to embrace all 'persons', the SEA's codification of the free movement of persons and ECJ enforcement of the principle of non-discrimination among member state nationals (see Plender 1976, 1988: ch. 6; Meehan 1993; Koslowski 1994, 1998; Wiener 1998a). In addition to codifying these norms, the Maastricht Treaty introduced new political rights for resident aliens in fellow EU member states (Art. 8b, TEU 1992).

On the face of it, EU citizenship was a minor provision largely adopted as a symbolic gesture that would slightly ease the democratic deficit of the approximately 4.5 million nationals of EU member states who lived in another member state. Indeed, Hans Ulrich Jessurn d'Oliveria called EU citizenship 'nearly exclusively a symbolic plaything without substantive content' and argued that Maastricht added little 'to the existing status of nationals of Member States' (d'Oliveria 1995: 82–3). Nevertheless, EU citizenship became very controversial when its constitutive implications were fully considered. For example, during the House of Lords debate on ratification of Maastricht, Baroness Thatcher argued,

> If there is a citizenship, you would all owe a duty of allegiance to the new Union. What else is citizenship about? There will be a duty to uphold its laws. What will happen if the allegiance to the Union comes into conflict with the allegiance to our own country? How would the European Court find them? The Maastricht Treaty gives this new European Union all the attributes of a sovereign state.
>
> (Thatcher 1993: 564)

Similarly, during the first Maastricht ratification campaign, many Danes apparently viewed EU citizenship as a replacement for Danish citizenship, thereby prompting fellow EU member states to accept a Danish 'reinterpretation' of EU citizenship at the Edinburgh Summit as a prerequisite to gaining a ratification in a second referendum. Indeed, the Maasticht ratification experience prompted the subsequent IGC to steer clear of some of the proposals to expand EU citizenship and, rather, simply reaffirm that 'Citizenship of the Union shall complement and not replace national citizenship' (Amsterdam Treaty 1997).

Despite the similarities with traditional models of federalism followed in the United States or Germany, EU citizenship renders a very different form of polity (Koslowski 1994). EU citizenship binds political units so that the composition of European Parliamentary and local electorates does not necessarily overlap with national and regional electorates – depending on the level of intra-EU migration. For example, a German national from Frankfurt who has lived in London for more than five years may vote in elections for a London city council, the Hesse *Landtag*, the German *Bundestag* and the Member of the European Parliament from the London district in which he or she lives. If member states follow the recommendations of some federalists (Wistrich 1991: 90) and establish a form of EU citizenship that gives full political rights to residents of one EU member state who move to another (i.e. the German who moved to London could then also vote for a member of the British Parliament), such full political rights would, practically speaking, extend citizenship to non-nationals. Hence the European *demos* would more closely resemble traditional federal models and its complexity would be reduced. The 1996–7 IGC and the agreement forged at the Amsterdam Summit indicate that such an outcome is not likely anytime soon. For the foreseeable future, EU citizenship is likely to remain in a permanent state of tension with member state nationality (for elaboration, see Koslowski 1999).

This tension may well be sustainable. To imagine its persistence is to imagine the continued evolution of the EU outside established statist categories and to consider routine contestation as an ongoing reality of the European polity and a process of legitimization rather than as evidence of its impending demise (see Banchoff and Smith 1999). Along these lines, Joseph Weiler suggests considering the constitutive dimension of a Union citizenship that separates citizenship from nationality and contemplating the Union outside of a state-centric constitutionalism.

> On this view, the Union belongs to, is composed of, citizens who by definition do not share the same nationality. The substance of membership (and thus of the *demos*) is in a commitment to the shared values of the Union as expressed in its constituent documents, a commitment, *inter alia*, to the duties and rights of a civic society covering discrete areas of public life, a commitment to membership in a polity which privileges exactly the opposites of nationalism – those human features which transcend the differences of organic ethno-culturalism.
>
> (Weiler 1997: 119)

In this view, EU citizenship embodies both a type of general European 'constitutional patriotism' (Habermas 1992) as well as the delineation of rights and duties in the discrete jurisdictional spaces allocated between member states and the EU by treaty. Political identification with the values embodied in the EU's constituent documents represents one potential source of legitimacy, while another source is found in the politically contested practical realization of the rights and duties of citizens within the jurisdictional spaces created.

5. SUBSIDIARITY, REGIONALISM, NON-TERRITORIAL FEDERALISM AND EUROPEAN CONSOCIATIONALISM

These newly created jurisdictional spaces are not just limited to the lines drawn between the EU and its member states in large measure because of the incorporation of the federal principle of subsidiarity[19] into integrative processes, especially with the way in which subsidiarity was formulated in the Maastricht Treaty. The compromise clause insisted on by the UK which removed the word 'federal' from the preamble of the Treaty on European Union states: 'This Treaty marks a new stage in the process creating an ever closer union among the peoples of Europe, in which decisions are taken as closely as possible to the citizen' (Art. A, TEU 1992). Further defined in Art. 3, TEC, subsidiarity means that in those areas outside of its exclusive competence, the EU 'shall take action only if and in so far as the objectives of the proposed action cannot be sufficiently achieved by the member-states and can therefore, by reason of the scale or of the effects of the proposed action, be better achieved by the Community' (Art. 3b, TEC). By providing a rule to divide jurisdiction over policy areas between the EU and its member states, subsidiarity helps to delineate competencies in terms of levels of government and, therefore, territorially as well. By guiding the EU and its member states in the exercise of their competencies, subsidiarity functions as a federal principle governing the scope of EU policy-making and thereby frames the political relationship between the EU and its member states in federal terms.[20]

The British government supported the adoption of subsidiarity with the intention of restricting the EU's authority and retaining as much authority as possible for the member states themselves. However, subsidiarity also had some unintended side effects as it legitimated several federal practices within and among member states. Taking decisions 'as closely as possible to the citizen' can be, and has been, interpreted to mean greater authority for subnational governments. This interpretation has, in turn, prompted moves to greater constitutionalized power-sharing within EU member states. Ironically, the unitary British government has not been immune to such movements as the reopening of a Scottish Parliament amply demonstrates. Of particular importance are subnational political movements and their interaction with European integration as well as non-territorial federalism and consociationalism operating on a Europe-wide scale.

The interpretation of subsidiarity to mean greater subnational authority changes the dynamics of the integrative practices of member states, particularly those that are themselves federations (Scharpf 1988; Jeffery and Savigear 1991; Leonardy 1996; Rack 1996). In some cases, political leaders within subnational units have promoted European integration in contrast to the national governments of the member state to which they belonged. For example, during the 1980s while Margaret Thatcher's Conservatives applied the brakes to a Franco-German coalition for further integration, the previously anti-integration Scottish National Party adopted its 'independence in Europe' policy and became a pro-European factor within British politics (Lynch 1996: 36–49). Although Scottish 'Euro-subnationalism' may have had only a marginal impact on the unitary British government's bargaining position at the European level, subnational politics may have a significant impact on the bargains hammered out by the most powerful of EU member states, particularly if that state is a federation. Moreover, the subnational politics need not be a force for greater European integration. For example, during the 1996–7 IGC, the German federal government led the drive to communitarize parts of JHA – migration and asylum policy in particular – and argued for permitting a subset of member states to forge ahead with communitarization if all members could not agree. In the face of

British intransigence, Germany and France formed a coalition that struck a bargain for communitarization of migration and asylum policy with opt-outs available for the UK and Ireland (Gaunt 1996). Ironically, however, the bargain was modified at the Amsterdam Summit at the insistence of Germany. Since the German Constitutional Court's ruling that upheld Maastricht ratification reinforced the role of the German *Länder* in German–EU relations, the *Länder* were able to put sufficient political pressure on Helmut Kohl to make him insist that the shift to qualified majority voting on immigration and asylum policy, scheduled to take place five years after the Amsterdam Treaty went into effect, could only come after a unanimous vote (see *Financial Times* 1997). This retreat on Germany's previous advocacy of communitarization reversed Germany's position among those member states that had decided to go ahead with communitarization from that of the driver of the process to that of the brake.

Moreover, member state acceptance of the subsidiarity principle lends legitimacy to subnational autonomy movements within unitary member states (Marks *et al.* 1996), i.e. their 'federalization' (Friedrich 1968; Hesse and Wright 1996). Member state acceptance of subsidiarity combined with the introduction of the Committee of the Regions (Art. 198, TEU) further legitimates and provides institutional support for linkages between European integration and subnational political activities, which, in effect, bypass the member states themselves. For example, by 1996 some fifty-four subnational units had established offices in Brussels to represent regional rather than national interests and to lobby EU officials directly (Marks *et al.* 1996: 46–8). If the forces of economic globalization lead business activity to gravitate toward regional economic units that span existing international borders (Ohmae 1993), a transgovernmenal dimension enters into federal relations among centres of authority as well (Duchacek 1986; Newhouse 1997; Slaughter 1997). Subnational units of EU member states are increasingly organizing on a transgovernmental basis as, for example, the Conference of Peripheral and Maritime Regions, the Association of Cross-border Regions and the Network of Regions of Technological Innovation (see Loughlin 1996: 157). An increase in subnational political practices that bypass the member states (whether to the supranational level or on a transgovernmental basis) demonstrates both the limitations of state-centric conceptualizations of European political space and the promise of constructivist approaches to understanding regionalism and the development of a 'Europe of Regions' (see, e.g., Christiansen 1997).

A major advantage of a non-state centric constructivist approach to federalism is that it also enables consideration of what may be considered an oxymoron to some – non-territorial federalism. The Austro-Hungarian Empire actually practised non-territorial federalism to an extent that was sufficient to generate an alternative conceptualization of the relationship between federalism and democracy in the context of a non-contiguous geographical dispersion of the *demos* (Renner 1918). Similarly, Belgium practised non-territorial federalism (Lijphart 1984: 28) before reconstituting itself as a formal federation and, together with Austria, the Netherlands and Switzerland, it serves as a model of consociational democracy.

Elsewhere, I have argued that one possible trajectory for the evolution of the

European *demos* that had been restructured by EU citizenship was towards a type of non-territorial federalism or European consociationalism in which there are multiple overlapping *demoi* and multiple access points of interest articulation on all levels of governance (Koslowski 1994: 394–6). Moreover, the patterns of EU politics at the level of member states and élites in many ways follow consociational principles (Taylor 1990, 1996). Consociationalism is based on four principles: executive power-sharing, or grand coalition, a high degree of autonomy for parts of the society, proportionality and minority veto (Lijphart 1977). For example, even with the introduction of qualified majority voting, consensus-seeking within the Council is the norm that produces over-sized coalitions, if not unanimity, even when a qualified majority would technically suffice. Similarly, recruitment to positions in the Commission follow informal norms, if not formal decisions, requiring proportional representation from the member states, even though members are supposed to leave their member state's interests behind when they become European civil servants (Taylor 1996: 85–90). Perhaps most importantly, the idea of European consociationalism frames the 'end state' of European integration as a polity between confederation and a federal state – a polity that is as stable as existing consociational democracies but at the same time one characterized by continual internal contestation on a variety of political dimensions along non-territorial as well as territorial lines.

CONCLUSION

Federalism provides an important perspective on European integration, even if that has yet to be acknowledged in mainstream IR theory. Constructivism helps to retool federal theories for more persuasive analysis of the EU by refocusing attention on political practices, intersubjective meanings and informal norms. Furthermore, an explicitly non-state centric constructivist approach to federal theory helps one to escape the domestic hierarchy/international anarchy conceptual dichotomy that, unfortunately, often leaves analysis stuck in debates over whether or not a given polity is a confederation of sovereign states or a federal state itself. The confederal/federal theoretical distinction loses much of its analytical utility except as ideal types, given that the reality of European political practices remains in between the two.

Despite its resistance to traditional taxonomies of federal theory, the emerging European polity can be understood in federal terms. Member states have agreed to establish federal institutions and abide by federal principles (even if some member states attempt to hide the fact from themselves through verbal gymnastics) which include: a European Central Bank; Union citizenship; frameworks for co-operation and eventual integration of foreign policy, defence and internal policing; and the principle of subsidiarity to guide policy-making throughout the Union. Perhaps even more importantly, federal political relationships have developed through the routinization of certain political and legal practices over time and the resulting institutional framework has had its effect on the meaning of member state bargaining. Given the legitimization of subnational and non-territorial political actors, it may no longer be sufficient to only analyse the bargaining of member states to understand the political dynamics of the European polity as a whole.

The challenge of analysis, of course, is to resist teleological explanations, accept the 'in betweenness' of the European polity and settle for understanding the European polity for what it currently is, rather than try to explain European integration toward some hypothetical 'end state' that it may never reach. If an 'end state' is necessary for analysis, perhaps the best alternative is to conceive of it in terms of a form of European consociationalism that is neither a confederation nor a federation. Nevertheless, some scholars may persist in envisioning the realization of a federal European state through wholesale redesign of European political institutions via constitutional convention. They may have the laudable aim of streamlining the unintended agglomeration of complex and overlapping institutions, rationalizing the policy-making processes and lines of bureaucratic authority, codifying EC law, subordinating member state judicial structures and vesting popular sovereignty in a democratically elected European Parliament through giving it the requisite powers that would resolve democratic deficits. If, however, Alfred North Whitehead was correct in arguing that 'Civilization advances by extending the number of important operations which we can perform without thinking about them',[21] well-meaning efforts to design an optimal European federation run the risk of its construction on the rubble of taken- for-granted social institutions and unintended federal political relationships upon which politically sustainable European integration may depend.

ACKNOWLEDGEMENTS

I am grateful to Anne-Marie Slaughter, Alexander Wendt, and to the authors in this volume for comments and suggestions.

NOTES

1   For a general overview of federal thought on European integration as well as statements of policy-makers, see Burgess 1989. For a sample of more country-specific overviews, see Ransom 1990; Burgess 1995 for the British federalists; Levi 1992 for the Italian; Roemheld 1990 for the French tradition of 'integral federalism'; and Jeffrey and Savigear 1991 for the German perspective.
2   For an overview, see Greilsammer 1976; Pentland 1973.
3   On the distinction between federalism and federation, see King 1982; Verney 1993.
4   On the distinction between federations and confederations, see Forsyth 1981.
5   Federalists of the inter-war period agreed with realists on the anarchical nature of international politics (Robbins 1939: 104–9) and, together with the realists, helped to establish the Hobbesian paradigm in the post-Second World War era (Jennings 1949: 1). Sharing this paradigm, realists and federalists could only conceive of international politics as complete anarchy and international organizations as a leap into complete order analogous to that of states, even if only federal states such as the United States. Federalism then dropped out of the general IR literature as the political agendas of European and world federalists failed to be realized with the demise of the European Defence Community and the European Political Community in 1954 (Hansen 1969; von Krosigk 1971), and the marginalization of the United Nations accompanying

the intensification of the Cold War during the 1950s (Kratochwil and Ruggie 1986; Rochester 1986).

6   The contemporary debate over the EU echoes the nineteenth-century *Bundestaat/ Staatenbund* debate. Drawing on the authors of the *Federalist*, Georg Waitz (1853) made the distinction between *Bundestaat* (federal state) and *Staatenbund* (union of states). Drawing on Calhoun, Max von Seydel (1872) countered that the concept of *Bundestaat* was nonsensical because statehood and sovereignty were inseparable.

7   See Bowie and Friedrich 1954; Macmahon 1955.

8   See, for example, Haas 1958. On the implicit federal goal of neo-functionalism, see Groom 1978.

9   Hoffmann 1966: 909–10.

10 I owe this point of clarification to Friedrich Kratochwil.

11 The following discussion draws freely from Koslowski and Kratochwil 1994.

12 For an elaboration of the constructivist approach, see Onuf 1989; Wendt 1987, 1992; Dessler 1989; Koslowski and Kratochwil 1994; Onuf 1998b. For recent overviews, see Adler 1997b; Checkel 1998; Kubalkova *et al.* 1998; Gould 1998.

13 This constructivist conceptualization parts company with the state-centric approach taken by Alexander Wendt in Wendt 1994.

14 For example, the Schuman declaration states: 'The pooling of coal and steel production should immediately provide for the setting-up of common foundations for economic development as a first step in the federation of Europe' (Schuman 1994: 12).

15 Case 186/87, *Reports of the European Court of Justice*, 1989.

16 In the discussion following Dr Lenaerts' presentation of this argument, he agreed that many of the cases critical to the constitutionalization of the Treaty involved intra-EU migration.

17 Implementation is done in conjunction with national courts and the ECJ has marginal enforcement powers, although the Maastricht agreement enables the Court to fine states. Hypothetically, member states may therefore not comply. In practice, however, they have. It is the steady reproduction of the practice of compliance that ultimately counts more in analysis of the present polity than projection of a hypothetical with-drawal from Community obligations as proof of 'sovereignty'.

18 For a discussion of how bargaining is evidence of federalism and a discussion of bargaining within federal relationships, see Riker 1964.

19 The modern concept of subsidiarity comes from Catholic social doctrine articulated in Pope Leo XIII's 1891 encyclical, *Rerum Novarum, Quadraesimo Anno*, which was influenced by German Jesuits who identified subsidiarity with federalism. See Kuehnhardt 1992: 82–4.

20 See definitions of Wheare (1964: 2) and Riker (1964: 11) quoted above.

21 Whitehead quoted in Hayek 1945: 528.

4
Social Construction and European Integration
Jeffrey T. Checkel

INTRODUCTION

Over forty years after the European project began, it is striking how little we know about its socialization and identity-shaping effects on national agents. Indeed, prominent Europeanists are themselves deeply divided on this question, with some arguing that integration has led to a fundamental shift in actor loyalty and identity, while others claim the opposite. The basic premiss of this chapter is that both schools are right: constructing European institutions is a multi-faceted process, with both rationalist and sociological toolkits needed to unpack and understand it.[1]

Put differently, much of European integration can be modelled as strategic exchange between autonomous political agents with fixed interests; at the same time, much of it cannot. Constitutive dynamics of social learning, socialization, routinization and normative diffusion, all of which address fundamental issues of agent identity and interests, are not adequately captured by strategic exchange or other models adhering to strict forms of methodological individualism. For these constitutive processes, the dominant institutionalisms in studies of integration – rational choice and historical – need to be supplemented by a more sociological understanding of institutions that stresses their interest- and identity-forming roles.

After briefly addressing definitional issues and the literature on integration, I argue that social construction, a growing literature in contemporary international relations (IR), can help students of integration to theorize and explore empirically these neglected questions of interest and identity. Specifically, the chapter shows how a social constructivist cut at institution-building explains key aspects of Europeanization – social learning and normative diffusion – better than its rationalist competitors, with the practical goal being to elaborate the specific methods and data requirements for such work.

Before proceeding, three comments are in order. First, my analytic starting point is that research on integration should be problem-, and not method-, driven; the goal is to encourage dialogue and bridge-building between rationalists and social constructivists. By itself, each school explains important elements of the integration process; working together, or at least side-by-side, they will more fully capture the range of institutional dynamics at work in contemporary Europe. Indeed, too many constructivists are themselves method-driven, ignoring the obvious empirical fact that much of everyday social interaction is about strategic exchange and self-interested behaviour.[2]

Second, and following on the above, the constructivism favoured in this chapter belongs to what has been called its modernist branch. These scholars, who combine an ontological stance critical of methodological individualism with a loosely causal epistemology, are thus well placed, within the integration literature, 'to seize the middle ground' – staking out a position between positivist and agent-centred rational choice, on the one hand, and interpretative and structure-centred approaches on the other.[3]

Third, the chapter's central focus is theoretical and methodological, and not empirical. My concern is how one could develop and apply, in a systematic manner, constructivist insights to key puzzles in the study of integration. Empirically, I seek only to establish the plausibility of such propositions, and do so in two ways: (1) by drawing upon arguments and evidence from a wide range of existing studies on European integration; and (2) by reference to my own work in progress.

INSTITUTIONS AND EUROPEAN INTEGRATION

Of the many institutionalisms floating around these days in economics, political science and sociology, I need briefly to discuss three: rational choice institutionalism, historical institutionalism, and sociological institutionalism. For rational choice scholars, institutions are thin: at most, they are a constraint on the behaviour of self-interested actors – be they interest groups or unitary states in IR. They are a strategic context that provides incentives or information, thus influencing the strategies that agents employ to attain given ends. In this thin conception, institutions are a structure that actors run into, go 'ouch', and then recalculate how, in the presence of the structure, to achieve their interests; they are an intervening variable.[4]

For historical institutionalists, institutions get thicker, but only in a long-term historical perspective. In the near-term here and now, they are thin – structuring the game of politics and providing incentives for instrumentally motivated actors to rethink their strategies; they are a constraint on behaviour. Over the longer term, however, institutions can have deeper effects on actors as strategies, initially adopted for self-interested reasons, get locked into and institutionalized in politics. Institutions thus can be both intervening and independent variables.[5]

Sociological institutionalists are unabashedly thick institutionalists. Not only in the distant future, but in the near-term, institutions constitute actors and their interests. What exactly does it mean for institutions to constitute? It is to suggest that they can provide agents with understandings of their interests and identities. This occurs through interaction between agents and structures – mutual constitution, to IR scholars. The effects of institutions thus reach much deeper; they do not simply constrain behaviour. As variables, institutions become independent – and strongly so.[6]

In our research and theorizing about Europe, should one of these institutionalisms be favoured, serving as the baseline? The answer here is 'no', for ultimately this is an empirical question. No doubt, there are many situations and aspects of integration where agents operate under the means-end logic of consequences favoured by rationalist choice and some historical institutionalists (meetings of the European Council or the hard-headed interstate bargaining that features prominently in intergovernmentalist accounts). At the same time, the less static perspective favoured by sociologists reminds us that much social interaction involves dynamics of learning and socialization, where the behaviour of individuals and states comes to be governed by certain logics of appropriateness (informal communication in working groups of the Council of Ministers, European-level policy networks centred on the Commission). Unfortunately, these latter logics, while equally compelling and plausible, have received little systematic theoretical attention in studies of Europeanization.

Indeed, to students of international politics well versed in the never-ending neo-realist–neo-liberal controversy, the debates over Europeanization and European integration produce an eery feeling of *déjà vu*. On the one hand, the discussion has helped advocates of opposing approaches to sharpen their central arguments and claims; similar intellectual clarifications have occurred over the past decade in the debate between neo-realists and neo-liberals in IR.

At the same time and in a more negative sense, the debate over Europeanization, like any academic discourse, has emphasized certain methods and actors at the expense of others. To my reading, much of the discussion has been about institutions – be they encompassing governance or federal structures, historically constructed organizational and policy legacies, or, more narrowly, bodies of the European Union (EU) such as the Commission or European Council. Moreover, in most cases, the analysis is about how such institutions structure the game of politics, provide information, facilitate side payments or create incentives for agents to choose certain strategies.

Such an emphasis, however, comes at a cost. It short-changes the role that institutions can play in politics, or, more to the point, in European integration. In particular, their constitutive role, typically stressed by sociologists, is neglected. If the neo-debate in contemporary IR can be accused of neglecting fundamental issues of identity formation, much of the current discussion about European integration can be accused of bracketing this constitutive dimension of institutions. Put differently, the great majority of contemporary work on European integration views institutions, at best, as intervening variables. Missing is a thick institutional argument, derived from sociology, that demonstrates how European institutions can construct, through a process of interaction, the identities and interests of member states and groups within them.[7]

SOCIAL CONSTRUCTION AND INTEGRATION

In this section, I develop an approach that addresses the above-noted gaps, and do so by drawing upon a growing and vibrant body of IR scholarship: social constructivism. As presently elaborated, constructivism – at least the modernist branch of concern here – is an argument about institutions, one which builds upon the insights of sociological institutionalism. It is thus well suited, in a conceptual sense, for expanding our repertoire of institutional frameworks for explaining European integration. Moreover, modernist social constructivists remind us that the study of politics – or integration – is not just about agents with fixed preferences who interact via strategic exchange. Rather, they seek to explain theoretically both the content of actor identities/preferences and the modes of social interaction – so evident in everyday life – where something else aside from strategic exchange is taking place.[8]

So defined, constructivism has the potential to contribute to the study of integration in various areas. Below, I consider two: learning and socialization processes at the European level; and the soft or normative side of Europeanization at the national level. In each case, I explore what a constructivist approach entails, how it could be carried out empirically and its value added compared to existing work on integration. I also address and counter the argument that my results cannot be generalized. The section concludes by noting how a constructivist approach to integration can build upon and systematize theoretical arguments and descriptive insights advanced by a growing number of Europeanists; I also argue that the whole exercise is not one of reinventing the wheel.

Learning and socialization

What does it mean for an agent to learn? Social learning involves a process whereby actors, through interaction with broader institutional contexts (norms or discursive structures), acquire new interests and preferences – in the absence of obvious material incentives. Put differently, agent interests and identities are shaped through interaction. Social learning thus involves a break with strict forms of methodological individualism. This type of learning needs to be distinguished, analytically, from the simple sort, where agents acquire new information, alter strategies, but then pursue given, fixed interests; simple learning, of course, can be captured by methodological-individualist/rationalist accounts.[9]

Consider small group settings: it is intuitively obvious that there are times when agents acquire new preferences through interaction in such contexts. This is not to deny periods of strategic exchange, where self-interested actors seek to maximize utility; yet, to emphasize the latter dynamic to the near exclusion of the former is an odd distortion of social reality. Now, the perhaps appropriate response is 'so what?' In an abstract sense, it readily can be appreciated that social learning takes place at certain times, but how can one conceptualize and empirically explore whether and when it occurs? Luckily, there is a growing literature in contemporary IR – by constructivists, students of epistemic communities and empirically oriented learning theorists – that performs precisely this theoretical/empirical combination.

More specifically, this research suggests four hypotheses on when social learning occurs; these could be translated to empirical work conducted at the European level.

1   Social learning is more likely in groups where individuals share common pro-fessional backgrounds – for example, where all/most group members are lawyers or, say, European central bankers.
2   Social learning is more likely where the group feels itself in a crisis or is faced with clear and incontrovertible evidence of policy failure.
3   Social learning is more likely where a group meets repeatedly and there is high density of interaction among participants.
4   Social learning is more likely when a group is insulated from direct political pressure and exposure.[10]

Clearly, these hypotheses require further elaboration. For example, can a crisis situation be specified a priori and not in a *post-hoc* fashion as is typically done? When is the density of interaction among group participants sufficiently high for a switch to occur from strategic exchange to interactive learning? These are difficult issues, but they are only being raised because a first round of theoretical/empirical literature exists. Europeanists could build upon and contribute to this work – for example, by exploring and theorizing the impact, if any, of different EU voting rules (unanimity, qualified majority voting) on these group dynamics.

The deductions also point to a powerful role for communication. However, in keeping with this chapter's attempted bridging function, it is a role between that of the rationalists' cheap talk, where agents (typically) possess complete information and are (always) instrumentally motivated, and the postmodernists' discourse analyses, where agents seem oddly powerless and without motivation. Yet, this role itself requires further unpacking: underlying my communication/learning argu-ments are implicit theories of persuasion and argumentation.[11]

On the latter, students of integration can and should exploit a rich literature in social psychology, political socialization and communications research on persuasion/argumentation. At core, persuasion is a cognitive process that involves changing attitudes about cause and effect in the absence of overt coercion; put differently, it is a mechanism through which social learning may occur, thus leading to interest redefinition and identity change. The literature suggests three hypotheses about the settings where agents should be especially conducive to persuasion:

1   when they are in a novel and uncertain environment and thus cognitively moti-vated to analyse new information;
2   when the persuader is an authoritative member of the in-group to which the persuadee belongs or wants to belong; and
3   when the agent has few prior, ingrained beliefs that are inconsistent with the persuader's message.[12]

While these deductions partly overlap with the first set, further work is still needed – for example, how to operationalize 'uncertain environments' and integrate political context. On the latter, my strong hunch is that persuasion will be more likely in less politicized and more insulated settings. All the same, both sets of hypotheses do elaborate scope conditions (when, under what conditions persuasion and learning/socialization are likely), which is precisely the promising middle-range theoretical ground that still awaits exploitation by both constructivists and students of European integration.[13]

What are the data requirements for research based on the above hypotheses? Essentially, you need to read things and talk with people. The latter requires structured interviews with group participants; the interviews should all employ a similar protocol, asking questions that tap both individual preferences and motivations, as well as group dynamics. The former, ideally, requires access to informal minutes of meetings or, second best, the diaries or memoirs of participants. As a check on these first two data streams, one can search for local media/TV interviews with group participants. This method of triangulation is fairly standard in qualitative research; it both reduces reliance on any one data source (interviewees, after all, may often dissimulate) and increases confidence in the overall validity of your inferences.[14]

For students of integration, is this a feasible undertaking? Drawing upon my own work in progress, I suggest that the answer is 'yes'. In a larger project, I am studying the appearance and consolidation of new European citizenship norms; an important concern is to explain, at the European level, whether and how new understandings of citizenship are emerging. To date, my focus has been on Strasbourg and the Council of Europe (CE), for this has been where the more serious, substantive work has occurred. When the CE is trying to develop new policy, it often sets up committees of experts under the Committee of Ministers, the intergovernmental body that sits atop the Council's decision-making hierarchy. In a sense, then, these committees are the functional equivalent of the working groups of the EU's Council of Ministers.

I have been examining the Committee of Experts on Nationality, the group that was charged with revising earlier European understandings of citizenship that dated from the 1960s. My particular interest was to describe and explain what occurred in this group as it met over a four-year period: for example, why did it revise existing understandings on dual citizenship to remove the strict prohibition that had previously existed at the European level? To address such issues, I did the following. First, three rounds of field work were conducted in Strasbourg; during these trips, I interviewed various individuals who served on the Committee – members of the Council Secretariat and experts. Second, I conducted interviews in several member state capitals, meeting with national representatives to the committee of experts. Third, as a cross-check on interview data, more recently I was granted partial access to the confidential meeting summaries of the Committee.[15]

This was a considerable amount of work, but the pay-off was high. Over time, particular individuals clearly shifted from what they viewed as a strategic bargaining game (for example, seeking side payments to advance given interests) to a process where basic preferences were rethought. This shift was particularly evident on the question of dual citizenship, where a growing number of committee members came to view the existing prohibition as simply wrong. Processes of persuasion and learning were key, and such dynamics were greatly facilitated by a growing sense of policy failure – the number of dual nationals was climbing rapidly despite the existing prohibition – and the committee's insulation from publicity and overt political pressure. Indeed, the committee benefited from the public perception of Strasbourg as a quiet backwater of Europeanization – with the real action occurring in Brussels. This allowed it to meet and work out revised understandings on citizenship prior to any overt politicization of its work.

At the same time, it should be stressed that not all committee members learned new interests. Indeed, the national representative of one large European state held deeply ingrained beliefs that were opposed to arguments favouring a relaxation of prohibitions on dual citizenship. Consistent with the above deductions, there is no evidence that this individual was persuaded to alter his/her basic preferences.

The point of this example is not to dismiss rationalist accounts of strategic bargaining. Rather, it is to note the value added of a middle-range constructivist supplement to these more standard portrayals: it led me to ask new questions and employ a different set of research techniques. The result was to broaden our understanding of how and under what conditions new European institutions – norms – are constructed through processes of non-strategic exchange.

Whether or not one accepts my particular arguments, the basic point remains. In making claims about socialization, learning, persuasion or deliberation promoted by, or conducted within, European institutions, students of integration must theorize these dynamics. In recent years, it has become almost a cottage industry to cite such processes as central, while simultaneously failing to elaborate their theoretical underpinnings. The result has been a near total disconnect between analytic claims and empirical documentation that such dynamics are at work. As one scholar has correctly noted in reference to the EU, 'what is needed is a decision-making theory which includes in its analysis the ways in which preferences, beliefs and desires are shaped by participation in the decision-making process itself.'[16]

Socialization/Diffusion pathways

Constructivists view norms as shared, collective understandings that make behavioural claims on actors. When thinking about norms in the EU context, two issues must be addressed: (1) through what process are they constructed at the European level; and (2) how do such norms, once they reach the national level, interact with and socialize agents? Now, the distinction between European and national levels is false, as multiple feedback loops cut across them; at the same time, the dichotomy can be justified analytically as it helps one to unpack and think through different stages in the process of European norm construction. In what follows, I am less interested in formal legal norms developed and promulgated, for example, by the European Court of Justice; a growing body of literature in both law and political science already addresses such understandings and their impact. Rather, the constructivist value added comes from its focus on the less formalized, but pervasive social norms that are always a part of social interaction.[17]

On the first issue – the process of norm development – constructivists have theorized and provided empirical evidence for the importance of three dynamics. First, individual agency is central: well-placed individuals with entrepreneurial skills can often turn their individual beliefs into broader, shared understandings. The importance of this particular factor has been documented in case studies covering nearly a one-hundred year period and a multitude of international organizations and other transnational movements. In the literature, these individuals are typically referred to as moral entrepreneurs; in the language of my earlier discussion, they are the agents actively seeking to persuade others.[18]

Second, such entrepreneurs are especially successful in turning individually held ideas into broader normative beliefs when so-called policy windows are open. This means that the larger group, in which the entrepreneur operates, faces a puzzle/problem that has no clear answer, or is new and unknown. In this situation, fixed preferences often break down as agents engage in cognitive information searches. While the policy-window concept was first elaborated by public policy (agenda-setting) and organizational theorists (garbage-can models), it was only more recently that constructivists applied its insights in the international realm to explain norm formation.[19]

Third, processes of social learning and socialization (see the previous section) are crucial for furthering the norm creation process first begun by individual agents exploiting open policy windows. The basic point is that individual agency is insufficient to create durable social norms. A brief example clarifies the point. In the mid-1980s, several close advisers to Soviet leader Gorbachov played the part of entrepreneurs seeking to advance new ideas about international politics. In the near-term, such individually held beliefs, which were influential in shaping Gorbachov's own preferences, were decisive in bringing the Cold War to a dramatic, peaceful and unexpected end. Yet, once the USSR collapsed and Gorbachov was swept from power, these ideas largely vanished, as many analysts of Russian foreign behaviour have noted. Put differently, absent social learning among a larger group of actors – that is, the development of norms – the particular ideas held by specific agents had no real staying power.[20]

When and if new European norms emerge, one must still theorize about the mechanisms through which they diffuse to particular national settings and (perhaps) socialize agents. Here, constructivists have identified two dominant diffusion pathways: societal mobilization and social learning. In the first case, non-state actors and policy networks are united in their support for norms; they then mobilize and coerce decision-makers to change state policy. Norms are not necessarily internalized by the élites. The activities of Greenpeace or any number of European non-governmental organizations (NGOs) exemplify this political pressure mechanism.[21]

The second diffusion mechanism identified by constructivists is social learning, where agents – typically élite decision-makers – adopt prescriptions embodied in norms; they then become internalized and constitute a set of shared intersubjective understandings that make behavioural claims. This process is based on notions of complex learning drawn from cognitive and social psychology, where individuals, when exposed to the prescriptions embodied in norms, adopt new interests.[22]

A key challenge is to develop predictions for when one or the other of these mechanisms is likely to be at work. To date, constructivists have been silent on this issue; however, my work on European citizenship norms suggests a possibility. I hypothesize that the structure of state–society relations – domestic structure – predicts likely diffusion pathways, with four categories of such structures identified: liberal, corporatist, statist and state-above society. From these, I deduce and predict cross-national variation in the mechanisms – social mobilization and social learning – through which norms are empowered.[23]

A brief example highlights the utility of the approach as well as the attendant data requirements. In the project on European citizenship norms, I have explored whether and in what way they diffused to several European states, including the Federal Republic of Germany. Consider this German case. I first did research on the basic structure of state–society relations in the country; like many others, I concluded that the polity is corporatist. That is, it possesses a decentralized state and centralized society, with a dense policy network connecting the two parts; both state and society are participants in policy-making, which is consensual and incremental.

Given this coding of the German structure, I next advanced predictions on the expected process whereby norms would have constitutive effects, arguing that societal pressure would be the primary and (élite) social learning the secondary mechanism empowering European norms in Germany. The logic is as follows. In a corporatist domestic structure, state decision-makers play a greater role in bringing about normative change than in the liberal case, where policy-makers are constantly pressured by social actors; however, this does not mean that they impose their preferences on a pliant populace. A hallmark of corporatism is the policy networks connecting state and society, with the latter still accorded an important role in decision-making. In this setting, I thus hypothesize that it is both societal pressure (primary) and social learning (secondary) that lead to norm empowerment.

With these predictions in hand, I then conducted extensive field work in the Federal Republic. To date, this research has confirmed my working hypotheses: emerging European norms on citizenship are diffusing and being empowered in Germany primarily via the mobilization of societal pressure; social learning at the élite level has been secondary. More specifically, these norms are connecting to a wide variety of social groups and individuals: NGOs favouring the integration of Germany's large resident foreigner population; activists in the churches and trade unions; and immigrant groups. At the decision-making level, one finds isolated evidence of élites learning new preferences from the norms (for example, a small group of Christian Democratic Bundestag deputies).[24]

Two streams of evidence are important for establishing the presence of these diffusion mechanisms, as well as their relative weighting. Most important were structured interviews with a wide range of actors – both societal and state. As at the European level, these discussions were designed to probe the degree to which agent preferences were changing and the motivations for such change. However, as the rationalists remind us, talk is cheap. Therefore, as a cross-check on the interview data, I consulted a wide range of primary documentation – official summaries of

Bundestag debates, media analyses, and interviews given in newspapers or on TV.

What is the value-added of all this work? It convincingly demonstrates that a rational choice institutionalist understanding of the role that norms play in social life (norms as constraint) missed an important part of the story in the Federal Republic. I indeed found instances where domestic agents simply felt constrained by the European norms (for example, a number of officials in the Federal Interior Ministry); yet, in many other cases, I uncovered evidence of non-strategic social learning where agents, in the norm's presence, acquired new understandings of interests. Clearly, much theoretical work remains to be done – in particular, elaborating scope conditions for when norms have constraining as opposed to constitutive effects. Addressing this latter point is crucial for, again, the obvious empirical fact is that norms do not always constitute.

Extending the argument

Perhaps, though, my constitutive analysis of European institutions only works because of the particular organization and policy area from which I drew empirical examples: the Council of Europe and human rights. Such arguments are largely irrelevant for the EU – a special type of institution with very different policy domains. Two responses counter such a critique.

First, there are well-established theoretical reasons for suspecting that Europe, especially Western Europe, is a most likely case for international institutions to have constitutive effects. Most important, it is an institutionally dense environment, one where theorists predict high levels of transnational and international normative activity. This logic, precisely because it is a particular way of viewing the social world, is in principle equally applicable to a variety of European institutions – whether their focus is human rights (CE) or political and economic affairs (EU).[25]

Second, assume, despite the foregoing, that differences in policy domains do matter. That is, arguments about social learning or the constitutive effects of European norms just do not work when applied to the EU. After all, the process of European integration has largely been about market integration, where national and transnational business interests have played key roles. Such groups are quite different in structure and goals from the actors of civil society – domestic NGOs, churches – highlighted in several of my examples. However, if the institutional (enhanced role of the European Parliament) and substantive (third pillar of justice and home affairs) innovations of Maastricht and Amsterdam continue to evolve, new actors and policy issues are increasingly likely to make themselves felt. Moreover, the current interest in Brussels, London and elsewhere in moving the EU away from a strict regulatory role to one emphasizing standard-setting and so-called 'soft law' plays to the strength of social actors like NGOs: it is precisely the promotion of such informal practices and norms where they are most influential.[26]

In fact, human rights pressure groups have begun utilizing the European Parliament as a means of generating precisely the sort of normative pressure-from-below documented in my CE example. Moreover, immigration, which is now on the third pillar agenda, is an issue where previous studies have documented the extensive degree to which European state interests are constituted by broader international norms. On the related issues of citizenship and racism, recent work establishes that the 1996–7 Intergovernmental Conference (IGC) saw extensive mobilization by NGOs and other transnational movements, and their qualitatively different, when compared to the past, interaction with EU institutions, as well as the IGC itself. Thus, even if differences in policy domains are important, these are at present being blurred if not erased.[27]

Summary

My purpose in the foregoing was constructive. The goal was not to dismiss rational choice or historical institutionalist work on integration; those literatures are rich and offer many insights. Yet, because of their adherence to variants of method-ological individualism, certain analytic/empirical issues – interest and identity formation, most importantly – are bracketed. A more sociological and con-structivist understanding of institutions as constitutive allows one to address such questions. Constructivism, however, need not and, indeed, should not be viewed as *terra incognita* to Europeanists. In fact, a constructivist cut at integration is already evident, albeit implicitly, in both theoretical and empirical studies.

Theoretically, one has the recent work of Olsen, Kohler-Koch and Fligstein. Olsen's writing, including that on the EU, has been concerned with broader institutional environments – how they provide the very basis of action for political agents, how they lead to rule-governed behaviour, which may supplant instrumental, strategic calculation, and how they promote learning. Yet, he has failed to explicate, in a theoretical sense, the processes through which such insti-tutional dynamics occur. The constructivist work reviewed above suggests a number of ways in which these micro–macro linkages could be developed in a specifically European context.[28]

Much of the analysis in recent work by Kohler-Koch and Knodt is also premissed on sociological assumptions – in particular, their exploration of the domestic normative impact of EU institutions, where they do not simply constrain, but constitute agents and their preferences. Unfortunately, this argument is much less clear about the process through which, and the conditions under which, EU norms have such effects. Here, constructivist hypotheses on the mechanisms through which national level socialization and social learning occur might be relevant.[29]

Fligstein is also interested in constitutive dynamics but, in contrast to Kohler-Koch and Knodt, the focus is on Brussels. In his work on the Commission, he argues that, under certain conditions marked by crisis and uncertainty, it can play an entrepreneurial role in helping to culturally construct political action. Less clear, however, are the specific processes through which such construction takes place, as well as his theoretical understanding of an agency's role. All the same, this analytic move hints at rich possibilities for a dialogue with those social constructivists who theorize the role of individual agency, entrepreneurs and policy windows in their work on normative change.[30]

Empirically, the last decade has seen an explosion of work on institutional fusion, policy networks, comitology and informal communication patterns centred upon and generated by EU institutions. While this research is extraordinarily rich in a descriptive sense, it is often under-theorized. To be fair, solid empirical work is often a prerequisite for theory building. All the same, more attention to theory would help these scholars to systematize their implicitly sociological view of institutions – and constructivism has much to offer here.

Consider three examples. Wessels, Rometsch and their collaborators have made a powerful and well-documented case for institutional fusion within the EU context, where the density of interaction between European and national institutions is such that old distinctions between the two levels no longer hold. These analysts ascribe an important symbolic and identity-shaping role to institutions – to constructivists, a constitutive role. Yet, they are silent, theoretically, on when, how and why such identity formation occurs, which leads them to advance an under-specified convergence thesis, where 'the constitutional and institutional set-up of [EU] member states will converge towards one common model.' Given that constructivists have already begun to specify scope conditions regarding institutions and identity change, the potential for theoretical cross-fertilization seems significant.[31]

In a second example, recent work by Beyers and Dierickx on the EU Council and its working groups suggests that informal communication is key for understanding their operation. Yet, this research, despite its empirical richness, neglects a crucial theoretical question: under what conditions – if at all – does this communication lead political agents away from situations of strategic exchange and into those marked by social learning, socialization and communicative action? For both theoretical (debates over the consequences of integration) and policy reasons (explaining when and why member state interests change), this issue is fundamental. However, because of their reliance on a methodologically individualist ontology, Beyers and Dierickx seem simply unaware that they are in fact well placed to address it. The point is not that they get the story wrong; rather, it is incomplete. And constructivism, with its concern for modelling modes of social interaction beyond strategic exchange, could provide analytic tools for filling out the picture.[32]

Research on so-called comitology represents a third example where constructivist theorizing and empirical integration studies could profitably interact. Comitology refers to the complex set of committee rules that have evolved to implement EU policy and procedures; the system stems from a 1987 European Council decision in which member states made clear their unwillingness to lose control of the implementation process – in particular, by ceding too much power to the Commission. These committees, by member state dictate, are composed of government representatives and, occasionally, additional experts; yet, the growing empirical literature on them notes how these representatives must often turn elsewhere for information and, more important, interpretation. Indeed, two analysts argue that 'scientific evidence' is accepted as the most valid currency for 'effecting convincing arguments' in comitology.[33]

The last point suggests a link to my earlier hypotheses on small groups, communication and social learning. Indeed, constructivist deductions on the role of common backgrounds, crisis, density of interaction, etc., could readily be exploited by these Europeanists to explore more systematically the conditions under which European committees, through learning and argumentation, socialize their participants.[34]

A final issue is not so much one of new theoretical directions for analyses of integration, but, instead, a look back. Simply put, is my call for bringing constructivist insights to bear on the study of the EU a short-sighted reinventing of the neo-functionalist wheel? After all, over thirty years ago, Haas and others were writing about the identity-shaping effects of the European project. Indeed, collective identity was to emerge via a 'process whereby political actors in several distinct national settings are persuaded to shift their loyalties, expectations and political activities towards a new centre, whose institutions possess or demand jurisdiction over the pre-existing nation-states.'[35]

While references to social learning and socialization are evident in the work of many early neo-functionalists and regional integration theorists, the differences with constructivism are significant. Most important, the latter is not a general substantive theory that predicts constant learning or a growing sense of collective identity; rather, its aspirations are more modest. As currently being developed, it is a middle-range theoretical approach seeking to elaborate scope conditions for better understanding precisely when collective identity formation occurs. Constructivism is thus agnostic as to whether the endpoint of social interaction is greater common interests and identity. Neo-functionalists, at least implicitly, were not neutral on this question; there was a clear normative element to their scholarship.[36]

In addition, despite the strong allusions to identity formation and change, neo-functionalists failed to develop explicit micro-foundations that moved them beyond an agent-centred view of social interaction. In fact, there is a strong element of rational choice in their research. While considerable work remains, constructivists are attempting to elaborate such alternative foundations – their stress on logics of appropriateness and communicative action, for example.[37]

CONCLUSIONS

My arguments throughout this chapter were based on an obvious but too often neglected truism about our social world: the most interesting puzzles lie at the nexus where structure and agency intersect. The real action, theoretically and empirically, is where norms, discourses, language and material capabilities interact with motivation, social learning and preferences – be it in international or European regional politics. Research traditions such as rational choice, postmodernism and, more recently, large parts of constructivism, which occupy endpoints in the agent–structure debate, have life easy: they can ignore this messy middle ground. Yet, the true challenge for both rationalists and their opponents is to model and explore this complex interface; this article has suggested several ways in which this could be done.[38]

As one scholar recently put it, 'regional integration studies could uncharitably be criticized for providing a refuge to homeless ideas.' While constructivism is certainly not homeless, Europeanists should resist the temptation simply to pull it off the shelf, giving it a comfortable European home in yet another N = 1, non-cumulative case study. Rather, these scholars have the opportunity – given their immensely rich data set – to push forward one of the most exciting debates in contemporary international and political theory.[39]

NOTES

1   For the diverging views among Europeanists, compare Wessels 1998 and Laffan 1998. Thanks to Johan P. Olsen for alerting me to this latest round in a long-running and seriously under-theorized debate.

2   For example, Christiansen 1997.

3   On the different schools within constructivism, see Adler 1997b: 335–7. Checkel 1998 provides a critical overview of the modernist branch. The phrase 'seizing the middle ground' comes from Adler.

4   My analysis here and in the following paragraphs draws upon DiMaggio and Powell 1991: ch. 1; Longstreth *et al.* 1992: ch. 1; Koelble 1995; Kato 1996; Katzenstein 1996a: ch. 2; Finnemore 1996b; Hall and Taylor 1996.

5   For historical institutionalists employing a thin conception of institutions, see Immergut 1992 and Pierson 1994. Thicker conceptualizations are found in Hattam 1993 and Goldstein 1993. Consistent with my near/long-term distinction, the analysis in Immergut and Pierson is contemporary, while that in Hattam and Goldstein spans decades.

6   Students of organization theory should recognize these arguments: they have roots in sociological work on organizations. See DiMaggio and Powell 1991 *passim*; Dobbin 1994; March and Olsen 1998.

7   Elsewhere, these claims are documented in some detail. See Checkel 2000, where I review work on integration by proponents of multi-level governance, historical institutionalists, supranational institutionalists, neo-functionalists, intergovernmentalists, rational choice theorists and neo-realists.

8   For detailed overviews of the epistemological, ontological and methodological emphases in the work of modernist constructivists, see Adler 1997b; Checkel 1998; Ruggie 1998: 35–6.

9   Levy 1994 is an excellent introduction to the learning literature.

10 These hypotheses derive from a number of sources. See DiMaggio and Powell 1991 *passim*; Haas 1990, 1992; Hall 1993; Risse-Kappen 1996b; Checkel 1997a: chs 1, 5.

11 Johnson 1993 provides an excellent and balanced discussion of the theoretically incomplete role accorded communication in rational choice analyses.

12 On these deductions, see Zimbardo and Leippe 1991; Johnston 1998: 16–25.

13 Checkel 1998. On the insulation/persuasion connection, also see Pierson 1993: 617–18.

14 Also see the excellent discussion in Zürn 1997: 300–2.

15 Checkel 1999b: 94–6 provides full documentation for the claims advanced in this and the following paragraphs.

16 Kerremans 1996: 221. For evidence of this analytic–empirical disconnect, see, among many others, Wincott 1995: 603–7; Kerremans 1996: 222, 232–5; Öhrgaard 1997: 15–16, 19–21; Cram 1997 *passim*; Jørgensen, 'PoCo: the diplomatic republic of Europe', in Jørgensen 1997a: 174–5; Wessels 1998: 227; Laffan 1998: 242–3; Falkner 1998: 6–7, 12, 17 *passim*. The few exceptions to this critique are considered below. On the centrality for Europeanists of the challenges raised here, also see Olsen 1998: 31–2.

17 Mattli and Slaughter 1998 provide a detailed review and critique of the literature on the Court of Justice. On constructivist definitions of norms, see Katzenstein 1996a: ch. 2.

18 On entrepreneurs and the role, more generally, of individual agency in processes of norm development, see Nadelmann 1990; Finnemore 1996a; Florini 1996; Finnemore and Sikkink 1998.

19 The epistemic and ideational branches of constructivism are especially helpful here. See Haas 1992; Checkel 1997a: ch. 1.

20 Checkel 1997a: chs 5, 6.

21   Keck and Sikkink 1998: ch. 1 *passim*; Risse and Sikkink 1999, for example. See Checkel 1999a: 3–8, for a full discussion of these two diffusion pathways.

22   Stein 1994; Risse-Kappen 1995b; Robert Herman, 'Identity, norms and national security: the Soviet foreign policy revolution and the end of the Cold War', in Katzenstein 1996a: ch. 8, for example.

23   For details, see Checkel 1999b: 87–91.

24   For extensive documentation of these points, see Checkel 1999b: 96–107, where I also consider alternative explanations for the results presented here.

25   See Weber 1994; Risse-Kappen 1995a: ch. 1; Adler and Barnett 1996: 97 *passim*.

26   The issue and actor expansion noted here has already begun. See Hooghe and Marks 1996, and, more generally, the entire literature on multi-level governance. Indeed, the June 1997 Amsterdam Treaty, by incorporating the social policy articles of Maastricht directly into the Treaty on European Union, codified the access of various non-state actors to EU decision-making in that area (Obradovic 1997). On the growing interest in seeing the EU move to a soft law, standard-setting role, see Lionel Barber, 'A punctured image', *Financial Times*, 15 June 1998; and George Parker, 'Foreign Secretary urges curb on Brussels', *Financial Times*, 14 August 1998.

27   See Soysal 1994; Roula Khalaf, 'Call to strengthen rules on human rights and democracy', *Financial Times*, 11 February 1997; Emma Tucker, 'European Union asylum seeker policies slammed', *Financial Times*, 4 December 1997; 'The Brussels lobbyist and the struggle for ear-time', *Economist*, 15 August 1998; Favell 1998: 5–6, 10–14.

28   Olsen 1995, 1996, 1998.

29   Kohler-Koch and Knodt 1997. Similarly, Conzelmann 1998: part IV *passim*, while making a convincing empirical case for national-level policy learning in the EU, fails to explicate testable scope conditions for when such dynamics are more or less probable.

30   Fligstein 1998 *passim*. See also Öhrgaard 1997; Cram 1997, where the authors, like Fligstein, stress constitutive processes at the European level, but fail to specify the conditions and mechanisms through which they occur.

31   Rometsch and Wessels 1996: preface, chs 1–2, 14 – quote at p. 36.

32   See Beyers and Dierickx 1997, 1998. More recently, Beyers has addressed the possibility of socialization in Council working groups; unfortunately, his operational measure of it – the number of years an individual participated in such a setting – continues to bracket the interaction context in the group itself. See Beyers 1998. Hooghe 1998: 5–6, 8–9 offers a similar measure of socialization – in this case, for individuals working in the Commission. Not surprisingly, her important study thus suffers from the same bracketing problem as noted for Beyers.

33   Joerges and Neyer 1997b: 617. Useful introductions to the comitology system are Pedler and Schaefer 1996; Dogan 1997.

34   While several students of comitology have hinted at the importance of such factors for generating learning dynamics, to my knowledge they have not been operationalized and empirically tested. See Pedler and Schaefer 1996: 47; and, especially, Joerges and Neyer 1997a: 291–2, 1997b: 618.

35   Haas 1958: 16.

36   On neo-functionalism's in-built bias toward viewing integration as a 'perpetual [forward] motion machine', see Caporaso 1998a: 6–7.

37   On the rational choice foundations of neo-functionalism, see Burley and Mattli 1993: 54–5. An excellent review and comparison of the neo-functionalist, integration and constructivist literatures, one which reinforces the points made in the preceding paragraphs, is Pollack 1998 *passim*.

38   On the need to explore this interface in the context of debates over European integration, see Hix 1998: 55–6. More generally, see Checkel 1997b.

39   For the quote, see Caporaso 1998a: 7.

Part 2

SOCIAL CONSTRUCTIVIST PERSPECTIVES
IN STUDIES OF EUROPEAN INTEGRATION

5

Postnational Constitutionalism in the European Union
Jo Shaw*

[G]iven the propensity of [politicians and academics] to fall back on law, with its seemingly vast regulatory potential, as a mechanism of social engineering, it would be surprising if many were not tempted to invoke the spirit of constitutionalism and the substance of constitutional doctrine in their efforts to foster the legitimacy of the new order.

(Walker 1996: 272)

I. INTRODUCTION: CONSTRUCTIVISM AND EU LEGAL STUDIES

Constitutions, constitutionalism and constitutional politics have become common currency of debate and discussion in European Union (EU) studies.[1] In this chapter, I want to develop an argument in relation to these issues which draws upon emerging interdisciplinary and constructivist lines of thinking within EU legal studies. The specific task is to re-examine the challenges *of* and *to* the concepts of constitution and constitutionalism when they are used as terms of analysis in the postnational setting of the EU. Working within the framework of a set of assumptions about legal and political categories as socially constructed and about the need for legal ideas to be understood both sociologically (Cotterrell 1998a) and in relation to concepts of political power, the chapter seeks to identify a frame of reference which links ideas about integration as a process (and in particular the legal dimensions of that process), with constitutionalism as a process of accommodation of diverse interests within society.[2]

As the chapter shows more specifically in relation to the articulation and understanding of issues of EU constitutionalism, methods of legal study overly focused on the authoritative legal text, seen in isolation from its (social, economic, political or cultural) context or studied without the interpretative aid of other types of social scientific knowledge, in general encounter many difficulties.[3] It may be unfair and indeed excessively schematical, but none the less legal positivism, as an approach to law, 'has come to be identified with empty formalism, theorizing by definition, morally detached linguistic analysis, and the unreflective science of calculable observations' (Campbell, I., 1998: 65). Similarly, the 'doctrinal' or 'black letter' approach to law – one based on the assumption that in the words of the judges and the text of the law a set of meanings is to be found and can in turn be explicated by the academic commentator – has been increasingly criticized as providing too limited a set of intellectual tools or insights. Perhaps the most celebrated and certainly most oft-quoted exposition of the core problems of these approaches as they apply to European Community (EC) law comes from Martin Shapiro. He sharply criticized a work which was

> a careful and systematic exposition of the judicial provisions of the 'constitution' of the [EEC] . . . But it represents a stage of constitutional scholarship which American constitutional law must have passed about seventy years ago . . . It is constitutional law without politics. [The work] presents the Community as a juristic idea; the written constitution as a sacred text; the professional commentary as a legal truth; the case law as the inevitable working out of the correct implications of the constitutional text; and the constitutional court as the disembodied voice of right reason and constitutional teleology . . . [S]uch an approach has proved fundamentally arid in the study of individual constitutions.
> (Shapiro 1980: 538)[4]

The academic scene has changed since that time. By the end of the 1990s, the field of EU legal studies had come to be characterized by a notable pluralism of approaches and intellectual influences. It now draws upon both the ever greater eclecticism of the discipline of legal studies itself, in which debates about the relationship between the legal, social, human and even natural and physical sciences have never been more intense, and upon the very clear imperative within European (Union) studies to develop interdisciplinary approaches to the multifaceted and sometimes contradictory phenomena of the integration and disintegration of European nation states and the emergence of a 'European polity' (Mayes 1994). Some might regret the passing of some of the old certainties evident when EC law scholarship was court-centred but allegedly more rigorous in its adherence to the demands of legal texts and the possibilities of legal interpretation. Criticisms of the so-called 'new approaches' could, perhaps, more justly be aimed at a continuing willingness simply to define the 'new' negatively by reference to the 'old' (in other words, as work which *does not* accept the assumptions of doctrinal and positivist scholarship on legal rules and institutions, and in particular rejects an essentialist view of legal categories and definitions). There has been a consequent failure to map out the 'new' terrain more self-consciously or consistently by reference to well-established or newly emerging currents of theory. In other words, EU legal studies would be a stronger discipline if it encompassed more constructive efforts towards theory building.

If it were to undertake this task, EU legal studies would be following the lead of (UK national) public lawyers in confronting the challenge of theory to ask the questions 'what is [public] law for?' and 'how do we escape the trap between a conception of law as normative which loses sight of the social significance of law and a functionalist view of law as the handmaiden of politics which omits a normative perspective?' (Loughlin 1992: 243–4; see also Prosser 1982, 1993; Harvey 1997; Harden and Lewis 1986; Morison and Livingstone 1995). A greater degree of intellectual self-awareness in relation to parallel questions is now gradually emerging among those looking outwards from the discipline of EU legal studies towards the challenges of theory, notably sociological theory, but also economic and political theory,[5] following the lead of scholars such as Christian Joerges, Francis Snyder, Joseph Weiler and Bruno de Witte, pioneers in very different ways of a more reflective conception of the discipline. Furthermore, legal and social theorists coming from a wide variety of well-established positions have examined segments of the field of inquiry constituted by EC law, including Zenon Bańkowski, Peter Fitzpatrick, Jürgen Habermas, Karl-Heinz Ladeur, Neil MacCormick, Bert van Roermond and Gunther Teubner. These interventions have notably broadened the terrain and parameters of the debate.

These comments are not intended to set out a contemporary canon for interdisciplinary legal work on the EU, but merely to highlight some newly emerging patterns where intersections may be evident with constructivist traditions in liberal and critical theories of law, democracy and constitutionalism (Rawls 1993, especially Lecture III; Habermas 1996, especially ch. 6; Teubner 1989) as well as in other disciplines. These are intellectual patterns where neither the shapes nor the colours are yet fixed or even wholly clear. For the purposes of this chapter, they suggest at a minimum the need for a critical perspective when applying apparently well-established concepts such as 'constitution' or 'democracy' to unfamiliar circumstances such as the newly emerging 'postnational European polity', and in the particular institutional context of the EU legal order which privileges the role of the Court of Justice as 'constitutional court'. Such concepts and adjudicatory roles may need to be reconsidered and reconstructed when applied away from the national context. Beyond a conceptual critique, this chapter makes greatest use of the general 'procedural turn' visible in many recent studies of law and the exercise of public power (including work on the EU, such as Scott 1998), in which it is acknowledged that conventional 'parliamentary' approaches to democracy represent inappropriate attempts to offer legitimate anchorage to the activities of non-state entities such as the EU. This shift in turn leads to inquiries into alternative forms of participation and representation which examine the roles of the states and sub-state entities such as regions, the 'people' themselves, as well as intermediate and representative associations such as non-governmental organizations (NGOs), trade unions and firms.

Accordingly, in Section II of the chapter I shall set constitutional approaches to the EU against the backdrop of the central strands of thinking on constitutionalism more generally, identifying some of the principal weaknesses in current approaches. In Section III, I broaden the debate by interrogating briefly the nature of 'postnationalism', highlighting how this concept throws open many established categories and schemes of thinking. In Section IV I bring constitutionalism and post-nationalism together by examining approaches to constitutionalism as process and as the accommodation of diversity in contested and divided communities including the EU. Finally, in Section V I bring the argument to a conclusion, highlighting the possibilities and limitations of a procedural approach to constitutionalism.

II. CONSTITUTION AND CONSTITUTIONALISM IN THE EUROPEAN UNION

Joseph Weiler is celebrated for noting that 'Europe' has developed 'a constitution without constitutionalism' (Weiler 1995: 220). Building on this comment, Michelle Everson (1998b: 408) critiques traditional approaches to the task of consti-tutionalizing the EU legal order which rely too heavily upon the 'traditional com-parative tools of constitutional analysis, trawling through existing "black- letter" constitutions in an endeavour to identify the formal constitutional mechanisms which might aid them in overcoming the immediate apparent problems of European integration'. Constitutionalism, then, is troubling to the EU.

But for many scholars of the EU the trouble with many standard versions of the concept of constitutionalism is that they often beg as many questions as they answer. For example, from a normative perspective, constitutionalism is said to be about 'the political/philosophical theories of social and private ordering underlying the law of the constitution' (Everson 1998b: 389). In similar terms, consti-tutionalism is termed 'the set of beliefs associated with constitutional government' (Walker 1996: 267) or 'the set of ideas and principles which form the common basis of the rich variety of constitutions which we find in many countries of the world' (Preuß 1996: 12). More precisely, it has been defined as

> the creed according to which political power ought only to be exercised under constitutional provisions and subject to constitutional restrictions, where such restrictions include a separation of powers and its corollaries, effective checks and controls among the branches of government, security at least of the rights allowed for by the theory of constitutionally derivative rights.
>
> (MacCormick 1993b: 135)

A similar definition comes from Rosenfeld (1994: 3): 'in the broadest terms, modern constitutionalism requires imposing limits on the power of government, adherence to the rule of law, and the protection of fundamental rights.'

Constitutionalism is, of course, as contested as it is closely studied. So, like the concept of citizenship, it can be imbued with quite different meanings and functions depending upon the underlying world-view of the commentator. Thus, for example, constitutions can be seen through liberal lenses as the expression of individual freedom and, implicitly, the degree of order necessary to achieve and protect that freedom. In contrast, communitarian lenses render the constitution the instrument of societal organization for the common good. Yet a third set of lenses, often donned in conjunction with one or other of the first two sets, those of the nationalist, sees the constitution as the expression of a national ideal or consciousness.

However, there are other ways to 'cut' the concept of constitutionalism. Especially when understood in a legal sense, constitutions also have an institutional dimension. They are the basic rules of design of a society; according to Ivo Duchacek they constitute the 'power map' (Duchacek 1973: 3 quoted in Banting and Simeon 1985: 3), including the framework for government and a body of rights operating according to the rule of law. The constitution may be seen as the means for protecting rights against the possibilities of unjust majoritarianism. Ronald Dworkin (1995: 1) aptly suggests that constitutionalism is less about majoritarianism as such than about *legitimate* majority rule. Alternatively, constitutionalism may be driven primarily by a republican concern for the form of society and the form of politics and government. Constitutionalism is not, however, just about institutions and structures, but also about ideas and values – 'the basic ideas, principles and values of a polity which aspires to give its members a share in government' (Preuß 1996: 12). In other words, to use the example of democracy, if a constitution provides for a structure of popular participation, for example through elections, it does so for a particular reason because of the value which a given society ascribes to democracy (i.e. government by the people). It does so because this is linked to the need for social legitimacy and the acceptance of a given order by 'the people'.

Political and legal science offer yet other ways of understanding constitutions and constitutionalism. There is, for example, the 'rationalist' notion of the link between constitutionalism and societal bargains. This is perhaps most classically expressed by Robert Dahl, who argued that 'constitutional rules are not crucial, independent factors in maintaining democracy'. Nor are they from this perspective important as 'guarantors of either government by majorities or of the liberty from majority tyranny' (Dahl 1956: 137). Instead 'constitutional rules are important in determining the bargaining advantages of groups within the political process' (Cohen and Fung 1996: xliv). Similarly functional is the view of written constitutions emerging from the theory of autopoetic social systems; it sees constitutions as mechanisms of structural couplings of the legal and political systems, which lead to increased autonomy within the legal system through the internal control of legal change (e.g. judicial review) and more limited autonomy in political systems by restricting political choices (Luhmann 1990, 1993: 468–81).

Yet when scholarship on the EU begins to engage with constitutionalism, it is evident that the literature frequently slips between three distinct levels of analysis influenced by different strands of constitutional thinking:[6] the discussion of aspects of the 'EU constitution' as empirical fact; the articulation, within a normative project, of the *desiderata* of a constitution for the EU as legal, political and economic integration project; and the use of political theories of constitutionalism (particularly in their liberal and communitarian guises, and less often in the guise of (neo-)republicanism) to analyse the politics, practices and institutions of the EU especially in comparison to nation states. Each of these three levels of discussion poses distinct challenges, but represents an inadequate starting or ending point for the discussion.

Unlike the study of constitutionalism in the United States, there is no firm empirical base such as an EU equivalent of the American constitution which would serve as a point of departure for any analysis. The Court of Justice might call the EC treaties the Communities' 'constitutional charter',[7] and indeed the EU legal order as a whole may operate in many respects in a manner which is recognizably 'constitutional' (e.g. acceptance of the rule of law; a discourse and practice of legal rights; allocation of competences to different institutions and different levels; emergent conceptions of citizenship rights and relations, etc.). In fact, what constitutional framework does exist actually comprises a wider variety of sources than those posited by the Court, including not only the founding treaties and the Court's own case law, but also other forms of institutional practice including legislation and measures akin to constitutional conventions which govern the conduct of the member states and the Union institutions themselves. Moreover, clear aspects of an economic constitution, through the creation and regulation of the single market and the recent arrival of economic and monetary union based on the institutional core of an independent central bank are visible (Sauter 1997). Finally, at the level of political capacity and accountability, the Union's treaties are now peppered with references – some of a more or less rhetorical nature – to rights, democracy, liberty, citizenship, and so on.

Yet despite these features, I would argue that overall this conception of the EU legal system as constitution lacks the degree of clarity in relation to its external or internal contours as well as the degree of coherence, consistency or completeness which one would normally associate with 'a' constitution in the classic sense. The framework is looser and much less clear than the Court has (for rhetorical purposes?) suggested. The Court does not consistently track either an integrationist or a disintegrationist *telos*, but is subject to a number of varying political influences from within and without the Union (de Búrca 1998; Shaw 1996). For example, it has not always adopted an expansionist vision of the EC's external powers, and in the field of internal market law it has, in the 1990s, adopted a more nuanced approach to the balance between liberalization promoted through uniform regulation at EU level and local diversity of regulatory conditions.

In addition, there is a deeply ambiguous relationship between the EU and notions of 'stateness' (*Staatlichkeit*) and related questions of nation, *demos* and *ethnos*. In formal terms, the first level at which the EU operates is between the (member) states as an entity based on international treaties; moreover, it is not, and is probably never likely to be, a state – at least in the conventional sense. Yet that statement underestimates the extent to which the member states have – internally as well as in their external relationships – been 'europeanized' at all levels through membership and its legal, political and socio-economic consequences. However, these governance processes, under which the member states are tied in so many ways, to adopting a 'European' *modus operandi* and participating in a radically new practice of polity formation, are not anchored in any of the conventional forms or symbols of legitimacy, through notions of political or pre-political community. At the political level, this lack of anchorage often manifests itself in forms of Euroscepticism, sometimes also coupled to a strong reaction against the allegedly expansionist tendencies of the Court of Justice (Hartley 1999).

It is the combination of the lack of an empirical base and the uncertainty generated by the EU's relationship with the paradigm of stateness which often makes it difficult to establish a clear and secure terrain in which discussion framed in terms of constitutionalism can be seen as a useful part of political and legal theorizing on the EU; on the contrary, much work slips too easily from the descriptive to the normative register of 'Europe needs (or does not need) a constitution'.

Alongside the three levels of analysis, there are also three distinctive substantive concerns which have dominated much writing and thinking about the EU and its 'constitution': issues of sovereignty, and the authority of Community law; the questions of government and governance; and the debate about rights in the EU. In many instances, the scholarly debate – especially but not solely in the field of legal studies – has been led by discussions of the way in which the Court of Justice has developed the legal order of the EU as the cornerstone of constitutional development, in relation to both the treaties as 'constitution' and the evolving competence structure of the EU. So, for example, the constitutionalism debate has been led at many junctures by the debate entitled 'the constitutionalization of the treaties'. In reality, this is the sovereignty debate: the Court of Justice's creation of a 'supreme' EU legal order, taking effect within the national legal orders and empowering national courts as 'Community courts'. In other words, the first conceptualization of constitutionalism in the European Communities came through the prism of sovereignty and legal power. Likewise, much of the debate over governance has been dominated – from many scholars' perspectives – by the debate over the Court of Justice's policing of inter-institutional relationships, rather than by constructive consideration of the link between governance and forms of (post-national) democracy. And finally, what 'rights debate' has existed in the EU context has been dominated by the concern that EC law almost by definition creates individual rights in the national context, which national courts must protect. In other words, it is another version of the story of EC law dominated by the constitutionalization of the treaties. It has been less concerned to identify and critique the precise content of those rights which have, hitherto, been predominantly market-oriented, or to allow a sceptical perspective on the very notion of rights in a postnational legal order.

Thus each of these three substantive concerns regarding EU constitutionalism has been notably undertheorized by reference even to standard accounts of constitutionalism, still less by reference to a reworked notion of constitutionalism which takes into account the *sui generis* nature of the Union. Yet where attempts have been made to link constitutional reality and constitutional theory, the point has been well made by writers such as Richard Bellamy and Dario Castiglione (1996b: 2) that: '[t]he European Union has highlighted the inadequacies of certain key concepts of constitutional and democratic thought outside the context of relatively homogeneous nation states, such as the sovereignty of the people and the link between citizenship and rights.' Such attempts to match theory and reality have quickly demonstrated that constitutionalist ideas and thinking are not capable of simple transmission to the supranational level, without a full consideration of how many of the conditions underpinning them at national level are changed by the shift in register. These are important difficulties which go beyond the question of finding the right version of the standard theory, and these difficulties have so far been insufficiently addressed in the literature on constitutionalism.

This chapter also seeks to demonstrate that, however important, the difficulties revealed by Bellamy and Castiglione's comment are only the beginning of the challenge posed in relation to the development of postnational constitutionalism. In making the argument, I hold that, despite the difficulties already encountered and likely to be encountered in the future with the normative position which speaks in favour of some form of EU constitutionalism, it is possible to derive from the languages and ideas of constitutionalism tentative responses to some of the enduring conundrums posed by the EU. This admittedly normative argument is strongest when constitutionalism is articulated by reference to certain conceptions of 'common constitutionalism' and constitutionalism as intercultural dialogue (Tully 1995). This allows us to confront the question: if the EU is indeed more than an international organization but less than a state, how is it to proceed in terms of political organization? It simply begs the question to describe the EU as an emergent postnational non-state polity. That does not solve any of the crucial questions of political power and responsibility, or indeed settle conflicts of legal hierarchy. Constitutionalism in its modern guise cannot on its own provide the answers, and leaves untouched the key questions because it is impossible to make in the EU context many of the assumptions about notions of political community which implicitly drive much liberal or communitarian political theory. The challenge for the EU is that of capturing the essence of postnationalism, and combining it with understanding the process of building a new kind of polity which is based on the existing diversity of the member states. This is the challenge of building a link between integration and constitutionalism.

The particular focus on constitutionalism in this chapter is thus not with reworking and applying standard liberal or communitarian accounts. Rather it is with the essential preliminary question of considering the relevance for the EU of the dialogic character of constitutionalism and constitutions as process, and as a framework within which differences and similarities between social groups are uncovered, negotiated and resolved. This is vital in a polity such as the EU where the very social basis of the polity remains highly contested and very fluid (and the geographical boundaries themselves likewise remain unresolved as enlargement negotiations continue). Thus closest attention will be paid to 'the proper role of constitutions and constitutionalism in forging a fruitful interplay between the reinforcement of identity and the preservation of diversity' (Rosenfeld 1994: 3). The argument constructed in this chapter builds upon earlier work in related fields by constitutional scholars and legal theorists, in particular James Tully, Zenon Bańkowski and Emilios Christodoulidis. However, there are also clear links to arguments developed by scholars of discourse and deliberative theories of democracy and ethics such as Jürgen Habermas and Seyla Benhabib, communitarians such as Charles Taylor, cosmopolitans such as Andrew Linklater, liberals such as Rawls and those whose work sits at the cusp of liberalism and republicanism, and of communitarianism and cosmopolitanism, notably Richard Bellamy and Dario Castiglione.

III. THE POSTNATIONAL DIMENSION

Before engaging with the task of recovering the discourse and practices of constitutionalism for the EU, it is essential to inquire more closely into the 'postnational'
setting of the EU, so that we can begin to see what a concept of postnational constitutionalism might involve.

To speak of *post*nationalism would be to pose, it appears, first and foremost
a direct challenge to nationalism. Postnationalism may be seen as the denial of
nationalism, or, perhaps more appropriately, as the attempt to recover and rethink
some of the core values of nationalism as lending meaning to a particular community with shared practices and institutions, without the necessary institutional
baggage or ideological weight of the modern (nation) state or a negative sense of
nationalism as exclusion.[8] For Deirdre Curtin (1997: 51), for example, the term
'postnational' 'expresses the idea that the link implied by nationalism between
cultural integration and political integration can be prised open'. Postnationalism
articulates an idea of change and transformation in relation to the nation state
(change *of* or *to* the nation state; change at the supra- or sub-state level *because of*
changes in the nation state), and not merely an alternative use of its political forms
and cultural signifiers such as identities or legal orders in another *inter*national,
*trans*national or even *sub*national context.

It seems useful, however, to distinguish a number of different elements or
dimensions of postnationalism. The first concerns the institutional dimension of
handling and managing power in a world where states are highly interdependent
and are not the only *loci* and foci of political activity and processes. In particular,
there exists an increasingly global economy, which demands institutional innovation in response to novel problems of control. In the context of the EU, part of
that institutional dimension (which in itself also has a substantial market management dimension) may be reflected by a shift – perhaps semantic only or perhaps
reflecting a deeper change in the conceptualization of political and legal forms –
from presenting what is studied by scholars as concerned with the 'integration of
states', towards an emphasis on studying the governance of an 'emerging non-state
polity'. Increasingly, ideas such as Philippe Schmitter's (1996) *condominio* as a future
form for the 'Euro-polity' or the suggestions based on consociationalism and related
ideas put forward by writers such as Dimitris Chryssochoou (1997; also Gabel
1998) represent the basis for creative thinking about the institutional demands of
and possibilities for such a 'postnational' polity.

However, the institutional dimension – while essential when thinking con-
structively about the uses of postnationalism – is not alone. There exists also a
dimension to postnationalism which relates to the nature and structure of communities and the reflection that, in respect to questions of attribution, identity and
affinity, issues of political community should more accurately be described in plural
rather than singular terms, with the increasing emergence or re-emergence of local,
linguistic or cultural, regional, national and even supra-state identities, in each case
outside the formal framework of the state (Breton 1995). Furthermore, one should
not neglect the geographical dimension of postnationalism, where writers have

argued that the conceptualization of space needs to be described in terms of shifting non-state territorialities (Anderson 1996). A closely related turn can be discerned in some international relations scholarship (Ferguson and Mansbach 1996).

Law has a complex relationship with postnationalism, which goes beyond the conventional link drawn between legal authority and nation states. For example, some would argue that there are strict *limits* to legal postnationalism. There remains an unresolved debate between conceptions of the EU and national legal orders as binary opposites in which one but not both can be sovereign (which in turn are linked to acute challenges to EU constitutionalism – or more precisely the authority of EC law – such as that of the German Federal Constitutional Court in its decision on the Treaty of Maastricht[9]) and more pluralist conceptions of law. A pluralist idea of law sees it as a 'complex of overlapping, interpenetrating or intersecting normative systems or regimes, *amongst which relations of authority are unstable, unclear, contested, or in the course of negotiation*' (Cotterrell 1998b: 381; emphasis in the original). Under the latter conception, the possibilities of non-state law admitting of flexible architectures which express the nature of sovereignty in different and non-binary ways have been explored by writers including Neil MacCormick and Zenon Bańkowski (MacCormick 1997; Bańkowski 1994; Bańkowski and Scott 1996; see also Walker 1998; Richmond 1997; Maher 1998). If legal orders can be overlapping and do not stand in a hierarchy or an arrangement which is either strict or fixed, it is possible to see the EU as an entity of 'interlocking normative spheres'; what is significant is that no particular sphere is seen as privileged or predominant.

Even more radically, the EU can be seen as one element of what Gunther Teubner calls 'global Bukowina', a conception of 'legal pluralism within emerging world society' (Teubner 1997a; Maher 1998). Teubner dubs the central thesis of this trend of work the argument that 'globalization of law creates a multitude of decentred law-making processes in various sectors of civil society, independently of nation-states' (Teubner 1997b: xiii). What is termed *lex mercatoria* – the law of international commercial transactions – is the most advanced manifestation of this phenomenon of *global* rather than *international* law. However, aspects of the phenomenon can be found in relation to the regulation of multinational enterprises, aspects of legal and other professional practice, labour law and the protection of human rights with the increasing role of non-state actors. Since Teubner specifically distinguishes this phenomenon from (official) international politics and international law (*between* states rather than within the emerging world society), this version of postnationalism should be distinguished from a version of liberal internationalism, theorized by international lawyers such as Anne-Marie Slaughter (Slaughter 1995; Helfer and Slaughter 1997) and based on an argument about 'civil' behaviour of nation states accepting the international rule of law. This is strongest in relation to international trade law (the emergence of the World Trade Organization and the pre-eminence of the General Agreement on Tariffs and Trade (GATT) (Petersmann 1995)) and to a certain extent in relation to international human rights law (the war crimes endeavours of the United Nations and national reactions such as the House of Lords judgments in the *Pinochet* case[10]). However, as Teubner (1997a: 3) suggests, it is easy to be cynical and to view this form of legal postnationalism as another version of American (political, military and moral) hegemony.

It is possible that some of the difficulties in resolving all these opposing views on law and postnationalism may stem from the ambiguities attendant in much thinking which invokes the concepts of sovereignty (Walker 1998). There is also an unfortunate bifurcation (Himsworth 1996) between legal scholarship which observes the transformation of the state from a sovereignty-based perspective (MacCormick 1993a) and scholarship in political science, international relations, and political economy which observes the 'decline' of the nation state in the face of economic and cultural globalization (Tsoukalis and Rhodes 1997; Axtmann 1998).

In sum, it must be concluded that postnationalism is neither a fixed or defined concept within academic writing and thinking, nor a certain and empirically observable phenomenon of law or politics. For the purposes of this chapter, therefore, it will be defined dispositively as an open-textured concept used to express many of the dynamic and *sui generis* elements of the EU as *integration* project involving the *process* of polity formation and in particular constitutional processes. It is precisely these elements which reinforce that, as a political and legal entity, it does not merely replicate the states out of which it first emerged and to which it remains indissolubly linked, but is sustained by a separate logic. Indeed, the institutional and constitutional processes of polity formation demand to be understood on their own terms, but in a way which respects the diversity of the member states themselves. It suggests the need for a perspective which captures precisely the indeterminacy of the political community which is implicated by the constitutional settlement in the EU and the complexity of its institutional arrangements. We need a perspective which allows for the definition and redefinition of community as the process of constitutional settlement continues. We turn now to seek such a perspective.

IV. CONSTITUTIONALISM, POSTNATIONALISM AND THE ACCOMMODATION OF DIVERSITY

There is a well-established inclination in EU studies to assert that issues of process are the key to understanding EU constitutionalism. That point has been well made by a number of writers, such as Dario Castiglione, who argues that

> if the European polity suffers from a 'constitutional deficit', this needs to be addressed not simply by discussing the contents of a constitution for Europe, but also the political process through which such a constitution must be put in place. The forms of such a process do not just depend on expediency and particular circumstances, they can be the subject of principled discussion and of imaginative political psychology.
>
> (Castiglione 1995: 74)

Similarly, Luigi Ferrajoli brings the question of process to the fore, using the concept of constitutional patriotism developed in the German context originally by

Jürgen Habermas (Habermas 1996: 491–515) and subsequently applied to the EU:

> The sole democratic foundation of the unity and cohesion of a political system is its constitution, and the type of allegiance it alone can generate – the so-called 'constitutional patriotism'. For this very reason, it seems to me that the future of Europe as a political entity depends to a great extent on developing a constituent process open to public debate, aimed at framing a *European constitution.*
>
> (Ferrajoli 1996: 157; emphasis in original)

These are examples of pragmatic criticisms of the absence of a sustained debate on constitutionalism within the EU, doubtless because of the lack of a 'European' public space, sphere, opinion, *polis*, *demos*, or whatever, pointing along the way to all manner of gaps and deficits. That observation has been widely made – and could perhaps be restated as the mathematical perspective of seeing the 'European constitution' as a vector, rather than as a point.[11] It is a different matter entirely to link this observation to a theorization of constitutional politics or to develop from this a perspective upon the role of law. In what follows, I shall examine some work which has, in my view, uncovered the key problems and suggested some useful avenues for further inquiry.

We begin with James Tully's frontal assault on modern constitutionalism and underlying positions of liberal political philosophy (Tully 1995). The essence of Tully's challenge is a rejection of many of the premises of modern constitutionalism which focus essentially on the importance of the separation of powers, legitimate government, the protection of rights, and the operation of institutions under the rule of law. In stark contrast, Tully asserts that argument must begin by positing constitutionalism as a discursive process. For him:

> A constitution should be seen as a form of activity, an intercultural dialogue in which the culturally diverse sovereign citizens of contemporary societies negotiate agreements on their forms of association over time in accordance with three conventions of mutual recognition, consent and cultural continuity.
>
> (Tully 1995: 30)

Tully's argument concentrates for the most part on presenting how the traditions of 'modern' constitutionalism have undermined the position of indigenous peoples, and ignored the voices of intercultural minorities and women. However, the frame within which it is developed includes the challenges of supranational association as just one of the six sets of claims for cultural recognition 'which gather together the broad and various political activities which jointly call cultural diversity into question as a characteristic constitutional problem of our time' (Tully 1995: 1–2).[12] He argues that these challenges demand an alternative mode of understanding and doing constitutional politics and it is my contention that the type of analysis employed by Tully is relevant and useful in the EU context.

Tully's argument is based on a very strong critique of modern constitutionalism as fostering imperialistic cultural practices. In societies composed of diverse groups, dominant groups engaging with the traditions of modern constitutionalism seek to 'assimilate, integrate or transcend' differences, rather than to 'recognize and affirm' cultural diversity (1995: 44). This is because the practice is driven by the unexamined conventions and traditions of modern constitutionalism, which crucially include an assumption that there is a single comprehensive form of constitutional dialogue, and by theories of 'progress' which associate the ancient with the irregular and the modern with the uniform. Such practices, conventions and traditions quickly lose sight of many historical and cultural continuities or the meaning of real 'consent'. Constitutional moments thus occur which constitute – typically – nations out of a society of individuals presumed to be both equal and in a state of nature, yet bound together by some implicit common good (1995: 62–70). These types of dialogue are in truth more monological in character. For as Tully argues:

> The presupposition of shared, implicit norms is manifestly false . . . in any case of a culturally diverse society. Also, the aim of negotiations over cultural recognition is not to reach agreement on universal principles and institutions, but to bring negotiators to recognise their differences and similarities, so that they can reach agreement on a form of association that accommodates their differences in appropriate institutions and their similarities in shared institutions.
>
> (Tully 1995: 131)

In his detailed case studies – which are both historical and contemporary in nature – Tully finds examples of practices predicated on these principles of what he calls 'common constitutionalism' (mutual recognition, consent and cultural continuity). Equally, he observes how badly 'modern constitutionalism', based on the foundational paradigms of liberal and communitarian political theory, spiced by a heady dose of nationalism, has served the indigenous inhabitants of North America during the long-running periods of constitutionalization of the nation states of the United States and Canada. In many cases, such constitutional practices have been used to legitimate wholesale genocide.

The vehemence of Tully's argument has, naturally, attracted comment and criticism. William Scheuerman (1997), in a review essay, rejects his characterization of liberalism particularly in regard to the (mis)reading of classic sources. There are, in addition, accounts of the accommodation of difference and multiculturalism within liberalism to which Tully could, perhaps, lend greater credence (e.g. Kymlicka 1991). Kymlicka's approach specifically endorses a developed notion of community within liberalism which means that his practical approaches (and, indeed, his refusal to make outright prescriptions) find him not so distant from Tully (Kymlicka 1996). Hence, for these purposes, the interest of Tully's work lies less in his attacks upon modern constitutionalism or liberalism, but more in the urgency with which he seeks to prise open the very notion of constitutionalism, and the methods he applies to this end.

The details of Tully's alternative mode of constitution-building (common constitutionalism) are derived from critical concepts of understanding, definition and description drawn from the philosophy and philosophical practices of Ludwig Wittgenstein. He summarizes it thus:

> Wittgenstein's philosophy is an alternative worldview to the one that informs modern constitutionalism. First, contrary to the imperial concept of understanding in modern constitutionalism . . . it provides a way of understanding others that does not entail comprehending what they say within one's own language of redescription, for this is now seen for what it is: one heuristic description of examples among others; one interlocution among others in the dialogue of humankind. Second, it furnishes a philosophical account of the way in which exchanges of views in intercultural dialogues nurture the attitude of 'diversity awareness' by enabling the interlocutors to regard cases differently and change their way of looking at things.
>
> Finally, it is a view of how understanding occurs in the real world of overlapping, interacting and negotiated cultural diversity in which we speak, act and associate together.
>
> (Tully 1995: 111)

Crucially, Wittgenstein's *Philosophical Investigations*, from which Tully draws the strength of his argument, are themselves dialogic in character. There is more than one voice, since any use of a general term – such as those which permeate the language of contemporary constitutionalism, including rights, citizenship, culture, institutions, justice, and so on – is no more, on Wittgenstein's view, than 'one heuristic way of characterising the case in question among others, not a "preconceived idea to which reality *must* correspond"' (1995: 110).[13] As many have observed, the interest and provocation of Wittgenstein lie as much in his way of putting things, its essentially dialogical character, and in his reconfiguration of philosophical method as in what he actually says (Stern 1996). As Hacker puts it, 'his bequest is a vision of philosophy as the pursuit not of knowledge but of understanding' (Hacker 1996: 272–3).

Returning to the EU's constitutional and politico-legal evolution, we can blend these insights with the intellectual framework developed by Bańkowski and Christodoulidis (1998) in a recent article, where they argue for the EU to be understood as an 'essentially contested project'. In an argument which derives its starting point from the investigation of the limits of legal postnationalism using the prisms of sovereignty and legal pluralism, they argue that

> the whole point of trying to describe the EU in terms of 'interlocking normative spheres' is to be able to see the whole system as a continuous process of negotiation and renegotiation; one that does not have to have a single reference point to make it either a stable state system or one that is approaching that end.
>
> (Bańkowski and Christodoulidis 1998: 2)

It is the archetypal contrast to the strongly teleological 'integration through law' movement, which saw the development of law as self-consciously tracking substantive integrationist outcomes. Rather it is 'essentially contested', both in terms of its end point (it does not have one, or at least not one which is fixed), and in terms of the dialogic processes which underpin its evolution.[14] In focusing upon essential contestability as – to use their example – European identity understood in the process of the renegotiation of different identities which they call the process through which 'we get what we can call Europe' (1998: 348) Bańkowski and Christodoulidis are departing from W.B. Gallie's original notion of the essentially contested concept (see Gallie 1955–6; Hurley 1989: 46). Distinguishing their approach from that of Gallie, they remind us that his notion was intended to demonstrate how two people could disagree substantively about a certain concept and yet agree that some example could be a paradigm for the concept (e.g. democracy, perhaps subsidiarity in the EU context). In the conception worked through by Bańkowski and Christodoulidis, the crucial element is 'doing', not 'being'. In other words, it is *contestation* not *contestability* which is the key. Moreover, it is not achieving some fixed notion of what 'Europe' is to become. Consequently, it is not doing something with a predetermined end, but acknowledging that the end, if there is one at all, is continuously renegotiated through the doing.

Bańkowski and Christodoulidis elaborate their ideas by drawing on the theory of autopoetic social systems, reminding us that the concept of a 'European community' (in the sense of a 'people') is a functional term for the purposes of integration. The concept of a people underlying the possibilities of a European Union is used by a system of meaning to effect the structural coupling of different legal and political systems, even though in reality, because there are no shared meanings across the systems (legal and political systems having, for example, fundamentally different views of 'the people' in a constitution), at most there are 'constructive' misreadings which allow continuous readaptations of systems over time. They conclude that 'the European *demos* is forever caught up in the definition of systems that articulate around it by simultaneously defining and undercutting the privilege of its naming' (Bańkowski and Christodoulidis 1998: 349). However, their approach is not a systems theoretical explanation of the EU, but a use of systems theory in order to make 'more precise the kind of reflexive and eschatological view' they wish to propound (1998: 354).

Combining these two insights, we begin to see that constitutionalism is not about – in its core – the design of 'good' institutions for a European society or new Euro-polity or the placing of potentially arbitrary power under reasonable restraint. In fact, it is not about 'an' end, or 'the' end, at all. Pragmatically, of course, many people would broadly accept that it is important to ensure that what power is wielded at the EU level is subjected to principles which the Western liberal heritage of democratic constitutionalism would recognize and acknowledge. Thus, a system of judicial review is in place, along with formal acknowledgements of the rule of law, the importance of justice, the separation of powers amongst institutions, and respect for human rights and democracy. The reality of representative democracy is, in fact, much more keenly in question. But little more than 'paper' progress can be made on any of these fronts until the reality of EU-based constitutionalism is fully recognized. Indeed, these reflections may be part of an intellectual inquiry which carries us away from the accepted conventions of liberal democracy as the basis for constitutionalism, perhaps towards the republican notion of democratic liberalism suggested by Bellamy and Castiglione (forthcoming). Their reasoning bears strong parallels to that of Tully, and Bańkowski and Christodoulides. It is wrong to assume that the body politic can necessarily bring different social groups into balance with each other. Rather, it may be necessary to acknowledge that this equilibrium cannot occur or can only occur after very sustained dialogue. It is important to avoid perceiving or positing a fixed desirable outcome for that dialogue, but rather it should be left 'free form'. They distinguish, significantly, between bargaining on the one hand, and negotiation and argument on the other, with a focus in the latter case on compromise (Bańkowski and Christodoulidis 1998: 20).

These reflections carry us back to Tully's refutation of the assumption of shared values and goals. The accommodation of the diversity which underlies the social, political, economic and legal framework of the EU must not be the attempt to persuade the member states to adopt a pre-defined template of 'integration'. Similarly, the pursuit of constitutionalism must not be driven by a set of assumptions about the 'good' constitution. So, Tully reminds us that:

> The presumption of an implicit consensus or a universal goal mis-identifies the *telos* of this type of constitutional dialogue, filtering out the diverse similarities and differences the speakers try to voice. Universality is a misleading representation of the aims of constitutional dialogue because, as we have repeatedly seen, the world of constitutionalism is not a universe, but a multiverse: it cannot be represented in universal principles or its citizens in universal institutions.
>
> (Tully 1995: 131)

Constitutionalism, on Tully's view, is precisely the intercultural dialogue and the process of negotiation and renegotiation (and even contestation), and the only values it should be underpinned by are those of mutual recognition, consent and cultural continuity, Tully's three conventions of common constitutionalism. This is different to the traditions of modern constitutionalism, which Tully criticizes as 'laying down simplistic concepts of popular sovereignty and constitutional association as premises' for constitutional dialogue (1995: 131). He also criticizes them for their concepts of dialogue in which 'the participants aim to reach agreement either on universal principles or on norms implicit in practice and, in both cases, to fashion a constitutional association accordingly' (1995: 131).

Once these misconceptions about the nature of constitutional dialogue are cleared out of the way, it becomes possible to make some preliminary suggestions about what these conventions might signify in the EU context. Thus, if mutual recognition is more than assimilation and implies a responsibility to listen to others speaking in their own language and not in a dominant language, this brings the unresolved problems of language and translation to the fore in the expanding, multilingual EU. If consent is indeed very different to coercion, that raises the question of 'whose consent', and demands a review of the nature of participation in EU constitutional processes recognizing that the EU implicates not only states but also 'their' peoples. And, finally, the notion of cultural continuity recognizes that EU constitutionalism is not built in a political, legal or intellectual vacuum, even if the European constitutional ship has to be constantly rebuilt at sea because of the realities of the context in which constitution-building actually occurs.[15] There are the constitutional practices of the member states, of the EU itself and of other European/international political entities all to be taken into consideration. Each national constitution creates a different 'gateway' for the EU legal order. In that sense, EC law has a different constitutional meaning in each legal order, despite the attempts of the Court of Justice to preach the gospel of uniform interpretation and application. Yet disintegration (or non-integration) can be as valuable as integration itself (Shaw 1996) in the formulation of a constitutional settlement which is more than a simple statement of constitutional principles, but incorporates also subjective elements of values and legitimacy (Snyder 1998).

V. CONCLUSION

Section IV has dwelt upon the creative and positive dimensions of understanding constitutionalism in process-oriented terms informed by the types of intellectual framework used by Tully, Bańkowski and Christodoulidis, as well by Bellamy and Castiglione. Moreover, I argued at the outset for constitutionalism in the EU to be understood explicitly within its postnational context and that context has been drawn into the analysis throughout. I have attempted to suggest that there are some useful intellectual avenues of inquiry which avoid the pitfalls of simply assimilating EU constitutionalism into the 'mainstream' of modern constitutionalism – whatever its inspiration. These avenues of inquiry emerge from one reading of con-stitutionalism, which reflects the need to ensure mutual recognition, consent and the continuity of constitutional practices. In the EU context, a necessary element is the rejection of a fixed teleology of integration – whether towards a federal or intergovernmental goal – in favour of a fluid understanding of postnationalism, coupled with a critical focus on processes of polity formation emerging from the constant negotiation and contestation of interests. Accordingly, approaches to constitutionalism in this spirit may appear strongly attached – perhaps even too strongly – to the spirit of proceduralism (Habermas 1996) in their focus upon deliberation, discourse and communication. They concentrate less upon formu-lating answers and more upon opening up 'spaces' of deliberation (Curtin, forth-coming).

This chapter does not try to suggest either that the procedural approach is free from pitfalls or that it represents the end of the story as far as constitution-building is concerned in either the EU or any other political space (Scott 1998). The 'space' for deliberation may be opened up, and that space may in due course be occupied by an emergent civil society, as postulated by Curtin (forthcoming). But a procedural approach alone gives no simple solutions to enduring problems such as ensuring 'inclusiveness' and civility in divided societies. A procedural approach based on the types of principle advanced by Tully may, as I have implied, make it possible to distinguish 'good' debate from 'bad', and legal rules are essential in order to make this a reality. Such rules can, for example, confer legal rights to be heard or rights to information which go beyond the veneer of transparency which currently characterizes the EU's approach to this question and gives rise to relationship of clientelism which so often links the EU's institutions with many associations and NGOs. Likewise, there is civic republicanism's strong attachment to the role of judicial review with the courts embodying a version of public reason. The courts can be employed in the context of a procedural approach to constitution-building to deal with issues as diverse as accession and secession, conflicts between individual and group rights whenever participation within the intercultural dialogue becomes contested, and perhaps most controversially to manage the structures of flexibility and differentiation which are probably both an inevitable and even desirable feature of a large and diverse EU.

We can pragmatically observe how far the current institutions and procedural frameworks of the EU diverge from the ideals of participation and representation postulated by writers such as Tully for constitution-building. We can suggest piecemeal improvements, or alternatively adopt a position inimical to any claim on behalf of the EU to be on a constitutional road, insisting instead that its pathway continues to be that of diplomacy not politics, based on an ethics of integration and not (yet) an ethics of participation (Bellamy and Warleigh 1998). For as long as that is the case, the argument can run, the language of constitutionalism should be eschewed as misleading and unhelpful. The argument sketched in this chapter, and the frameworks which the argument implies, are not intended to be an alternative normative and Utopian vista for the evolution of the Union. Rather, the argument is developed because it is an essential preliminary step, in a constructive analysis of constitutionalism in the postnational forum of the Union, towards uncovering the reality of constitutionalism as intercultural dialogue and as contestation between interests.

NOTES

* Professor of European Law, University of Leeds. Earlier drafts of this chapter were delivered at the King's College London Legal Theory Seminar, 'Constructing Constitutions', 11 November 1998 and at a staff seminar in the Law School of Queen's University Belfast, February 1999; I am grateful to participants at both events for their comments. Thanks also to John Bell, Damian Chalmers, Colin Harvey and Neil Walker for helpful and stimulating comments on earlier drafts, and to the anonymous reviewers and the editors for their comments on the penultimate draft. The usual caveat applies.

1 See Moravcsik and Nicolaïdes (1998) for an example of the mainstreaming of these debates.

2 This is preparatory work for a broader project, tentatively entitled *Constitutionalism and Integration in the 'New European Polity'*.

3 This section draws upon earlier expositions of the necessity of an interdisciplinary approach to the study of European Community law, notably: Shaw 1995, 1996, 1997; Armstrong and Shaw 1998.

4 The statement was directed principally at Barav 1980 but is applicable also to a wider range of scholarship.

5 A partial list (limited, for example, to work in English) would include the work of Kenneth Armstrong (1998a, 1998b), Damian Chalmers (1997, 1999), Deirdre Curtin (1997, forthcoming), Michelle Everson (1998a, 1998b), Imelda Maher (1998), Miguel

Poiares Maduro (1998), Inge-Johanne Sand (1998a, 1998b), Harm Schepel (1998), and Joanne Scott (1998). See also Neil Walker (e.g. 1996 and 1998), whose theoretical work on constitutionalism within a tradition of (reformed) legal positivism has emerged in a context specifically informed by the multi-level and pluralist challenge of EU governance, and Cathy Richmond, whose work on the EU legal order as system begins with, but goes beyond, the jurisprudential challenge of Hans Kelsen (Richmond 1997).

6   For examples of work on EU constitutionalism from the fields of law and political theory, see Weiler 1995, 1996, 1997; Walker 1996; Weale and Nentwich 1998; Bellamy and Castiglione 1996a; Eleftheriadis 1996, 1998; Snyder 1998.

7   See Case 294/83 *Parti Ecologiste 'Les Verts'* v. *European Parliament* [1986] ECR 1339; Opinion 1/91 *Re. the Draft Agreement on a European Economic Area* [1991] ECR I-6079.

8   In that sense it is close to the concept of 'supranationalism' developed extensively by Joseph Weiler, which paradoxically sees the development of the EU as an integral part of the 'national project' within Europe; for a summary, see Weiler 1998a.

9   *Brunner* [1994] 1 CMLR 57. For an extended treatment largely accepting these premises as the starting point for analysis, see Eleftheriadis 1998.

10 *Regina* v. *Bow Street Metropolitan Stipendiary Magistrate, ex parte Pinochet Ungarte* [1998] 3 WLR 1456 (no. 1); [1999] 2 WLR 272 (no. 2); [1999] 2 WLR 827 (no. 3).

11 I owe this point to Daniel Farber.

12 The six examples of the politics of cultural recognition are: claims of nationalist movements to be constitutionally recognized as independent nation states or as autonomous political associations within federal systems; pressures to recognize and accommodate supranational associations such as NAFTA and the EU; the claims of long-standing linguistic and ethnic minorities to constitutional recognition; the claims of 'intercultural' minorities, such as immigrants, refugees and exiles; the demands of feminist movements for recognition and women's struggles for autonomy within politics; the demands of Aboriginal or indigenous peoples for recognition and accommodation of their diverse cultures, governments and environmental practices.

13 The quotation is from L. Wittgenstein, *Philisophical Investigations*, translated by G.E.M. Anscombe, Oxford: Basil Blackwell, 1967, s. 131.

14 Compare, in conception, Ian Ward's notion of the EU as a 'post-modern polity' (Ward 1996: 173–9).

15 A useful metaphor which I owe to Neil Walker, in a comment on an earlier draft.

6

Speaking 'Europe': The Politics of Integration Discourse

Thomas Diez

NAMING THE 'BEAST'

Suppose a zoologist reveals the existence of an animal so far unknown to mankind. In an article, she describes its features and gives the beast a name. It is classified and categorized, put into the framework of zoological knowledge. In recent years, there have been many attempts at 'exploring the nature of the beast' (Risse-Kappen 1996b) in European integration studies. In many of them, the European Union (EU) is dealt with as if it were our zoologist's unknown animal. It is compared to other polities and international organizations, its organizational mechanisms are described and categorized. And there is much effort to name this unknown beast. Debates abound as to whether it is a 'postmodern' or 'regulatory state' (Caporaso 1996), a 'confederatio', 'consortio' or 'condominio' (Schmitter 1996), a system of 'multi-level governance' (Marks 1993) or a 'multiperspectival polity' (Ruggie 1993).

But as long as there is such a proliferation of names, and conceptualizations of what the name 'EU' means, the EU remains beyond the framework of our political knowledge. While the efforts of categorization and naming are most often presented as pure descriptions, i.e. as mirrors of reality, the discrepancy between the existence of the beast and our knowledge of it suggests that reality is not so readily observable as it may seem. Instead, even the zoologist needs a given system of language, constituting the body of zoological knowledge, for her categorizations. Language is thus central to our knowledge of reality. It does not only serve as a 'mirror of nature' (Rorty 1979). Rather, it is possible to know of reality through linguistic construction only.

This chapter explores the role of language in the construction of the EU. Its main argument is that the various attempts to capture the Union's nature are not mere descriptions of an unknown polity, but take part in the construction of the polity itself. To that extent, they are not politically innocent, and may themselves become the subject of analysis, along with articulations from other actors. My plea is therefore to include discourse analysis in the canon of approaches in European studies. With a few exceptions, and in contrast to the field of international relations, such work is currently missing. Closing that gap would both enlarge our understanding of the integration process, and insert a reflective moment in our analyses. First, it adds an important dimension to the predominant focus on ideas and institutions within social constructivist studies of European integration, arguing that they cannot exist apart from discourse. Second, it introduces a new 'face of power'. Analyses of European integration have so far by and large focused on (absolute or relative) material capabilities as power, and on the interests behind the application of such power. Against such an understanding, Steven Lukes once put his 'radical' view of power that works through preventing individuals or classes from realizing their 'real' interests in the first place (Lukes 1974). The notion of power employed in this chapter follows the line of Lukes but doubts that there is such a thing as a 'real' interest independent from the discursive context in which interests emerge. The power of discourse then becomes crucial.[1] Third, it allows for an analysis of the contestedness of certain concepts, and thus points towards possible integration alternatives. Finally, it brings with it a reflective dimension to the research processes, particularly necessary in a field in which many researchers have traditionally been directly entangled with the political process of integration.

Throughout the chapter, I will restrict myself to providing some illustrations of the argument and not conduct a discourse analysis as such. Instead, my aim is to lay down the theoretical groundwork that relates a constructivism focusing on language (variously called 'radical' or 'epistemological' constructivism, among other labels) to European studies.[2] The argument proceeds in three moves, each of which I associate with the name of a certain philosopher or social/political theorist whose writings have contributed to the elaboration of these moves. The first move is labelled 'Austinian' and introduces the notion of a performative language. The second move is called 'Foucauldian' and points to the political implications of the performativity of language through the definition of meaning. The third move takes up 'Derridarean' themes and discusses the possibilities of change, opening up space for the articulation of alternative constructions of European governance.

I introduce these moves as a way of developing and introducing a certain approach. There are various problems attached to such a procedure. Most importantly, it is not at all clear whether the work of the respective theorists is compatible. On the contrary, it has been claimed that lumping together Foucault and Derrida, for instance, is to ignore the disagreements both of them expressed *vis-à-vis* each other (see Marti 1988: 167, fn. 2). The exchange between Derrida and Searle (who uses an Austinian understanding of language) has become a linguistic classic (Derrida 1977; Searle 1977). It is, however, also the case that the works associated with each of the three moves are, at least in part, shaped by the others. The order in which they are presented here roughly follows the historical chronology of their development, in particular in relation to when each move was taken up by the social sciences in general, and international relations in particular. Thereby, it will become clear how the debate proceeded from insisting on the relevance of language *per se* to clarifying its power and potentials to change. Each move will therefore refine, transform and thus move somewhat away from the insights gained from earlier steps. All of them push the argument in a certain direction, with other paths available. Readers may thus want to leave the proposed tour of inquiry at a certain point, and prefer other possibilities opened up by then. None the less, I propose that the approach I will have elaborated in the end is valuable in that it provides a new perspective on the development of European governance.

THE AUSTINIAN MOVE: THE PERFORMATIVE LANGUAGE

The common sense of language is that it describes or takes note of a reality outside language. It is, in other words, 'constative' (Austin 1975: 3). The search for the nature of the beast EU is in this tradition: European governance is something 'out there', the nature of which needs to be captured by language, i.e. by the definitions and observations entailed in our analysis. But there are several cases in which language, even to the casual observer, seems to go beyond its constative function. Examples are the declaration of a child's name at her baptism, the issuing of an order, or the formulation of a treaty through which a new political organization comes into existence. In his lectures at Harvard in 1955, J.L. Austin thus introduced the notion of 'performative' sentences (Austin 1975: 6). In the examples above, language is performative in that it does not only take note of, say, the founding of the European Economic Community (EEC). Instead, it is *through* language that this founding is performed. Apart from the act of speaking itself (which Austin labelled a 'locutionary act'), in these cases it is '*in* saying something [that] we do something' (Austin 1975: 94). There is an 'illocutionary force' to language. Furthermore, what we say may have an effect on other people; by saying something, we may not only act ourselves, but also force others to do so.

Austin and his student John Searle contributed significantly to the development of a theory of 'speech acts' – acts performed through speech. On the basis of this theory, Jürgen Habermas was later to develop his theory of communicative action (Habermas 1984), the influence of which one may trace to his current concerns for a European citizenship linked to a European politico-communicative space (Habermas 1992a, 1992b). It is, however, important to note the 'through' in the above definition of speech acts. In contrast to the following moves, the Austinian move does not locate action on the level of language as such. Instead, language serves as an instrument of will and intention: the question posed by Austin is, 'how to do things *with* words', and not, 'how are things done *by* words'. To the extent that this presupposes language as a carrier of meaning, the 'principle of expressibility', formulated by Searle (1969: 19–21), is of crucial importance: It is 'in principle' possible to say what one means. Habermas's discursive ethics, after all, relies upon exactly this possibility of expression in a discursive space ideally situated outside coercive power relations (Habermas 1990).

Although speech acts are never purely particularistic but rule-governed and thus performed within a certain social context, they none the less flow, seen from this perspective, from the individual. But to the extent that they are conceptualized as rule-governed, meaning in Searle's work is already 'at least sometimes a function [and not the origin] of what we are saying' (Searle 1969: 45). Speech act theorists are concerned with politics *through*, not politics *of* discourse. But they recognize that language is not always a neutral and purely descriptive device. Instead, it may contain evaluations and serve political purposes (Searle 1969: 132–6).

When it comes to politics, it is probably uncontested that most articulations, in the form of negotiation statements, laws, treaties or the like, do or at least intend to do something. Introducing speech act theory to international law, Nicholas Onuf cites the statement of rules as an example of typical illocutionary acts (Onuf 1989: 83–4). The signing of the treaty on the European Coal and Steel Community, for instance, founded the first European institution on the way to what is now the EU, and served France's interest of controlling an important base of German industry, while it helped Germany to return to the international scene. The system of governance established since then can be presented as a remarkable collection of speech acts and their effects, be it in the form of declarations, further treaties, decisions by the European Court of Justice, or Community legal acts.

In contrast to other attempts to analyse European governance, an approach informed by speech act theory would pay more attention to language. In looking for the nature of the beast, Thomas Risse-Kappen, for instance, is mostly concerned with the domestic structure of certain policy fields and their degree of 'Europeanization' (Risse-Kappen 1996b). The role of language in governance seems to be as much underplayed as it is in social constructivist scholarship in international relations more generally speaking, starting with Alexander Wendt's focus on state interaction through 'gestures', not speech (Wendt 1992: 404; see Zehfuß 1998: 125–8).[3]

A most interesting story in this respect is how citizenship developed from concerns about Europe's political future and role in the world, via the necessity to regulate membership of a single market, to being a response to questions about legitimacy and democracy within the EU. During this process, speech acts performed by a variety of actors, often with different intentions, not only led to the establishment of EU citizenship, but also to the reformulation of the concept of citizenship, with consequences for the shape of the Euro-polity.[4] More generally speaking, the whole history of European integration can be understood as a history of speech acts (following Onuf: rules) establishing a system of governance (which, after all, is about rules that are binding for the members of the system; see Kohler-Koch 1993).

We should not, however, overstate the distinction between locutionary and illocutionary acts. In fact, one of Austin's central propositions concerned the practical difficulties in distinguishing between constative and performative sentences (Austin 1975: 94). First, even locutionary acts are performative to the extent that to state something is to do something: it is to locate something in a specific context, following certain rules and depending on the given circumstances (Austin 1975: 146–7; Searle 1969: 22). Second, the notion of locutionary and illocutionary acts is an abstraction. Speaking more generally includes both acts (Austin 1975: 147).

In the same vein, Searle insisted that the idea that descriptive statements could never entail evaluative ones amounted to what he called the 'naturalistic fallacy fallacy' (Searle 1969: 132).

Consider that it was common in the British debate of the 1960s to refer to the EEC as the 'Common Market', whereas in Germany the term most often used was 'Gemeinschaft' ('Community').[5] One can reasonably assume that, to most people, the utterance of these words seemed innocent and descriptive, but they were not. First, in locating the EEC in different contexts according to the rules and circumstances of their respective national debates, they established a specific reading of the Treaties of Rome. Second, in the case of Britain, this partial fixation of meaning, together with a referendum as a means of legitimization, served to structure the evolving debate about possible European Community (EC) membership, dividing the broad spectrum of opinions into two simple camps: 'pro-' and 'anti-marketeers'.[6]

Even if their illocutionary force is not as readily visible as in the case of rules, such speech acts have important social and political consequences. Whereas the Austinian move helped us to understand that speaking Europe is to do something, the Foucauldian move will help us to understand better the political force of such performative language.

THE FOUCAULDIAN MOVE: DISCOURSE, POWER AND REALITY

The British example is, of course, well known and not very original. But it seems that its implications are rarely understood. More often than not, the British are taken to be 'natural' Eurosceptics, owing to their history or geographical status.[7] But on closer inspection, the problem is less to do with different attitudes towards Europe, but with the concept of 'Europe' itself. It has to be stressed that neither the 'Common Market' nor the 'Gemeinschaft' conception was 'correct' or 'false'. Rather, they were possible readings of the system of Western European governance. In other words, 'Europe' is not a neutral reality but a 'contested concept', the meaning of which is not (yet) fixed (Connolly 1983; see Schäffner et al. 1996: 4). Even assuming (as I will do in the following) that it is somehow related to a system of governance does not help that much: there are still numerous ways to construct such a system, in content, nature and scope. It is such constructions that the speech acts discussed at the end of the last section were about.

'Europe' might be one of the most typical examples of contested concepts, but the argument can be made on a more general level. The central proposition is that 'reality' cannot be known outside discourse, for the moment broadly defined as a set of articulations. In the words of Michel Foucault:

> We must not imagine that the world turns towards us a legible face which we would have only to decipher; the world is not the accomplice of our knowledge; there is no prediscursive providence which disposes the world in our favor. We must conceive discourse as a violence which we do to things, or in any case as a practice which we impose on them.

> (Foucault 1984: 127)

In many ways, this is merely a more radical reformulation of Austin's observation that to state something is to do something. But to phrase it in such radical terms brings to the fore the political relevance of language beyond the concept of rhetoric as a means to political ends, and towards a power that rests in discourse itself. This power makes us understand certain problems in certain ways, and pose questions accordingly. It thereby limits the range of alternative policy options, and enables us to take on others. The contest about concepts is thus a central political struggle (Connolly 1983: 30), not only between individuals and groups defending one meaning against another, but also between different ways of constructing 'the world' through different sets of languages. These different languages are not employed by actors in a sovereign way. It is the discursive web surrounding each articulation that makes the latter possible, on the one hand (otherwise, it would be meaningless), while the web itself, on the other hand, relies on its reproduction through these articulations.

Discourse in this Foucauldian reformulation is thus more radical than the speech act tradition in that more emphasis is put on the context in its relation to the individual actor. Although it is 'we' who impose meaning, 'we' do not act as autonomous subjects but from a 'subject position' made available by the discursive context in which we are situated (Foucault 1991: 58). The speech act tradition emphasized the rules and contexts of speaking; the discursive tradition furthermore emphasizes the constitutive role of discourse in the production of subject identities. Discourse then takes up a life of its own. It is not a pure means of politics – instead, politics is an essential part of discourse. The struggle to impose meaning on such terms as 'Europe' is not only a struggle between politicians but also between the different discourses that enable actors to articulate their positions (Larsen 1997a: 121–2).

In a way, this notion amounts to what one may call a 'linguistic structurationism', adding to Giddens' theory the crucial importance of language (see Giddens 1984). Giddens' central aim, shared by Foucault, was to move beyond structuralism and to reconceptualize the duality of structures and agency. His theory of structurationism, imported into international relations by Alexander Wendt (1992), argues that both, structure and agency, were mutually dependent on each other. Whether Giddens was successful in this endeavour is contested. It has been argued, for instance, that structurationists eventually privilege structure by making it their ontological starting point whereas, in a Foucauldian perspective, more emphasis is put on practice in that structures are always reinterpreted and thereby transformed (Ashley 1989: 276–7). The major point in the present context, though, is that Giddens does not take language seriously enough (Zehfuß 1998), whereas a focus on discourse attributes a central importance both to the practice of speaking and the linguistic context in which articulations emerge and are read.

Before I move on to show the relevance of this to European integration studies by way of some more examples, I need to clarify that to say that any talk about reality will always be a specific construction of the latter is not to deny the existence of reality itself (Laclau and Mouffe 1985: 108; Potter 1996: 7). When entering a different country, confronted with very 'real' physical barriers, one has to present a passport. While the Schengen agreement has eliminated borders between some of its signatory states, it has led to the intensification of such controls at the outside borders of 'Schengenland'. But there is no 'neutral language' to convey the meaning of these 'real' borders. Their construction as guarantees of welfare provisions or illegitimate walls depriving people of their right to move are both speech acts within a specific discursive context. Furthermore, discourse itself is part of reality. In that sense, discursive approaches do not fit into the old dichotomy of idealists versus realists. In fact, the example of 'Schengenland' nicely illustrates this: it emanates from and reifies a specific discursive construction of European governance.

'EURO-SPEAK'

After the Foucauldian move, any 'description' of European governance participates in the struggle to fix the latter's meaning, and thus is a political act. This is hardly ever recognized. Philippe Schmitter, for one, explicitly acknowledges the role of language in European integration. He identifies the development of a 'Euro-speak' defining the space for political action within the EU, while often being hardly comprehensible to an outsider (Schmitter 1996: 122–7; see also Schäffer et al. 1996: 8). Elements of this 'Euro-speak' range from 'acquis communautaire' to 'co-decision', from 'subsidiarity' to 'supranationalité' (Schmitter 1996: 137). At the same time, however, Schmitter sees a need 'for labels to identify the general configuration of authority that is emerging' in the case of the EU, and doubts that this can be done by a mere aggregation of currently existing 'Euro-speak' (Schmitter 1996: 137).

But following the Austinian and Foucauldian moves, the 'new vocabulary' that Schmitter is looking for cannot be used simply to 'pick up such developments' as the emergence of 'a new form of multi-layered governance', and to 'describe the process of integration' (Schmitter 1996: 132–3). Instead, such developments are only knowledgeable to us within specific discursive contexts, and to label them from our various subject positions is to engage in the 'struggle for Europe' (Wæver 1997b). This struggle is not restricted to the realm of political 'practitioners' – as academics dealing with matters of European integration, we are also part of it.[8]

Consider the conceptualization of the EU as a system of 'multi-level governance' (e.g. Marks 1993; Christiansen 1997). The image created by this account is one of a set of various separated levels of governance (local, regional, national, European) that interact with each other in some issue areas and follow their own course in others. This has by now become something of a 'textbook image' of the EU. It would be naïve to assume that this image directly becomes the ground on which politicians in the EU base their decisions. This is not what is claimed here. Rather, the point is that such conceptualizations are part of a wider discursive context and do not 'stand aside' from their object of analysis. They take up the claims made by German Länder about their role in the overall system, or by various national governments leading to the specific construction of subsidiarity in Art. 3b TEC.[9] It is these 'multi-level' representations taken together that reify a notion of politics working on separate planes. The development of the EU towards such a system that way becomes a self-fulfilling hypothesis.[10]

The power of discourse is that it structures our conceptualizations of European governance to some extent, rather than us simply employing a certain language to further our cause. The multi-level language gives preference to actors on various 'state' levels and is linked to an extension of the classical federalist practice of territorial representation on the 'highest' organizational level, now with three representational bodies instead of two. What happens if for a moment we employ a different language and speak of a 'network polity' instead? Our conception of the EU changes, and instead of 'levels', we find a more open political space, both geographically and functionally diversified, undermining the territorial notion of politics that is still upheld by the multiple levels concept (Kohler-Koch 1999).[11]

Which of the two languages should be preferred is contestable, and need not be discussed at this point. Both have their own political consequences in that they enable different kinds of political actors to claim legitimate existence in different kinds of decision-making processes. A functional body such as the Economic and Social Committee does not, of course, simply disappear once the multi-level language is employed. But it does not figure too prominently in our representations of the EU, and this quasi non-existence is being reified.

The language of neo-functionalism provides a second illustration. One of the distinctive features of neo-functionalism was its proposal to bridge the gap between functional and political association in classic functionalism by transforming the concept of 'spill-over' (i.e. the notion that integration processes, once started in a field of 'low politics', will create a dynamic of their own and sooner or later affect other policy fields) by adding to it an explicit political content and agent, working towards the eventual establishment of an overall federal, or at least supranational, system (Caporaso and Keeler 1995: 33–4; Kelstrup 1998: 29; Zellentin 1992: 70–1). Again, the question is not whether those expectations were right or misplaced. Instead, my proposition is that while neo-functionalism might thereby have closed one gap, it opened up another one, and that this is because of the language employed.

On the one hand, the reformulated spill-over concept had to include democratic processes at one point or another. Economic policy might well be legitimized by references to economic output – the guarantee of welfare. But this leads to the construction of Europe as an 'Economic Community' (Jachtenfuchs 1997b; Diez 1999; Jachtenfuchs et al. 1998). While legitimation through output is already a position hardly accepted universally in relation to economic policy, things become even more problematic if one moves into other policy fields. Thus, the inclusion of participatory elements was unavoidable if spill-over was to be sustained. But, on the other hand, the language of neo-functionalism was all very technical, the name of the approach itself being no exception. Accordingly, the central institution in the emerging polity was given the name of a 'commission', and the means of governance were called 'directives' and 'regulations' (Art. 189 TEC). Such terms are hardly reconcilable with the current language of democracy without a redefinition of democracy itself. That, however, was not what was proposed – in fact, classic functionalism might have been more apt to such a redefinition by changing the territorial organization of societies into a functional one, whereas neo-functionalism proposed using the latter to achieve the former.

The 'democratic deficit' charge that has haunted the EU ever since its inception at Maastricht seems to be directly connected to this problematic. Its citizens claim that the EU is far too bureaucratic, technical, distant, and its decision-making procedures too intransparent (see Weiler 1998b: 78). This might be the case or not – it seems at least questionable whether politics in any of the national capitals is more transparent. But the institutional language of neo-functionalism has prevailed until today, and provides the ground to continuously reconstruct the EU as a monster bureaucracy concerned with technical matters that increasingly affect the everyday life of its citizens without their formal consent, while the nation state carries with it the ideals of self-determination and democracy.

In such a setting, it is hard to make the case that the initiative for a substantial number of directives can be traced back to member state governments, or that the size of the EU administration is smaller than that of a single member state such as Germany's federal bureaucracy (Wessels 1996: 182–4), or that non-governmental organizations are heavily involved in the making of EC policies (Jachtenfuchs and Kohler-Koch 1996: 24; Kohler-Koch 1998). Surely, none of this makes the EU a heaven of democracy – not on the basis of the predominant current understanding of democracy, in any case. Instead, the point of this discussion is that the language of neo-functionalism enables one reading of the EU rather than another. And furthermore, this language seemed right and innocent (in the sense of being the objectively best available way) at one point – much in the same way as the language of multi-levellism today.[12] In each case, the Foucauldian move points to the politics involved in discourse, a politics that we are often unaware of and that does not come to our attention as long as we equate politics with interests and intentions.

THE DERRIDAREAN MOVE: CONCEPTUALIZING CHANGE AND OPTIONS FOR ALTERNATIVES

Within a universe of discourses, change is only possible if meaning is not eternally fixed and if the lines of contestation between various discourses are allowed to shift. Only if this is the case will there be a chance for the development of a new 'Euro-speak', and thus for the development of alternative constructions of European integration. On the other hand, the meaning of words needs to be relatively stable in a given context for communication to be possible. In his structural theory of language, Frédéric de Saussure argued that national languages 'work' because they represent crystal grids in which each word has its proper place. It takes on meaning through the firm opposition in which it stands towards another word in this grid (Frank 1983: 32–4). In such a 'crystal grid' model, change is hard to conceive of. But we all know that meaning is not eternally fixed: dictionaries provide us with contested meanings of a single word, and, once in a while, such entries have to be changed because the word is now used in a different or additional sense. Furthermore, we do experience breakdowns of communication.

This is the reason for a third and final move, which I will call Derridarean.

Change was not absent from the Austinian and Foucauldian moves. They emphasized the role of action in a continuous reconstruction of and struggle for meaning. But in order to conceptualize the interplay of structure and agency in linguistic terms, the Derridarean move will be more helpful. In contrast to Saussure, French philosopher Jacques Derrida conceptualized language not as a closed and more or less rigid grid, but as a series of open-ended chains (Derrida 1977). With each articulation, there is at least a potential of adding new oppositions to the already existing chain, and thereby of altering it (see Potter 1996: 84). This does not necessarily result in a breakdown of communication. In fact, communication does not have to rest on a concept of 'understanding', assuming the correspondence of what is said and received in the speaker's and receiver's minds. Instead, it can be conceived of as operating on the level of language, where the decisive factor is the affinity of discourses and thus their mutual translatability (see below). Furthermore, change and continuity always go hand in hand with each other. Although the overall discursive space is not as volatile as Derridareans sometimes suggest, and each addition to a linguistic chain seems to be minor at first, it may indeed be part of a major transformation, the importance of which becomes clear only in the long run.

An example of such a change is the development of the construction of European governance as an economic community in the form of a 'common market' in the British case. There, the predominant concept of European integration in the 1950s was indeed a classic 'Eurosceptic' one of pure intergovernmental co-operation. But at the same time, economic considerations played an increasing role in the overall political debate. This led to the reformulation of co-operation as a free trade area. The language in which this area was constructed centred around economic output. Its basic mechanism was still intergovernmental, but this economic focus laid down a trace that soon made it possible to articulate supranational governance in the economic realm. And indeed, this is how Macmillan presented his 'bid for membership' in August 1961 (Hansard 1961: 1481, 1490; see Diez 1999: ch. 3).

Put in a simple way, we all enter into a conversation with a set of preconceptions from which we set out to reconstruct other articulations. Thus, we not only receive them passively, but regularly add to the linguistic chain unless our set of preconceptions (or at least those relevant for the given conversation) are exactly the same as the ones of the speaker. Borrowing a conceptualization from the radical constructivist branch of systems theory (Hejl 1987), we may think of ourselves as being situated in, and our preconceptions resulting from, a node of discourses providing the basis for our interaction in communication. In other words, our preconceptions are nothing other than objects of particular discourses, which in turn are linked to a number of other discourses in what I call a 'discursive nodal point' (Diez 1998a, 1998b, 1999: ch. 2). There is a simple reason for such linkages between discourses: the conceptualization of objects in one discourse follows a set of rules, which, in turn, result from 'metanarratives' providing meaning to the latter, etc. This creates a web in which discourses are bound up with each other, and which is held together by nodal points.

The latter, given the Derridarean move, are potentially unstable, but will usually not change in a radical way. Shifts seem most likely if there is a considerable overlap between the rules (and therefore the metanarratives) of the two discourses in question, both in terms of content (that is, concerning the objects of the metanarratives) and in terms of structure (that is, some overall principles to which the rules adhere). This overlap makes articulations translatable. On the basis of such similar 'languages', it is possible from one nodal point to make sense of articulations resulting from another one, so that the latter are not rejected right away, opening up the possibility of (ex)change. Seen from such an angle, the language of a free trade area in the British case facilitated the move towards the articulation of an economic community that would otherwise have been much harder, if not impossible.

Finally, the Derridarean move also allows us to address possible alternatives to the federal state and economic community conceptions that currently dominate the debate (see Jachtenfuchs *et al.* 1998). Recent years have witnessed an emerging 'Euro-speak' that focused on subsidiarity and flexibility.[13] Most well known are the introduction of the principle of subsidiarity into the Treaty of Maastricht, accompanied by the establishment of the Council of the Regions, and suggestions ranging from the '*Kerneuropa*' and 'concentric circle' visions of German Christian Democrats Karl Lamers and Wolfgang Schäuble and former French Prime Minister Eduard Balladur to the demands for more flexibility by former British Prime Minister John Major. All of them, in one way or another, are set in opposition to 'centralization' and a further unitary development of the EU, either because the latter are linked to hindrances for further deepening and widening of integration, or because they are associated with a neglect of nation state identities. While potentially undermining the *acquis communautaire*, the emergence of this new 'Euro-speak' in parts also serves to reify the 'nation state' as a central concept in politics. Nowhere is this clearer than in the way 'subsidiarity' is invested in legal discourse through Art. 3b and its sole stress on member states' competences.

In terms of the centrality of territorial statehood in political discourses, the change brought about by these terms thus seems to be of a rather marginal kind. It is easier to see the problems they pose to the construction of European governance as a federal state in the making than to the territorial organization of politics as such. Rather, their usage seems to follow rules similar to those of 'multi-level' constructions. But seen from the perspective outlined above after the Derridarean move, these seemingly marginal changes might bring with them more fundamental transformations in that they lay out a linguistic trace that can be seized upon by alternative constructions.

Consider the rules of the network discourse. It, too, is set against centralization, but also against purely territorial politics, and includes both territorial and functional divisions. Network-like constructions of European governance have traditionally been marginalized in the overall integration debate. Members of the Integral Federalists, for instance, argued at the Congress of The Hague in 1948 for the encouragement, 'regardless of frontiers, [of] the spontaneous articulation of interests, energies and hopes' (Lipgens and Loth 1985: 49), and stated their 'wish to be as far as possible decentralized, both regionally and functionally; not a superstate but a real democracy, built up of self-governing communities' (Lipgens and Loth 1985: 45). But their influence within the federalist movement was never strong, and if anything became weaker over time.[14] Their construction of 'federalism' was too far apart from that of the dominant discourse, the discursive nodal point from which they argued too different and outlandish for those used to talking in terms of modern territorial statehood. The language of the latter is clear, orderly and relatively parsimonious – the waters of the network discourse are much more muddied. They do not provide a clear outlook and focus on terms such as 'spontaneity' or 'living, supple complexity' (Lipgens and Loth 1985: 50). From the discursive nodal point of a federal state conception, it is hard not to see this as a deficiency. To put it simply, the language of vagueness did and does not translate well into a language of clear borders, hierarchy and uniformity. The language of neo-functionalism, in contrast, was in a much better position, having a clear overall programme. In the same vein, 'multi-level governance' is still a pretty much ordered one in that it implies, for instance, the clear separation of a minimum number of levels.

But remember that the exact meaning of a term is context-bound, while at the same time it can be transformed through the reinvestment of the terms in question from different discursive positions. Hence, it may turn out to be of some significance that the terms 'subsidiarity' and 'flexibility' are contested concepts that are not alien to the network language. Instead, they are much closer to it than, for instance, neo-functionalist language. This increases the translatability of network articulations into dominant 'Euro-speak'. Much like the movement from free trade area to economic community in the British case, there is a trace that can be seized upon by actors working from the network's discursive nodal point.

This is, of course, not to say that, in due course, the debate will have changed so much that it becomes common to construct European governance in such terms. The notion of 'linguistic structurationism' reminds us of the need for these terms to be reinvested by actors from such a discursive position. What is important, however, is that the current transformations in 'Euro-speak' allow for such a reinvestment. Thus, the language of day-to-day politics may well be ahead of our minds in trying to figure out the 'nature of the beast'.

THE IMPORTANCE OF LANGUAGE

My attempt in this chapter was to make a case for the importance of language in the process of European integration. By way of three moves (Austinian, Foucauldian and Derridarean), I argued that language does more than describe; that all our accounts of the world (and thus of European governance) are embedded in certain discourses; that the meaning of words is dependent on their discursive context; that this context is not rigid but in constant, if only slow, flux; and that recent transformations of the discursive context enable the construction of Europe as a 'network'. I have illustrated this string of arguments with a number of examples, but there is no doubt that there needs to be more research into the workings of each of the moves in the context of European integration. Among the research questions that emanate from the above line of argument are the following:

- What are the terms with which we speak about European integration? How did 'Euro-speak' evolve?
- What are the political pre-decisions implied in those terms?
- What are the alternative meanings of these terms in various contexts?
- How are these terms invested? Which rules do they follow? From which contexts do they emanate?

Substantiated by such research, there are at least two further 'practical' implications, besides the enablement of the network alternative.

First, the future development of the EU will not depend solely on member states' interests, but also on the translatability of the discourses on European governance that the relevant political actors are embedded in. It seems that the EU is a 'multi-perspectival polity' not only because of its lack of a single centre of decision-making, but also because it allows for conceptualizations from various angles. The issue for institutional development is not whether these conceptualizations are identical, but whether they can make sense of the Treaties and other basic texts at the core of integration (Wæver 1990).

Second, there might be too much focus these days on the change of institutions in the narrow, organizational sense of the term. The change of institutions, from the perspective developed above, is not interesting as a fact in and of itself, but as part of a broader set of practices in which language plays a crucial role. Institutions cannot be separated from the discourses they are embedded in, and rather than a formal change of institutions, what seems necessary is a change in the discursive construction of these institutions, of which the former would only be one particular component. Such change is obviously problematic, for no one can control language, but everyone contributes to it in each new articulation.

The academic attempts to categorize the EU and give it a place in our order of political systems are nothing but such contributions. They are attempts to fix the meaning of European governance, so that we know what the latter 'is', but they are not just 'objective' analyses of a pre-given political system. This does not make them worthless; on the contrary, they are as essential for our knowledge as the zoologist's classification of her 'beast' is, and they are probably more relevant to our daily lives. Eventually, a further difference to what the zoologist does with her words is that while it may be relatively easy for her to take the lead in constituting the first dominant discourse on the newly discovered animal, the many voices involved in the construction of European governance will ensure that the fixation of meaning in this case is much harder.

What is the politics involved here? On one level, the answer that this chapter has given is that it is a politics *of* discourse, that within the language in which we operate lies a set of choices about the political decisions of our day. Since I started out from the observation that this discursive dimension is largely neglected, it was my attempt to bring the latter to our attention by focusing on these pre-decisions. But are we then, according to the above line of argument, *dependent* on the discourses of the nodal points in which we are situated? Addressing these questions is a thorny undertaking, and I can only sketch my (preliminary) answer. But however thorny, they are of the utmost theoretical and practical relevance. After all, the post-structuralist work in the theory of international relations, from which my argument is largely derived, set out as a critique both of individualized conceptions of political agency and of the structuralism of neo-realism, which seemed to undermine any attempts to change the anarchical international system (Ashley 1989: 273–4).

My sketch draws on two distinctive features of discourse at it was set out above. First, I pointed out that discourses do not 'cause' but *enable*. They do have a structural quality in that they are more than the sum of individual acts, but they are at the same time dependent on the latter. They set limits to what is possible to be articulated (Wæver 1998: 108), but do also provide agents with a multitude of identities in various subject positions, and are continuously transformed through the addition and combination of new articulations. In spite of all the epistemological and ontological differences, their work is thus none the less similar, for instance, to the structures in Robert Cox's work on international relations, in which structures predispose, but do not determine (Mittelman 1998: 76). There is room for creativity on behalf of political actors in the model of discursive nodal points. In Ernesto Laclau and Chantal Mouffe's conceptualization, stressing the practice of articulations, the latter are even the means to link various metanarratives in order to fix meaning (Laclau and Mouffe 1985: 113). But this creativity is not unlimited, and it does not *originate* within the individual because the latter operates from a subject position that is in itself discursively produced (Laclau and Mouffe 1985: 109, 115), and so each articulation will already flow from a discursive nodal point. Neither needs articulations that lead to a reformulation to be consciously conceived of as such. Their meaning cannot be fixed, and thus they might induce changes beyond original intentions – actors, as Foucault once remarked, may well know what they do, 'but what they don't know is what they do does' (quoted in Dreyfus and Rabinow 1982: 187).

Second, it needs to be recalled that, following the Derridarean move, discourses are different from traditionally conceptualized structures in that they are not rigid. Their contents can thus only be approximated, and not be once and for ever determined. The concept of discourse itself might help us to think in novel ways of structure and agency, since each articulation (a political *act*) is in itself a constitutive part of discourse. It is essential to note the extent to which articulations combine linguistic elements in novel ways, or whether they largely reproduce the prevailing rationalities. In that respect, the social constructivisms of Alexander Wendt (1992), or Jeffrey Checkel (1998; this volume), stressing the co-constitution of structure and agency and asking for greater attention to be paid to the processes of this co-constitution, are closer to the discursive constructivism espoused in this article than is often assumed, again despite their differences. Surely, I cannot claim to have finally solved the general puzzle of transcending the duality of structure and agency. But the purpose of this article was a more limited one. It was to foster in European studies, on the ground of theoretical reflections largely taken from the current debate in international relations, the awareness of the power of language, and of the discursive situatedness of our articulations and their readings. Speaking 'Europe', I hope I have shown, is always to participate in a struggle, as much as is practised from within a discursive context. The politics of integration discourse should not be underestimated.

ACKNOWLEDGEMENTS

Previous versions of this chapter appeared as a paper for the 'Social Constructivism in European Studies' workshop in Ebeltoft, Denmark, July 1998, and as COPRI Working Paper 26-1998. For their helpful comments and suggestions, I am indebted to Thomas Christiansen, Lykke Friis, Knud Erik Jørgensen, Markus Jachtenfuchs, Marlene Wind, Maja Zehfuß, two anonymous referees and the workshop participants.

NOTES

1   For a discussion of these various kinds of power, see Hindess 1996. The latter are not necessarily mutually exclusive, but my point in this context is to introduce the notion of discursive power. A discussion of how the different 'faces of power' are related is an interesting task beyond the scope of this chapter.

2   It should be noted that discourse is not reducible to language. But since the latter is a crucial element of the former, I will restrict myself in this chapter to the role of language.

3   Generally, though, the use of speech act theory is more widespread in international relations than in European integration studies. Examples are the already quoted work by Nicholas Onuf on international norms, Friedrich Kratochwil's study on international law (Kratochwil 1989), or more recently the conceptualization of security as a speech act called 'securitization' by Ole Wæver and the so-called Copenhagen School (Wæver 1995; Buzan et al. 1998; see Huysmans 1998). Wæver and his colleagues have also been among the so far few to analyse the role of language in constructing European governance (Holm 1997; Larsen 1997a, 1997b; Wæver 1990, 1997b, 1998).

4   This builds upon Antje Wiener's work (Wiener 1997, 1998a), although she does not use speech act theory explicitly in this context.

5   Until today, the major British-based political science journal dealing with European integration is called the *Journal of Common Market Studies*, and the major law journal *Common Market Law Review*, whereas the major German journal dealing exclusively with European integration simply bears the name of *Integration*.

6   The pro-/anti-dichotomy may be seen as an effect of having a referendum as such. On the other hand, referenda themselves depend on the prior formulation of alternatives.

7   This is analysed in greater detail in Diez 1999: ch. 1.

8   On the question of the problematic division between a realm of practitioners and a purely 'theoretical' academic realm, see Ashley 1989: 280.

9   TEC: Treaty establishing the European Community, as amended by the Treaty on European Union.

10 A more general example is even more intuitive: the notion that we live in an age of globalization has become one of the most important justifications for economic policies, never mind the question of whether the phenomenon itself is 'real' or not; see Hirst 1997: 206–14.

11 Schmitter suggests the network-like 'condominio' as one possible future development path of European governance. However, in the line of the above argument, he does not treat it as a different reading of what the EU is (Schmitter 1996: 136). For other conceptualizations of the 'network', see Diez 1996, 1997; Jachtenfuchs et al. 1998: 421–2.

12 It should be recalled that, in the heyday of neo-functionalism, trust in technology

and science reached a peak in Western development, for instance in relation to nuclear energy.

13   Out of a rich literature on this issue, see Adonis 1991; Endo 1994; Hüglin 1994; Stubb 1996; van Kersbergen and Verbeek 1994; Wilke and Wallace 1990; Wind 1998.

14   Integral federalism experienced a small renaissance, though, in the European governance models of Green Parties in the 1980s, see Diez 1996, 1997.

7

Constructing Europe? The Evolution of Nation-State Identities

Martin Marcussen, Thomas Risse, Daniela
Engelmann-Martin, Hans Joachim Knopf and
Klaus Roscher

INTRODUCTION[1]

This chapter investigates the impact of deep-rooted identity constructions relating to 'Europe' and of ideas about European political order on the way in which political élites in France, Germany and Great Britain have constructed nation state identities since the 1950s. We seek to understand:

- why two dramatic shifts in French nation state identity occurred – one with the emergence of the Fifth Republic under President de Gaulle in the late 1950s and early 1960s, the other during the 1980s and 1990s when political élites increasingly incorporated 'Europe' in the nation state identity of the Fifth Republic;
- why (West) German political élites have shared a consensual and thoroughly Europeanized version of German nation state identity since the end of the 1950s as a way of overcoming the country's own past;
- why the English[2] nation state identity which continues to dominate the British political discourse on Europe has remained virtually the same since the 1950s and why Europe still constitutes the, albeit friendly, 'other'.

We argue that a combination of three factors helps us to get a better understanding of this variation. First, new visions of political order need to *resonate* with pre-existing collective identities embedded in political institutions and cultures in order to constitute a legitimate political discourse. Second, political élites select in an instrumental fashion from the ideas available to them according to their perceived *interests*, particularly during 'critical junctures' when nation state identities are contested and challenged in political discourses. Third, once nation state identities have emerged as consensual among the political majority, they are likely to be *internalized* and institutionalized, as a result of which they tend to become resistant to change.

The chapter proceeds in the following steps. We begin with some conceptual clarifications of the notion of 'nation state identity'. Second, we present a brief overview of the empirical material. Third, we offer a theoretical approach to explaining change as well as continuity of nation state identities in the three countries.

NATION STATE IDENTITY: CONCEPTUAL CLARIFICATIONS

The concept of 'collective identity' we apply in this chapter draws on social psychology, particularly social identity and self-categorization theories (Oakes *et al.* 1994; Abrams and Hogg 1990; Turner 1987). Social groups tend to define themselves on the basis of a set of *ideas* to which members can relate positively. These ideas can be expressed directly in the discourse of the members and in their ways of interacting and communicating, or indirectly through the application of common symbols, codes or signs. The function of these ideas is to define the social group as an entity which is distinct from other social groups. The members thereby perceive that they have something in common on the basis of which they form an 'imagined community' (Anderson 1983). In this chapter, we look at discourses among *party élites* in France, Germany and Great Britain in order to understand their identity constructions with regard to the nation state and to Europe (see also Wæver 1996; Wæver *et al.* 1993; Wæver and Kelstrup 1993). Party élites are major actors in a country's political discourse and, contrary to other types of élites (academics and artists, for instance), they are constantly required to justify their actions in order to gain the support of their electorates and constituencies. In Europe at least, parties have always been major vehicles for the transmission of ideas between society and the state, rather than being confined to electoral organizations and, as mass integration parties, they instigate, shape and reflect major political debates.

Social identity and self-categorization theories also argue that, apart from being defined by a set of shared ideas, the sense of community among members of a social group is accentuated by a sense of distinctiveness with regard to *other social groups*. In other words, a social identity defines not only an 'in-group', but also one or several 'out-groups'.[3] When speaking about the political order during the Cold War, the élites in the three countries collectively shared an 'Other', communism and the Soviet Union. Moreover, British political élites have continuously considered 'Europe' as the friendly 'out-group', whereas German élites have seen the country's own catastrophic past as 'the other', and French political élites have traditionally added the US to their list of 'others'.

Furthermore, individuals are members of several social groups, which may or may not overlap. In other words, they hold *multiple identities*. Depending on the immediate context and the various roles that individuals play, they can be expected to invoke different elements of their social identity in different situations. In this article, we deal specifically with one of these social groups – *party élites* – and their utterances in a specific context, i.e. political discourses. As a result, we have considerably narrowed down the number of social identities dealt with and, subsequently, also the number of possible 'others'.

Related to this previous point, individuals invoke different elements of their social identity depending on the *specific context*. Because we are interested in utterances about the state as well as political and social order, we have chosen to call this particular identity a *nation state identity* to distinguish it from other components of the national and other social identities of party political élites. We do *not* claim that the nation as such is carrying this identity. What we do claim, though, is that party élites express visions about the state and Europe and consequently give discursive expression to nation state identities.

Finally, social psychology theory tells us that social identities are *unlikely to change frequently*. Individuals cannot constantly adjust their cognitive schemes to the many complex and often contradictory signals from the social world around them, as a result of which these perceived signals are integrated into existing cognitive schemes and stereotypes or simply rejected outright if they seem to be incommensurable with existing world views.[4] Nation state identities therefore tend to be sticky rather than subject to frequent change (Fiske and Taylor 1991: 150–1). However, this does not mean that they are completely stable. They do indeed vary over time according to the following logic:[5]

- There is always some leeway for the purposive attempt of political actors to alter existing ideational frameworks and boundary definitions, but it is particularly during *critical junctures* that the likelihood of the success of such attempts is greatest. We define critical junctures as *perceived* crisis situations occurring from complete policy failures, but also triggered by external events. Nation state identities are likely to be challenged under such circumstances (Olsen 1996: 252–3). Empirical examples are the catastrophe of the Second World War and the Nazi regime for German nation state identity, or the end of the Cold War for the French nation state identity. Élites start promoting new ideas about political order and about nation state identity when the old concepts are commonly perceived as irrelevant or as having failed.
- New ideas about political order do not fall from heaven, but need to *resonate with existing identity constructions* embedded in national institutions and political cultures (Checkel 1997b; Soysal 1994; Ulbert 1997; Jetschke and Liese 1998). While existing identity constructions are broadly defined and can resonate with a whole series of new ideas, they nevertheless define the range of options considered legitimate for new nation state identities. There is no reason to believe that these existing identity constructions are 'givens', which are elevated above identity politics and contestation.[6] But we argue that élites cannot construct new identities at will. Rather, new ideas about social order

and the nation state need to resonate with previously embedded and institutionalized values, symbols and myths. In our case, ideas about Europe
and European identity usually appear in various 'national colours' in order to
appeal to élite groups and to the larger public opinion.

- When promoting new ideas about political order during critical junctures, we
  expect political élites to act on the basis of what they perceive to be in their
  interest. These can be concerns about political power, but also economic or
  security interests. An *'interest-based'* account essentially argues that nation
  state identities are instrumental social constructions developed by élites in their
  struggle for political power in so far as they rationalize and legitimize the
  instrumental and material 'taken-for-granted' preferences of actors (Haas 1997;
  Goldstein and Keohane 1993; Garrett and Weingast 1993; Jacobson 1995). We
  do not promote an 'interest vs. identity' account, but try to figure out the
  precise way in which both interact. On the one hand, embedded identity
  constructions, mentioned above, define the boundaries of what élites consider
  to be legitimate ideas – thereby constituting their perceived interests. On the
  other hand, perceived interests define which ideas political élites select in their
  struggle for power among those available to actors. The precise relationship
  remains a matter of empirical study.

- A *'socialization'* argument claims that ideas and identity constructions become
  consensual when actors thoroughly internalize them, perceive them 'as
  their own', and take them for granted (Schimmelfennig 1994; Finnemore and
  Sikkink 1998; Risse *et al.* 1999). Once a set of ideas about political order have
  become consensual, they are likely to be *embedded in institutions* and in a
  country's political culture. By 'institutions' we refer to both formal organizations, procedures and rules, as well as routines and collective understandings
  about 'ways of doing things' (March and Olsen 1989, 1998). As a result, the
  number of legitimate ideas available in a political discourse decreases and the
  institutionalization of ideas in institutions and political culture makes them
  resistant to challenges. In other words, we would expect the developing institutional set-up of a state to reproduce and consolidate taken-for-granted
  visions about the 'state and Europe'.

A EUROPEANIZATION OF NATION STATE IDENTITIES? EMPIRICAL EVIDENCE FROM FRANCE, GREAT BRITAIN AND GERMANY[7]

In the following, we illustrate our argument with regard to the discourses of political élites in France, Great Britain and Germany from the 1950s on. Concerning the
1950s, we distinguish among five ideal-typical identity constructions in the various
discourses (Risse 1998; for a similar attempt to categorize visions of political order
see Jachtenfuchs *et al.* 1998). While their origins can be found in the inter-war period
(and earlier), they were widely contested at the time, particularly in France and
Germany. For these two countries, then, the 1950s constitute a 'critical juncture'
where ideas about political order and nation state identity were contested and

challenged. We identified the following identity constructions (for details, see Engelmann-Martin 1998; Knopf 1998; Roscher 1998):

- *Liberal nationalist* identity constructions (on liberal nationalism, see Haas 1997) whereby the 'we' is confined to one's own nation state and where political sovereignty resides in the nation state. This concept is compatible with a 'Europe of nation states' and, as we argue below, still prevails in Great Britain, while it dominated in the French political discourse during de Gaulle's presidency.
- A wider *Europe as a community of values* 'from the Atlantic to the Urals' embedded in geography, history and culture. This concept attracted some support during the early years of the Cold War and re-emerged to some extent after the end of the East–West conflict, particularly in France and Germany.
- *Europe as a 'third force'*, as a democratic socialist alternative between capitalism and communism, thus overcoming the boundaries of the Cold War order. This concept prevailed among French socialists and German social democrats during the early 1950s, but then virtually disappeared when these parties reconstructed their collective identities.
- A *modern Europe as part of the Western community* based on liberal democracy and the social market economy. This concept became consensual in the Federal Republic of Germany towards the late 1950s and to some extent also underlies the more recent changes in French collective nation state identity.
- A *Christian Europe (Abendland)* based on Christian, particularly Catholic, values including strong social obligations. This identity construction was common among the Christian Democratic parties in France and Germany during the 1950s, but then increasingly amalgamated with the modern Westernized idea of Europe.

While these five conceptions of the state and of Europe were heavily contested during the 1950s, only two competitors remained in the dominant discourses of the three countries during the 1990s: the *liberal nationalist* identity and the modern Western idea of *Europe as a liberal democracy*. However, both concepts come in distinct national colours.

THE EUROPEANIZATION OF FRENCH EXCEPTIONALISM

Constructions of French nation state identity by political élites have undergone considerable change over time. Policy-makers of the Third Republic, such as Aristide Briand and Eduard Herriot, were among the first to embrace a federalist vision of *États Unis d'Europe* during the inter-war period (Bjøl 1966: 172–3). Their vision did not become consensual within their own parties until after the Second World War. During the 1950s and in conjunction with the first efforts toward European integration, a national debate took place, which concerned French nation state identity and basic political orientations in the post-war era.

The Second World War and the German Occupation served as traumatic experiences and as 'critical junctures' so that French nation state identity became deeply problematic. Many controversies centred around how to deal with Germany as the most significant 'other' for the French at the time.

There was no consensus among the French political élites at the time about European integration as a solution to the German problem. All five identity constructions outlined above competed among one another during the 1950s. Each resonated with elements of the previous identity constructions embedded in political institutions and culture. The French Gaullists (RPF) embraced a strictly nationalist view of France based on the values of republicanism, while de Gaulle himself occasionally supported a wider vision of Europe 'from the Atlantic to the Urals'. The Christian Democrats (MRP) promoted the Christian vision of Europe together with the modern Westernized concept. Finally, the French Socialists (SFIO) tried to push a concept of France as part of a European socialist 'third force' beyond the two blocs of the Cold War (details in Roscher 1998).

The war in Algeria and the ongoing crisis of the Fourth Republic only added to the crisis of French nation state identity. When the Fifth Republic came into being in 1958, its founding father, President Charles de Gaulle, reconstructed French nation state identity and managed to reunite a deeply divided nation around a common vision of France's role in the world. His successful reconstruction of French nation state identity constitutes a prime example of the instrumental selection of a particular discourse as outlined above:

> When one is the Atlantic cape of the continent, when one has planted one's flag in all parts of the world, when one spreads ideas, and when one opens oneself to the surrounding world, in short, when one is France, one cannot escape the grand movements on the ground. One has to play one's role straightforwardly and comprehensively in order not to be crushed and, at the same time, to serve the cause of all mankind.[8]

De Gaulle's identity construction related to historical myths of Frenchness and combined them in a unique way. As the leader of the French *résistance* during the Second World War, he overcame the trauma of the Vichy regime and he related the French *état-nation* – comprising a specific meaning of sovereignty – with the values of enlightenment and democracy (Bédarida 1994; Kelly 1996). The notion of sovereignty – understood as national independence from outside interference, together with a sense of uniqueness and '*grandeur*' – was used to build a bridge between post-Revolutionary Republican France and the pre-Revolutionary monarchy. The French *état-nation* connoted the identity of the nation and democracy as well as the identity of French society with the Republic. Finally, de Gaulle reintroduced the notion of a French '*mission civilisatrice*' for the world destined to spread the universal values of enlightenment and the French Revolution. '*L'Europe des nations*' became the battle cry during de Gaulle's presidency. None of these identity constructions was particularly new, but de Gaulle combined them in a particular way and managed to use them in order to legitimize the political institutions of the Fifth Republic. By the mid-1960s, the Gaullist understanding of French nation state identity had carried the day in France and won out against the other four identity constructions.

But this nation state identity construction only remained consensual among political élites for about another ten years after de Gaulle's resignation. Beginning in the late 1970s, a gradual Europeanization of French nation state identity took place among élites which came about as a result of French experiences with European integration as well as two more 'critical junctures' – the utter failure of Mitterrand's economic policies in the early 1980s and the end of the Cold War in the late 1980s (Schmidt 1996, 1997). De Gaulle's immediate successors incrementally changed French policies toward the European Community adopting a more pro-active stance. It was only a matter of time until the European integration process became incompatible with the particular nation state identity of the Fifth Republic. The inconsistency between the liberal nationalist identity and French attitudes toward European integration became apparent when François Mitterrand was elected as the first French Socialist president in 1981.

As the new leader of the Socialist Party, he initially pushed the pro-European SFIO of Guy Mollet towards a more reluctant stance, thereby accepting the Gaullist legacy (Cole 1996: 72, 1999). When Mitterrand and the Socialist Party came into power in 1981, they initially embarked upon creating democratic socialism in France based on leftist Keynesianism. This project bitterly failed, so in 1983 Mitterrand had no choice other than to change course dramatically if he wanted to remain in power (Uterwedde 1988). This political change led to a deep identity crisis within the Socialist Party which moved towards ideas once derisively labelled 'Social Democratic'. Mitterrand now reverted to a more pro-European discourse:

We are at the moment where everybody unites, our fatherland, our Europe – Europe our fatherland – the ambition to support one with the other, the excitement of our land and of the people it produces, and the certainty of a new dimension is awaiting them.

(Mitterrand 1986: 104)

The Socialist Party's move toward Europe was motivated by instrumental concerns of remaining in power. The change included an effort to reconstruct French nation state identity. French Socialists started highlighting the common European historical and cultural heritage. They increasingly argued that the future of France was to be found in Europe. As Mitterrand once put it, 'France is our fatherland, Europe is our future.'[9] The French left also started embracing the notion of a 'European France', extending the vision of the French *'mission civilisatrice'* toward Europe writ large. The peculiar historical and cultural legacies of France were transferred from the 'first nation state' in Europe to the Continent as a whole, because all European nation states were children of enlightenment, democracy and Republicanism. France imprints its marks on Europe. This identity construction used traditional understandings of Frenchness and the French nation state – sovereignty understood as enlightenment and republicanism, the French *mission civilisatrice* – and Europeanized them. By the end of the 1980s, the French Socialists had thoroughly embraced a particular French vision of Europe as part of modernity and the Western community of liberal democracies.

Similar changes in the prevailing visions of European order combined with reconstructions of French nation state identity took place on the French right, albeit later. The heir of Charles de Gaulle's vision of a '*Europe des patries*', the *Rassemblement pour la République* (RPR), provides another example of the French political élite changing course. In this case, the end of the Cold War was the decisive moment constituting a crisis for French nation state identity. When the Berlin Wall came down, Germany was united, and the post-Cold War European security order was constructed, France – *la grande nation* – remained largely on the sidelines (Zelikow and Rice 1995). As a result, large parts of the political élite understood the grand illusion of '*grandeur*' and '*indépendence*'. The way out was Europe (Flynn 1995). The political debates surrounding the referendum on the Maastricht Treaties in 1992 can be seen as an identity-related discourse about the new role of France in Europe and the world after the end of the Cold War. As in the 1950s, fear of German power dominated the debates. Supporters of Maastricht and economic and monetary union (EMU), particularly on the French right, argued in favour of a 'binding' strategy, while opponents supported a return to traditional balance of power politics. This time, however, and in contrast to the 1950s, the binding argument carried the day, i.e. support for European integration.

Competing visions about European order held by RPR leaders corresponded to differing views of Frenchness and French nation state identity. President Jacques Chirac, who at the end of the 1970s and beginning of the 1980s echoed the Gaullist legacy (Shields 1996: 90–1), now expressed similar ideas about the Europeanization of French distinctiveness as his counterparts among the French left:

> The European Community is also a question of identity. If we want to preserve our values, our way of life, our standard of living, our capacity to count in the world, to defend our interests, to remain the carriers of a humanistic message, we are certainly bound to build a united and solid bloc ... If France says Yes [to the Treaty of Maastricht], she can better reaffirm what I believe in: French exceptionalism.[10]

In contrast, a minority of RPR 'Eurosceptics' such as Charles Pasqua and Philippe Séguin stuck to a traditional Gaullist understanding of sovereignty and a nationalistic view of collective identity during the Maastricht debates (Joas 1996).[11]

In sum, French nation state identity was heavily contested both in the 1950s and during the 1980s and early 1990s. Each time, however, political élites selected different identity constructions in accordance with what they perceived as their instrumental power interests. In the early 1960s, the Gaullist vision of the French *état-nation* as the Fifth Republic's particular identity prevailed over rival visions. Thirty years and two more 'critical junctures' later, however, a Europeanization of this particular nation state identity won out, one which gradually embraced the modern Western vision of Europe, albeit in French colours.

GERMANY'S PAST AS EUROPE'S 'OTHER'

The German case is one of thorough and profound reconstruction of nation state identity following the catastrophe of the Second World War. Thomas Mann's dictum that 'we do not want a German Europe, but a European Germany' became the mantra of the post-war (West) German élites. Since the 1950s, a fundamental consensus has emerged among political élites, and has been generally shared by public opinion, that European integration is in Germany's vital interest. Simon Bulmer called it the 'Europeanization' of German politics (Bulmer 1989; see also Hellmann 1996; Katzenstein 1997).

Chancellor Konrad Adenauer, who regarded the integration of the German nation state and society in the West as the best means of overcoming Germany's past, initiated the multilateralization of German foreign policy (for details of this and the following, see Engelmann-Martin 1998). Adenauer had been active in the pro-European wing of the *Zentrum*, the Catholic predecessor of the German Christian Democrats (CDU) during the Weimar Republic (Baring 1969; Schwartz 1966). Adenauer's thinking was heavily influenced by the Rhinelandish *Zentrum* where Europeanism and Catholicism went hand in hand with a distinct anti-Prussian connotation (Bellers 1991), but also by the transnational European movement, in particular the *Paneuropean Union* founded by Count Richard Coudenhove-Kalergi (Coudenhove-Kalergi 1982).

After 1945, the newly founded Christian Democratic Party (CDU) immediately embraced European unification as the alternative to the nationalism of the past (Paterson 1996). As Ernst Haas put it, 'in leading circles of the CDU, the triptych of self-conscious anti-Nazism, Christian values, and dedication to European unity as a means of redemption for past German sins has played a crucial ideological role' (Haas 1958: 127). As the Bavarian Christian Social Union (CSU) declared in 1946, 'Europe is a supranational community among the family of nations. We support the creation of a European confederation for the common preservation and continuation of the Christian Occidental culture' (Eichstätt Basic Programme 1946).

Christianity, democracy and social market economy became the three pillars on which to base a collective European identity which was sharply distinguished from both the German nationalist and militarist past and – increasingly so during the late 1940s and early 1950s – from communism and Marxism. In other words, Germany's own past as well as communism constituted the 'others' in this identity construction.

When Chancellor Adenauer came to power in 1949, he built upon and expanded these identity constructions. He amalgamated the Christian vision of Europe (see above) with the modern Western concept in one identity construction. He considered the firm anchoring of post-war Germany in Western Europe as the best way to overcome another German *Sonderweg* (Baring 1969: 57; Bellers 1991: 27–8).

But throughout the early 1950s, there was no élite consensus on German post-war identity. While political élites shared the belief that the German past of militarism and nationalism had played havoc and had to be overcome, they drew different lessons from this legacy. Within Adenauer's own party, Jacob Kaiser, the

CDU leader in Berlin, favoured a German policy of 'bridge-building' between East and West including neutrality between the two blocs. Similar concepts originally prevailed among Adenauer's coalition partner, the Free Democratic Party (FDP) (Glatzeder 1980). However, the FDP leader at the time, Thomas Dehler, promoted a German nationalist identity, albeit embracing democracy and liberalism, which closely resembled Gaullist visions.

The Social Democrats (SPD) were the main opposition party to Adenauer's policies. During the inter-war period, the SPD had been the first major German party to support the concept of a 'United States of Europe' in its 1925 Heidelberg programme. When the party was forced into exile during the Nazi period, the leadership embraced the notion of a democratic European federation which would almost naturally become a Socialist order. As in the case of the CDU, 'the "European idea" was primarily invoked as a spiritual value in the first years of the emigration. In this period, Europe was seen as an antithesis to Nazi Germany' (Paterson 1974: 3; see also Bellers 1991; Hrbek 1972). Thus, the Europeanization of German nation state identity originated from the experiences of exiled political leaders – both SPD and CDU – in their resistance to Hitler and the Nazis (Voigt 1986). For them, Europe's 'other' was Nazi Germany. Consequently, the first SPD post-war programme supported the 'United States of Europe, a democratic and socialist federation of European states. [The German Social Democracy] aspires to a Socialist Germany in a Socialist Europe'.[12] SPD leaders saw Europe, Germany, democracy and socialism as identical. The German Social Democrats under their first post-war leader, Kurt Schumacher, supported an identity construction which closely resembled the French Socialists' view of a 'third force' Europe – and always interlinked with the issue of German unification.[13] Schumacher, a survivor of the Dachau concentration camp, argued vigorously against the politics of Western integration, since the latter foreclosed the prospects of the rapid reunification of the two Germanies (Moeller 1996; Paterson 1974; Rogosch 1996; Schmitz 1978). At the same time, he denounced the Council of Europe and the European Coal and Steel Community (ECSC) as 'un-European', as a 'mini-Europe' (*Kleinsteuropa*), as conservative-clericalist and as capitalist (Hrbek 1972). However, the SPD was at great pains to argue that it did not oppose European integration as such, just *this* particular vision.

Two major election defeats later (1953 and 1957), the SPD slowly changed course. In this case again, instrumental power interests led party élites to pick a different identity construction. There had always been an internal opposition to Schumacher's policies. Party officials such as Ernst Reuter (the legendary mayor of Berlin), Willy Brandt (who later became party chairman and, in 1966, Chancellor), Fritz Erler, Herbert Wehner, Helmut Schmidt (Brandt's successor as Chancellor in 1974) and others supported closer relations with the US as well as German integration into the West. These Social Democrats were strongly influenced by the Socialist Movement for the United States of Europe founded in 1947 and by Jean Monnet's Action Committee. By the late 1950s, they took over the party leadership. The German Social Democrats thoroughly reformed their domestic and foreign policy programme. In the domestic realm, they accepted the German model of welfare state capitalism, the social market economy. With regard to foreign policy, they became staunch supporters of European integration. The changes culminated in the 1959 Godesberg programme. Two years earlier, the SPD had already changed course regarding European integration and supported the Treaty of Rome in the German parliament (Bellers 1991; Hrbek 1972; Paterson 1974; Rogosch 1996).

From the 1960s on, a federalist consensus (the 'United States of Europe') prevailed among the German political élites comprising the main parties from the centre-right to the centre-left. In contrast to Gaullist France, German nation state identity now embraced the modern Western vision of Europe, with Europe's 'other' being both Germany's past and communism. This consensus outlasted the changes in government from the CDU to the SPD in 1969 as well as the return of a CDU-led government in 1982. It also survived a major foreign policy change towards Eastern Europe, East Germany and the Soviet Union. When Chancellor Willy Brandt introduced *Ostpolitik* in 1969, he made it very clear that European integration efforts were untouchable and had to be continued (Hanrieder 1995).

Even more significantly, German unification twenty years later did not result in a reconsideration of German European orientations. With the unexpected end of the East–West conflict and regained German sovereignty, a broad range of foreign policy opportunities emerged, creating a situation in which the German élites could have redefined their national interests. But not much happened. Germany did not reconsider its fundamental foreign policy orientations, since Germany's commitment to European integration had long outlived the context in which it had originally emerged (see Hellmann 1996; Katzenstein 1997; Müller 1992; Rittberger 1993). The majority of the German political élite continued to share Chancellor Kohl's belief that only deeper political and economic union can anchor Germany firmly in the West and strengthen European institutions to ensure peace in the years ahead (Banchoff 1997). German support for a single currency and for a European political union was perfectly in line with long-standing attitudes toward integration and the country's Europeanized nation state identity. The German political élite – in contrast to German public opinion – shared a consensus that the Deutsche Mark should be given up in favour of the Euro. This stubborn support for the single currency by the vast majority of the political élites can only be understood with reference to their Europeanized nation state identity (Risse *et al.* 1999). While the new 'red–green' coalition under Chancellor Schröder has altered some details in German policies toward the European Union (EU), it did not touch the élite consensus concerning Germany's European identity.

EUROPE AS BRITAIN'S 'OTHER'

In sharp contrast to both France and Germany, the fundamental British élite attitudes toward European integration have remained essentially the same since the end of the Second World War. More than twenty years after entry into the European Community (EC), Britain is still regarded as 'of rather than in' Europe; it remains the 'awkward partner' and 'semi-detached' from Europe (Bailey 1983; George 1992, 1994). British views on European integration essentially range from those who objected to British entry into the EC in the first place, and who now oppose further Europeanization (the right wing of the Conservatives, Labour's far left and far right), to a mainstream group within both main parties supporting a 'Europe of nation states'. European federalists remain a distinct minority in the political discourse. The two leading parties share a consensual vision of European order:

> *Labour Party:* 'our vision of Europe is of an alliance of independent nations choosing to co-operate to achieve the goals they cannot achieve alone. We oppose a European federal superstate.'
> *Conservative Party:* 'the government has a positive vision for the European Union as a partnership of nations. We want to be in Europe but not run by Europe . . . Some others would like to build a federal Europe. A British Conservative government will not allow Britain to be part of a Federal European State.[14]

Surprisingly, the general attitude apparently has not changed much since the 1950s and despite Britain's entry into the EC in the 1970s. Take the following quotation from Sir Winston Churchill:

> Where do we stand? We are not members of the European Defence Community, nor do we intend to be merged in a Federal European system. We feel we have a special relation to both. This can be expressed by prepositions, by the preposition 'with' but not 'of' – we are with them, but not of them. We have our own Commonwealth and Empire.[15]

British attitudes toward the European project reflect collectively held beliefs about British, particularly, *Anglo-Saxon* identity, which, as William Wallace put it, 'is as old as Shakespeare, matured through the experiences of the English Civil War and the struggles against the threat of Catholic absolutism, first from Spain and then from France: a free England defying an unfree continent' (Wallace 1991: 70). There is still a feeling of 'them' vs. 'us' between England and the Continent. In the political discourse, 'Europe' continues to be identified with the Continent and perceived as the, albeit friendly, 'other' in contrast to Anglo-Saxon exceptionalism, as the following two quotations illustrate:

> Labour Minister of State, Kenneth Younger, in 1950: 'We *and*, even more, *our friends in Europe* are entitled to adequate guarantees against the revival of the German war potential, and until we can be satisfied that Germany is able and willing to take her place as a part of the Western community we do not intend to be stampeded into ill-considered action.'

> Labour Foreign Secretary, Robin Cook, in 1997: 'because one of the things that those of us *who have gone to Europe* have learnt is that there is also a change of opinion in Europe. As it happens, when *I first went to Europe*, the first European politician I met was Lionel Jospin.'[16]

Neither Younger nor Cook forty-seven years later consider themselves 'Europeans', even though they both view Europe as part of the Western community.

The collective identification with *national* symbols, history and institutions is far greater in the British political discourse than a potential identification with *European* symbols, history and institutions. The social construction of 'exceptionalism' as the core of British nation state identity comprises meanings attached to institutions centring around a particular understanding of national sovereignty which is hard to reconcile with a vision of a European political order going beyond functional co-operation over borders (see Lynch 1997; Lyon 1991; Mitchell 1992; Schauer 1996; Schmitz and Geserick 1996). 'Europe' simply does not resonate well with identity constructions deeply embedded in national political institutions and in political culture. For instance, the Crown symbolizes 'external sovereignty' in the political discourse, in terms of independence from Rome and the Pope as well as from the European continent since 1066. Élites continue to construct parliamentary or 'internal sovereignty' as a constitutional principle relating to a 700-year-old parliamentary tradition and hard-fought victories over the King (Wallace 1994). English sovereignty is, thus, directly linked to myths about a continuous history of liberal and democratic evolution and 'free-born Englishmen' (Langlands 1999). It is not surprising, therefore, that parts of English nation state identity are often viewed as potentially threatened by European integration. Objections to transferring political sovereignty to European supranational institutions are usually justified on grounds of lacking democratic – meaning parliamentary – accountability. As a result, it is difficult to link this notion of parliamentary sovereignty to notions about a European political order except from one comprising independent nation states. The following quotes from 1950 and from the 1990s illustrate this point again:

> Sir Stafford Cripps, Labour Chancellor of the Exchequer, 1950: 'Thus the history of the advance in European co-operation since the war . . . is largely the history of a series of practical steps which have gradually extended the mutual trust and confidence in political and economic co-operation . . . It does not, however, seem to us . . . either necessary or appropriate . . . to invest a supra-national authority of independent persons with powers for overriding Governmental and Parliamentary decisions in the participating countries.'

> Prime Minister John Major, 1993: 'Britain successfully used the Maastricht negotiations to reassert the authority of national governments. It is clear now that the Community will remain a union of sovereign national states. That is what its peoples want: to take decisions through their own Parliaments . . . It is for nations to build Europe, not for Europe to attempt to supersede nations.'[17]

These and other statements show a remarkable continuity of British attitudes toward the EU and related identity constructions from the 1950s (and earlier) until the present time. This is particularly striking, since the political context of these speeches has changed dramatically. In 1950, there was no 'supranational authority' in Europe, while John Major's assertion that Maastricht reaffirmed 'the authority of national governments' mainly represents wishful thinking. Contrary to other advanced industrial societies, British élites have not attempted to discuss or redefine the century-old identity constructions and myths underlying post-war foreign policy (Wallace 1991, 1992). It seems as if these identity constructions are so embedded in the national political culture that not even dramatic geo-strategic developments trigger discursive contestation. It remains to be seen whether British entry to the monetary union in the next century will change the identity discourse among political élites which so far has remained stable.

EXPLAINING CONTINUITY AND CHANGE IN NATION STATE IDENTITIES

The brief and extremely simplified description of almost fifty years of nation state identity constructions in France, Germany and Britain reveals continuity and change. To explain this 'puzzle', we can probably dismiss two rival approaches out of hand. First, neo-functionalism expected that European integration would gradually lead to the transfer of loyalties to the European level, particularly among those élite members involved in the European policy-making process (Haas 1958, 1964; Lindberg and Scheingold 1970). Our evidence does not support such claims. On the one hand, more than twenty years after Britain joined the EC, its collective nation state identity remains firmly anchored in a peculiar notion of Anglo-Saxonism. On the other hand, German collective identities became European at a time when the European integration process was too weak to exert any independent effects on identity constructions. Only the French case might be consistent with a neo-functionalist path.

Second, one could deduce from intergovernmentalism – either its realist (Hoffmann 1966) or liberal versions (Moravcsik 1993, 1997) – that European integration should not affect nation state identities, since the European polity consists of intergovernmental bodies which do not require much loyalty transfer to the European level. The French and the German cases appear to contradict this argument.

However, the three propositions which we developed above and which delineate conditions under which a change in collective nation state identities is to be expected, can be taken together to explain the variation in our findings.

We take the *resonance* assumption as our point of departure. Élite groups promoting a specific nation state identity or a concept of political order need to make these new ideas fit with pre-existing identity constructions embedded in political institutions and culture. New ideas about just political order have to resonate with these classical notions of political order and, if the fit is not commonly perceived to be evident, national élites will attempt to construct a compatibility between new and old ideas (Bartram 1996).

As argued in the empirical section, classical *Anglo-Saxon* notions of political order emphasize parliamentary democracy and external sovereignty. It is not surprising, therefore, that only an intergovernmentalist vision of European political order – in which politically sovereign states co-operate pragmatically across borders –

resonates fully with internal and external sovereignty. Thus, there is not much space for 'Europe' or 'Europeanness' in this particular British political discourse.

In the *French* case, state-centred republicanism – the duty to promote revolutionary values such as brotherhood, freedom, equality and human rights, in short, 'civilization' – constituted a continuous element in the discourse about political order (Kelly 1996). Therefore, political élites can legitimately promote any European idea which resonates with French exceptionalism and which does not violate the particular concept of republicanism, including a Europeanization of French exceptionalism.

Finally, *German* concepts of a social market economy, democracy and political federalism were central elements in the discourse of German exiled élites during the war and among the entire political class after the Second World War. Ideas about European political order resonated well with these concepts. In addition, a nationalist view of Germany was thoroughly discredited by militarism and Nazism. Europe provided an alternative identity construction and, thus, a way out.

In short, the 'resonance assumption' seems to account for the variation between Great Britain, on the one hand, and France as well as Germany, on the other. European identity constructions have so far remained incompatible with Anglo-Saxon exceptionalism, while French and German élites could easily embrace these notions and incorporate them into their political discourses. But this argument does not explain why different identity constructions dominated in the two latter countries towards the end of the 1950s, and why it took French élites thirty years longer than Germany to incorporate 'Europe' into their nation state identity and their exceptionalism. As we argued above, five different identity constructions were considered legitimate in the German and French political discourses of the 1950s. The 'resonance assumption' does not tell us which carried the day.

Here, the concept of 'critical junctures' becomes relevant, indicating that party élites convince themselves that existing visions of political order are inapplicable or dysfunctional in a specific political context. They shop around for alternative ideas about political order and nation state identity provided that these are compatible with pre-existing beliefs and deeply embedded identity constructions. Above, we used the 'interest-based' literature on the role of ideas and identities to argue that political élites are likely to select those among the legitimately available ideas and identity constructions which suit their perceived power interests.

Thus, we argue that the German SPD reached such a point in the mid- to late 1950s when more and more members of the party leadership recognized that the vision of 'Europe as a third force' – unconditionally linked with German unity – was no longer a viable option given the ECSC, the Treaty of Rome and two federal election defeats in a row. At the same time, the modern Western concept of European identity resonated well with the domestic programme of the party reformers supporting liberal democracy, market economy and the welfare state, while giving up more far-reaching Socialist visions. The German SPD thoroughly reformed its programme and Europeanized its party identity, because its leaders reckoned that this was the only way to win elections.

A critical juncture of a different kind occurred in France during the late 1950s with the war in Algeria and the crisis of the Fourth Republic bringing Charles de Gaulle into power. His notions of French *grandeur* and *mission civilisatrice* complemented and legitimized the institutions of the Fifth Republic by supplying the French public with a consistent and comprehensive identity construction which resonated well with French traditions of republicanism and the *état-nation*. De Gaulle then used the identity constructions of the Fifth Republic to consolidate his power.

The French case reveals two more crises leading to reconstructions of French nation state identity. When President Mitterrand's economic policies had to confront the European monetary system (EMS) in 1982–3, he was forced to choose between Europe and his socialist goals. He readily opted for Europe and set in motion a process which the German Social Democrats had experienced twenty-five years earlier – the parallel turn to social democracy and to Europe. Mitterrand changed policy and reformed the ideology of the French socialists, because he wanted to remain in power. Incorporating Europe into French nation state constructions later extended to the centre-right when the RPR and its leader Jacques Chirac realized, at the end of the Cold War, that French exceptionalism was nothing but a Utopia without Europe. In other words, it took another critical juncture *and* the initiatives of nation state leaders, who pursued what they defined as being in their party's interest, to place Europe almost consensually within the French nation state identity.

But perceived instrumental interests can only explain the variation in our cases *in conjunction* with the other factors. First, party leaders are not free to manipulate nation state identities at their convenience. Rather, they can only try to promote those identity constructions which resonate with pre-existing views among the public and the political élites. To posit a European 'civilizing mission' would be considered preposterous in the German political context (where missions of a different kind ruined the country and Europe earlier in the century), while it constitutes a perfectly legitimate idea in the French political discourse. To worship European unity publicly can be a dangerous proposition in the British debate, while it is regarded as perfectly normal in Germany. In short, the resonance assumption explains which identity constructions are available, considered appropriate and legitimate in a particular political discourse, while perceived interests might elucidate *which* of these identity constructions are then selected and promoted by party élites.

Second, as argued above, 'critical junctures' provide a window of opportunity for party élites to deconstruct, reconstruct and manipulate given nation state identities. Of course, such crises again do not fall from heaven, but are only 'real' in so far as they are perceived and constructed as such. The end of the Cold War and German unification, for example, represented a 'critical juncture' for the French élites, while these events did not trigger a major debate among the German élites concerning their collective Europeanness and their foreign policy orientation. This does not mean, however, that political leaders can single-handedly manipulate such crisis phenomena. At the very least, they must be able to convince a wider audience that a particular moment in history indeed constitutes a crisis whereby nation state identities are up for negotiation. In the German case, for example, one could argue that the end of the Cold War and German unification reinforced rather than challenged the (West) German nation state identity, precisely because élites could celebrate the fall of the Berlin Wall as a major policy success (cf. Risse 1996b). For the French élites, however, the end of the Cold War symbolized the ultimate failure of the Gaullist and nationalist nation state identity.

Finally, we need to distinguish between 'open' and 'closed' political discourses. When nation state identities are challenged or contested, and compete with each other, as was the case in Germany and France during the 1950s as well as in France during the 1980s and 1990s, strategic interests might explain which parties chose which identity construction and promote it. Once the range of available nation state identities narrows down and a particular construction becomes consensual and prevails over others, the discourse closes. Challenging the prevailing consensus becomes much more difficult.

Here, the *socialization hypothesis* mentioned above has to be considered, focusing on internalization processes. This explains the stickiness of identity constructions which can no longer be manipulated by political élites. Rather, the collective identity itself can now be exploited for instrumental purposes. The latter was the case in Germany under Helmut Kohl. Given the thorough Europeanization of German nation state identity, the German Chancellor was able to silence critics of the single currency extremely effectively by arguing that 'good Germans' had to support the Euro, as any 'good European' would do. Against this powerful construction, critics had to make the far more complicated argument that 'good Europeans' could disagree over the merits of the single currency (Risse *et al.* 1999).

The British case also illustrates the point. When old visions about political order remain unchallenged, they tend to become increasingly embedded in national institutions and political cultures, as a result of which they become difficult to deconstruct and to replace.[18] Studying the remarkable similarity of identity-related statements by British party élites from the 1950s to the present, it seems as if the longer old ideas about political order remain unchallenged, the more room for manoeuvre narrows. Traditional British notions of external and internal sovereignty still seem to be relevant today. A recent example of this is Prime Minister Tony Blair's difficult attempt to prepare the British public for membership of EMU. At least at the discursive level, it is still contentious to speak about transferring political authority to Brussels and replacing a national symbol of unity and sovereignty, such as the British pound, with the Euro (Featherstone 1999: 7).

CONCLUSIONS

In this chapter, we tried to explain continuity and change in the extent to which 'Europe' enters collective nation state identities in the discourses among political élites. We suggested a four-step process. First, new ideas about European identity and European political order are usually transmitted through discourses in transnational organizations and movements. Second, these ideas are transferred to national discourses to the extent that they resonate with given and pre-existing consensual identity constructions and concepts of political order embedded in a country's institutions and political culture (*resonance* assumption). Only those ideas that resonate are considered legitimate in a political struggle. Third, perceived 'critical junctures' define situations in political discourses when identity constructions are open to being challenged and contested. Under such circumstances, political élites select among the available and legitimate identity constructions according to their perceived power interests (*interest* assumption). Thus, perceived interests and ideas' resonance together determine which nation state identity construction carries the day. Fourth, however, once identity constructions have become consensual and, thus, collective views, they tend to be internalized by actors as well as institutionalized (*socialization* assumption). As a result, the range of legitimate identity constructions in a political space narrows, until the next 'critical juncture' occurs.

Our empirical findings run counter to two prevailing, but competing, views in the literature. Conventional wisdom holds that either there is no European collective identity to speak of at all in the European polity (cf. Smith 1992; Kielmansegg 1996), or that there is some convergence among the various European nation state identities toward a common identity. We disagree with both views. The British example shows that there is not much convergence toward a common European nation state identity. But the German and French cases show that some collective nation state identities have thoroughly integrated ideas about Europe and the European order. One could go even further and argue that the modern Western concept of European identity incorporating values of liberal democracy, market economy and the welfare state provides common ground among the political élites in France and Germany, if not elsewhere. But these European nation state identities come in distinct national colours. French Europeans remain French, and German Europeans remain Germans (and Bavarians and Rhinelanders, and so on), i.e. people hold multiple identities, as social psychology theory would lead us to expect. In a certain sense, multiple European and nation state identities might actually be appropriate for a multi-level system of governance, such as the EU.

NOTES

1   This chapter presents results from a research project on the Europeanization of nation state identities in France, Germany and Great Britain which has been funded by the German Research Association (*Deutsche Forschungsgemeinschaft*) and the European University Institute, Florence. We thank Walter Carlsnæs, Thomas Diez, John A. Hall, Ulf Hedetoft, Iver B. Neumann, Bo Stråth, Antje Wiener, Mette Zølner, the participants in the panel 'Identity and International Theory' at the Third Pan-European Conference on International Relations, Vienna, 16–19 September 1998, and the panel 'Social Constructivist Approaches to European Integration', ECSA, Pittsburgh, 2–5 June 1999, as well as two anonymous referees for their many comments on earlier versions.

2   Until the end of the 1980s political élites in Britain used the terms 'British' and 'English' interchangeably when speaking about political order in a European context. In this chpter we refer to a myth of Englishness as the basis of varying ideational expressions. We call this myth 'Anglo-Saxon exceptionalism'. Subsequently, we do not discuss Welsh, Scottish and Northern Irish élite discourse, how and when various British

political actors apply these terms strategically in a domestic political game, or the impact that these notions might have on Welsh, Scottish and Irish élites – as opposed to English élites – and European attitudes. Instead, we focus on (i) the definition of the myth of Englishness, (ii) the way party élites replicate the myth in their discourse about political order and thereby make claims about Great Britain, and (iii) the necessity for party-political élites to construct a 'fit' between Anglo-Saxon exceptionalism and ideas about political order with a view to gaining a reputation as responsible speakers. Therefore in terms of terminology, we refer to 'party élites', analyse '*British* élite attitudes and views', '*British* political discourse', 'the *British* debate', '*British* notions', and conclude that the concept of the 'Europe of nation states still prevails in *Britain*'. This implies that, first, whenever we speak about 'Anglo-Saxon exceptionalism' we refer to the myth which is underlying party élites' claims about British nation state identities. Second, when we describe British nation state identity as essentially 'English', we refer to the observation that Anglo-Saxon exceptionalism characterizes British nation state identity. Finally, it is important to emphasize that we do not suggest that myths – be they century-old as in the case of Great Britain, or more recent as in the German case – are necessarily exogenous elements for the analysis of nation state identities. Instead, we assume that national myths as well as the ideas based on them are socially constructed. Since it is beyond the limited framework of this chapter to elaborate on this question, we have chosen to focus on party élites' attempts to base their discourse on a 'pre-defined' set of national myths with a view to gain popular support, understanding and legitimacy after the Second World War.

3   On the self–other dichotomy in international relations, including a discussion of social-psychological approaches, see Neumann (1996).

4   At this point, a theoretical approach to political discourses, which is informed by insights from social psychology, differs sharply from other – particularly postmodern – approaches to discourse. This is a major theoretical disagreement among various constructivist approaches. For a different conceptualization of discourse, see Thomas Diez's chapter in this volume.

5   Martin Marcussen has developed the concept of an 'ideational life-cycle' in this context (Marcussen 1998a, 1998b, 1999).

6   See Cederman and Daase (1998) for an attempt to endogenize such deep-rooted identity elements – they call this aspect 'corporate identity' – in policy analysis. Their purpose is to theorize about the '*longue durée*' whereas we aspire to theorize about medium-term 'identity politics' in which one specific social identity is at stake – the nation state identity.

7   The following part summarizes Risse (2000).

8   President de Gaulle, speech in Lille, 11 December 1950, D.M. II, p. 393.

9   Quoted from *Le Monde*, 4 September 1992.

10   Jacques Chirac, *Liberation*, 11 September 1992.

11   It seems that in recent years Euro-sceptic Philippe Séguin of the RPR, in the context of the 1999 elections to the European Parliament, is increasingly leaning away from the traditional Gaullist line, towards President Jacques Chirac's more accommodating European strategy.

12   Political guidelines adopted at the Hanover Party Congress, May 1946.

13   In a speech in Berlin on 20 June 1946 Schumacher said, 'Die Einheit Deutschlands bedeutet die Einheit Europas. Ein zerrissenes Deutschland wuerde nur ein uneinheitliches Europa zur Folge haben' (cited in Hrbek 1972: 37).

14   The first quote is from the Labour Manifesto 'Britain will be better with new Labour': http://www.labourwin97. org.uk/manifesto/index/html. The second quote is from the Conservative Manifesto 'Our Vision for Britain': http://www.conservative-party.org.uk/manifesto/defe3.html.

15   Speech on 11 May 1953, House of Commons, vol. 513, col. 895.

16   (Emphasis added in both quotes.) The first quote is from Mr Younger (Labour Minister

of State), House of Commons debate on Foreign Affairs, 28 March 1950, col. 216. The second quote is from Robin Cook, Speech in the House of Commons, 9 June 1997, col. 801, http//:www.parliament.the-stationery-office.co.uk/pa/cm199798/cmhansrd cm970609/debtext/70609-08.htm.

17   The quote from Sir Stafford Cripps, House of Commons debate on the Schuman Plan, 26 June 1950, cols 1946–50; the quote from John Major: 'Raise your eyes, there is a land beyond', *The Economist*, 25 September – 1 October 1993, p. 27.

18   We will not be able to expand on this point in this chapter, but we have a broad range of institutions in mind, such as the media, the educational system, the electoral system, the legal system, political decision-making procedures, etc. What they have in common is that they tend to consolidate and reify existing and consensually shared ideas about just political order.

8

Constructing Institutional Interests: EU and NATO Enlargement

K.M. Fierke and Antje Wiener

INTRODUCTION

The eastward enlargement or expansion of the European Union (EU) and the North Atlantic Treaty Organization (NATO), respectively, are likely to transform the political and economic landscape of Europe. Yet there has been little analysis of the relationship between the two parallel processes. Instead, two separate literatures approach eastward enlargement from different angles. The literature on accession to the EU focuses primarily on more institutional, formal agreements and procedures, and less on the politics of the accession process.[1] Indeed, there has been little attention to the politics of European enlargement, that is, how it came about.[2] The question is important because neither EU enlargement nor NATO expansion was clearly envisioned in the immediate aftermath of the Cold War. The EU had taken steps, with the Single European Act, the common market project of 'Europe 92' and the Maastricht Treaty, to deepen European integration; many saw the potential of widening to a group of 'fragile democracies' in the East as undesirable if not destabilizing.

The somewhat more lively political and academic debate over NATO expansion has tended to revolve around the question of whether this move eastward will recreate the division of Europe or bring greater peace and stability to a fragmented region.[3] In the immediate aftermath of the Cold War, western publics were questioning why NATO, as a defensive alliance set up to contain the Soviet Union, was even necessary or relevant in the absence of its Cold War enemy. Many, at the time, assumed that the more comprehensive Conference on Security and Co-operation in Europe (CSCE) would provide the framework for future security co-operation in a larger Europe, including Russia (Havel 1991: 35).

As a result, one can question how and why the expansion of both institutions is proceeding despite questions about the material interest in doing so and in the face of increasingly negative public opinion.[4] In other words, why does it appear to have become 'inevitable' to the actors involved in enlargement politics? The empirical question relates to a larger theoretical issue about how organizations know their interests and how these interests are transformed.

Based on the observation that the existence of the Union's *acquis communautaire* provides a normative basis for expansion eastward,[5] constructivists have argued that enlargement of one of the institutions, the EU, can more readily be explained by normative considerations than in terms of objective interests (Schimmelfennig 1998). In this respect, a difference between the two institutions is apparent. Enlargement has been at the heart of the European Community's (EC's) identity from the start. There have been a range of accessions to the EC, and now the EU, since it began with the original six in 1957. In the process, the EU has defined itself as a 'widening' organization in so far as any 'democratic nation' of Europe was a potential member. The *acquis communautaire* provides an important normative basis for enlargement, although the current potential is qualitatively different in scope than past accessions, which have only involved a few countries at a time. Enlargement could incorporate up to fourteen new countries, which is double the current membership, and is likely to transform dramatically the institutions of the community.

NATO, by contrast, lacks any formal equivalent of the *acquis*. While the idea of adding new members is not by definition in conflict with alliance formation, the expansion of NATO, as a Cold War alliance, had been largely unthinkable. In contrast to the classical European balance of power, characterized by states continuously joining or leaving alliances, the nuclear stand-off between the two superpowers froze a particular pattern of allegiance in place; in that context, a request by Poland to join NATO could have provided the impetus for nuclear war. Since the end of the Cold War, and the disappearance of the Soviet Union, this concern has faded. The key issue for the alliance is less one of adding new members than whether it is possible to do so without drawing clear boundaries between those 'inside' and 'outside' the alliance. As an alliance defined in defensive terms, NATO's central task – and that of alliances historically – has been one of protecting the sovereignty of individual states. Subsequently, security practice has involved the drawing of clear boundaries, specifying who was protected by the American security guarantee and who was outside. The current challenge is to expand without reviving Cold War tensions or recreating a divided Europe. The purpose of the organization is now being defined less in terms of defence than of providing an anchor of stability. This raises fundamental questions about the meaning of security and NATO's identity as a security organization.

The difference between the two organizations only highlights the question of how the parallel processes of expansion became possible. Our argument relates both processes of expansion to the social construction of European *identity* during the Cold War. We seek to demonstrate that, in that context, both organizations developed a specific western identity that was embedded in the construction of shared democratic norms. Crucially, these norms were the result of both social practices and the definition of the democratic western political order, as different from the communist eastern political order. The East was therefore an important reference point for the social construction of western Europe. As this chapter will demonstrate, the post-Cold War context poses a dramatic challenge to this identity which is most clearly demonstrated by the respective enlargement processes. Now, the eastern Europeans, previously the West's Other, seek membership in western organizations. In this respect, the empirical question relates to a larger theoretical issue about how institutional identities and interests are transformed.

The chapter is divided into three sections. Section 1 explores the theoretical question at the core of the rationalist–constructivist debate as it relates to NATO and EU expansion. Section 2 builds a theoretical argument about the relationship between speech acts, norm construction and institutional interests. Section 3 develops a research agenda for comparing the expansion of the EU and NATO within this framework.

1. THE THEORETICAL QUESTION

A rationalist approach to interests or preferences might proceed as follows. If we assume that the preferences or interests of actor A are X, that is, if we take these preferences as given, we can expect a particular outcome. For instance, if the EU, in the late 1980s, had an interest in deepening, as opposed to widening, we could expect an outcome that would contribute to the realization of this interest. Rationalists make an argument that, given a set of preferences or interests, we can anticipate certain rational outcomes. The problem, in this case, is not to explain outcomes given a set of stable preferences; rather, it is to gain some insight into the changing identity and interests of NATO and the EU. We therefore approach the problem from a slightly different angle than the rationalists. Rationalists take the context as given; we want to problematize the context. Rather than taking the rules of any particular game for granted, and focusing on the rationality of decisions within an assumed context, we want to elaborate on the context itself within which the changing identities and interests of both organizations were invested with social and political meaning. To do so, we suggest elaborating on a Wittgensteinian constructivist approach.

Constructivists have challenged the rationalist assumption of exogenously given interests, arguing that interests are constructed in historically specific circumstances, that is, a context of social and cultural norms shapes actor identity and behaviour.[6] Consistent with this assumption we explore interest formation and change in the process of eastern enlargement. We ask how and why eastern expansion became part of the policy agenda despite serious doubts, in the early aftermath of the Cold War, that expansion was in the interest of either organization. Sociological constructivists such as, for example, Emmanuel Adler (1997) and Alexander Wendt (1992) have explored the nature of changing games, and of the reconstitution of identities and interests; however, in these constructivist accounts, meanings are instrumentally deployed by rational actors or rationality appears to be prior to the development of any shared context of meaning.[7] For instance, Wendt's analysis of the first encounter between alter and ego emphasizes the rational cost-benefit calculations of the two players. Alter and ego begin without a common language or history but possess a desire to survive and certain material capabilities. Through a process of signalling and interpreting, alter infers the costs and probabilities that ego's intent is malign or friendly. Wendt focuses on an originary situation, before the development of any kind of relationship, and is therefore not easily adapted to a situation where alter and ego have a past and are, therefore, already embedded in a context of social interactions. Doty (1997: 387), by contrast, points out that encounters '[a]lways take place in a context wherein traces of prior meanings and representations are already in place and become interwoven in new experiences'. She argues that a priori meanings constrain reasoning about the other not an a priori rationality.

We argue that a sociological constructivist approach provides only limited understanding of the current enlargement process. For instance, EU enlargement can in part be explained by the commitment to widen to other democratic states in Europe. This commitment is embodied in the *acquis communautaire*, that is, the legal provisions, procedures and rules of the Treaty of European Union. Enlargement fits within the shared norms of the Union, and these norms have a stronger pull than 'objective' interests. There are two problems with this argument, however. First, the institutionalist argument begs the question of why the rules and norms of the *acquis communautaire* would override other interests. Second, if NATO, as an institution that lacks the formal equivalent of the *acquis communautaire*, is also expanding, the explanation must in part lie elsewhere. Given the parallel processes of expansion we raise a question about the role of another level of norms *shared by the two organizations*, which may be propelling the expansion process.

To provide an explanation of both processes of enlargement, our argument draws on a Wittgensteinian constructivism where meaning and language are central to the constitution of identity and interest (Fierke 1998; Kratochwil 1989; Onuf 1989; Zehfuss 1998). Wittgensteinian constructivism provides an important point of departure for the analysis that follows. In contrast to sociological constructivists, who often treat norms as causes (for a critique, see also Checkel 1999), scholars in this tradition have argued that once one enters the realm of social action and language, norms cannot be reduced to causes. Thus, Kratochwil argues, for example:

> that our conventional understanding of social action and of the norms governing them is defective because of a fundamental misunderstanding of the function of language in social interaction, and because of a positivist epistemology that treats norms as 'causes'. Communication is therefore reduced to issues of describing 'facts' properly, i.e. to the 'match' of concepts and objects, and to the ascertainment of nomological regularities. Important aspects of *social* action such as advising, demanding, apologizing, promising etc., cannot be adequately understood thereby. Although the philosophy of ordinary language has abandoned the 'mirror' image of language since the later Wittgenstein, the research programmes

developed within the confines of logical positivism are, nevertheless, still indebted to the old conception.

(Kratochwil 1989: 5–6; emphasis in original)

Building on this opening towards language, our theoretical argument seeks to push the constructivist argument further, by examining the process of norm construction in the dialectical relationship between context, speech acts and institutional transformation. While the rationalist asks what outcome, given a set of preferences, can be expected, we instead ask in what kind of context the expansion of NATO and EU would be meaningful and rational.

In other words, we are not looking for a unidirectional relationship between preferences and outcomes, but rather at a changing context within which identities and interests are mutually constituted through a process of interaction. If the meaning of a speech act is dependent on a context, it follows logically that, if the context changes, so will the meaning of an act. The purpose of this analysis is to reflect on how, given the dramatic change of context resulting with the end of the Cold War, the meaning of the Cold War 'promise' of Helsinki was transformed into a threat. We have chosen to focus on Helsinki because it is a promise that transcended both organizations, yet, given its three baskets, was related to the mandates of each.

2. SPEECH ACTS, CONTEXTUAL CHANGE AND INSTITUTIONAL INTERESTS

This section outlines the contours of a more extensive empirical research programme. Three concepts – speech acts, contextual change and institutional interests – are developed against the background of the Cold War and post-Cold War transformations. We use these alternative categories to reconstitute the relationship between identity, norms and practices, reinforcing the constructivist point regarding the inseparability of identity and interests, and how their mutual transformation was constituted out of the dialectical relationship between the three concepts. The empirical examples illustrate that the rationality of both decisions has to be situated in a context of a priori and changing meanings in regard to the identity and norms of the West.

While the EU and NATO are usually studied as separate phenomena, there is a historical relationship between the development of their respective roles and practices. The creation of western institutions such as the EC and NATO in the late 1940s and early 1950s was inspired by a notion of security that was both economic and military. The European Coal and Steel Community, the first institution of the EC, was set up in the hope of binding the economic fate of Germany and France such that they would have a common interest in avoiding war. NATO was established for the purpose of protecting western Europe from the Soviet Union. The security provided by the one organization faced inward; the security provided by the other faced outward. Both notions of security formation stress the importance of a *border of order* provided by the two, which ran through the centre of Europe. Referring to the discourse of citizenship as constructing the 'border of order',

Kratochwil (1994) argues that within a political community the discourse of citizenship creates a border of order by defining who is inside and who is outside. This perspective on political community formation includes the observation that a community is more than the sum of its parts. That is, the discourse of citizenship reaches beyond the definition of rights. It also creates a notion of belonging which is constructed through practice.[8]

The 'iron curtain' represented a border of order for the EU and NATO, in so far as it played a crucial role in the process of identity formation for both organizations. States became members of each and, akin to the political rights of citizenship, acquired – *qua* membership – the right to vote within the order of each respective organization. Through political practice, NATO and EU member states have created a notion of belonging to a community within a particular order. This order was built on liberal democratic principles that were, to a large extent, established and sustained by negative definition with the other side of the Iron Curtain, the communist East. The specific institutional identities were profoundly challenged by the post-Cold War situation. Enlargement is not simply a means to extend membership to a new member state; it also involves incorporating what was previously the Other, i.e. including members from another type of order. Enlargement in the post-Cold War context hence not only poses the challenge of a missing Other; both organizations also face a second challenge of having to incorporate members whose notion of belonging developed in a different context. Transgressing the Cold War borders of order, therefore, raises the question of belonging anew.

In the context of the Cold War, aside from early talk about the 'rollback' of Communism, eastern Europe became the largely forgotten half of Europe, invisible against the background of the Soviet Union's dominating presence. The containment policy of NATO, which necessarily involved the US, was defined primarily in relation to the Soviet Union. Until the period of *détente*, EC policy was largely inward looking, preoccupied with the re-emergence of western European economies. The self-definitions and normative ideals of both NATO and the EU were defined in opposition to the East. The openness, democracy and freedom of western societies were contrasted with their closed totalitarian neighbour. The articulation of the West's normative ideals served primarily to reinforce its own identity *vis-à-vis* the Other.

Prior to *détente*, there was some hope that the two Germanies would be reunified and this was reflected in the failure to recognize the new German Democratic Republic (GDR). This hope of obliterating the division of Europe subsided with *détente*. Eastern and western European states created a framework of peaceful coexistence. The common principles which would guide their relationship were embodied in the three baskets of the Helsinki Final Act, which was signed by states in both the East and the West in 1975. Expansion was a non-issue; *détente* cemented the division of Europe, granting communist regimes in the East a legitimacy they had not previously enjoyed. None the less, the Helsinki process was highly politicized from the start, as states in each bloc selectively interpreted the document (Bloed 1990: 283). Western states emphasized western values, and in particular the primacy of human rights, while eastern states emphasized disarmament provisions, non-interference in their affairs and the hope of economic aid. For the West, Helsinki represented the embodiment of western ideals of the free flow of information, people and goods across the division of Europe as well as the possibility of greater respect for human rights. The 'promise' articulated in the human rights basket of the Final Act first came back to haunt the eastern European communist regimes during the last part of the Cold War and later, after its end, western institutions. In what follows, we articulate the theoretical relationship between speech acts, contextual change and the challenge to institutional identity by reflecting on the 'promise' of Helsinki.

Speech acts: the promise of Helsinki

An article in *NATO Review*, entitled 'The implementation of the final act of the CSCE' (1976), referred to the significance of the document as follows (see also Luns 1976: 6):

> The ultimate significance of the Final Act of the Conference on Security and Cooperation in Europe, signed in Helsinki on 1 August 1975, depends on the degree to which all its provisions are implemented by all the participants. Although the Final Act does not, in Western eyes, have the force of law and its implementation is voluntary, there is nevertheless a strong *moral obligation* on signatories to translate its *promises* into reality [emphasis added].

The significance of the Final Act lay less in the force of law than in constructing a moral obligation. The goal was to translate the promise of Helsinki into reality.

This promise is an example of a speech act. There is a long tradition of speech act theory, which has recently begun to seep into the IR literature.[9] Several ideas at the core of this theory are relevant to our analysis. First, certain categories of speech do not simply describe or convey information, but are acts in and of themselves. Acts of this kind are referred to as 'performatives'. Saying something is doing something (Kratochwil 1989: 8). For instance, when someone says 'I do' in the context of marriage, they undertake an act which has a range of moral and legal consequences; the act constitutes the marriage, or brings it into being. The second point, which flows from this, is that speech acts are dependent on a context for their meaning. The meaning of a promise in the context of a marriage is quite different from a promise to pick up clothes at the dry cleaner's or the promise of Helsinki. It is by virtue of the context that acts, such as promises or threats, have illocutionary force and perlocutionary effects. The two can be distinguished by the *force* of variously promising, ordering, threatening, and the meaning attached to these actions, as opposed to the *effect* of promising, forcing or frightening on the addressee, or the bringing about of effects on an audience (Levinson 1983: 236). Both the illocutionary force and perlocutionary effects are dependent on context. The third point, which is somewhat less obvious, is that speech acts do not necessarily presuppose any face-to-face communication between communicants. All that matters is that the content of the speech act is conveyed from one party to another. If state X targets its missiles on state Y, for instance, a threat may be communicated, even if the threat was not spoken.[10] The propositional content of a promise or threat may also be conveyed through public discourse toward an other, rather than in a direct face-to-face exchange. In this light, it is perfectly reasonable to understand the commitment of states, in the context of the Helsinki Final Act, as the expression of a speech act of 'promising' to undertake a range of activities. This promise was communicated both to other states involved in the process and to their respective publics.

The human rights example is particularly interesting when examining the relationship between speech act and context. The illocutionary force and perlocutionary effect of the eastern promise to respect human rights manifested itself on two levels, that is, toward eastern European citizens' initiatives, which pointed out the discrepancy between the promise and corresponding acts by eastern governments, and western countries, who, given the priority attached to human rights, encouraged the dissident eastern Europeans. By 1976 and 1977 the Workers' Defence Committee (KOR) in Poland and the Charter 77 in Czechoslovakia were pointing out the discrepancy between the promise of eastern governments to respect human rights and the abusive treatment they were receiving for exposing violations. In this respect, eastern citizens' initiatives magnified the moral obligation which the promise entailed.

Western countries reinforced this breach of promise by referring back to Helsinki. For instance, in response to the Declaration of Martial Law in Poland in December 1981, the Special Ministerial Session of the North Atlantic Council stated that: 'The process of renewal and reform which began in Poland in August 1980 was watched with sympathy and hope by all who believe in freedom and self-determination; it resulted from a genuine effort by the overwhelming majority of the Polish people to achieve a more open society in accordance with the principles of the Final Act of Helsinki.'[11] The West not only recognized the role of the Helsinki principles in encouraging this dissidence, but also the commitment to accept the right of individuals to help in ensuring full implementation,[12] and the responsibility of the West toward those attempting to uphold 'western' ideals. As Lord Carrington stated:

> We must face squarely the complex moral and political dilemmas which developments in Eastern Europe pose for the West. Whatever we do, the Soviet Union will accuse us of subverting these countries. They are bound to say this because they cannot contemplate the enormity of their own failure in the area. Free societies have a power of attraction of which it would be perverse to be ashamed, and we should not be afraid to subvert by example. Our prime concern must be for the peoples of these countries themselves. *We have a historical duty, and a political and moral responsibility to uphold their right to freedom and self-determination.*
>
> (Lord Carrington 1983: 2; emphasis added)

In making this statement, Carrington emphasized that the West should not encourage revolution in the East, but rather reform. Consistent with *détente*, the goal was not to overturn the eastern order (and therefore the western border of order) but to open it up so that the people there might live under freer conditions. The recognition of a moral obligation toward the eastern dissidents, who were exposing the eastern failure to abide by its promise of human rights, manifests a further illocutionary force in this context. The praise of eastern human rights dissidents was situated again and again within a larger argument about the need for western activists, who were questioning their own governments' policies in the area of disarmament, to recognize what precisely NATO, in particular, was defending, i.e. western ideals of democracy and human rights (Levi 1982; de Carmoy 1982; Carrington 1983; Defois 1984). In both these respects, the promise of Helsinki, articulated in the context of the Cold War, served primarily to reinforce the border of order separating East and West.

Changing contexts, changing meaning

From 1989 to 1991, the political landscape of Europe was transformed with the dismantling of the Berlin Wall and the collapse of the Warsaw Pact and the Soviet Union. Both the EU and NATO were forced to redefine their identities as a result. For the EU, the dramatic changes accompanying the end of the Cold War created pressures to expand the Community at a time when it had been preparing to 'deepen' further the integration of existing members. For NATO, as a military alliance, designed for the defence of the West within the Cold War, the key issue in the immediate aftermath was less whether NATO would expand than whether the Alliance was necessary in the absence of its former antagonist (Lubkemeier 1991; Ando 1993). Against the background of a series of unanticipated changes that raised questions about the future identity of both organizations, past promises became one of the stable features in an otherwise uncertain situation. These promises were reinforced by the conceptualization of the end of the Cold War as a 'victory' for liberal democracy, capitalism and western values. Dissidents had acted in the name of liberal democratic principles. Western leaders had recognized their responsibility to those upholding their ideals. With the collapse of Communism, the West declared a victory. Each of these factors contributed to a transformation – once the context had changed – of promises from the past into threats. At this point we emphasize the eastern European context; in the next section, we return to an analysis of the two western organizations.

With the end of the Cold War, the countries of Central and Eastern Europe (CEECs) referred to their liberation from Communism as a return to an original state, for instance, a return to the natural geographical and historical boundaries of Europe (Melescanu 1993), or a return to democracy, after a historical detour, or a return to capitalism and to history (Jeszenszky 1992). This ideal healthy state was not, however, primarily a geographical or physical category; it was normative. As Romanian Foreign Minister Melescanu stated: 'today's Europe is to be found where its democratic, liberal and humanist values and practices succeed in shutting the door on the nightmare of authoritarian regimes, command economies, and a disregard for human rights and fundamental freedoms' (Melescanu 1993: 13). The model for this ideal healthy state was a set of shared western values going back to the

Enlightenment and the democratic revolutions of the eighteenth century. The problem in the years following the collapse was that western Europe was not doing enough to contribute to this outcome and in fact appeared to be isolating itself behind a new cordon sanitaire from the problems of post-Cold War Europe (Suchocka 1993: 6). The Cold War victor, who had challenged eastern bloc leaders to tear down the walls that kept eastern Europeans in, appeared, in the immediate aftermath of the Cold War, to be constructing barriers to keep them out.

The western effort to reconstruct a new border of order flew in the face of everything that the central and eastern Europeans had expected from the West. Vaclav Havel, speaking before NATO in the early 1990s, presented this expectation and, like Lord Carrington earlier, the responsibility that flowed from it:

> The democratic West ... was for years *offering sympathies* to the democratic forces in the countries of the Soviet bloc ... The protection of democracy and human liberty to which it has been committed *has given encouragement and inspiration* to citizens of our countries, too ... The determination to resist evil has been a source of hope for millions of people who had to live under a yoke. Because of that, the West *bears a tremendous responsibility* ... To the West, whose civilisation *is based on universal values*, the fate of the East *cannot be a matter of indifference* for reasons of principle, and for practical reasons either. Instability, poverty, misfortune and disorder in the countries that have rid themselves of despotic rule *could threaten* the West just as the arms arsenals of the former despotic governments did.
>
> (Havel 1991: 35; emphasis added)

The West, and its institutions, represented a normative ideal. The CEECs were encouraged to act in accordance with these ideals in resisting totalitarianism. Now that 'containment' of the Soviet Union was no longer necessary, the West had a responsibility to assist the CEECs in the recovery, to help them in upholding these values. Havel's appeal to western responsibility mirrored Carrington's recognition of this responsibility a decade earlier. In the aftermath of the Cold War, democracy was presented as a cure for eastern ailments, but, given the painful nature of the reforms, and the unhealed wounds reopened by the spirit of freedom, democracy would potentially give rise to – and by 1993 had given rise to – social unrest and national conflict, most notably in the former Yugoslavia where war had broken out (Gazdag 1992). The West had encouraged the adoption of ideals, had celebrated the hope and possibility of prosperity and democracy, but the prescribed cure, rather than contributing to recovery, was exacerbating tensions. The EU was accused of only a lukewarm response to eastern problems, and NATO of isolating itself behind a new cordon sanitaire from the problems confronted by the CEECs since the fall of Communism (Suchocka 1993).

The existence of norms supporting eastward enlargement was dramatized by central and eastern Europeans who pointed to the discrepancy between western promises and actions. The Cold War promise to eastern Europe became, in a new context, a threat of instability should the West fail to act. But the threat went even deeper. As we will argue in the next section, a failure to act on the promise became a threat to the identity of both institutions.

Redefining interests: the challenge to institutional identity

The point of the last section was to illustrate how actors used the past promises of states to hold a mirror up to current practices. The mirror was first held up to the eastern European regimes, who in signing the Helsinki Final Act promised to respect human rights and then proceeded to abuse the rights of dissidents who – morally supported by western governments – pointed out the discrepancy. In the immediate aftermath of the Cold War, these same dissidents, many of whom had become state leaders, held a mirror up to western governments, arguing that they, as the embodiment of the victory of liberal ideals in the Cold War, had a responsibility to those whom they had encouraged to adopt those ideals. These processes of mirroring provide a point of departure for rethinking the role of norms in processes of interest transformation.

These acts of exposing a discrepancy cannot be accounted for by rationalist theories. Given the emphasis on individuals or states as purely self-regarding ego-ists, it is assumed that promises will not be respected if they are in conflict with one's self-interest, regardless of others. However, if one's identity and ability to act are understood to be fundamentally social and, therefore, dependent on the recognition of others, promise-keeping becomes extremely important. It is at the point that others recognize the violation of normative expectations, or the failure to live up to previously stated ideals, that shame or disrespect are experienced. As Honneth (1995: 259) points out, it is not in the positive affirmation of norms that one's constitutive dependence on recognition from others is evident, but in the inability to continue with action once confronted with the discrepancy. The ability of states or alliances to act is as dependent on the positive recognition of identity as it is for individuals. Both rely on some measure of acceptance of an alignment between ideals or moral argument and practice.

In the aftermath of the Cold War the CEECs were seeking recognition from the West. But western identity was also dependent on recognition. Too great an inconsistency between the normative ideals which the West represented and its practices toward the CEECs would be damaging to the identity of the EU and NATO, not to mention those élites in the CEECs who were attempting to provide a democratic carrot rather than a nationalist stick (Allin 1995). The institutional challenge, however, took a somewhat different form for the two organizations.

In the case of the EU, the prospect of inclusion by way of enlargement was offered to all European states which shared the goals of the EC (Preamble to Single European Act, 1987). The responsibility of Europe as a whole to speak increasingly in one voice and the necessity for all democratic European states to be represented by and through the European Parliament became constitutionally entrenched with the Maastricht Treaty on European Union (TEU) in 1991 which states that '[A]ny European State may apply to become a member of the Union' (Article O, TEU). The promise was enhanced in the 'Conclusions of the Presidency' at the Copenhagen Summit in June 1993, which stipulated that 'membership requires that the candidate country has achieved stability of institutions guaranteeing democracy, the rule of law, human rights and respect for protection of minorities.'[13] The Amsterdam Treaty restates the intention of enlargement and explicitly the democratic condition, stipulating that '[A]ny European State which respects the principles set out in Article 6(1) may apply to become a member of the Union' (Article 49, TEU).[14] The promise of enlargement is hence firmly expressed in the Treaty, on the condition that the candidates are European states, governed democratically, and based on the principle of law.

The key issue in the current context of EU enlargement is less the uniqueness of adding new members than the changing context in which it takes place. While the sheer number of accession candidates certainly plays a role in the complexity of this process, we argue that the absence of the Cold War border of order has influenced how this process proceeds.[15] Candidate states have historically been required to accept the *acquis communautaire* in joining. The same is true in the current membership negotiations. However, an accession of this size and scope poses a challenge to the institutional capacities of the EU. It hence requires a reshuffling of the EU's institutional balance before accession can proceed. The 1996–7 intergovernmental conference (IGC) at Amsterdam postponed a decision in this respect, however, no later than the point when EU membership would exceed twenty.[16] As one observer remarked, it was not obvious why twenty members should come to an agreement that fifteen could not reach.[17] At any rate, the unresolved question of institutional balance at Amsterdam does present a hurdle in the enlargement process. To postpone the decision reflects a creeping insecurity in handling the process among EU member states. Effectively, this insecurity means a gradual move away from previous promises of enlargement that were uttered in the Cold War context. This new stress on the conditions for enlargement, rather than the promise to do so, suggests that the EU is now less ready to take on the responsibility which it had assigned for itself earlier when eastern enlargement was not yet in sight.

Indeed, more recent documents point to the development of a policy of conditionality which involves adding conditions for enlargement. One such condition, for example, regards a respect of minorities; candidates have to comply with this condition before joining the club. While the condition as such fits well into the shared norms of liberal democracy, it is striking that, while respect for minority rights is a condition to be accepted by the eastern candidates of the EU, it is not explicitly mentioned in the *acquis communautaire* to which the western members have adhered. We can, therefore, speak of hurdles being constructed for eastern candidate countries. There is a clear tension between the promises of the past and the slow emergence of present concerns. This shift was expressed during the Austrian Council Presidency of the EU at the beginning of actual accession negotiations with individual candidate countries on 10 November 1998. With the actual accession in view, worries about EU security, human rights, minority politics, and threats to EU employment security have led to an increasing number of key political actors cautioning against enlarging too rapidly.

For example, on 1 July 1998, the Austrian Council President, Foreign Minister

Wolfgang Schüssel, stressed that 'concern is now mounting that the date for the enlargement of the EU to take in countries from eastern Europe and Cyprus will be put back as the countries concerned struggle to meet EU standards.'[18] While negotiations were formally opened under the British presidency over a whole series of policy areas, Mr Schüssel warned that not only would the new countries have to make strenuous efforts but the EU would have to undertake major reforms before enlargement could go ahead. He said that *'Even the Union itself is currently not yet in any fit state to take in new members.'*[19] And, later in the process, supporting Chancellor Victor Klima, Austrian MEP Hannes Swoboda stressed that 'not only Austrians but also people in the candidate countries were anticipating this project of the century [EU enlargement] with concern. It would be irresponsible to forcefully push both EU and the candidate countries towards hastened enlargement.' At the same time, the beginning of the accession negotiations were praised as a 'historical day', as an achievement that had been 'a particular concern of the Austrian presidency' according to Council President Wolfgang Schüssel. As Schüssel stressed, the accession conferences beginning in Vienna signified the 'return to Europe of Hungary and other eastern European partners after more than eighty years of the breakdown of the Austrian-Hungarian monarchy'.[20]

Since the beginning of the German EU Presidency in January 1999 the main hurdle to compliance with previous promises has become the financial burden of enlargement. Next to the issue of 'institutions', 'minority rights' and 'security', 'money' now appears to be the major constraint in the process of enlargement. Instead of speaking with one voice, seeking to include the newly democratized central and eastern European states in the project of European integration, the EU member states appear to be quarrelling among themselves over who has to bear the financial brunt of eastern enlargement. The German ministry of state expressed the suspicion that other member states have high hopes that the Germans will 'pay it all' (*Die Woche*, 5 February 1999, p. 21). But quite to the contrary, the 'favourite toy of the Germans is now the calculator' (*Die Woche*, 5 February 1999, p. 21), and it is clear that, without successful budgetary reforms, enlargement is not likely to happen soon. Chancellor Gerhard Schröder of Germany, for example, painted a dire picture of European integration, lest the financial burden was reshuffled, pointing out that '[T]he century of European integration will see little success if burden-sharing is not distributed on a more equal basis' (*Die Woche*, 8 January 1999, p. 4). Despite these financial constraints, the German Presidency of the EU continued to reassure the CEECs with statements about the duty to enlarge. As German Council President, Foreign Minister Joschka Fischer stated:

> After the Cold War the EU must not be limited to Western Europe; instead, at its core the idea of European integration is an all-European project. Geopolitical realities do not allow for a serious alternative anyhow. If this is true, then history has already decided about the 'if' of eastern enlargement, even though the 'how' and 'when' remain to be designed and decided.
>
> (*Die Zeit*, 21 January 1999, p. 3)

The at times contradictory comments on enlargement as a historical opportunity to reintegrate the eastern European countries, on the one hand, and a concern of the West regarding issues of security, institutions and finance, on the other, point to the conflicting interests in the context of the enlargement discussion. An EU identity based on western democratic principles, and the related promise of enlargement, are at odds with emerging practical policy problems. A discursive analysis reveals that continuity in the enlargement process, despite frequently raised concerns, can be explained in terms of an EU identity rooted in shared norms and values. The strong emphasis on the norms structuring EU policy strategy was expressed in the European Parliament's Oostlander Report, in which the author cautioned against 'manoeuvring' aimed at postponing the opening of negotiations until there are precise details about the cost of enlargement. With too much manoeuvre, the author maintains that 'enlargement will never take place.'[21]

The issues raised by the dramatic end of the Cold War were somewhat different for NATO. As a military alliance, designed for the defence of the West within the Cold War, the key issue in the immediate aftermath was less whether NATO would expand than whether the Alliance was necessary in the absence of its former antagonist. Lacking the institutional equivalent of the EU *acquis* in regard to new members, the idea that NATO should expand was far from apparent. While the end of the Cold War brought the relationship between widening and deepening back on the EU's political agenda, the military security question was initially less one about expansion than about the relationship between NATO and the larger Organization for Security and Co-operation in Europe (OSCE), which already included the CEECs. NATO had 'won' the Cold War but, despite this apparent success, its continuing relevance was being called into question. The central problem was the reluctance of publics and parliaments on both sides of the Atlantic to direct resources to the organization in the absence of any apparent threat (Lubkemeier 1991; Ando 1993). Neither NATO nor the countries of central and eastern Europe assumed from the beginning that NATO would militarily expand to the East. Through a series of moves over several years the expansion became inevitable.[22] The motor of this transformation was the conflict between two promises.

In the last section, we explored how the CEECs gave meaning to their struggle for recognition by the West during this period. The CEECs argued that failure to expand would give rise to disorder. By contrast, one of NATO's arguments against military expansion was that it would arouse fears in Russia that the West sought domination over its former enemy, and exacerbate xenophobic sentiments and a reluctance to proceed with cuts in defence spending on the part of the Russian population (Taylor 1991; Holst 1992). Russia had articulated its opposition to the expansion of NATO but then made a surprise move in August 1993 in signing the Russian–Polish declaration which granted Poland leave to join the Alliance. Yeltsin's act was viewed hopefully by the CEECs, but not by Russia. Instead, 'non-democratic' forces interpreted the possibility of NATO expansion as a move to re-establish the Cold War and isolate Russia (Ignatenko 1994; Sturua 1994).

The strong Russian reaction created some nervousness in the West, which was reflected in NATO's Brussels Summit in January 1994. Faced with pressure from the CEECs to join the Alliance, and with the prospect that a decision to expand would mobilize nationalist forces in Russia, NATO mapped a middle course by creating the Partnership for Peace (PfP). The PfP would make it possible to delay the decision about expansion but, at the same time, would allow the CEECs to prepare for such an eventuality. While the West initially sought to mollify nationalist and communist forces in Russia through the PfP, the CEECs, concerned about the same development, emphasized the promise of the Partnership to prepare candidates for future membership. The Polish Minister of Defence, Piotr Kolodziejczyk, referred to the January Summit and the proclamation of the PfP by the Alliance: 'We expect and would welcome NATO expansion that would reach to democratic states to our East.' He further stated that Poland undertook the Partnership as 'the best route towards its goal of full integration in the Alliance' (Kolodziejczyk 1994). Poland drew on the promise of the PfP to press Polish interests.

At the beginning of 1994, NATO said that there would be no immediate enlargement. By mid-1994, after Clinton's speech in Warsaw, momentum had shifted towards enlargement.[23] At the December 1994 Brussels meeting of NATO foreign ministers, a decision was made to proceed with expansion. The enlargement of NATO was placed in the context of building a European security architecture which would extend to the whole of Europe. While enlargement was initially avoided out of fear that it would re-create the division of Europe, by 1996 it was said to have rendered the idea of dividing lines in Europe 'obsolete' (Moltke 1996). Any distinctions between countries as a result of expansion would be 'contours' indicating 'degrees of difference' rather than dividing lines. By developing a 'true partnership' with Russia and making a conceptual linkage between the enlargement of the EU and NATO, the expansion was to communicate the parallelism of integration and co-operation: the integration of new members and the deepening of co-operation with those nations who are not, or not yet, ready or willing to join (Voigt 1996).

Like past applicants to the EU, the CEECs viewed membership of the two organizations as part of the same package. Even though the initial concern of the CEECs was an economic one, the challenge was raised to both organizations. Through a series of incremental decisions, not least of which was the creation of the PfP, the Visegrad countries emphasized those parts of the promise which would contribute to their eventual membership. Once a decision had been made to include the Visegrad countries, the threat began to focus on a more traditional security concern and the promise to avoid new 'spheres of influence' in Europe, as leaders of the Baltic states pointed to promises by American leaders that 'No nation in Europe should ever again be consigned to a buffer zone between great powers or related to another nation's "sphere of influence".'[24] The problem that NATO currently faces is the conflict between its promise to expand to the Baltic states and its promise of genuine partnership with Russia, which opposes a further wave of expansion.

While NATO's interests may have originally been driven by a survival concern, the contradictions of the present situation open up two alternatives which are contrary to this interest, in so far as survival, in this case, is primarily a question of *institutional* relevance rather than military. One is to transform the survival problem into one of military survival by respecting the promise to the Baltic states at the expense of its promise to Russia of genuine partnership. The other is to deepen the partnership with Russia at which point NATO's identity, and therefore survival as *NATO*, may become doubtful; the deeper the co-operation with Russia, the less need there is for an organization focusing on the North Atlantic area as opposed to a pan-European security organization, such as the OSCE.[25]

In conclusion, it is interesting to look at the relationship between contextual changes, normative ideals and institutional expansion for each of the three players: the EU, NATO and the CEECs respectively. This approach provides insight into the rationale for the expansion of both western organizations by placing them in a changing intersubjective context, which has been transformed through the interaction of the different players. The changing context, while more dramatic for the CEECs than the West, constructed the possibility for the former to articulate two *compatible* interests, i.e. inclusion in both NATO and the EU, while it created *conflicting* interests for both western organizations. The changing context disrupted the future plans of the EU and NATO, presenting an entirely new situation to which they had to respond. In order to maintain their identity as victors in the Cold War, western institutions had to act with some semblance of consistency with the normative ideals which they represented. The promise of prosperity and democracy was a stable and constant feature against a backdrop of material disarray. The CEECs drew on these normative ideals to pressure the West to keep their promises. While failing to provide the massive assistance reminiscent of the Marshall Plan, both the EU and NATO did reinforce the promise of eventual inclusion. By making the CEECs responsible for their own readiness to join, the West also provided a carrot that would, it was hoped, dampen the conflicting tendencies toward disintegration in the East. The promise constituted the possibility of expansion. Against the background of a dramatically changed context, the CEECs transformed the promise into a threat, making maximum use of their compatible interests in expansion with both institutions. By contrast, NATO and the EU were pulled toward expansion against the background of conflicting interests.

3. THE CHALLENGE OF EASTERN ENLARGEMENT AND THE CONSTRUCTIVIST RESEARCH PROGRAMME

The comparison of EU and NATO expansion provides an insight into the expansion process in a way that an analysis of either organization, in and of itself, cannot. Based on this brief comparison of the two cases of enlargement politics, we have argued that an explanation of both processes, against the odds, requires embedding these policy decisions in a *normative order* which does not exclude the EU's *acquis* but is larger and encompasses NATO as well. When embedded in this larger normative order, moves by NATO and the EU to redefine their interests regarding expansion can be understood as emerging out of the tension between past promises and on-going practice in a context of dramatic change, which, in the absence of the old border of order, constituted a challenge to the Cold War identities of the two institutions. To this end, we examined a process of norm construction which preceded the critical juncture of the end of the Cold War. In doing so, our analysis fits squarely within the constructivist debate but pushes further. We elaborate the relationship between norms, practices and identity, and how interests were transformed in the dialectical relationship between the three.

The constructivist emphasis on identities, norms and practices provides an important point of departure for understanding the expansion process; at the same time, we note that this literature has not sufficiently addressed issues raised by a context of dramatic change where the 'other' disappears or undergoes significant transformation. Building on the strengths and expanding on the weaknesses of this tradition, our argument includes the following components. First, the enlargement decisions have to be embedded in a longer process going back to the construction of norms during the Cold War. The key issue is how the meaning of speech acts embodying these norms changed with the end of the Cold War, and how this constructed the conditions for eastern enlargement. The argument rests on a dialectical relationship between *context*, *speech acts* and *institutional change*. The rationality of moves by either organization has to be situated in a context of past meanings.

Second, we emphasize that context and speech acts are explicitly intersubjective. As a result, we assume the importance of the meanings that actors bring to their own actions and the material world around them. This points to one other crucial element that has not been adequately addressed in some of the constructivist literature, that is, the role of language. The reluctance to take language seriously undoubtedly relates to a widespread acceptance of the realist assumption that the primary speech act of diplomats is the lie and that states will break promises if it is in their interest to do so. The following turns the realist argument about language on its head, analysing 'promises' as a specific form of action, and looking at processes by which the two institutions were held to account for their promises and normative ideals.

Third, if meaning is dependent on context, it follows logically that, as a context changes, so will the meaning of acts. We argue that the promise of western institutions, held out to the former eastern bloc during the Cold War, was transformed into a threat, by both East and West, with the dismantling of the European division and the Soviet Union. This new threat gave rise to a conclusion that the CEECs could not be excluded, over the long term, from western organizations. If western acts were not consistent with past promises, the consequence would be a loss of popular support for democratic institutions and a free market economy, which would exacerbate nationalist tensions and ethnic rivalries in the region, creating a security threat for the West. The threat not only took the form of potential instability in the East, however; the failure to fulfil the promise, and the exposure of this failure, presented a threat to the identity of the two organizations.

ACKNOWLEDGEMENTS

We would like to thank William Wallace and Jan Zielonka for encouragement to move ahead with the project. We would also like to thank the Politics Group at Nuffield College for providing Antje Wiener with access to logistics and the opportunity to carry out joint work at Nuffield in the summer of 1998, while Karin Fierke was a Prize Research Fellow there. The chapter has previously been presented at the University of Aarhus workshop on Constructivism and European Integration at Fenmøller, Denmark, June 1998, and the British International Studies Association meeting at the University of Sussex, December 1998. We thank the participants for their comments. Specifically, we thank two anonymous reviewers, as well as Knud Erik Jørgensen, Veronique Pin-Fat, Jeff Checkel, Frank Schimmelfennig, Thomas Diez and Ulrich Sedelmeier for concise comments. The responsibility for this version is ours.

NOTES

1   See Avery and Cameron 1998; Grabbe and Hughes 1998; Mayhew 1998; Preston 1997; for conceptual work, see Schimmelfennig 1998; Sedelmeier 1998.
2   For an exception, see Sedelmeier 1998.
3   See Brown 1995; MccGwire 1998; Mandelbaum 1996; Asmus *et al*. 1995; Glaser 1993; Sloan 1995, respectively.
4   See, for example, public opinion changes which show an increased scepticism towards NATO enlargement. Surveys of the UKS Information Agency show that, while in 1996 majorities of 56 per cent in France, 61 per cent in Germany, and 66 per cent in Britain welcomed enlargement, these percentages changed significantly to 39 per cent in France, 38 per cent in Germany and 42 per cent in Britain in favour of NATO enlargement in 1997. (See European Opinion Alert, USIA Office of Research and Media Reaction, 7 February 1997, cf. Statewatch, DB2WEB 2 October 1998.)
5   The *acquis communautaire*, or the shared properties of Community law and legislation, has come to be the guiding framework for enlargement procedures in particular (Michalski and Wallace 1992). Indeed, the accession *acquis* has been identified as the oldest form of *acquis*, entailing 'the whole body of rules, political principles and judicial decisions which new Member States must adhere to, in their entirety and from the beginning, when they become members of the Communities' (Gialdino 1995: 1090).
6   For a more in-depth elaboration on the distinction between various strands of constructivist approaches in international relations (IR), see Christiansen *et al*. 1999.
7   Doty (1997) and Campbell (1998) discuss this critique in greater detail.
8   These practices include two conceptions of practice: one is the republican notion of identity formation by way of political debates among citizens (see, for example, Preuss 1995; Habermas 1992); the other has been defined as 'the conflictive process of establishing the institutional terms of citizenship, i.e. citizenship practice' (Wiener 1998a: ch. 2, 1998b: 305).
9   See Austin 1962; Searle 1969; Levinson 1983; Duffy *et al*. 1998; Kratochwil 1989; Buzan *et al*. 1998.
10   We would like to express our thanks to Gavan Duffy both for this particular example and for clarifying this point.
11   Special Ministerial Session of the North Atlantic Council, 11 January 1982, 'Declaration of Events in Poland,' *NATO Review*, vol. 30 no. 2 (1982), p. 28.
12   See Solesby 1978; Luns 1979; Nimetz 1980; de Carmoy 1982.
13   *Bulletin of the European Communities* 6, 1993, point I.13.
14   See also Article 6, paras 1, 2, the TEU stipulates '1. The Union is founded on the principles of liberty, democracy, respect for human rights and fundamental freedoms, and the rule of law, principles which are common to the Member States. 2. The Union shall respect fundamental rights, as guaranteed by the European Convention for the Protection of Human Rights and Fundamental Freedoms signed in Rome on 4 November 1950 and as they result from the constitutional traditions common to the Member States, as general principles of Community law.'

15 Past accessions have not involved more than a few countries at a time. By contrast, now, with the Cold War over, expansion will potentially incorporate up to fourteen new countries which is almost double the current membership. Ten candidate countries are from Central and Eastern Europe including Bulgaria, the Czech Republic, Estonia, Hungary, Latvia, Lithuania, Poland, Romania, Slovakia and Slovenia.

16 On the IGC's failure to prepare the EU's institutional balance for enlargement, see Sedelmeier 2000; Falkner and Nentwich 2000; Moravcsik and Nicolaidis 1998.

17 See European Policy Center, September 1997, http://europa.eu.int/en/agenda/igc-home/instdoc/universe/europe.htm, pp. 1 and 2 respectively.

18 See *EP News*, July 1998, p. 1.

19 See *EP News*, July 1998, p. 1; emphasis added.

20 All citations from *Der Standard*, 10 November 1998; this and the following translations from German into English by A.W.

21 See *Together in Europe. European Union Newsletter for Central Europe*, No. 88, 1 May 1996, p. 5. Rapporteur Arie Oostlander, report approved by EP on 17 April 1996.

22 For a more in-depth analysis of the processes underlying NATO expansion, see Fierke 1999.

23 The American Congress and public opinion were once again asking why they should continue to invest in the Alliance, given the failure to take effective action in Bosnia (Sloan 1994; Aspin 1994). At the same time, Alliance countries were faced with major cuts in defence spending and renewed questions about the relevance and need for NATO in the absence of a Soviet threat (Bruce 1994; Sloan 1994; Rose 1994). Expansion was the answer to these problems. The desire of the CEECs to join the Alliance became proof of its continuing relevance and mission (Aspin 1994).

24 See Warren Christopher, as quoted in Stankevicius 1996; see also Golob 1996.

25 For a more in-depth analysis of this conflict, see Fierke 1998: chs 10 and 11.

9

Reconstructing a Common European Foreign Policy

Kenneth Glarbo

INTRODUCTION

Theories levelled at the study of integration within the European Union (EU) have recently begun to display a refreshing diversity, especially in opening up a host of non-state centric and non-objectivist approaches. However, the study of what is perhaps the most political of all subfields within the EU, i.e. common foreign and security policy (CFSP) – previously European political co-operation (EPC), still lags behind this development.[1]

When subjected to theoretical analysis, European political co-operation has traditionally been the prerogative of realists. Arguably, the realist narrative of political co-operation, however diverse in appearance, can be reduced to a 'hard core' hypothesis, from which all the realist theoretical statements of EPC/CFSP are derived. Adopting a nation state unit and rationality assumptions, this core proposition simply states that the interests of single European nation states will eternally block integration within the high politics realms of foreign, security and defence policy.

Realist students of the EPC/CFSP supply convincing evidence to back this core proposition. As they point out, the institutional setting of European political co-operation has been intergovernmental throughout its history; and interstate negotiation remains the norm within present-day CFSP (see, e.g., Pijpers 1990, 1991; Ifestos 1987). Where, recently, Maastricht and Amsterdam Treaty provisions have warranted more supranationality within political co-operation, this has been far from successful (Regelsberger and Wessels 1996). In fact, where common positions and common actions should be obvious, they are repeatedly made impossible by displays of national interests; and when common opinions – on rare occasions – are actually forged, unilateral defection often follows (e.g. Keukelaire 1994; Jakobsen 1997).

Even where the European partners do succeed in implementing common action, and hence where realism should be put to its hardest test, this is quite naturally interpreted as reconcilable with national interest. Realists have two favoured strategies for circumventing this anomaly. One is to subscribe successful common actions to an underlying preferential fit or to a tactical manoeuvring among major partner states. For example, this has been the case with theoretical explication of the EU recognition of the reasserted states of Slovenia and Croatia in 1991–2, where the common position finally adopted has been widely interpreted as the partners simply bowing to German preference for recognition against the background of prolonged interstate haggling on the matter (e.g. Lucarelli 1997: 36–43; Owen 1995: 376–7).

The second strategy for a realist reduction of successful political co-operation focuses on the alleged low salience of such agreement or, if this cannot be established, on the frailness of the common positions adopted. This latter accusation of EPC/CFSP impotence frequently resurfaces in the realist depiction of European political co-operation as merely '*demarchés* and declaratory diplomacy' (e.g. Forster and Wallace 1996: 416–20).

Admittedly, this brief description paints an idealized image of political co-operation literature, much of which, in fact, contains a great deal more nuance than stipulated here.[2] But the dominance of realism remains, not only as the explicit orientation of the more deliberately theoretical interventions in the field, but also as the implicit premiss of many analytical accounts of the EPC/CFSP.[3]

In this chapter, the aim is to show that there is much more to European political co-operation than suggested by realism. More specifically, it is suggested that European political co-operation should rather be viewed as a case of social construction. For the present purposes, this can be demonstrated simply by taking another look at the heralded realist history of European political co-operation – this time, however, from a constructivist vantage point. Accordingly, the first and major purpose of the chapter is to shed a new and broader theoretical light on the history of European political co-operation, which promises to deliver a more faceted theoretical knowledge of the political co-operation process than is provided by realism.

Two arguments are intrinsic to the constructivist perspective. The first of these, theoretical in nature, is that important junctures in EPC/CFSP history are not the simple products of national interests. Rather, they emerge as social constructions, that is, as the results of national diplomacies intentionally and unintentionally communicating to themselves and to each other their intents and perceptions of political co-operation. Alternatively, they appear against the background of inter-subjective structures built up by such previous communication. These mechanisms might work only as a supplement to instrumental rationality but, nevertheless, play crucial roles in accounting for important turns in political co-operation history.

Second, as an unconventional empirical corollary to this, I shall argue that integration *does* prevail within European political co-operation, or at least within the CFSP of recent years, even if this does not totally refute the importance of national interest. Despite interest, however, constructivist theory argues that political co-operation leaves room for a *social* integration that stems from diplomatic communication processes set up through political co-operation history, and which is not easily discernible from the intergovernmentalist formal codes of CFSP.

In attempting to apply 'constructivist' theory the chapter has a second purpose, which is mostly of an implicit nature. Recent years of meta-theoretical debate within international relations (IR) have shown 'social constructivism' to be a rather vacuous, if not a downright tautological term, that can be adapted to fit almost any pre-given theory or empirical phenomenon (Glarbo 1998b). Hence, the purpose here is not to develop a full-blown constructivist theoretical body but, on an explorative level, to begin suggesting how a truly theoretical constructivism could be set up. For this important second purpose, I reserve an equal amount of effort and space in the following.

After briefly sketching the theoretical framework and an ontological model to accompany this, in the following sections I investigate chronological periods of EPC/CFSP history in order to present the argument. It should be noted that, owing to the task taken on, neither of the two purposes envisaged is arguably fully accomplished in this study. In order to avoid disappointing the empirically and theoretically interested reader respectively, the following remarks should then be read – empirically – as suggested notes on the history of EPC/CFSP and – theoretically – as milestones for an operable IR constructivism.

CONSTRUCTIVISM AND EUROPEAN POLITICAL CO-OPERATION

The still young constructivist intervention within IR is undergoing a severe transformation. Starting with radical criticism, levelled at a hegemonic rationalist mainstream (Keohane 1988; Onuf 1989; Wendt 1992), constructivist scholars are now beginning to face up to the difficult task of systematically defining, operationalizing and applying constructivist first order theory to empirical analysis.

In the hope of contributing to this, this constructivist inquiry applies a set of sociological categories, all somehow grappling with the social conversion or construction of reality, to the case of European political co-operation. In particular, I draw on the phenomenology of Alfred Schutz (1972 [1932]) and the symbolic interactionism of George Herbert Mead (1967 [1934]) and Herbert Blumer (1969; see also Ritzer 1992: 326–92).

Phenomenology and symbolic interactionism are both theories of social action. As such, they both lend first order theoretical categories to social constructivism which, in itself, is arguably nothing but a hollow philosophical postulate (cf. Adler 1997b; Collin 1997; Lose, 2001).[4] Moreover, phenomenology and symbolic interactionism are both predominantly suited to the study of individuals in their capacities as social agents, and confronted by social structure. This does not supply a satisfactory ontological gallery for an inquiry into European political co-operation, however. Instead, we need to harness constructivism to a distinct and relevant ontology for political co-operation in order to get theoretical analysis under way.

For this purpose, it is suggested that we merge constructivist theory in the shape of phenomenology and symbolic interactionism with the simple ontology set out in Figure 1. Besides operating with individuals in their capacities as social and diplomatic agents, the model also incorporates an anthropomorphized collective 'national diplomacy' agent, this state-centric move on agency already being a familiar feature within IR constructivism – a move which especially goes to sharpen dialogue with realism (cf. Wendt 1992). Their agency capacities aside, national diplomacies are conceived, subject to closer theoretical specification, as also appearing in the shape of national social structure. Finally, at the upper tier of ontology, one should expect a social structure characteristic of political co-operation to emerge some time along EPC/CFSP history.

No propositions should be drawn solely from this model. Rather, the constructivist rendition of EPC/CFSP history and the relation of this to traditional narratives should merit attention here, not the ontological levels simply applied to this. Figure 1 hence only serves heuristic purposes.

On the other hand, a clear-cut and specified ontology is arguably imperative for the accomplishment of operable constructivist analysis. This becomes evident if one considers more closely the meta-theoretical virtues of constructivism itself. In contrast to rationalist IR theories, constructivism should accommodate the variability of both agency and structure (Onuf 1989: 52–62; Wendt 1992: 394; Risse 1997: 6). This is a very sympathetic principle in abstract, which has nevertheless

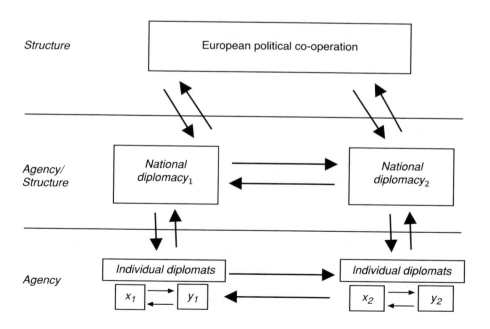

Figure 1 An overview of agents and structures within European political co-operation

proved to be a severe stumbling block for constructivist empirical analysis, mostly because it demands great attentiveness to methodological rigour.

Without elaborating this problem any further, let us just stress that the onto-logical model proposed here fits one of the few viable methodological means of accommodating such variability in empirical analysis. This is the 'analytical bracket-ing' strategy proposed by Anthony Giddens (e.g. 1983; Archer 1982; Thompson 1989). Bracketing entails the continuous reversal of the causal order among agents and structures in empirical analysis. As will be demonstrated, this allows for both a theoretical and periodic inquiry into political co-operation, as analysis progresses up through the history of political co-operation by tracking, in turn, the effects of agency upon structure and vice versa.[5]

THE GENESIS OF POLITICAL CO-OPERATION

A constructivist study of EPC/CFSP history must begin by investigating social agency. In other words, social structure is deliberately 'bracketed' in this first section.

At the agency level, Figure 1 presents only two of the current fifteen national diplomacies within CFSP and the respective individual diplomats in these. For our purposes, each diplomacy could be seen as comprising the *corps diplomatique* of state foreign offices, including incumbent ministers and civil servants designated to the Brussels representation, but also other individuals in positions that allow them to affect the foreign policies of member states. Such individuals could be members of cabinets or even influential members of national parliaments. A watertight definition is not imperative here. What is envisaged are simply different groups of policy-makers granted the right to formulate national foreign policy on a day-to-day basis.

At first glance, both the run-up to and the launch of the EPC in 1969–70 appear clearly as conducive to state interests. Besides a shared interest in relaunching the European project after the 'empty chair' crisis of 1965–6, each of the participating states arguably had credible motives for opting for formalized political co-oper-ation at this particular historical juncture (Allen and Wallace 1982).[6] As such, these initial phases of European political co-operation should pose severe difficulties for constructivism.

At this point, it should be remembered that both phenomenology and symbolic interactionism are theories of social *interaction* (Blumer 1969: 8). By logical exten-sion, the constructivist story of the pre-EPC period is therefore a negative one. Considering now national diplomacies in their agency capacities, phenomenology and symbolic interactionism both illustrate how regularized interaction between West European diplomacies was practically absent before the onset of EPC. On the contrary, interaction between European national diplomacies was irregular in nature and mostly extended only to what was required by a traditional bilateral agenda of intermittent confrontations. In the words of Schutz, before EPC, respective diplo-macies belonged to each other's *Mitwelts*, i.e. their 'world of contemporaries', characterized by a simultaneous and an equal presence in time, but also by a per-manent spatial 'separation' and thus no regularized interaction (Schutz 1972: 176–207).

This reasoning does not depart drastically from realist wisdom on European post-war diplomacy. Concurrently, diplomacies had begun to interact on a regular basis within NATO, thus also facilitating an institutionalization of democratic norms and even a degree of collective identity which is necessary for explaining the later persistence of this institution (Risse-Kappen 1996a). Moreover, regular cross-diplomatic interaction took place within bilateral foreign policy settings such as the Brussels Treaty. But these alliances aside, post-war interaction between West European states rarely extended all the way to co-ordination based on intense contact and between fixed groups of partners, and the international climate was hence predominantly based on state autonomy and self-help.

In phenomenological terms, national diplomacies, given such relative isolation, forge perceptions of each other on the basis of 'typifications'. Typifications refer to ideal typical charts of reality, which are held as integral, not only to a diplomatic agent's way of viewing the international system and its elements, but also more broadly to any social agent's method of grasping social reality; for example, through the application of labels – such as 'dog' or 'house' – or simply through the use of language (Ritzer 1992: 376). The active operation of 'typifying' hence embodies phenomenology's theoretical strategy for capturing how agents manage to conduct a social existence.

As a basic phenomenological premiss, typifications are produced and stocked with agents on the basis of *social interaction*. Social interaction thus holds the key to both the creation and the altering of typifications. By extension, integration, in the sense of converging typifications, stems directly from social interaction. If, on the other hand, typifications are not moulded by an agent's social interaction with others, the available typifications describing these contemporaries should be expected as relatively fixed with the agent. Correspondingly, in the *Mitwelt* condition characterizing the relation between national diplomacies before 1970, the typifications stocked with each agent of any other diplomacy should logically display a fundamental suspiciousness.

This is clearly visible from a brief rereading of what is the appropriate empirical context here, namely the multiple attempts to create an institutionalized European political co-operation *prior* to EPC. On at least two grand occasions, models for a formalized political co-operation had been proposed, only to be withdrawn after intense inter-diplomatic conflict and mutual suspicion. In the early 1950s, negotiations on a European Defence Community (EDC), providing, *inter alia*, for a European army alongside common defence institutions, were subject to heated diplomatic disagreement, and the plans were ultimately withdrawn after the failure of the French Assembly to ratify the EDC draft treaty. Throughout the 1950s new proposals for political co-operation reappeared and continued to spark strong disagreement, in particular between de Gaulle's France and the more 'integrationist' member states. The culmination of this was the Dutch veto of the so-called Fouchet proposals for a political union in June 1962 (Willis 1968: 131–84, 305–11; Nuttall 1992: 30–50).

As should be evident from this, the constructivist account finds some common ground with a default realist rendition of European high politics prior to EPC. But grave theoretical differences also persist. In the constructivist version, it is not sufficient to view the recurrent breakdowns of initiatives before EPC as the simple products of the interests of the states involved. Rather, failure seemed to stem from the historical reproduction of a negative typification of mutual suspiciousness. Once consolidated, this typification spurred national diplomacies towards conducting policy on the basis of rational calculus, thus again solidifying negative typifications, etc. (cf. Wendt 1992: 405).

THE FORMATIVE YEARS

The 1970 Luxembourg Report did provide rough formal guidelines for political co-operation, but no social practice had yet consolidated understandings and routines for the conduct of common foreign policy. In this section, as in the previous one, the agency viewpoint is thus preserved, keeping a bracket on structure. In this section, however, the *positive* social interaction between the diplomatic agents of EPC from 1970 onwards is in focus.

From the very beginning, EPC brought member diplomacies and their diplomats together in space and time on a regular basis. Constructivism argues that this provided completely different terms for the social interaction between both national diplomacies and their individual diplomats. First, neighbouring diplomacies became part of each other's direct phenomenological environments (*Umwelts*). Recalling the ground hypothesis, their daily contact should allow for an alteration of mutual typifications and, in turn, for integration.

Before turning to the empirical side of this, it is necessary to add some constructivist theoretical substance to the – strictly phenomenological – typification terminology. Symbolic interactionism adds a more nuanced description of the social integration forestalled here. In the words of Mead, interacting diplomacies and diplomats are expected to establish meaning recursively on the basis of their engagement in a mutual exchange of 'gestures' and 'significant symbols' (Mead 1967: 75–82; Blumer 1969: 8–9).

Contrasting with merely unreflected 'gestures', which can only inadvertently give cause to meaning during interaction, significant symbols are characterized by the immediate requirement of *interpretation*. Moreover, Mead highlights the way in which even the eliciting agent himself, along with receivers of the symbol, is able to reflect on and respond to the significant symbol, as this latter acquires an autonomous existence or – importantly – as he watches other agents take on attitudes towards his initial actions (Mead 1967: 46–7). The agentic self-surveillance implied by this takes the shape of a 'looking-glass self', i.e. a developing process in which the agent keeps tabs on his own behaviour according to the reactions of the surrounding social world. With Mead, essentially, this leaves the agent leaning towards an increasing social conformity.

Returning to early EPC, it seems evident that diplomacies spent just as much time studying their own as well as others' actions, adjusting their own eliciting of symbols to fit interpretations of emergent meaning, as they spent on counting national interests. The contours of such mutual symbolic signalling can be saliently traced from both the institutional and the heralded substantial policies of EPC during the early years.

On the former of these, symbolic interaction was generally evident from the institutional evolution of EPC between the Luxembourg Report and the ensuing codification of EPC formalities in the 1973 Copenhagen Report. The initial development of formal EPC procedures, as mentioned, could not build on the loose provisions of the Luxembourg Report. Beyond the setting-up of a council of foreign ministers and a political committee, the Report did not lay down strict provisions for a political co-operation process. Instead, the EPC process evolved largely on a trial-and-error basis, with presiding states continuously probing new routines for solving co-ordination problems. For instance, the working group formula, which later on proved crucial to diplomatic integration, was effectively the product of the French 1971 presidency's effort, not to exercise national inter- est, but to propose or construct a model that would allow for a degree of European Community involvement in political co-operation, while not dispensing with an autonomous and functional EPC structure. As it turned out, this model, originally consisting of a set of subcommittees to the political committee and a so-called *ad hoc* group allowing for Commission representation, was successfully put to work during the Conference on Security and Co-operation in Europe (CSCE) process and was hence silently endorsed by all fellow member states (Nuttall 1992: 62–3).

On the level of ministers, ground rules for co-operation were also constructed virtually from scratch between the Luxembourg and Copenhagen Reports, only a few discernible national interests seemingly gaining ground in this process. As a rather curious example of this, the first conference of ministers in November 1970, contrary to later practice, was held in Munich rather than in the West German capital of Bonn. Nuttall notes that this point is neither anecdotal nor trivial, but bears witness to the probing nature of EPC institutional development. In his words, given that 'ministers had never met before in that format; they were not certain what they were supposed to achieve nor in what conventions they would be operating' (1992: 55).

The initial formal innovations of EPC were hence levelled as significant symbols and gestures rather than as interests. Symbols were then subjected to interpretation by other diplomacies, initial misunderstandings being a recurrent feature of this. With time, reciprocal interpretation would have the effect of partner states accept- ing and accommodating routines, and a common symbolic content of the inno- vation could steadily be adjusted and stabilized by its recurrent employment in institutional practice.

As it happens, the symbolic process was crowned by the member states seem- ingly 'proposing' and codifying in the Copenhagen Report what was already a fully institutionalized set of formal procedures for the EPC, including intensified meeting schedules for ministers and the political committee, the setting-up of the group of correspondents, working groups, the involvement of representations and ambassadors, etc. (Allen and Wallace 1982: 26). As suggested by Jørgensen, this method of constructing and affirming institutional innovation has, in fact, been an integral part of EPC policy-making, at least up until the 1986 Single European Act (Jørgensen 1996: 43).

After the adoption of the Copenhagen Report, national interest and negotiated compromise continued to play major parts in EPC institutional politics. A realist flavour was, for instance, noticeable during the creation of a European Council at the 1974 Paris Summit. The design of this institutional novelty, which was also to be the superior political decision-making body within political co-operation, was essentially intergovernmentalist, and promised to preserve traditional national prerogatives within foreign policy.

However, symbolic processes were paramount in another institutional context, which is at least of equal importance to the European Council, namely during the creation and institutionalization of the so-called 'Gymnich' formula for meetings between foreign ministers. Launched by the West German presidency also in 1974, the extremely informal and relaxed design of the semi-annual Gymnich meetings, envisaging face-to-face contact between foreign ministers without fixed agendas and surrounding diplomats, was initially a deliberate means of remedying short-term disagreement over the Middle East and energy policy (Allen 1982: 85–8; Nuttall 1992: 90–3). To the surprise of the EPC partners, however, this highly unorthodox institutional novelty soon enjoyed formidable success, not only in clearing up internal differences, but also in restoring American–West European relations. Moreover, the Gymnich formula apparently achieved this without jeopardizing existing typifications of how diplomacy could work. Later, the Gymnich formula, originally only an idiosyncratic solution to short-term problems, was communicated and reproduced as a central part of the institutional structure of European political co-operation – a part which has persisted, in fact, to the present day.

The rapid symbolic reproduction of the Gymnich method for EPC provides an important early example of the constructed element within political co-operation. However, in the mid-1970s there were still tangible restrictions to the leeway for national symbolization and gesturing, even on formal EPC matters. These restrictions can be viewed from the way in which political co-operation was always vigorously dissociated from Treaty matters by practically all member states. Also, the supranational associations attached to plans for an EPC political secretariat led to the recurrent downfall of such plans, from the 1972 Paris Summit onwards (Jørgensen 1996: 32–3; Nuttall 1992: 71–4).

If social construction did not entirely sum up EPC formal matters during its formative years, on the level of EPC policy substance national interest also prevailed during the early 1970s. But, concurrently, common typifications began to materialize where single diplomacies proposed – and hence spurred on – symbolic exchanges on the first areas for concerted action. The launching of these issues clearly displayed the characteristics of a proto-communicative process where the pre-existing interests and typifications held and the gestures and symbols levelled by national diplomacies seemed to play equally vital roles.

During the first years of EPC, the agenda of potential concertation was virtually subsumed by the CSCE and Middle East issues. Recalling general realist strategy, co-operation in these fields has frequently been explained away with reference to the relatively low salience of the CSCE process within the context of global power politics (Kohler 1982: 92), with reference to the converging interests of European partners in the Middle East, or by exposing the feeble, insubstantial nature of results achieved by co-operation (Allen 1982; Nuttall 1992: 56).

Naturally, there was much more at stake here than envisaged by these realist reductions. Constructivism points to how, given the youth of the EPC institution, the *exclusive* dedication to only CSCE and Middle East issues was soon felt as an 'appropriate' profile for European political co-operation. The CSCE question, proposed for EPC by the Belgians, was quickly conceived and communicated to the partners, not as a special priority for Belgium or any other individual state, but as a field in which EPC had reasonable chances of playing a role, namely acquiring an autonomous identity (e.g. von Groll 1982: 63–9).

On the Middle East question, internal dissension was traditionally more on the cards, and the view to launch this issue as a success agent for EPC is perhaps hardly as credible. However, member states subsequently came to notice how EPC commanded instrumental leadership in the CSCE process and how, partly because the European stance became defined in opposition to the Americans, an aggregated European policy became surprisingly operational in the Middle East.

Initial diplomatic practice in both these areas thus quickly came to solidify the appropriateness of what was otherwise a completely arbitrary and restricted EPC agenda. Notably, as EPC history testifies, this appropriateness could not be entirely reduced to the interests and rationalities of single diplomacies. Rather, it evolved as the result of a probing symbolic interaction which, eventually, as the success of co-operation was interpreted and communicated by the partners, transformed into a firm common typification of the substantial content of political co-operation.[7]

Regularizing diplomatic interaction: co-ordination reflexes

The hard evidence of diplomatic interaction in the constructivist vein remains, however, in the realm of the formal guidelines for co-operation. In the literature on the formative years of EPC, there is a conceptual theme that goes a long way towards illustrating important constructivist dynamisms even within the long-lasting bureaucratic practices of EPC/CFSP. This theme deals with the prevalence of a diplomatic 'co-ordination reflex'.

Curiously, the occurrence of a co-ordination reflex among member diplomacies was normatively forestalled by the so-called Copenhagen Report – an official EPC document – as early as 1973. Empirical descriptions of the reflex have since been a recurrent feature of the EPC literature (e.g. von der Gablentz 1979; Allen and Wallace 1982: 25–6; Tonra 1997: 191–2). By definition, the reflex refers to a reciprocal, yet *in-built*, disposition of national diplomacies. It thus still adheres to the agency level while bracketing structure.

In substance, the co-ordination reflex dictates policy proposals originating in single states or in subgroups of states to be aired with political co-operation partners before an ensuing unilateral/bilateral action is implemented. This feature of political co-operation provides a highly interesting feature of diplomatic integration for the present theoretical purposes. As a matter of fact, the existence of such a reflex, calling for a regularized and socially sanctioned communication and the adjustment of views among diplomacies, amounts to a rather clear-cut empirical equivalent of the phenomenological typification process.

This theoretical fit is exacerbated by a more elaborate comparison with mere realist interstate 'negotiation'. Notably, the co-ordination triggered by the reflex is *habitual*. It hence refers to a permanent inclination of diplomacies that is not captured by the utilitarian counting of benefits controlling negotiation processes within realist and intergovernmentalist theory. In other words, within EPC, co-ordination is not a deliberately chosen means of pursuing preferences; it is, rather, a naturally 'done thing'. In the words of an insider: '[l]'habitude de travailler ensemble rend plus facile, et aussi plus normale, la recherche d'un consensus dans une situation nouvelle' (de Schoutheete, quoted in Öhrgaard 1997: 20; also Wessels 1982: 15).

Second, the co-ordination entailed here is not exhausted by the intergovernmentalist stipulation of a 'breaking of interests', i.e. the production of strategic outcomes through negotiation on the basis of given utility functions (Moravcsik 1993). Crucially, the co-ordination reflex adds to this a continuous communicative process during which the basic political convictions of agents are shifted in a convergent direction (cf. also Kratochwil 1993; Müller 1994). This is central to most insider descriptions of the reflex phenomenon, and is also integral to the generally benevolent atmosphere surrounding political co-operation. Ben Tonra's study of the negotiating climate within political co-operation documents how sensible references to national interest or public opinion, rather than to abstract principle, generally manage to persuade and accommodate diplomatic partners. Commenting on this, an anonymous official notes how 'if a country has a very real problem very few people will fail to try to come to terms with this . . . I think that is a very strong principle' (quoted in Tonra 1997: 195–6).

Both these important – and inextricably 'social' – qualities of the co-ordination reflex correspond with phenomenological and symbolic interactionist presuppositions of agent interaction. At the same time, they point to serious omissions within rationalist treatments of EPC. But the in-built, habitual nature of the co-ordination reflex and the moulding of attitudes taking place through political co-operation interaction only testify to the natural alteration of typifications that results from iterated symbolic interactions within any social setting.

In the early days of EPC, as already indicated, national interests continued to play their major parts. But alongside this, a 'constructed' dimension of EPC, within which national diplomacies built up this institutional body through an explorative and mutual probing of viable formal routines and substantial domains of co-operation, was also quick to emerge. Hence, a firm agenda and a relatively consolidated co-ordination reflex, as argued, had already been constructed for the EPC towards the mid-1970s.

POLITICAL CO-OPERATION STRUCTURED

Until now, references to structure have been dodged. However, and arguably as a matter of definition, constructivism posits that a structural outcome emerges from the initial diplomatic agency of political co-operation (Glarbo 1998b). Accordingly, in this next analytical and historical section, agency is now bracketed, a grasp on such structure is set out, and the broad outlines of an inverted causality of structure upon agents is sketched.

Implicit references to a social structure within political co-operation abound in a good many insider accounts of EPC (esp. von der Gablentz 1979; Nuttall 1992). These works, while all recognizing the pertinent intergovernmental restrictions of EPC, began to notice a growing ensemble of *gemeinschaft* phenomena evident from the institutional set-up of political co-operation. As these effects took on increasing salience, academics also picked up this thread in trying to conceptualize what had then been increasingly perceived as a social effect exerted by political co-operation *on* diplomats (e.g. Tonra 1997; Jørgensen 1997a; Öhrgaard 1997).

None of these works, however, pays much attention to theoretical conceptualizations of social structure, in itself only an empty meta-theoretical phrase. In this study, constructivist first order theoretical categories are drawn from phenomenology and symbolic interactionism. Accordingly, when elucidating the theoretical meaning of social structure within European political co-operation, I shall rely on the phenomenological notion of 'intersubjectivity'. This Schutzian notion refers to a reified condition in which social and societal characteristics deliver similar 'schemes of interpretation' to groups of human agents (Bernstein 1976: 145), and where, crucially, the terms of this similar perception are equally recognized/interpreted by agents (Schutz 1962: 10; Berger and Luckmann 1966: 37). As it turns out, this amounts to a rather neat theoretical depiction of the nature of the social world set up and reproduced by diplomatic co-operation within EPC.

The argument here, in other words, is that the diplomatic intersubjectivity envisaged by political co-operation supplies social and professional codes to diplomats and diplomacies for the conduct of common foreign policy and that, characteristically, this leaves open the possibility of diplomatic agents interpreting even the most fundamental social terms of their dealings with the EPC/CFSP machinery.[8] I pursue this latter part of the hypothesis further within the ensuing 'bracket' of political co-operation history.

The moulding of diplomatic identity: bureaucratic socialization

In order to empirically track intersubjectivity and its effects on agents, one may distinguish between hard (behavioural) and soft (identity-level) evidence. On the former, straightforward elements of intersubjectivity are crystallized even in the rigid formal design of EPC/CFSP institutions, as provided for by the treaties and reports formally guiding political co-operation. Pre-scheduled meetings in the European Council, the council of foreign ministers, the political committee, the working groups, the group of correspondents and the CFSP unit within the

Council Secretariat all add up to a salient framing of political co-operation even before diplomats begin interacting. The vital effect of these institutions is simply that they provide stable arenas and temporal rhythms to social interaction between diplomats from different national diplomacies. As such, institutions in themselves hold a latent promise of social integration.

The same can be said of the cumulated stock of previous political stances and actions undertaken within political co-operation, as set out primarily in joint declarations and in common positions and common actions. In Euro-speak, this is normally referred to as the *acquis politique* of political co-operation. Past actions provide real restrictions and possibilities for the diplomats involved in political co-operation and, in so doing, already in themselves make for social integration.

Corresponding with behavioural indicators of intersubjectivity, one may find equally behavioural evidence of the outcome expected, i.e. social integration. It is well known, for instance, how foreign ministries have reorganized in a convergent direction to fit emergent political co-operation institutional structure, how modes of national decision-making have changed, or even how EPC/CFSP bodies themselves have intensified activity and undergone a physical centralization in Brussels (Regelsberger 1997: 68–71; Tonra 1997; Jørgensen 1997a).

However, the crucial vindication of our hypothesis of social integration lies, of course, not in behavioural regularities, but in the exposure of the 'soft' social fabric of intersubjectivity, or, better still, in the shifts in diplomatic agency *identity* caused by intersubjective social structure (Wendt and Duvall 1989).[9] Again, the empirical task envisaged cannot be entirely lifted by this study. But, as in the case of co-ordination reflexes, we may find some help within other non-behaviourist writings on the EPC/CFSP. Among these, evidence of altered diplomatic identities has traditionally been cloaked in the language of a European political co-operation 'socialization'. Arguably, intersubjectivity is intrinsic to this jargon. Socialization within political co-operation can thus be viewed as the process through which intersubjectively shared understandings of political co-operation supply codes to be drawn upon by diplomats when conducting common foreign policy.

This sort of blind or 'first order' socialization, where agents are viewed as the numb victims of social structural intersubjectivity, has been thoroughly demonstrated by students of diplomatic interaction within EPC/CFSP. In fact, it has been said of the early 1990s EPC that socialization 'is real, and has become an effective substitute for traditional bilateral diplomacy among the Twelve' (Nuttall 1992: 312). Otto von der Gablentz was the first to launch a consistent focus on EPC socialization, which unsurprisingly began on the formal aspects of European foreign policy (1979: 688–91). With the 1970s' EPC being subjected to 'only very few rules of procedure', diplomats quickly developed a special 'code of conduct' for undertaking common foreign policy (von der Gablentz 1979: 691). Among several elements in this, von der Gablentz refers to a commitment to informal decision-making and a consistently communitarian tone of negotiation where, as a general rule, *fait accomplis* are rarely launched by single diplomacies, even if national interest is felt to be salient. Simon Nuttall has later supplied an updated and more differentiated picture of EPC socialization, noting how a communal identity has spread among the bureaucratic bodies of the Political Committee and the Group of European Correspondents (Nuttall 1992: 23).

Equally, the history of political co-operation has seen a devotion to socialization even among foreign ministers and heads of government. This is evident from the good or even 'special' personal links frequently forged here, but also from the institutional arrangements set up for the comfort of such good personal relations. Again, the practice of Gymnich meetings is worthy of attention. Analysing the content rather than the historical creation of this practice, Gymnich meetings provide a strictly informal arena – conducive to 'fireside chatting' – for interaction among foreign ministers. The significance of these meetings should perhaps not be overestimated on account of the regular Council sessions, but there is no doubt that their informal format was meant to cultivate personal friendships and an *esprit de corps* among ministers (cf. Hill and Wallace 1996: 7; Nuttall 1992: 15). The success of the Gymnich formula is evident not only in the breakthroughs accomplished at these meetings, but also in their importance to ministers, even when agendas are relatively trivial.

From this brief summary, it can be detected that socialization – which is reminiscent of intersubjectivity – is an ongoing and wide-ranging mechanism within political co-operation, stretching all the way from convergence on formal routines through commonly held political convictions to downright camaraderie, and encompassing both the bureaucratic and the political strata of political co-operation.

For our meta-theoretical and theoretical purposes, it should be recalled that intersubjectivity and socialization did not appear out of nothing. Structural intersubjectivity, crucially, was gradually set up and reproduced by regularized agent (diplomatic) interaction, as described in the previous sections. As the history of political co-operation progresses, the virtues of agency/structure-variability attached to constructivism and the bracketing strategy are slowly beginning to prove their value for both a historical *and* theoretical inquiry into European political co-operation.

The three periods analysed still far from fully depict the history of EPC/CFSP. This would, in fact, paint a far too romanticized picture of political co-operation integration. More alarmingly, on the level of theory such a conclusion would malign constructivism with a sort of over-socialized determinism that is entirely contradictory to the very meta-theoretical essence of constructivism.

At this point, it should be asked whether constructivism and the analytical framework proposed here are able to accommodate even the tangible restrictions on social structural socializing powers. In the remainder of this article, I shall suggest two ways in which this question may be answered in the affirmative. One possibility will only be levelled as a suggestion, as it moves along analytical lines fairly well established in the previous sections. This is the possibility of national diplomacies also acting as a social *structural* constraint on individual diplomats. This possibility, as will be recalled, is provided for in the ontological model. Structural intersubjectivity on the national level might be diversified, but should at the very least highlight the intersubjectively consolidated imperative of looking out for national interest.[10] As such, national diplomacies in their structural capacities – however theoretically conceived – always provide important restrictions on political co-operation socialization.

Apart from this, the constructivist theoretical framework applied here points to a second, and less trivial, reason why diplomats are not fully socialized by political co-operation interaction. This reason, however, has to refer to the dispositions of individual diplomats themselves. The next section hence draws the constructivist tale of political co-operation integration to a (provisional) close by revisiting the level of diplomatic agency, this time as it works through individual diplomats' self-reflection to modify the increasing prominence of political co-operation structure.

THE CONSTRUCTED STATE OF CFSP: 'WIDE-AWAKE' DIPLOMACY

By intuitive standards, it should already be evident how the double structural influence of political co-operation and national diplomacies does not fully account for the diplomatic identity of individual diplomats. Such determinist reasoning defers any sort of personal integrity from diplomats and suggests treating these as merely 'structural dopes'.

In reality, diplomats are highly educated people, and their subjection to structural pressures is far from exclusively a cause for blind action. It is equally, and very importantly, a systematic cause for *reflection*. Notably, it is constructivist theory that alerts us to this. As already mentioned, symbolic interactionism and phenomenology are both distinguished among sociological theories by their emphasis on *self-reflection*, i.e. the capacity of agents to interpret their own thoughts and behaviour within social contexts (e.g. Mead 1967: 144–52). Schutz, in particular, has put self-reflection at its most succinct through his ideal typical notion of the 'wide-awake' individual (1962: 213), conducting a continuous social existence through uninterrupted processes of interpretation and self-interpretation (Schutz 1972: 83). As, according to constructivist theory, self-reflection describes a general disposition with human agents, the proposition of this final bracket is that it should also be expected from diplomatic agents within the social setting of European political co-operation.

On the empirical side of this, diplomats' reflections focus, in fact, on several different aspects within political co-operation. First, how participants not only act, but also ponder, the endless counting of national benefits going on within the CFSP process is usually overlooked. This phenomenon does not *only* endorse political realism, because the pursuit of national interest in realism only envisions a first order in-built inclination of state representatives. Here, in contrast, an altogether more elaborate sense of self-interest is on the cards. Political co-operation diplomats know the intergovernmental score of the negotiation game they are supposed to play, and they know which benefits, even symbolic ones, they are expected to reap for their national audiences. Thus, diplomats note themselves how a reference to salient national interest, rather than to abstract principle, is necessary, not only for achieving leverage in CFSP negotiations, but also for maintaining credibility and status *vis-à-vis* domestic and international publics (Tonra 1997: 197). Hence, support for political co-operation is always *deliberately* cloaked in nationally instrumental terms.

More significantly, diplomats systematically recognize even the sociological dynamisms of the political co-operation process, largely as these are set out in the above. This is a vital, yet rarely noticed, feature of political co-operation integration. In Tonra's survey of CFSP, the unfolding of such 'second order' interpretation is nevertheless outlined in the utterances of diplomats. A Danish official '*recognizes* that political co-operation "is in fact determining the agenda of this [department]"' (Tonra 1997: 184; emphasis added). Similarly, a Dutch colleague, commenting on the Treaty on European Union's possibility of qualified majority voting within CFSP, notes how this mechanism 'is *designed* to create habits of thinking, it has no legal effect, but in practice that might be very much like a consensus procedure' (Tonra 1997: 182; emphasis added; see also 192–4).

As a more aggregated indication of this, the lively tradition for EPC/CFSP insiders to sit down and embark on written analysis of political co-operation, and to participate in the epistemic community surrounding this field, is both highly unusual in its own right and, at the same time, a remarkable feature of diplomatic self-reflection. To be sure, much of the socialization noted in the above draws on the analytical records of CFSP diplomats themselves.

Diplomats' analytical knowledge of the political co-operation process, and their frank communication of this knowledge, provide distinguishing empirical features of political co-operation integration. Moreover, when captured by theoretical categories, as here by phenomenology and symbolic interactionism, it promises to ameliorate the sort of over-socialized account typically expected from constructivist explanations of social integration.

CONCLUSION

The reflective corrective to structural, socializing powers brings the constructivist narrative of political co-operation forward to present-day CFSP. Corresponding with the primary purpose of this chapter, and in contrast with traditional approaches to European political co-operation, the constructivism proposed here has tried to shed a new optimist light on the integration stocked within CFSP. Specifically, it has been suggested that social integration is emerging as the natural historical product of the day-to-day practices of political co-operation. Diplomats and national diplomacies have internalized, in particular, the formal requirements of a CFSP. On the level of foreign policy substance, a fully-fledged European identification is not yet discernible. But an institutionalized imperative of 'concertation' is vividly evident from the interaction within political co-operation.

In addition to this, a forgotten dimension alluded to by constructivism is the transcendence of a mere blind socialization within political co-operation. The diplomats of present-day CFSP, besides being affected by the structural surroundings of political co-operation and national diplomacies, are also well aware of the deep social demands levelled at them for conducting both 'national' and 'European' foreign policies. In the future, this enhances the ability of diplomats to *control* reflexively their own diplomatic undertakings and, in turn, to manipulate the political co-operation environment itself. Highly interesting implications for the future of CFSP may be drawn from this.

The second purpose of the chapter, which was mostly implicit, was to contribute to the grand disciplinary project of an operable IR constructivism. It was suggested that we view constructivism as a meta-theoretical category that must be converted into real first order (IR) theory in order to be made amenable to empirical analysis. It might be argued that the first order theories appropriated for the study of EPC/CFSP history – phenomenology and symbolic interactionism – could have been specified in a more narrow or parsimonious vein. On this still preliminary stage of IR constructivism, however, such positivist virtues should not be expected of theory. Future adherents of IR constructivism, or at least those who, on a similarly 'modernist' ground, aim at refuting realism and rationalism on its own empirical soil, will have much more to add, it is hoped, to the refinement of constructivist first order theory.

NOTES

1   Whereas I use 'political co-operation' as a general reference denoting European collaboration within foreign, security and defence policy at all times, the acronyms EPC and CFSP refer to concrete instances of European political co-operation. Briefly, the EPC was created at the Hague Summit in 1969 and inaugurated with the so-called Luxembourg (or Davignon) Report in 1970. EPC was substituted by the CFSP with the coming into force of the Treaty on European Union (TEU) in 1993. For more on history, see Allen and Wallace 1982 and Nuttall 1992, 1997.

2   As it happens, much EPC/CFSP literature is not interested in political integration *per se*, but in questions of a wider (global) leverage of a co-ordinated European foreign policy (cf. Glarbo 1998b: 13–15). Consequently, this sort of literature is not even state-centric, but tends to surpass the national level, taking the European tier as its point of departure (e.g. Allen and Smith 1991; Rummel 1990; Regelsberger *et al.* 1997). Besides this, of course, among theoretical studies one also finds the odd liberalist or structuralist approach to EPC/CFSP (e.g. Long 1997; Öhrgaard 1997; George 1991).

3   As noted by Holland (1991b) and Jørgensen (1996), European political co-operation is only rarely subjected to IR *theory*. Instead, most studies proceed from more concrete analytical presuppositions (cf. Jørgensen 1993: 212), allowing for a wider range of variables (e.g. Ginsberg 1989). Often, however, these studies emerge from rock-bottom realist premisses of state centrism, national interest, primacy of high politics, etc. Allen and Wallace (1982) and Hill (1996b) provide examples of this approach.

4   Elsewhere, I have elaborated some of the theoretical and meta-theoretical questions lurking behind this chapter (Glarbo 1998a, 1998b).

5   Within constructivist IR, analytical bracketing is arguably implicitly employed by the contributors to volumes such as Katzenstein (1996a) and by Finnemore (1996a; cf. Checkel 1998).

6   On such motives of West Germany, Great Britain and France, see e.g. Rummel 1996; Hill 1996a; Glarbo 1998b: 84–9.

7   The notion of 'appropriateness' is inspired by a new institutionalist vocabulary (March and Olsen 1989). But this description departs from new institutionalism in viewing this facet of political co-operation as a product of interaction rather than of individual

(bounded) rationality. Nevertheless, on the plausible affinities of new institutionalist 'logics of appropriateness' with constructivism, see Finnemore 1996b; Checkel 1998: 326.

8   Intersubjectivity has already been appropriated by others for the part of social constructivist structure. The most prominent scholars reifying phenomenological structure in this vein are Berger and Luckmann (1966: 97–109, especially 106; also Wendt 1992: 396–403). Within constructivist IR, social structure is most often viewed as materializing in norms and rules (Finnemore 1996a: 22–4; Wendt 1992: 399).

9   If the hard evidence envisaged above is not even accepted as indirectly reminiscent of intersubjectivity, it might alternatively be conceptualized as a *material* structure of political co-operation, complementary to the social structure of intersubjectivity, and also stemming from the previous social interactions of diplomatic agents. The existence of such objective givens interplaying with social constructions is a familiar feature within constructivism (Collin 1997; Adler 1997b; Glarbo 1998b).

10 For an explicit constructivist treatment of national interest, dealing also more thoroughly with the structural repercussions of the state entity, see Weldes 1996.

10

Discourses of Globalization and European Identities

Ben Rosamond

INTRODUCTION: GLOBALIZATION AND EUROPEAN INTEGRATION[1]

The European Union (EU) presents a number of beguiling problems for the student of international political economy (IPE). Not least among these problems is the question of how contemporary European integration can be understood in terms of the ongoing debate about the relationship between globalization and regionalization. While the acceleration in market integration and the associated drift of governance functions to the European level since the mid-1980s can be linked to the emergence and growth of other forms of (second wave) regionalism such as the North American Free Trade Agreement (NAFTA), Asia Pacific Economic Co-operation (APEC) and Mercusor, the EU studies literature in recent years has tended to shy away from international relations as a 'parent discipline'. The depth of economic integration encompassing the single market programme and (with effect from 1 January 1999) monetary union among the majority of member states, along with the associated growth of regulatory capacity at the European level, have combined to generate a large and increasingly dominant literature that focuses on the nuances of policy-making within the EU and matters of (multi-level) governance. This literature is important and insightful, but this should not mean that globalization–regionalization questions are ignored in the analysis of European integration. The challenge is to find a way to combine the subtleties of the 'governance turn' in EU studies with the more interesting research programmes emerging in IPE.

With that in mind this chapter represents an attempt to combine a social constructivist approach to the study of the EU with a contribution to the growing concern in the social sciences about 'globalization'. As such it offers (a) a particular view about how European integration can be investigated in the context of globalization and (b) some propositions about how constructivist insights can be used to study certain aspects of the EU in particular and forms of regionalism in the global political economy more generally. It draws on, and, it is hoped, develops, an understanding of globalization as discourse by contemplating the nature of the (inter)subjectivities generated within EU policy communities by the globalization debate. This stands in contrast to treating globalization as simply a matter of objective, exogenous or structural change. Rather the social construction of globalization and control over knowledge about globalization become matters of importance. Moreover, globalization comes to be construed as a zone of contestation rather than as a conditioning structure (Amin and Thrift 1994). The chapter explores the proposition that the social construction of external or structural context is an important element in the European integration process because it has helped to define the 'politically possible' within the EU polity. This has not been simply about the identification of constraints, but also about how globalization discourse might open strategic opportunities for certain types of policy actor and/or help to embed the case for rethinking the level at which the authoritative processes of governance can and should occur. More broadly, the EU may be seen as a venue for the development of a discourse of the superiority of one form of 'regionalism' over others.[2] A further proposition is that the EU may be seen as an important empirical venue for the investigation of the discursive strategies of so-called 'globalizing élites' (Gill 1996).

At another level, this chapter also deploys constructivism to find a way through the rather counterproductive 'inside–outside' dichotomy that seems to have arisen recently in some branches of EU studies. Few would say that global context – in some form or other – is unimportant in understanding the trajectory of European integration and the growth of supranational governance. Yet, fuelled by the important injection of policy analytical approaches to the study of EU governance, some have argued vehemently for the irrelevance of international relations (IR) as a parent discipline for 'EU studies'. This suggests that if the EU is a functioning polity where the questions motivating political action are not about 'more or less integration', but rather emerge around a politics of distribution, the tools of comparative political science matter most (Hix 1994). In response it has been argued that IR theories may be useful for understanding the external structural context within which the nested games of the 'Euro-polity' take place, and, therefore, may be helpful in explaining moments of epochal change such as the initiation of the Communities and subsequent treaty revisions (Hurrell and Menon 1996). Alternatively, European integration might be reconceptualized as a multi-level process within which shifts at the 'super-systemic' level should be the venue for the deployment of IR-derived integration theories such as neo-functionalism and forms of intergovernmentalism (Peterson 1995). A further strategy is to self-consciously 'bracket' external factors in pursuit of theoretical parsimony (Sandholtz and Stone Sweet 1998). It is suggested here that such depictions of the EU are unnecessarily rigid and perhaps help to reproduce rationalistic assumptions about the relationship between interests and behaviour. They treat changes to the policy environment as wholly external and direct discussion towards the reactions of actors 'inside' the EU to exogenous shocks rather than canvassing the ways in which environments might be shaped through internal processes of communicative action. With that in mind, the now pervasive metaphor of multi-level governance should mean rather more than the idea that the EU system is composed of distinct policy-making levels. Rather it should be used to explore the EU as a highly fluid system of governance, characterized by the complex interpenetration of the national, subnational and supranational; as a multi-perspectival domain of complex overlapping spaces with a multi-level institutional architecture and a dispersion of authority (Ruggie 1998: 173; see also Jachtenfuchs 1997a; Marks et al., 1996).

This is not to say that 'EU studies' has totally ignored the interplay between European integration and globalization. On the contrary, countless studies cite global economic change as a crucial determinant of the advances in formal economic integration such as the single market and the putative economic and monetary union (EMU) and others emphasize the changing context of European integration wrought by post-Cold War changes to the geopolitical structure (Keohane et al. 1993; Hyde-Price 1997). What may be called 'globalization', 'interdependence', 'competitive threat', 'informal integration' or 'global economic change' often appears in the literature as a form of 'external regulatory shock' that forces a policy response from within the EU. These changes 'outside' impact upon the interests of key policy actors and – in the last fifteen years or so at least – are said to have galvanized the momentum towards both the institutionalization of governance functions at the European level and the progressive 'deepening' of economic integration. Within this broad framework there are several alternative explanations. One is that global economic change – especially technological changes – affected the preferences of key sections of European business and opened a strategic opportunity for the development of alliances with the European Commission. This in turn generated the momentum for a single market programme combining (a) the de-fragmentation and liberalization of the European market and (b) the enhancement of European level regulatory capacity (Sandholtz and Zysman 1989). More state-centred accounts argue for the impact of global shifts upon either the executive capacities of (member state) national governments (Armingeon 1997; Schmidt, n.d.) or the interests of domestic constituencies that are central to the formulation of governmental preferences (Milner 1998; Moravcsik 1993). Another common line of argument is that the Europeanization of economic governance arose as national models of economic policy-making manifestly failed to cope with the pressures of globalization, a perception aided and abetted by the growth of informal transnational networks, especially within high technology sectors (Bressand 1990). A way of combining some of these ideas is to read European integration, and particularly that since the mid-1980s, in terms of the dilemmas of nation states emasculated, on the one hand, by the forces of globalization and overloaded by demands from the domestic arena, on the other. In such circumstances, it is argued,

European integration can be seen as a distinct west European effort to contain the consequences of globalization. Rather than be forced to choose between the national polity for developing policies and the relative anarchy of the globe, west Europeans invented a form of regional governance with polity-like features to extend the state and harden the boundary between themselves and the rest of the world.

(H. Wallace 1996: 16)

This raises the matter of the specificity of the European response to globalization, a debate that feeds into some work in contemporary IPE. Here, exogenous economic change is often thought of in terms of so-called 'informal' or *de facto* economic integration that creates pressure for 'formal' integration or *de jure* institutionalization. Indeed, William Wallace's definition of informal integration as 'those intense patterns of interaction which develop without the impetus of deliberate political decisions, following the dynamics of markets, technology, communications networks and social change' (W. Wallace 1990: 9) resembles what many have in mind when they speak of globalization. Regional integration (or regionalization), in the form of state-sanctioned decisions to institutionalize economic integration, is often seen as responding to the imperatives set by the market behaviour of private economic agents, especially where production processes – in response no doubt to technological change and capital liberalization – take on a trans-border form (Higgott 1997: 167; Bressand and Nicolaides 1990).

While these studies hint that globalization (or at least global economic context) matters, they tend to pose rather more questions than they answer. In part this is because 'globalization' (or the appropriate synonym) is often poorly specified. Indeed it is a process that is quite evidently, and sometimes consciously, externalized in many accounts. The analysis tends to begin once the external influence of 'the global' has been asserted. But this leaves open important issues, particularly (a) how globalization impacts upon the identities, interests and preferences of actors and (b) how globalization might then exacerbate the intensification of economic integration or the Europeanization of governance functions. The problem is difficult in the EU context because of the institutionalized importance of various non-state actors and the difficulty of establishing, for example, *whose* executive autonomy is at risk if globalization is a threat. Furthermore, there is the troublesome, but fundamental, question of whether contemporary European integration is best perceived as *a facilitator of* or as *a response to* globalization. Is globalization a process 'out there' embedded in the workings of markets to which 'politics' – in the form of intergovernmental bargains or strategically motivated networks of non-state actors – somehow responds? Or is integration a proactive stepping stone to globalization, thereby representing the capture of the EU-level institutional framework by 'globalizing élites'? Alternatively, regional integration in Europe can be read as policy response to the activities of globalizing élites *elsewhere*, notably in the United States, where the deregulatory momentum was first ignited (Oman 1993) (this debate shadows the more 'orthodox' discussions about the relationship between regionalization and free trade – see Anderson and Blackhurst 1993; Cable and Henderson 1994). Moreover, while integration might be seen as a facilitator of globalization, whether it is consciously proactive remains a moot point. One noted observer of the Commission has written:

European nations, reacting to the collapse of their earlier efforts to conciliate national political economies with a more open trade setting through the Common Market, renewed European integration to cope with this collapse. In the process they probably promoted globalization rather more than responding to it.

(Ross 1998: 169)

Alternatively, are there elements of both reaction and proactivity in the EU's relationship with globalization? After all, EU governance is segmented, multi-actor and multi-level, the spread of supranational rule-making is uneven and so different communities of actors may be playing very distinct sorts of games *vis-à-vis* globalization.

As discussions like this proceed, so the limits of rationalistic approaches become apparent. The externalization of globalization in mainstream accounts is related to the treatment of interests and identities as exogenous or prior to the processes of institutionalized interaction. The implication of much of the literature on globalization and European integration is that actors' interests are *affected* by globalization and/or that it is in some actors' interests to *promote* globalization. The role of globalization in actually constituting those interests and identities is largely ignored. This need not be so. Increasing attention is being paid to the complex effects of institutionalization in the EU, and particularly to the capacity of institutions to co-ordinate actor expectations, generate shared systems of belief and shape norms, values and conventions within policy communities (Cram 1997; Radaelli 1995; also Armstrong and Bulmer 1998; Garrett and Weingast 1993). It is here that constructivist approaches can add value by forcing an explanation of the social construction of the external environment as a means to understanding how particular identity claims and interests arise within a policy-making context. This is discussed further in the following section which elaborates briefly a case for the analysis of the discursive aspects of globalization and goes on to discuss how constructivism might be used to think about the usage of 'globalization' in the EU context. The third section of the chapter lays out some empirical material, with reference to the role of globalization discourses within the EU polity.

The argument is that our understanding of the global–European interface can be greatly enhanced by the application of a form of constructivism. More concretely, the argument builds the hypotheses that (a) the deployment of ideas about globalization has been central to the development of a particular notion of European identity among élite policy actors but that (b) 'globalization' remains contested within EU policy circles.

GLOBALIZATION AND DISCOURSES OF 'GLOBALIZATION': A CONSTRUCTIVIST ANALYSIS

Few concepts are more widely used and more hotly debated in the contemporary social sciences than 'globalization'. Indeed, the concept has spread well beyond the academic world and is frequently employed to signify worldwide economic changes of profound significance. This is not the place for a full rendition of the debate that has colonized literatures in a wide array of disciplinary environments

(Baylis and Smith 1997; Dannreuther and Lekhi 1999; Higgott and Reich 1998; Kofman and Youngs 1996). For the most part 'globalization' is used to signify a series of objective, material shifts bound up with the increasing mobility of capital, the multi- and transnationalization of production processes, shifting patterns of trade and technological changes that together eradicate the constraints of physical distance to economic interaction. Normal usage also refers to the gradual world-wide spread of neo-liberal policy norms, the decline of national executive autonomy and the retreat from the practices of the Keynesian welfare state and social democracy. Debate – especially in disciplines such as IPE and international econ-omics – has concentrated on the veracity of claims that globalization is taking place or has occurred (Boyer 1996; Boyer and Drache 1996; Hirst and Thompson 1996; Wade 1996). Those who claim that it might not be the harbinger of economic efficiency, wealth creation and prosperity challenge apologists for globalization. Others have questioned the historical novelty of the process and, therefore, query the significance of its impact, particularly upon the capacity of states to pur-sue autonomous economic policy-making (Abu-Lughod 1989; Hont 1994; Thompson 1997).

At issue is the extent to which a series of material shifts has rendered the world economy a singular entity, where territorialized control over economic governance ceases to be relevant or efficacious. The significance of this debate should not be diminished, but it trades very much on the question of the *objective* transformation of the global economic environment – the move to a 'world in itself'. But it is also useful to think about the subjective dimensions of globalization – a 'world for itself'. Here the key question is neither the longevity nor the empirical demonstrability of globalization, but rather the extent to which knowledge of globalization as *the* defining attribute of contemporary life has become widespread. Research from this starting point thinks less about material structures and more about ideational structures and patterns of political discourse. This discursive dimension can be thought about in two senses. The first concerns the use of 'globalization' as a discursive device to render the world manageable, to define the range of individual and collective policy choice, to clarify external threats and constraints and to imagine the repertoire of available strategic opportunities. The second sense treats globalization as a 'discourse of power' associated with the emergence of particular interests in the global political economy and the legitimation of neo-liberal policy solutions (Gill 1995). It is also striking how the debate within both large portions of the academic world and policy circles has been captured by a particular conception of globalization: globalization as the progressive spread of economic liberalization across the globe (Robertson and Haque Khondker 1997; Sjolander 1996). At one level the term has spilled out of the academic world into the world of policy dis-course, though, as Robertson and Haque Khondker note, in a highly corrupted fashion. The subtleties and nuances of sociological theories of globalization with their emphasis on dissonance, local mediation, particularization and com-plexity (Appadurai 1990; Lash and Urry 1994; Robertson 1992; Rosamond 1995) do not register. Economic globalization is privileged and is then redefined in simplistic terms as a form of homogenization of practices and policies which induces a 'logic of no alternative' in policy terms (Hay and Watson 1998). In other words, conceptions of globalization as discourse also need to think seriously about the sorts of knowledge that the term draws upon and signifies (Scholte 1996), especially since, as Nikolas Rose has observed, 'the truth effects of discourses of economic globalization are somehow independent of the reality of the analysis' (cited in Hay and Watson 1998: 26). Certain conceptions of globalization may be 'hegemonic', but this does not foreclose the possibility that alternative discourses may coexist and challenge the dominant strand. 'Globalization' may be used to signify market liberalization, but this may induce radically opposed interpretations of its significance and what policy options follow. Both 'embrace' and 'resistance' are possible. Moreover, 'globalizing élites' may engage in strategic theorizing about globalization, but this does not mean that they are immune from the shaping capacities of the intersubjective structures that their discursive practice creates.

One research strategy would be to explore globalization as rhetoric, as a series of compelling assertions about the world that serve the material interests of certain actors. However, this way of thinking separates the interests of actors from the discourses they articulate. The latter – in the case of 'globalizing élites' – is largely a derivative of the former. Constructivists have long argued that this kind of dichotomy is false. The basic constructivist proposition, as Checkel notes, is that the environment in which actors operate is given meaning through ongoing processes of social construction. This means that there is an inherent connection between the social construction of the 'external' environment and the interests that actors acquire (Checkel 1998: 325–6). Interests are best conceived of as endogenous, and not exogenous, to interaction. Constructivists attempt to dissolve the opposition between agency and structure. Agents' interests are not structured by their environment. They help to make their environment and their environment helps to make them. The environment within which actors operate is an intersubjective structure which also contributes to the creation of norms governing behaviour and the boundaries of the possible (Wendt 1992, 1994). This means that not just interests but also identities are bound up with these sociological processes. 'We' are what we make of ourselves, and what 'we' make of ourselves will be related to what 'we' make of our environment. Constructivist treatments of the staples of international politics such as 'anarchy' (Wendt 1992) and 'the national interest' (Weldes 1996) have tended to follow this pathway. 'Globalization' might be thought of as a similar sort of intersubjective structure that supplies a powerful ordering rationality and thereby helps to create a world defined by that ordering rationality as actors' behaviour and identities adjust accordingly (McNamara 1997). Actors assume themselves to be operating within a particular structure that regulates and constrains their behaviour and limits (though in some cases expands) policy options. To occupy a conventional rationalist vantage point loses sight of this important relationship between theories about the world and real world practices. The way in which the context of action is perceived and understood is vital to the conclusions that actors draw about their strategic location, their interests and who they are. Globalization discourse not only offers an account of new properties of external structure, but also opens up debate about the stability, usefulness and viability of established practices. In this sense globalization is a different sort of intersubjective structure to 'anarchy'. The social construction of a world built around unit inter-action with no overarching authority has the effect of reproducing the states system as *the* defining norm of world politics. Globalization, on the other hand, is usually a discourse of change and uncertainty. The acceptance of globalization as a structural property begets notions of contingency, crisis and the unbundling of the erst-while certainties of territoriality, national forms of governance, and so on (Higgott and Reich 1998). This opens up possibilities for claims about the efficacy of alternative policy arenas or, as Ruggie (1998) puts it, the social construction of 'nonterritorial functional spaces'. Indeed, in recent years, constructivists have become interested in the social construction of post-territorial regions (Adler and Barnett 1998; Higgott 1998; Higgott and Stubbs 1995). These are made up, as Adler (1997a) notes, of people sharing common identities and interests that are constituted by shared understandings and normative principles other than territorial sovereignty.

The question that follows is how do such regions arise? Constructivist reasoning suggests that the social construction of regional 'selves' requires the discursive elaboration of non-regional 'others' or the development of intersubjective under-standings about the context within which these selves are able to define themselves collectively. Constructivists tend to argue that these intersubjectivities occur in the context of communicative action involving processes of persuasion and advocacy that go well beyond the utilitarian exchange of preferences anticipated by ration-alistic accounts (Risse-Kappen 1996b; Risse 1997). Rationalistic perspectives tend to portray the growth of supranational governance as the consequence of actors seeking optimal solutions when confronted by sub-optimal conditions. This could be equally true for non-state actors engaged in transnational exchange (Sandholtz and Stone Sweet 1998) or for national executives dealing with the two-level game of domestic politics and international negotiations (Moravcsik 1998). The constructivist interest in processes of communicative action forces us to con-ceptualize the nature of actor interaction as about rather more than the exchange of preferences in an institutionalized environment. As Risse-Kappen comments:

> This does not mean that ideas cannot be used in an instrumental way to legitimize or delegitimize policies motivated by purely material interests. However, the 'power' of ideas in such instances is linked to their consensuality. Ideas become consensual when actors start believing in their value and become convinced of their validity. In other words, communicative processes are a necessary condition for ideas to become consensual (or to fall by the wayside, for that matter). Instru-mental use of ideas works, because their value has been previously established in discursive processes of persuasion and deliberation.
>
> (Risse-Kappen 1996a: 69–70)

This approach seeks a deeper explanation of the sources of policy convergence and the drift of governance functions and is well suited to the multiple levels of action and the mixture of formal and informal channels that characterize the Euro-polity.

Needless to say, this requires and deserves substantial empirical research and what follows can be read as a preliminary exercise.

DISCOURSES OF GLOBALIZATION AND EUROPEAN INTEGRATION

This part of the argument begins to think about how some of these ideas might be applied in the EU context, and thereby contribute to a more textured understanding of the connections between globalization and European integration. With that aim in mind, four preliminary questions are addressed:

1   What sorts of knowledge about 'globalization' are at work in EU policy-making circles?
2   Who uses this knowledge, how do they use it, why do they use it? Are there evident 'discursive strategies' at work?
3   What role is played by rhetorics of globalization within EU policy communities? Do they sanction particular policy solutions and foreclose others? Do they help to define 'Europe' as a valid regulatory space?
4   Are there discourse coalitions at work? In other words, do identifiable communities of actors within the EU polity cluster around particular conceptions of globalization and/or use the idea of globalization in distinct ways? In other words, is there 'one globalization or several?' in EU policy communities?

Needless to say, the answers to these questions require detailed and ongoing empirical research. However, initial investigations suggest that the approach outlined here may have significant empirical value. Writers on integration have identified connections between several phenomena in the EC/EU context since the early 1980s. These phenomena include (a) perceptions of inefficient European economic fragmentation, (b) the increasing persuasiveness of supply side economics to a range of policy actors, (c) the processes of globalization, (d) the redundancy of national economic solutions, and (e) the rise of European solutions. These independent variables are often brought together to explain the acceleration of integrative activity that became formalized in the Single European Act (1987) (Tsoukalis 1997: 137) and the 'loyalty transfers' undertaken by a host of governmental and non-governmental actors in the mid-1980s. The issue that the constructivist approach can try to explore is how these different elements were welded together discursively. It confronts head-on the issue of *how* actors become persuaded that the redundancy of national solutions should lead to the acceptance of the case for European solutions. Moreover, it helps us to think about why particular types of European policy response or activism become accepted in preference to others.

It is worth noting that the discursive deployment of 'globalization' or similar signifiers appears extensive in EU policy circles, but it is far from all-pervasive. The particular context provided by the EU policy process is also significant. The evidence presented here suggests that the use of discourses of globalization is most prevalent in agenda-setting contexts, in particular where elements of the Commission are engaged in semi-public utterances such as Green and White Papers and speeches of individual Commissioners. Indeed, the large-scale *absence* of globalization discourse from intra-community technical discussions is itself worthy of note. Most analysts, often drawing on the image of the EU as a system of multi-level governance (Marks *et al.* 1996a), note that the absence of fixed hierarchies and the polity's loose institutionalization mean that the manoeuvre of any particular policy option through the policy process can be difficult. Multiple points of access, the widespread segmentation of policy-making and the lack of policy clientelism aggravate the chances of defeat or subversion. As Peters notes, these peculiar facets render the EU policy process quite distinct from conventional (national) policy systems: '[i]n such a relatively unstructured situation there is an even more pronounced need for policy entrepreneurs than there is in other political settings' (Peters 1996: 63). In other words, there is much greater scope in the EU polity for 'strategic theorizing'. Indeed, the expectation is that rival acts of policy entrepreneurship will be found within the agenda-setting process. Given the formal concentration of initiation in the Commission and the segmented structure of its component Directorates-General (DGs), the marketing (as opposed to the technocratic discussion) of policy through discursive practice should be a feature of actors within the Commission. The issues at stake may have less to do with the discussion of the context of policy (for example, a 'globalized economy'). Rather, the practice of elaborating contexts may have more to do with the justification of a certain policy mode or the legitimation of European level action in a particular sector.

The usage of globalization as a signifier of the changing external context of European integration is comparatively recent, dating from the early 1990s rather than the mid- to late 1980s. This is hardly surprising since the 'first wave' of popularizing literature on globalization only began to appear in the late 1980s and early 1990s (Ohmae 1990, 1996; Thurow 1994; Wendt 1993). Having said that, much Commission discourse from the late 1980s was heavily concerned with making a linkage between external economic conditions and the need to give meaning to the European level of action. The external context, or the world economy within which the Community was located, was usually expressed in terms of the relative performances of discrete national economies (for example, CEC 1988b: 13–16). But the language of economies as congruent with national territories was not used to apply to the European Community (EC), which was treated as an empirical economic entity. Moreover, the policy frameworks that should be pursued by 'Europe' were unequivocally neo-liberal (CEC 1988a). The 'outside'–'Europe' linkage was central to the argumentation of the so-called Cecchini Report on the benefits of the single market (Cecchini 1988). The Report smacks of a deliberate strategic attempt to develop and verify the existence of a *European* economic space whose territorial reach corresponded to the actual and potential boundaries of the Community. Cecchini and his colleagues sought to reinforce the Commission case for the single market programme including both economic liberalization and the deepening of European level policy competence. Cecchini's rhetoric of 'Europe' as a unitary entity facing particular sorts of challenges was reinforced by the use of the ingenious counterfactual of 'non- Europe'. These efforts provide clear evidence of an attempt to justify a programme of economic and institutional reform corresponding to a 'Delorsian' vision of a continental market order. But it also represented a distinct discursive strategy on the part of the Commission (or at least its core 'economic' DGs) to place the idea of Europe as a single economic entity with discernible interests on to the policy agenda. This marked a discursive shift from the highly technical case for the single market that lay at the heart of the 1985 White Paper, *Completing the Internal Market* (CEC 1985). Here the persuasiveness of the case for pressing to complete the internal market drew heavily upon the fact that a series of European Council resolutions had made it a priority and not that the world outside was changing.

The construction of Europe as a valid space in the light of external challenge follows a discursive pattern in which three perceptions need to be embedded (see also Higgott 1998 for a comparative discussion):

1   the recognition of a particular problem, challenge or threat;
2   the perception of the need and/or right for there to be European level solutions (as opposed to separate national level strategies) and/or for the existing European level governance structure to undergo change to address the problem; and
3   the emergence of a consensus about a particular conception of a regional space in the minds of key actors.

The discovery of the concept of globalization has been especially important to the reinforcement of this logic. The 1993 *White Paper on Growth, Competitiveness and Employment* (CEC 1993) laid out clearly various perceived changes to the Community's environment or, as it put it, 'the universality of the trends which have been shaping the global economy and their acceleration since the 1970s'. The White Paper detailed these exogenous shifts as the emergence of new technologically advanced rival economic spaces, the end of Communism, the new skills revolution, the shift to a knowledge-based economy and growing market interdependence resulting from the widespread liberalization of capital movements. These various alterations to the EU's external 'décor' conspire to clarify 'Europe' as a meaningful entity that is more or less competitive and which should, therefore, command the loyalties and expectations of various actors. There is nothing intuitive or easily definable about 'European competitiveness', especially in an era of stateless firms and global corporate strategies (Strange 1998; Wyatt-Walter 1998). The idea is a social construction increasingly reliant on ideas about a globalized/globalizing external context, used to draw actors into the European arena. This sort of reasoning clarifies why certain actors might be persuaded to turn to 'Europe' in pursuit of rule-making. To take an example, the study of the telecommunications sector by Sandholtz (1998) offers a persuasive account of how processes of trans-nationalization in that industry led to actors seeking supranational rules that the Commission was able and willing to supply. Yet, Sandholtz's explanation cannot tell us why *European* rules were sought by these actors, rather than, say, global standards delivered via the World Trade Organization (WTO), something that might be anticipated in an evidently 'globalizing' industry such as telecoms. The existence of available supranational institutions may be part of the answer, but constructivists would want to probe more deeply about why those institutions were used. Thus another dimension of the explanation seems to reside in the identification of 'Europe' as a cognitive region and a plausible regulatory space.

The concept of globalization has been much used in DG Energy's analyses of the context of European energy policy. The familiar pattern of discourse is evident. Globalization, defined loosely in terms of radical changes in communications, transport and technology, has led to the erosion of discrete regional energy markets, meaning in turn that the *European* energy sector is coming under increasing competitive pressure. *It* requires structural and technological adjustment to meet these challenges (CEC 1995: 9–10, 1997b). These should be accomplished in line with broadly neo-liberal economic norms compatible with the achievement of the internal market (Benavides 1997; CEC 1997a). Discussions of renewable energy issues follow similar patterns but reveal some of the uncertainties and divergent logics that often follow from a discussion of globalization. For instance, DG Energy's original Green Paper on renewable energy (CEC 1996) explores various scenarios for the development of *European* policies on renewable energy in which globalization plays a role. The 'battlefield scenario' envisages the 'overstretch' of globalization leading to the fragmentation of the world into blocs. These blocs then pursue energy policies that seek to reduce external dependencies, thereby threatening projects associated with the greening of energy polices (CEC 1996: 15). The 'hypermarket scenario' depicts the free reign of global market forces, the withdrawal of state authority from the energy market and, thus, predicts threats to renewable energy policies since these might infringe the pure logic of markets (CEC 1996: 16). However, a third scenario depicts globalization as an incentive for global co-operation and innovation in energy policy-making. Here some sort of consensus about ecological imperatives is imagined. Globalization threatens this widely held policy preference, thereby inducing defensive collaboration. The reasoning here follows the standard patterns, to a certain degree. Globalization is defined in terms of hyperliberalization and the best safeguard in the light of this trend is the Europeanization of policy competence. But the debate on renewable energy is a clear instance where globalization is perceived as detrimental to Europe's needs. The creation of a European energy market is portrayed as a way of insulating against global pressures. An interim conclusion might be to agree that 'globalization is what we make of it' (McNamara 1997) and to add that a shared (if often implicit) definition can lead to significant divergences in terms of deductions about strategic or policy competence.

In much of the Commission literature, 'globalization' appears as little more than a largely 'empty' signifier. For example, the 1993 White Paper offers a reasonably elaborate discussion of competitiveness and occasionally drops in phrases such as 'the new globalized and interdependent competitive situation' without specifying what is meant by globalization. It denotes change and challenge, but what this process or condition means precisely is either left open or taken for granted. *Agenda 2000* is similarly vague about the concept, but logical about its conclusions: 'the process of globalization, from which the Union has benefited so much, also exposes it to both economic and political risks in the international arena' (CEC 1997d: 45). This can be read in two ways. The first is that there is some discursive leverage in leaving the concept under-specified. Strategic advantage might accrue from being able to define the 'outside' or 'the external environment' so straightforwardly. This is not to say that 'globalization' is used to denote a settled order but, as the example of DG Energy shows, the depiction of external turbulence and unpredictability is easily linked to arguments for 'European' consolidation or innovation. In other words, elusiveness, elasticity and under-specification can have their political uses. A second possibility is that 'globalization' is beginning to acquire the status of an intersubjective norm denoting new structural realities. The norm is reinforced through the frequent use of the concept by actors within policy communities rather than through a communicative deconstruction of its meaning.

The extent to which 'globalization' has risen to the status of a norm is hard to say, but the first of these readings certainly holds for the linkage between the frequent justifications for the growth of European level regulatory capacity and policy innovation and the practice of making assertions about external conditions. Analysts of globalization discourse have noted how the use of the concept by public officials can often be used to impose a logic of 'no alternative'. For example, Hay and Watson (1998) argue that the 'New Labour' government in the UK has often cited globalization as a process beyond its control which, therefore, thwarts social democratic policy options. Hay and Watson observe that a serious reading of the debates about globalization would cast grave doubts upon these claims. In this analysis, 'globalization' becomes a useful device for apologists of economic liberalism.

Yet globalization is not always such an 'empty signifier' in EU policy contexts. There are also instances of quite aggressive definition, particularly in the public iterations of senior Commissioners. A series of recent speeches by Commission Vice-President Leon Brittan gives a resounding sense of a serious attempt to present globalization as (a) desirable and (b) synonymous with global economic liberal-ization. At the World Economic Forum in Davos in 1997, Brittan defined global-ization as 'the dramatic acceleration and multiplication of economic activity which transcends national and regional markets, leading us towards a single global market' (1997a: 1). His argument deployed a fairly crude idea of commercial liberalism: economic openness is the most effective route to growth and benefits will flow from the exposure of market discipline to all parts of the world. Globalization is something that poses a challenge and to which there should be fashioned an effective response. The challenge is economic liberalization and the response appears to be further economic liberalization. Interventions like this are not simply hyper-liberal manifestos. As a more detailed speech a month later confirms, the elaborate discussion of 'globalization' is used to justify both European level regulatory competence and neo-liberal policy options (Brittan 1997b: 9–10). The discursive strategy here is to argue that globalization is good and should be encouraged, but that it attacks the capabilities of national governments. Moreover, national solutions are potential vehicles for protectionism and various forms of cultural fundamentalism. The EU, on the other hand, as evidenced by the single market pro-gramme, is the home of open regionalism and an established facilitator of 'liberal-ization, dynamism and flexibility'. Brittan's tenacious logic was not shaken by the Asian financial crisis. The cause, if anything, was not enough globalization: 'the real cause of the problems today in Asia and elsewhere is not excessive trade liberalization, or the freeing of international financial flows, but the imperfect application of the market economy and the distortion of liberalizing policies' (Brittan 1998: 1).

Brittan's speeches offer instances of the increasingly widespread articulation of globalization as an opportunity rather than a threat: a force for the creation of employment rather than a danger to jobs within the EU (ESC 1997; CEC 1997c, 1999; Cresson 1999). The tendency to engage in more elaborate definitions of globalization in the late 1990s is perhaps indicative of the growth of popular scepticism towards the alleged benefits of globalization. The truth claims of globalization discourse are less at stake here than the case for neo-liberal, market-driven policy priorities. The Economic and Financial Affairs DG's relatively elaborate discussion of globalization as an historical phenomenon is married to a defence of open markets, budgetary discipline and the growth potential that financial and commercial liberalization is said to bring (CEC 1997c). The con-clusions of the 1998 Cardiff European Council welcomed the reassertion by the Council of the primacy of strict budgetary discipline and saw the member states able to argue that '[s]ustained fiscal consolidation and economic reform are essential if the Union is to face successfully the challenges of globalization, competitiveness and promoting employment and inclusion' (European Council 1998; see also *Official Journal* C236, 2 August 1997 for similar statements from the Amsterdam European Council a year earlier). There is some evidence, therefore, of a shift in the terms of debate and the way in which globalization discourse is employed away from an external structural fact to which 'Europe' must respond towards a policy portfolio which the EU should seek to uphold. Yet it is obvious that, while there is a degree of consensus about what 'globalization' is (defined either as a structural property or as a set of policies), there is still normative divergence about its conse-quences. For example, the agenda laid out by the German government for its presidency of the Council of Ministers in the first half of 1999 uses 'globalization' to signal an opportunity. But this opportunity is defined less in terms of Brittan's cleansing waters of market liberalism and more as a chance to face up to the need for more solidaristic polices, both within the EU and globally (Germany 1999: 3–4).

In some instances, Commission-sponsored work has demonstrated an uncanny recognition of the powers of agents in relation to structures. The report of the research conducted under the auspices of a Commission task force called *Cellule de Prospective* (published in English as Jacquemin and Wright 1993) makes par-ticularly fascinating reading for the constructivist. The research aimed to identify two things: (a) the main 'shaping factors' in the economic environment at global, European and member state levels, and (b) the available and potential 'triggering mechanisms' by which awareness of new economic patterns could be made avail-able. The project also sought to establish whether actors (particularly firms) would find themselves in a largely reactive posture *vis-à-vis* economic change or whether they were strategically far-sighted. Indeed, one question posed by the project team was the nature of the likely response of public and private actors to their environment 'once awareness has been achieved': 'will they remain passive and simply adapt, or will they actually seek to impose their will, shaping the shaping factors after the event?' (Jacquemin and Wright 1993: xvi). In the same introductory section, the editors speak of 'shaping actors' becoming 'environment makers' as well as 'environment takers'. Two observations seem pertinent. The first is that projects such as this seek to define the EC/EU as an 'environment maker'. This is not simply a matter of asserting the capabilities of supranational/non-state agency to shape the structures within which it works. It is also a reflexive recognition of the idea that 'globalization is what we make of it'. There is deep ambivalence about globalization in reports such as this. On the one hand, it seems to denote a set of policy options that actors have the power to shape. On the other, it clearly signifies an increasingly risk-laden, competitive environment, to which European integration has contributed (Jacquemin and Wright 1993: 83). The second observation is that the research sought to ascertain the European priorities of businesses in various national contexts and in so doing went some way to constructing the idea of Europe as a meaningful policy-relevant space. The key point is that this can only be done in relation to the simultaneous social construction of global context.

CONCLUSION

This chapter posed four questions about the relationship between globalization discourses and European integration. The first question asked what kinds of knowledge about globalization exist within EU communities. The evidence suggests that there is widespread adherence to neo-liberal conceptions and that globalization appears as either/both (a) a structural fact associated with the development of circuits of capital, production, trade and technology, or/and (b) a set of policy preferences for economic openness and market-driven policies of budgetary restraint. It is used to signify external realities which define the EU's environment. But at a second level of analysis globalization is understood as having multiple and often contradictory consequences. In that sense, globalization has perhaps not acquired the status of a norm, that is if we define norms as 'collective expectations for the proper behaviour of actors with a given identity' (Katzenstein 1996b: 5). But – in response to the second and third questions – it is clear that strategically motivated actors within the EU have utilized the concept of globalization to create cognitive allegiances to the idea of 'Europe'/the EU as a valid economic space. This is not a matter particularly of defining a territorial space, but more a legitimate policy space which is a deeply normative issue, even if much of the debate is couched in technical terms (Fligstein and Mara-Drita 1996). Moreover, the policy mode (neo-liberalism) that emerges is also bound up in complex ways with the social construction of external threat (globalization). Globalization discourse has also been used to reinforce the case for neo-liberal policy solutions, a pattern that also appears in domestic political contexts. But this pattern is not uniform and the evidence suggests that different clusters of actors can deploy the idea of globalization with quite distinct effects. Notwithstanding the adherence to 'first wave' notions of globalization, there are – to respond to the fourth set of issues – potentially many 'globalizations' at work within the EU polity.

It remains obvious that detailed empirical work along the lines specified here would offer one way for constructivists to approach questions of European integration and to add value to the existing literature. The conventional theoretical tools used to study the European integration process tend to run into difficulty when we pose questions about the relationship between regional integration and globalization. First, they tend to 'exogenize' global change by treating it as something to which actors within the EU respond. Constructivism helps here because it suggests that 'external' factors are likely to be social constructions of 'internal' actors. The 'inside–outside' dichotomy is reinforced by a pervasive rationalism in conventional theoretical accounts. This underestimates the communicative processes within the EU polity that may shape actors' identities and interests. Constructivism also helps by building bridges between the nuanced work on multi-level EU governance and those strands of IPE that deal with regionalization as a process of collective imagination. In terms of 'globalization studies' a careful constructivist exploration of the EU might appear to side-step the objection that globalization remains an elusive and elastic concept that is still poorly specified. It offers a gateway to understanding the complex relationships between forms of knowledge and the 'real world' practices of policy actors.

NOTES

1   Earlier versions of this chapter were presented to the conference on Social Constructivism in European Studies, Ebeltoft, Denmark, 26–28 June 1998 and the JPSA-ECPR Joint Colloquium, Kumamoto, Japan, 13–15 November 1998. The author would like to thank two anonymous referees and the following for their comments on drafts of this chapter and on other work that feeds into the argument: Jane Booth, Thomas Christiansen, Charlie Dannreuther, Raymond Duvall, Ewan Harrison, Colin Hay, Richard Higgott, Knud Erik Jørgensen, Rohit Lekhi, Christian Lequesne, John Peterson, Timothy Sinclair, Akihiko Tanaka, J. Anne Tickner, Helen Wallace, Antje Wiener and Daniel Wincott.

2   The notion of regionalism is contested and is often defined in relation/opposition to globalization. For the purposes of this chapter it is used to denote the apparent trend towards the formal institutionalization of economic integration in various parts of the world through the likes of the EU, NAFTA, APEC, ASEAN, Mercusor and so on. For discussions see Fawcett and Hurrell (1997), Gamble and Payne (1996), and Mansfield and Milner (1997).

Part 3

DEBATING APPROACHES TO EUROPEAN INTEGRATION

11

Constructivism and European Integration: A Critique

Andrew Moravcsik

It has been over a decade since Alexander Wendt's article on the agent-structure problem signaled the advent of a self-conscious 'constructivist' theoretical approach to the study of world politics (Wendt 1987). Wendt, to be sure, has consistently presented constructivism not as an international relations *theory*, but as an ontology – a social theory. Yet he and other constructivists have nonetheless long claimed that their ontology facilitates the development of novel mid-range theoretical propositions.

This is a felicitous claim, for it promises to expand the debate among fundamental theories of world politics. Currently there are three. Realism highlights the distribution of resources. Institutionalism highlights the institutionalized distribution of information. Liberalism highlights the distribution of underlying societal interests and ideals as represented by domestic political institutions. The advent of constructivism promises to add a wider and perhaps more sophisticated range of theories concerning the causal role of ideational socialization.

For such theories, the European Union (EU) is as promising a substantive domain as we are likely to find. In few areas of interstate politics are ideals so often invoked, identities so clearly at stake, and interests so complex, challenging, and uncertain. In few areas is so much detailed primary data, historical scholarship, and social scientific theory available to assist analysts in tracing the role of ideas and the process of socialization. It is thus no surprise that there has been for some years an emerging constructivist analysis of European integration in security studies. This approach is often referred to as the 'Copenhagen school.' It is so named because the force of continental constructivist theories appears to radiate outward from the Danish capital, where it is the hegemonic discourse.

Thomas Christiansen, Knud Erik Jørgensen, and Antje Wiener, the editors of this volume, do us an important service by posing an intriguing and timely question: What has constructivist theory contributed to our social scientific understanding of the EU? In doing so, they have brought together a fascinating set of chapters most notable for their intriguing conjectures about the possible role of collective ideas and socialization in European integration. Ben Rosamond, for example, openly questions whether a compelling economic justification for internal market liberalization ever existed. Martin Marcussen, Thomas Risse, *et al.*, seek to rewrite the history of integration in terms of ideational shifts, rather than the succession of economic opportunities most analysts invoke. Thomas Diez reinterprets the first British bid for membership in the EEC as the action of a country caught in its own evolving discursive net. These are bold claims, and there are many more in this volume.

Despite high hopes for constructivism – hopes that any open-minded social scientist in the field must share – and the intriguing nature of some of the empirical claims above, however, my conclusion in this comment is a sobering one. Constructivists, to judge from the volume, have contributed far less to our empirical and theoretical understanding of European integration than their meta-theoretical assertions might suggest – certainly far less than existing alternatives. This disappointing finding may simply reflect the modest role of ideas in the process of European integration, but I doubt it. My analysis of this volume suggests that the true reason lies instead in a characteristic unwillingness of constructivists to place their claims at any real risk of empirical disconfirmation. *Hardly a single claim in this volume is formulated or tested in such a way that it could, even in principle, be declared empirically invalid.*

This failure to test stems fundamentally from the near absence of two critical elements of social science, each designed to put conjectures at risk: (1) distinctive testable hypotheses, (2) methods to test such hypotheses against alternative theories or a null hypothesis of random state behavior. Today most leading constructivists are committed to the proposition that their claims must be, in one way or another, subject to empirical confirmation – and, more important, disconfirmation. Most, including authors in this volume, accept that claims derived from constructivist-inspired theories compete with and should be tested against other mid-range hypotheses. This development is to be warmly welcomed, for it creates a common conceptual, methodological, and theoretical discourse among proponents and critics of constructivist theories alike.[1] It is in this spirit of internal, constructive criticism – that is, criticism of constructivism for failing to live up to its own publicly acknowledged standards – that I write.[2]

CONSTRUCTIVISM AND EUROPEAN INTEGRATION: ARE THE PROPOSITIONS TESTABLE?

The constructivist approaches to European integration represented in this volume, in my reformulation, share two core propositions. The first is that *governmental élites choose specific policies, policy ideas, strategies, and concrete interests because they (or their justifications) are consistent with more general, deeper, collectively held ideas or discourses.*[3] What is distinctive about this claim, it is essential to note, is not that interests are 'constructed' in 'historically specific circumstances.' Nearly all international relations (IR) theories, indeed nearly all social science theories, rest on the premise that actor policies, strategies, and even preferences emerge out of interaction with the external environment and, moreover, such interaction varies across time and space in response to complex social interaction. What is distinctive here is instead the claim that governmental élites calculate on the basis of consistency with collective ideas or discourses irreducible to material interests.

Whence do these ideas and discourses come? The second core proposition shared by nearly all participants in this volume states that *underlying ideas and discourses change only at rare 'critical junctures,' which arise in response to political crises.* In the interaction with the political world, policies may be perceived to fail, meaning that they may be perceived as inappropriate to the social circumstances. This inappropriateness may be perceived for instrumental reasons (the policies do not generate appropriate outcomes) or more sociological reasons (independent of substantive consequences, the policies are not those which other actors expect or appreciate).

The social scientific challenges facing those who seek to move from these two meta-theoretical claims to testable mid-range theory are clear. With regard to the first proposition, constructivists must specify concrete causal mechanisms through which the process of choosing policies and defining interests takes place, with the ultimate goal of saying something about *which* ideas and discourses influence (or do not influence) *which* policies under *which* circumstances. With regard to the second proposition, constructivists must seek to specify concrete causal mechanisms that help to explain *which* political crises lead to a change in *which* ideas and discourses under *which* circumstances. Propositions of this kind are testable.

How do the participants in this volume seek to meet these two theoretical challenges? What testable hypotheses result? In this section I seek to demonstrate that many chapters in this volume (despite their stated intent) advance no testable propositions at all, while many others advance testable propositions that are in no way distinct to constructivist theory.

Let us begin with those authors who advance theories that are *in principle* indeterminate and, therefore, untestable. These claims are not merely under-specified; they predict behavior that is *contradictory or in principle indeterminate* behavior *and* tell us nothing about how the contradiction and indeterminacy should be resolved. They are therefore in principle untestable. Space permits only two examples: the work of Rosamond, and Marcussen, Risse *et al.*[4]

Rosamond addresses the first theoretical challenge listed above, namely to specify the relationship between ideas and policy. In an explicit challenge to theories that explain European integration as a response to rising economic interdependence, Rosamond advances two central hypotheses. First, (see p. 162) 'the deployment of ideas about globalization has been central to the development of a particular notion of European identity among élite policy actors.' Second, '"globalization" remains contested within EU policy circles.' These two claims provide, at first glance, an intriguing speculation about where we might begin to look for the sources of state policy.

Taken together, however, Rosamond's two claims remain *in principle* indeterminate and therefore cannot be tested in any way, because between them they subsume the entire range of possible state behavior. Anyone, including Rosamond, seeking to assess the validity of these claims necessarily must resolve one fundamental theoretical issue. Should we expect any given situation to be a case of 'the development of a particular notion' (i.e. convergent views), a case of 'contestation' (i.e. divergent views), or some combination of the two? Absent a more precise specification, *any observed outcome* – except, perhaps, a policy debate with no reference to globalization or no contestation at all, which we would know to be false simply by glancing at the *Financial Times* – is 'explained' by this theory. It is inevitable, if a tribute to the author's honesty, that Rosamond's concluding summary is fundamentally indeterminate.

> [Globalization] is used to signify external realities which define the EU's environment [but] is understood as having multiple and often contradictory consequences . . . this pattern is not uniform and the evidence suggests that different clusters of actors can deploy the idea of globalization with quite distinct effects.
>
> (p. 173)

This in turn leads Rosamond to paper over perhaps the most intriguing and important question in modern studies of globalization. 'The evidence,' he concludes, 'suggests that there is widespread adherence to neo-liberal conceptions and that globalization appears as either/both (a) a structural fact associated with the development of circuits of capital, production, trade and technology or/and (b) a set of policy preferences for economic openness and market-driven policies of budgetary restraint' (p. 172). The relative weight of these two factors has been the subject of articles and books. Rosamond restates rather than resolves this fundamental theoretical issue.

The second example is the chapter by Marcussen, Risse *et al.*, who address both theoretical challenges. On the first major challenge, the relation between deep ideas ('identities') and policy (or policy ideas), they remain vague:

> We do not promote an 'interest vs. identity' account, but try to figure out the precise way in which both interact. On the one hand, embedded identity constructions, mentioned above, define the boundaries of what élites consider to be legitimate ideas – thereby constituting their perceived interests. On the other hand, perceived interests define which ideas political élites select in their struggle for power among those available to actors. The precise relationship remains a matter of empirical study.
>
> (pp. 103–4)

To be sure, it is always prudent to remember that the world contains more complexity than any single theory can encompass – a point to which I shall return below. Marcussen, Risse, *et al.* are also quite correct to insist on the need for empirical analysis. Yet theoretical innovation and empirical testing requires that we focus on specific causal mechanisms. In this context, the 'precise relationship' between ideas and interests or policies is not simply a matter for 'empirical study.' Instead, as Marcussen, Risse *et al.* concede elsewhere, *it is (or ought to be) one of two central theoretical issues in the constructivist research program*. Without a theory of the interaction between ideas and interests, it is not possible to generate hypotheses that distinguish views based on interests or institutions, and thus it remains impossible to confirm or disconfirm any one or combination of them. 'Empirical study' on this basis is of questionable utility, since any observation would confirm the underlying theory.

Marcussen, Risse *et al.* also address the second theoretical challenge, namely to explain why ideas and discourses change or remain stable in particular circumstances – with equally indeterminate results. The only attempt at a theoretical answer I can discern is buried in the final note, where they observe:

> When old visions about political order remain unchallenged, they tend to become increasingly embedded in national institutions and political cultures, as a result of which they become difficult to deconstruct and to replace. . . We will not be able to expand on this point in this chapter, but we have a broad range of institutions in mind, such as the media, the educational system, the electoral system, the legal system, political decision-making procedures, etc. What they have in common is that they tend to consolidate and reify existing and consensually shared ideas about just political order.
>
> (pp. 117, 120)

This construct evades theoretical analysis. Surely it is prima facie untrue as a general proposition that education, elections, law, and the media invariably have a conservative effect on existing social practices. (This is almost precisely the *opposite* of what conservative thinkers and professional sociologists alike have traditionally believed about liberal democratic societies, where their dynamics are often highly destructive of underlying social norms.) The only way we could know when the effect of these institutions is conservative and when it is dynamic would be to specify a theory of such socializing institutions. One would expect – and the authors appear to agree above – that this is the proper direction for constructivist theory. Yet their note tells us next to nothing about what such a theory or theories would look like. They neither set forth testable hypotheses, nor lay the theoretical foundation for the development of such hypotheses. Instead, they restate – albeit in an impressively sophisticated way – the basic theoretical problem.

Why so few testable propositions? Though some of the meta-theoretical speculations in this volume imply the opposite, there is no reason why claims about the 'constitutive' effect of ideas should be difficult to test. One piece of evidence for the ease with which hypotheses can be derived is the existence of promising propositions scattered throughout this volume. Two examples come from Jeffrey Checkel's analysis – in many respects a refreshing exception in its willingness to directly engage theoretical, as opposed to meta-theoretical, questions. Checkel advances at least two such distinctive and potentially testable propositions.

The first is that *an individual's specific policy ideas are most likely to change when other ideas are held by 'authoritative' members of an 'in-group' to which the persuadee belongs or wants to belong.* Institutional hierarchy imposes ideational conformity as a quid pro quo, implicit or explicit, for membership. Obviously this notion would require more elaboration, yet it points us in a clearly focused direction. We can easily imagine measuring the membership in in-groups (or the desire to do so) independently of ideas and tracing through the political consequences.[5]

A second causal proposition advanced by Checkel and others, most notably Marcussen, Risse *et al.*, is that *influential ideas about political order remain stable unless 'challenged' by a 'crisis.'* This is, in fact, the most common proposition found in the volume; hence I have treated it above as a core assumption. To be sure, at this level of abstraction, the claim is underspecified to the point of near-tautology. We can always find some sense of dissatisfaction, something that could be called a 'crisis,' motivating a change in ideas. And surely not all things that could be termed 'crises' lead to changes in relevant ideas. More precise specification is required for this insight to be useful. Still, the notion that crises are connected with change is *not*, in contrast to some of the claims we considered above, internally contradictory. We can imagine a more precise definition of crisis and a more precise specification of causal mechanisms that might generate testable causal propositions. Such work should be encouraged.

CONSTRUCTIVISM AND ITS CRITICS: WHERE ARE THE THEORETICAL ALTERNATIVES?

The assertion of a causal connection between crisis and ideational change has a second and more fundamentally troubling characteristic, however, in addition to its abstract character. *It is in no way distinct to constructivism.* Indeed, it is somewhat hard to see why it should be considered constructivist at all. To understand this criticism, it is instructive first to consider briefly the alternatives to a constructivist analysis of ideas.

Rationalist theories of integration, like rationalist theories of IR (realism, liberalism, and institutionalism, etc.), do not maintain that actors in international affairs have no ideas at all, as some authors in this volume would seem to imply. Collective ideas are like air; it is essentially impossible for humans to function as social beings without them. They are ubiquitous and necessary. In this (trivial) sense there is little point in debating whether 'ideas matter.' *Existing rationalist theories claim only something far more modest, namely that ideas are causally epiphenomenal to more fundamental underlying influences on state behavior.*[6]

To see precisely what this implies, consider, for example, a liberal intergovernmentalist (LI) analysis of European integration. Such an account seeks to explain decisions for and against deeper European integration in terms of three factors. These are: (1) underlying economic interests, with geopolitical ideas playing a distinctly secondary role; (2) relative power, understood in terms of asymmetrical interdependence; and (3) the need for credible commitments to certain policies, with ideology playing a distinctly secondary role (Moravcsik 1998). This explanation does not deny that individuals and governments have ideas in their heads or that we should observe them espousing ideas consistent with rational interests and strategies. It denies *only* that *exogenous* variation in other sources of those ideas decisively affects ideas and therefore policy. In sum, in the LI account of integration, ideas are present but not causally central. They may be irrelevant and random, or, more likely, they are important transmission belts for interests. In the latter case, they are endogenous to other underlying factors.[7]

One important implication is that *both an LI theory and constructivist-inspired theory* predict some correlation between collective ideas and policy outcomes.[8] What distinguishes rationalist and constructivist accounts of this correlation is *not,* therefore, the simple fact that state and societal actors hold ideas consistent with their actions, but the causal independence of those ideas – their source, variation, and the nature of their link to policy. *Hence the minimum we should expect of any effort to test constructivist claims is not just the derivation of fine-grained empirical predictions, examined above, but also the utilization of methods capable of distinguishing between spurious and valid attributions of ideational causality.* In short, studies that seek to show the impact of exogenous variation in ideas must be controlled for the causally epiphenomenal or 'transmission belt' role of ideas. In a social scientific debate, this is the minimum that proponents of a new theory owe those who have already derived and tested mid-range theories.

The chapters in this volume, I submit, do little to meet this minimum method-ological standard. Returning to the argument above, one example is the proposed link between political crisis (or policy failure) and changes in ideas – a link central to almost every chapter in the volume. This relationship is *precisely* what an LI account would predict. Indeed, one might argue that *only* an LI account generates such a prediction. Why should real world events undermine the confidence of decision-makers in their ideas if those ideas are not meant to be serving underlying instru-mental purposes? And if they are so intended, why is this causal argument presented as an alternative to, rather than a confirmation of, traditional theories of integration and international political economy? In this regard, it is striking that the number of *purely* sociological (or even clearly ideational) claims about variation in funda-mental discourses and state behavior in this volume is surprisingly low. Instead, we tend to see extensive, if somewhat *ad hoc*, recourse to rationalist and materialist (or formal institutionalist) causes – a tendency I shall document in a moment.

This dependence on (or, at the very least, ambiguity with respect to) the predictions of existing rationalist and materialist theories is disguised in part by the tendency of authors in this volume to misspecify alternative theories in a way that renders them little more than straw men. Such obfuscation is surely not deliberate, but the result is nonetheless to make it almost impossible to disconfirm con-structivist claims, since the stated alternatives are absurd or, in some cases, not theories at all. This undermines our confidence in the resulting empirical analysis. The editors of the volume go even further, seeking to make a virtue of this by seeking to demonstrate – unconvincingly, in my estimation – that *only* constructivist theory can explain many aspects of integration.[9] This tendency to reject alternative argu-ments without testing them takes a number of different forms.

The simplest way to reject alternative theories without testing them is to restate them as ideal types, rather than theories – that is, as constructs that do not explain variation in state behavior. Any variation – of course there is always variation – can thus only be explained by constructivist theory, which carries the day by default. We see this methodological move in the chapters of Kenneth Glarbo and Marcussen, Risse *et al.* Glarbo asserts that:

> When subjected to theoretical analysis, European political co-operation has traditionally been the prerogative of realists . . . however diverse in appearance, [the realist narrative] can be reduced to one 'hard core' hypothesis, from which all the realist theoretical statements of EPC/CFSP are derived . . . the interests of single European nation states will eternally block integration within the 'high politics' realms of foreign, security and defence policy.
>
> (p. 140)

This is manifestly incorrect as a statement about realism, which has in fact generated a number of highly refined theories of alliances. The most charitable thing that could be said is that it selects out of that extensive and sophisticated literature the *least* interesting and *least* plausible alternative hypothesis – namely a static ideal-type of non-cooperation. With this as the only alternative – for Glarbo ignores entirely institutionalist, liberal, and more sophisticated realist theories of alliances and collective security, as well as synthetic approaches like that of Stephen Walt – a constructivist theory need only explain some variation from 'eternal' non-cooperation to be 'proven' correct. If a fact already known to all – namely that the EU has taken some modest steps toward common foreign and security policy (CFSP) – settles the issue, why bother with empirical analysis?

Consider next Marcussen, Risse *et al.*'s chapter. These authors also do not take neo-functionalism and liberal intergovernmentalism seriously enough even to test them. They 'reject [both] out of hand' in the space of exactly seven sentences. This they do, moreover, by misspecifying each as an ideal-type assuming static, constant behavior, rather than as a theory – just as did Glarbo. LI gains the following treatment, *quoted in its entirety*:

> [O]ne could deduce from intergovernmentalism – either its realist (Hoffmann 1966) or liberal versions (Moravcsik 1993, 1997) – that European integration should not affect nation state identities, since the European polity consists of intergovernmental bodies which do not require much loyalty transfer to the European level. The French and the German cases appear to contradict this argument.
>
> (p. 114)

No effort is made to consider a more (if still minimally) sophisticated formulation of LI in which shared identities and symbols are correlated with policy but are epiphenomenal – as I have suggested above. Nor is any effort made to provide evidence of the causal importance of loyalty changes, beyond a conventional history of changing ideas about Europe over the past half century. Neo-functionalism gains the same cursory treatment – it purportedly predicts constant change and is therefore rejected. Constructivism prevails by default rather than by surmounting the challenge of honest empirical validation.

A more direct way to reject plausible alternatives without an objective empirical test is simply to ignore them entirely. We see this in the work of Diez, who maintains that new policies are more likely to occur if they are consistent with the underlying assumptions of prior ones – their language, symbolism, and images. An example is Diez's bold, parsimonious causal account of why the British applied to join the EC in 1961: '[T]he language of a free trade area in the British case facilitated the move towards the articulation of an economic community that would otherwise have been much harder, if not impossible' (p. 608). This is a refreshingly concise claim, yet Diez makes no effort whatsoever to substantiate it.

In particular, the unsuspecting reader would have no inkling that the existing literature contains at least two rationalist explanations far more strongly supported by the archival record. One is that Harold Macmillan was influenced by further relative economic decline and the rejection of his efforts to mediate between the superpowers, visible by 1960 (Kaiser 1996). The other is that Britain, skeptical of supranationalism and wary of any preferential trading area in agriculture, first attempted to negotiate its preferred policy, the free trade area (FTA), and, when it failed, sought the more onerous European Community (EC) in order to avoid economic and geopolitical isolation (Moravcsik 1998). Either renders linguistic and symbolic influences epiphenomenal. If language and symbolism also shifted, traditional accounts presume, it was because the government, business, and political parties were justifying self-interested policies that grew more pro-European over time. Perhaps they even manipulated the debate. British policy change was a strategic adaptation to new circumstances, rather than a shift in the deep structure of British values and preferences.

A simple empirical test can help to determine whether Diez's account or one of the traditional accounts is more accurate.[10] If the rationalists are correct that British policy was a strategic adaptation, not a fundamental transformation, British politicians and officials should have been able to foresee and plan for the future scenario. They should have understood *even before the FTA was proposed* that the failure of some commercial accommodation with the Continent would force a membership bid. If the alternative was linguistically and symbolically unthinkable, we should observe no such foresightedness. Unfortunately for Diez's claim, we observe the former. British officials argue as early as 1956 that if the EC negotiations succeed and any British alternative fails, Britain will soon be forced to join the EC. There is, moreover, considerable evidence that Macmillan, like subsequent leaders, considered élite and public opinion a constraint to be manipulated. One former top British adviser once told me that 10 Downing Street's working assumption was that public opinion could be moved to support any European initiative in eighteen months. Certainly Macmillan took this view.[11]

One could cite many other examples, but the central point is clear. Constructivists in this volume do not test their claims against plausible alternatives.

CONCLUSION: 'TO WHAT ISSUE WILL THIS COME?'

Given the multitude of citations to the likes of John Searle, Anthony Giddens, Alexander Wendt, and other social theorists, it would seem perverse to criticize constructivists for being insufficiently theoretical. Yet this volume reveals just that. We see a striking unwillingness to set forth distinctive mid-range hypotheses and test them against the most plausible alternatives in a rigorous and objective way. There is not a point in this chapter – with the single exception, perhaps, of Fierke and Wiener's claim about NATO and the EU, see chapter 8 – where one sensed that a claim by the author is in any danger (even in the abstract) of empirical disconfirmation.

This reticence to place empirical claims at risk cannot be explained as a function of the empirical material itself. Surely few domains are more promising than the study of ideas in the process of European integration. Even the most materialist explanations of European integration – such as those advanced by Alan Milward and myself – concede an important secondary role for ideas (Milward 1993). Nor can this unwillingness to test clear hypotheses be a function of the novelty of the claims being advanced. Surely few topics have been as extensively researched and subtly illuminated as the role of ideas in European integration – whether by historians like Walter Lipgens, political scientists like Stanley Hoffmann (1974), or practitioner-scholars like François Duchêne (1995).[12] Nor can this unwillingness be a function, as the editors imply in their introduction, of fundamental philosophical (ontological or epistemological) rejection of hypothesis testing. In fact when the authors in this volume turn to empirical analysis, they prove philosophically conventional, aspiring to test theories by presenting decisive evidence and so on. Nor, finally, can this unwillingness to test theories rigorously result, as authors in this volume repeatedly claim, from the inherent difficulty of testing ideational or sociological claims. Surely, as we have just seen in the case of Diez's analysis of Macmillan, the empirical material often lends itself to straightforward and decisive empirical tests easily within the grasp of anyone minimally acquainted with the archival and secondary sources. If this volume contains few such tests of competing theories, it is not because they are inherently difficult, but because authors chose not to conduct them.[13] Why?

The editors of this volume have an answer: Not enough meta-theory. They write in their introduction that the discovery of 'promising avenue(s) for future integration research' has been hampered by the lack of 'suitable meta-theoretical perspectives.' We need, they argue, 'heightened awareness of the implications of meta-theoretical positions.' Get the meta-theory right, they promise, and empirical theorizing will be 'important and fruitful.' This special issue provides a useful test of this claim. By my estimation, fully 50 percent or more of this volume is given over to meta-theoretical analysis, rather than theory or empirics – just as the editors recommend. A panoply of arguments drawn from ontology, social theory, epistemology, and philosophy of science are deployed. Yet the resulting empirical propositions are few, relatively conventional, and barely tested.

Perhaps, then, an opposite view is worth considering, namely that *meta-theory is not the solution but the problem.* Philosophical speculation is being employed not to refine and sharpen concrete concepts, hypotheses, and methods, but to *shield* empirical conjectures from empirical testing. Meta-theoretical musing does not establish but evades points of direct empirical conflict between sophisticated rationalist and constructivist theories. Abstract discussions of competing modes of positivism, ideational causality, rationalist explanation, the relationship between agents and structures, often serve as principled excuses for *not* engaging in competitive theory testing. At the very least, such speculation expends a great deal of time, effort, and space that might have been devoted to the elaboration of concrete concepts, theories, hypotheses, and methods.

All this distracts constructivists from the only element truly essential to social science: the vulnerability of conjectures to some sort of empirical disconfirmation. Only if one's own claim can be proven wrong are we able to conclude that it has been proven right. In this personal modesty and relentless skepticism toward the conjectures of any single scholar lies the real power of social science as a collective enterprise. Yet very few, if any, empirical propositions in this volume, I have sought to show, are advanced in this spirit or meet this standard. When constructivists 'wax desperate with imagination,' is it therefore not the responsibility of outside observers – most especially those, like myself, who wish the enterprise well – to ask, like Horatio and Marcellus watching Hamlet follow the ghost: 'To what issue will this come?'

NOTES

1   Five or ten years ago, even this minimal implicit commitment to theory testing – theories should be distinctive and tested against other theories – might have elicited spirited rejection. Yet leading constructivists have since broken with postmodernism and its rejection of any objective standards for empirical theory testing. Such attacks, generally based on the notion that ideational causation cannot be studied causally or objectively, were never very convincing anyway, given the extensive and refined empirical literatures in political science on public opinion, élite values, transaction costs, structure-induced equilibria, political culture, analogical reasoning, entrepreneurship, social capital, strategic culture, cognitive biases, symbolic politics, and other such topics.

2   In doing so, I have restricted my analysis to those in the volume that raise relevant issues. Other authors, in particular those engaged in purely normative analysis, I have unfortunately left aside. Jo Shaw's analysis is particularly interesting, not least because, in seeking a social theoretical grounding for a normative theory of European constitutionalism, she ultimately rejects a more 'constructivist' or 'top-down' sociological analysis. Instead she opts on normative grounds for a more liberal, 'bottom-up' view that privileges the pre-existing interests and identities of individuals and groups in civil society.

3   Some, such as Glarbo, flirt with the idea that constructivism does not explain state behavior at all, but just 'shifts in diplomatic agency *identity* caused by intersubjective social structure.' This view, not consistently pursued by any of the authors – and therefore – need not detain us.

4   Another example are Karin Fierke and Antje Wiener (Fierke and Wiener, in this book) addressing the link between the normative principles in the Helsinki Agreement and European willingness to enlarge to the East. This is a bold and intriguing interpretation

of a particular historical circumstance, but it does not appear to contain a testable general theoretical proposition.

5   This intriguing idea, also explicable in rational choice terms as an inter-temporal contract, has potentially wide applicability. See Bates 1996.

6   Note that other IR theories also specify a distinct role for ideas. For realists, broadly speaking, the distribution of ideas and information is a function of the underlying distribution of material power resources. For liberals, the distribution of ideas and information is a function of underlying social preferences and institutions, such as economic interests, structures of political representative, and fundamental ethnic and political identities. For institutionalists, the distribution of ideas and information is a function of international institutional commitments contracted by national governments.

7   There is, of course, at least one important exception. Liberal theories examine the exogenous impact of collective ideas concerning public goods provision, which help to define national preferences. These 'ideational liberal' (or 'liberal constructivist') factors include collective preferences concerning national, political, and socioeconomic identity. These ideas can be thought of as reflective of underlying societal demands and values – collectively determined, perhaps, but intelligible as individual political preferences.

8   Consider, by analogy, the telephone. Telephones have many characteristics generally applied to deep ideas and discourses. Telephones constitute an ubiquitous, absolutely essential network for collective decision-making in the EU. Their existence is a necessary condition for – indeed, it is constitutive of – social interaction as practiced in this particular historical context. The network of telephones collectively empowers individuals to speak and act; without them, social interaction would grind to a halt. Yet it would be absurd to argue that telephones 'caused' European integration.

9   The tendency of the editors of this volume, as well as some authors in it, to assume that no other theory could possibly explain the phenomena they observe or that no non-theoretical writing could offer the same conjectures amounts to a level of confidence in social science in general, and their own theory in particular, that can only strike an outside observer as astonishing.

10   There is, in addition, a materialist account of preference change. The direction of British exports was shifting, despite discrimination by the EEC, from the Commonwealth to the Continent. In 1955, around 25 percent of British exports went to Europe and twice as many to the Commonwealth. By 1965, these figures had reversed. See Moravcsik 1998: chs 2–3.

11   For detailed evidence, see Moravcsik 1998: chs 2, 3, also on later decisions, chs 6, 7.

12   The editors of this volume assert at one point in the introduction that constructivist theory is necessary to free us to think of explanations otherwise inaccessible to us. Yet few if any of the hypotheses in the volume hardly seem out of the ordinary in light of traditional history, daily journalism, or political criticism of the EEC in post-war Europe. This seems to place rather too much emphasis on the public influence and personal creativity of social scientists, as compared to others in society.

13   This is, of course, self-defeating behavior. The more generous the analyst is to opposing theories, the more confidence we should have in any positive empirical finding she reports. In *The Choice for Europe*, for example, I specify an alternative ideational explanation of national preferences and test it across the five most significant decisions in EU history, employing a method that, I maintain, is *biased in favor of ideational and geopolitical explanations* and against my economic account. The preponderance of evidence confirms three empirical conclusions: (1) Ideational factors played only a secondary or insignificant role in nearly all cases. (2) There is nonetheless interesting cross-national and cross-issue variation in how much ideational factors mattered, and I go on to suggest some hypotheses about the conditions under which ideas matter most. (3) One cannot trust the public rhetoric or interview statements of government officials and politicians. Politicians are professional experts at manipulating rhetoric

opportunistically; only confidential sources tell the real story. In that work, however, my primary concern was not to specify a detailed ideational theory. Hence there remains much room to improve such theories and engage in a far more intensive and focused *empirical* debate grounded in the rich archival sources available on European integration. On ideas, see also Moravcsik (2000).

12

Social Constructivisms and European Studies

Steve Smith

The chapters in this book lead to two main conclusions: first, social constructivisms offer considerably improved explanatory power for the study of European governance; second, there is no such thing as *a* social constructivist approach or theory of that or any other social process. My aim in this brief chapter is to comment on these two main conclusions from what can broadly be called a reflectivist theoretical stance. I will deal fairly briefly with the first conclusion, since I believe that the chapters so conclusively show their utility for dealing with European governance. The second point will take up more space because I feel that these chapters illustrate extraordinarily clearly a general problem of the social constructivist approach to international relations theory.

In many senses, my conclusions support the claims made by the editors in their introductory chapter. Like them I start from the premiss that it is paradoxical that constructivist scholars have largely ignored the study of European governance, of all subjects. Like them, I am convinced that social constructivisms offer much to this area of scholarship. Also like them, I think that social constructivism is more of an approach than a theory, and I agree that its central theme is the impact of the ideational on the material as seen in the host of social ontological features listed in the introduction (intersubjective meanings, etc.). Together these constitute the basis for a constructivist turn in European integration studies, and my firm prediction is that this turn will be the basis for much future work in the area. My only main point of departure from the arguments of the editors concerns whether or not the range of approaches used in the chapters in this book can really be subsumed under the title 'social constructivism'. I think that the range is so wide, and the metatheoretical assumptions so divergent, that the contributors are in fact dealing with very different theoretical positions.

This can lead to two conclusions: one (optimistic) reading would lead to the notion of *social constructivisms*, implying that the approaches did have something in common and that it made sense to talk of them as a set of related approaches. An alternative reading would be that the different approaches involve such mutually exclusive assumptions, particularly their ontological and epistemological ones, that they cannot be grouped together as approaches that share much at all. In this latter light, all they share is an opposition to the meta-theoretical assumptions of the dominant theories of European governance. My own view is that the chapters in this book start from a common point (of rejecting the assumptions of rationalist accounts) but then diverge considerably over how to characterize European governance; this is because they have different social ontologies.

SOCIAL CONSTRUCTIVISM AND INTERNATIONAL RELATIONS THEORY

As the editors note in their introduction, social constructivism has become a main approach in international relations in the last decade. It is self-consciously portrayed as an approach that lies between rationalism and reflectivism, and as such can be seen as a middle ground or a via media. I will cite five paradigmatic examples of this positioning, three from within the social constructivist literature (Wendt 1992; Adler 1997b; Checkel 1998) and two from important recent summaries of the state of the discipline of international relations (IR) (Walt 1998; Katzenstein *et al.* 1998). Wendt's self-proclaimed aim is to build a bridge between the two IR traditions of rationalism and reflectivism by developing a constructivism that builds on the shared features of the liberalist wing of the rationalist tradition and the modern constructivist wing of the reflectivist tradition (Wendt 1992: 393–4). Similarly, Adler sees constructivism, rather than any alternative such as the neo-institutionalist focus on the role of ideas (see Goldstein and Keohane 1993), as the 'true middle ground' between rationalist and relativist (his wording) approaches (Adler 1997b: 322). Checkel, in his survey of 'the constructivist turn' in IR theory, claims that 'Constructivists thus occupy a middle ground between rational choice theorists and postmodern scholars' (Checkel 1998: 327).

In his review of IR theory for the influential US journal *Foreign Policy* in its special issue on 'The Frontiers of Knowledge', Stephen Walt describes the key debate in international theory as being between realism and liberalism. But he notes that there is a third approach, constructivism, which he sees as the main alternative to these two. In his words the diplomat of the future should 'remain cognizant of realism's emphasis on the inescapable role of power, keep liberalism's awareness of domestic forces in mind, and occasionally reflect on constructivism's vision of change' (Walt 1998: 44). Katzenstein, Keohane and Krasner, writing in the fiftieth anniversary special issue of *International Organization*, offer a summary of the development of international theory which portrays the current theoretical scene as one dominated by two theoretical traditions, rationalism and constructivism. Specifically, they argue that 'constructivists have positioned themselves quite self-consciously between rationalist theoretical orientations, such as realism or liberalism, and postmodernist orientations' (Katzenstein *et al.* 1998: 678).

This is clearly the dominant portrayal of the place of social constructivism on the current theoretical waterfront, but the articles in this special issue reinforce my contention that this shared view of social constructivism as 'the middle way' is in fact deeply misleading. In my view, most social constructivism is far more 'rationalist' in character than 'reflectivist'; indeed I would go so far as to say that social constructivism in its dominant (mainly North American) form is very close to the neo-liberalist wing of the rationalist paradigm. This is precisely why it is seen by Walt, and by Katzenstein, Keohane and Krasner as the via media. One quote will suffice: 'In contrast to . . . constructivism, postmodernism falls clearly outside of the social science enterprise, and in international relations research it risks becoming self-referential and disengaged from the world, protests to the contrary not-withstanding' (Katzenstein et al. 1998: 678). For these three writers the journal International Organization has not published postmodernist work, because the journal 'has been committed to an enterprise that postmodernism denies: the use of evidence to adjudicate between truth claims' (Katzenstein et al. 1998: 678).

The same picture emerges from an examination of the work of leading constructivists. Adler, in his powerful manifesto for a constructivist research agenda, is explicit in differentiating it from what he terms relativist approaches (Adler 1997b: 330–7). These approaches are, he claims, based on 'untenable' assumptions that essentially deny the separate existence of both foundational truth and an independent reality. As Jeffrey Checkel puts it: 'It is important to note that constructivists do not reject science or causal explanation: their quarrel with mainstream theories is ontological, not epistemological. The last point is key, for it suggests that constructivism has the potential to bridge the still vast divide separating the majority of IR theorists from postmodernists' (Checkel 1998: 327). Wendt's work is explicitly based on epistemological assumptions shared with rationalist, not reflectivist, approaches (see Wendt 1987, 1992: 393–4, 422–5, 1994). As he comments in a recent paper, co-authored with Ronald Jepperson and Peter Katzenstein, 'The term identity here is intended as a useful label, not as a signal of commitment to some exotic (presumably Parisian) social theory' (Jepperson et al. 1996: 34).

Within the study of European integration, there has also been a considerable divide between constructivist and reflectivist approaches. The collection of essays edited by Jørgensen (1997b), Reflective Approaches to European Governance, is indicative since, despite the title, virtually all the essays are constructivist rather than reflectivist in orientation. Indeed the editor, in his introduction, notes that: 'Reflective scholars who wish to conduct theoretically informed empirical research on European governance cannot allow themselves the luxury of a comfortable, postmodernist position' (Jørgensen 1997b: 7).

THE CONTRIBUTION OF SOCIAL CONSTRUCTIVISM TO EUROPEAN INTEGRATION

What picture of the relationship between constructivism and the rationalism/reflectivism debate emerges from the chapters in this book? As noted above the most important conclusion is that social constructivist approaches have much to offer the study of European governance. The chapters show absolutely incontrovertibly both that the dominance of rationalist approaches has restricted the development of the literature on European integration, and that social constructivist approaches can offer convincing (and, I would argue, deeper) explanations of European integration. Indeed, the strength of the chapters in this book makes one wonder quite why it has taken so long for the constructivist turn to reach the study of European integration. I am not able to discuss each chapter in the length it deserves, but I do want to point to the specific advances made by each of them.

Checkel's chapter, based on a 'modernist' constructivism, makes a powerful case for the ways in which learning and socialization impact on actors' identities and interests. Rationalist accounts, he argues, miss an important part of the story, because they bracket identity and interest formation and because they are methodological individualist in character. Ultimately, he believes that constructivism can deal with the most interesting research questions because it operates at the intersection between structures and agents: in contrast, he claims, both rationalist and postmodern approaches 'have life easy', because they ignore the messy intersections and concentrate on one side of the story. In short, constructivist accounts offer alternative ways of conceptualizing the relationship between norms, discourse, language and material capabilities, and as such can work alongside rationalist accounts to 'more fully capture the range of institutional dynamics at work in contemporary Europe'. This results, he says, in better explanations than those provided by rationalism. I think that this claim is well founded, although I am concerned that Checkel's version of constructivism is very close in its assumptions to rationalist accounts: he speaks of favouring a constructivism based on methodological individualism (a limitation of rationalism, he later points out) and a 'loosely causal' epistemology. This, of course, is why he thinks that rationalists and constructivists can work hand-in-hand; but it is also a very specific take on constructivism and one that is very different indeed to some of the other constructivisms in this special issue.

Koslowski's chapter examines European Union (EU) federalism from a constructivist perspective, a perspective that involves a much more sophisticated treatment of institutions than is found in the federalist literature. Koslowski sees a constructivist account as one which is not wedded to existing legal structures and actors, and which focuses on institutions as routinized human practices. As such, a constructivist account looks at a wider notion of institutions and practices than is found in the rationalist literature, and thus helps to 'retool' federal theories for 'more persuasive analysis'; this is particularly noticeable in the case of Europe because it allows federalist writers to bypass the dichotomizing and limiting question of whether or not the European polity is a sovereign or a federal state, and at the same time to resist teleological analyses of the hypothetical end state of the European integration process. I found this a convincing argument, and accept that a constructivist notion of federalism offers a more subtle way of analysing European integration than that provided by the traditional literature. I have two worries, however: first, I am not clear that the traditional federalist literature is necessarily to be equated with rationalism. Second, the chapter makes a strong case for looking at federalism in this way, but I am not sure what it has to do with a thick constructivism. As was the case with Checkel's chapter, Koslowski seems to share many of the assumptions of rationalism, and his constructivism is a very 'thin' one. Note that I agree that his account of European federalism is a much richer one than provided by the traditional literature, but none the less his constructivism is firmly on the rationalist side of the rationalist/reflectivist divide.

Jo Shaw's chapter comes from a different intellectual tradition than the rest of the chapters in this book, but in my view it is a really sophisticated account of how constructivism can offer significantly better accounts of constitutionalism than can legal positivist approaches. I found the chapter extremely interesting in the way in which it moved beyond current approaches to studying the EU, finding in them a lack of clarity over the key elements of a European constitution. Building on the work of Bellamy and Castiglione, Shaw shows how the traditional literature on constitutionalism cannot be transferred to the EU in a postnational setting. Following Tully's work on constitutionalism in a multicultural polity, Shaw proposes a Wittgensteinian notion of constitutionalism as 'one heuristic' and not as a 'preconceived idea to which reality must correspond'. From this perspective, the EU and its constitutional development becomes an 'essentially contested project'. Shaw therefore sees the constitutional development of the EU as a process of negotiation and compromise rather than a development towards a preconceived end state, and as an ongoing contestation between interests rather than as a framework for eradicating these differences. I found this to be a very rich chapter and I thought the constructivism that underlies it to be rather more radical than that of the two preceding chapters. Shaw's use of Tully (and his reliance on Wittgenstein) offer a more intersubjective and constitutive account of European governance than either Checkel or Koslowski.

Thomas Diez's chapter is the most radical in the collection, in the sense that he is far removed from the assumptions of rationalism. I found his chapter to be convincing and enlightening. I have to confess that I am much more persuaded by the form of constructivism that he proposes than I am by many of the other forms found in this collection. Indeed, I would argue that he is engaged in a very different enterprise from most of the other authors. In his chapter, Diez looks at the role of language in constructing the EU. His main claim is that discussions on the EU are not simply descriptions of an existing reality but are instead part of the process of constructing that reality; as such these cannot be non-political discussions. For Diez, interests are inseparable from the discursive context in which they emerge. He illustrates this by three theoretical moves, building on the works of Austin, Foucault and Derrida, and outlines a set of research questions that come from this linguistic turn. Crucially, Diez argues that these discursive practices enable rather than cause, and this seems to me to imply a very different notion of the social world than that of most of the other contributors. What I particularly admired about his analysis was its clear empirical focus and its potential for analysing the nodal points of actual discourses. Having said which, I remain to be convinced that his work is as close to that of Alexander Wendt and Jeffrey Checkel as he argues to be the case.

The chapter by Martin Marcussen *et al.* is focused on a much analysed empirical problem, namely why French, German and British identities have developed in the ways they have since the end of the Second World War. Their account is constructivist in nature, relying on work from social psychology, and they convincingly show that it succeeds in offering a convincing explanation of their empirical questions. Importantly, they dismiss the two most obvious rival rationalist accounts, neo-functionalism and intergovernmentalism (in both realist and liberal versions), because the empirical record does not support the predictions offered by these theories for the three cases. Rather, their four-stage process model offers a detailed account of how the concept of 'Europe' becomes involved in national political debates. This is a persuasive account and I was most interested in the way in which it showed so clearly just where, how and why it offered a better explanation of the three countries' identities than did rationalist theories. Having said which, it is important to note that the social constructivism of this chapter is of a very different form to that of, for example, Diez: both use notions of discourse, but I think that Diez's use of Austin, Foucault and Derrida leads to a markedly distinct notion of what a discourse is. In my view, Marcussen *et al.* have a view of discourse and language that is more explanatory than constitutive in nature. Appeals to social psychology do not necessarily imply anything about the depth of the social construction involved, since that discipline is marked by exactly the same disputes about the relationship between the ideational and the material, and between structures and agents as apply to political science and IR.

Kenneth Glarbo's chapter looks at EU common foreign and security policy (CFSP), which he notes has traditionally been the preserve of one branch of the rationalist mainstream (realism). Realism's central prediction is that CFSP will be blocked by egoistic state actors fearful of a loss of sovereignty in a 'high politics' area. Despite the large amount of evidence that realists have to back up this contention, Glarbo offers a social constructivist account of integration in this policy area, pointing out that important aspects of CFSP have been social constructions rather than the products of national interests, and that integration has prevailed in the development of CFSP in recent years. In order to back up these assertions Glarbo uses the phenomenology of Alfred Schutz and the symbolic interactionism of George Mead and Herbert Blumer to develop an ontological model of structure/agency–structure/agency interactions. Using the methodology of analytical bracketing, whereby either agency or structure is in turn explicitly kept out of analysis, Glarbo looks at the history of political co-operation. What is most impressive about this account is that Glarbo's methodology does indeed produce a more sophisticated account of political co-operation than the rationalist account which, although it captures some of the main features, cannot account for the complexities and subtleties. In his conclusion he notes that his is a very preliminary attempt to develop constructivist theory, but it is clear from his chapter that he has opened up a most promising research agenda for future (modernist) constructivists. He is particularly concerned to move constructivism on from being a meta-theoretical orientation, and to develop it as first order theory. But it is also important to note that his constructivism is a very specific one, a self-consciously 'modernist' one, quite importantly distinct from some of the other constructivisms in this book. His constructivism is explicitly built on phenomenological and symbolic interactionist foundations, and these foundations are critically distinct from the foundations of the constructivisms of, for example, Checkel, Koslowski and Diez. Glarbo also makes a strong claim about the 'vacuous' nature of much social constructivist writing in IR, saying that it is so ill-defined 'that it can be adapted to fit almost any pre-given theory or empirical phenomenon'. This claim, of course, is broadly in line with the main theme of this chapter.

Ben Rosamond's chapter looks at how globalization is dealt with in accounts of the construction of European identities. This is a very strong chapter which charts the intersubjectivities developed in EU policy communities in response to globalization. Whereas the rationalist literature treats globalization as an external phenomenon, as a 'conditioning structure', he sees it as a 'zone of contestation', since it opens up space for some political actors rather than others. He is also concerned to use social constructivism to transcend the 'inside/outside' dichotomy that is found in much EU research, a view that ultimately reflects a comparative politics/ IR dispute over what kind of polity the EU is. For Rosamond, the traditional literature ignores both the impact of globalization on the identities, interests and preferences of actors and the question of how it might constitute governance and economic integration questions. As he notes, rationalist accounts are limited in their ability to deal with these kinds of question because they treat identities and interests as exogenous: they can deal with how identities and interests are affected by globalization but not with how it might constitute them. Rosamond's chapter looks in detail at the ways in which the discourses of globalization operate in EU policy-making communities. Although his is an initial analysis of the research question, his chapter makes an exceptionally strong case for the utility of social constructivist theories over rationalist accounts. His most significant conclusion is that globalization has been used by some actors to promote a specific set of neo-liberal economic policy solutions to this 'external threat'. In other words, the external becomes involved in the construction of internal actors, and whoever wins this rhetorical struggle gets to determine the appropriate policy response. I thought that this was an extremely persuasive account, and one that not only showed the power of social constructivist accounts over rationalist ones, but also showed the linkages between knowledge and real world practices. In terms of the form of constructivism involved, I thought that Rosamond's chapter was rather more reflectivist than most of the chapters in the book. But my main conclusion was that his was an excellent illustration of the utility of non-rationalist accounts of European integration.

As such, the chapters support the claims of Knud Erik Jørgensen (1997b) and Marlene Wind (1997) that reflectivist approaches offer deeper and improved accounts of European governance than do rationalist accounts. This, argues Jørgensen, is because reflectivist approaches, unlike rationalist accounts, are not based on an epistemology that contradicts their ontology: this problem with rationalist accounts was pointed out by Kratochwil and Ruggie in 1986, when they noted that the then-dominant rationalist account of institutions (regime theory) had an intersubjectivist ontology but a positivistic epistemology (1986: 764–5). The chapters in this book do not contain such a contradiction at their core, and as such are not subject to the same criticisms as rationalist accounts. Constructivism can offer powerful accounts of European governance precisely because it is based on a notion of intersubjective understandings and discourses being central in shaping over time the identities, interests and interactions of actors. As the editors note in their introduction, European governance is the exemplar of social constructivism in practice. It is also critically important to note that social constructivism is particularly good at generating *empirical research*. The chapters in this book stand in absolutely clear contradiction to the common rationalist claim that there is no alternative empirical research agenda coming from non-rationalist approaches. But the worry persists that the rationalist mainstream will follow Katzenstein, Keohane and Krasner in deeming only those 'modernist' constructivists as engaged in respectable social science.

But if the chapters all add significantly to the study of European governance, what is the picture of the nature of social constructivism that emerges from reading them all? I think that the inescapable conclusion is that there are indeed very different social constructivist approaches and theories underlying many of the chapters, so much so that I do not think that they add up to *a* social constructivist account. That is not really surprising as the editors were explicit in their introduction in saying that they were aware that there were varieties of constructivisms in the separate chapters. Yet I do think that it poses the important question of whether the different constructivisms are members of the same theoretical family. In my view they are not. The chapters reveal approaches based on a wide range of assumptions, and some of these seem to me to be mutually exclusive. To give just the most obvious example, I do not think that Diez shares the same view of the social world as the other contributors, despite the fact that he is dealing with similar sounding issues to many of the other contributors.

My own view is that the differences between the social constructivisms found in this book mirror exactly the division found in the literature generally. How then might we characterize the differences between social constructivist approaches? Many authors have attempted classifications of constructivist thought. It is sufficient for me to list the main ones: Ruggie (1998: 35–6) distinguishes between three variants of social constructivism: *neo-classical*, based on intersubjective meanings, and derived from Durkheim and Weber; *postmodernist*, based on a decisive epistemological break with modernism, and derived from the work of Nietzsche, Foucault and Derrida; and *naturalistic*, based on the philosophical doctrine of scientific realism, derived from the work of Bhaskar. Adler (1997b: 335–6), building on the work of Lynch and Klotz, distinguishes between four forms of constructivism: *modernist, rule-based, narrative knowing* and *postmodernist*. For Katzenstein, Keohane and Krasner (1998: 675–8) there are three versions: *conventional, critical* and *postmodern*. The editors of this book see two main groupings of approaches: *sociological constructivism* (meaning the institutional sociology of, among others, John Meyer) and *Wittgensteinian constructivism*.

Wendt (1987, 1992) relies at different times on the symbolic interactionism of Mead, the scientific realism of Bhaskar and the later work of Wittgenstein. The point of this list is not to argue for one classification over another, only to point out two features of this summary: first, there is little agreement over what social constructivism entails; second, despite all the differences, the lists point to very similar 'fault lines', mainly those between what I have elsewhere (Smith 1995) termed 'constitutive' and 'explanatory' theory. In other words, these classifications seem to contain within the term 'social constructivism' approaches resting on what I would term fundamentally opposed epistemological positions. There is no one social constructivism, instead there are many, and I wonder just how useful it is to continue to use the blanket term, as in talking of a 'constructivist turn'. Maybe this now obscures more than it reveals.

The reason for this can, I think, be further illustrated in Alex Wendt's map of international theory (see the discussion in Adler 1997b: 330–3): Wendt has a two-by-two matrix with the axes representing 'holism–individualism' and 'materialism–idealism', and he puts social constructivism in the holism/idealism box. But note that with it in that box are Gramscian Marxism, the English School, world society and postmodernism. A moment's reflection will show that these are approaches with very different epistemological and ontological assumptions. Therefore, despite the dominant portrayal of social constructivism lying between rationalism and reflectivism, in my view it is mainly a rationalist enterprise, because it shares methodological and epistemological assumptions with rationalism (and most effortlessly with neo-liberal institutionalism). The term 'reflectivist' is often used to encompass both social constructivism and more radical accounts such as critical theory, postmodernism and many forms of contemporary feminist work; however, I think that the gulf between social constructivism and these approaches is fundamental. In this book it is most obvious in the comparison between Diez's article and that of Checkel (compare his 'ontological stance of methodological individualism with a loosely causal epistemology', with Diez's notion of enabling (rather than causal) discourses operating in a setting that is anything but methodologically individualistic).

CONCLUSION

My conclusion is twofold: first, social constructivism has enormous potential for the study of the EU, and it is indeed likely that the next 'great debate' in EU studies will be between the more modernist social constructivism, represented in the bulk of the chapters in this book, and the neo-liberalist wing of the rationalist mainstream. My second conclusion is obvious from the preceding argument: it is that there is no one social constructivism, and that the current literature is more united on what is being rejected than on what is being proposed. The chapters therefore show both the promise of social constructivism and the false unity subsumed under its title. In my view, social constructivist work will split into two main camps, one broadly rationalist, the other more reflectivist. As I have argued elsewhere (Hollis and Smith 1990; Smith 1995, 1996, 1997) this split is necessary because the approaches adopt fundamentally different epistemological assumptions: the foundationalist, or modernist, constructivists can debate easily with rationalists because they share epistemological assumptions, whereas constitutive constructivists cannot do so. For me this all revolves around the question of whether reasons can be causes, and, as the contrast between the assumptions of Diez and Checkel illustrates so clearly, both cannot be easily or comfortably subsumed under the same social constructivist label. To the extent that constructivists can treat reasons as causes, they can debate easily with (neo-liberal institutionalist) rationalists, but to the extent that they cannot they are involved in telling a different type of story about the social world, one that differs from the rationalist story on ontological and epistemological grounds. At present social constructivism contains both sorts of stories, yet I believe that the future of constructivism in European studies, and in IR more generally, will be one of a division between at least these two camps with the new core debate in IR being between rationalism and 'reasons as causes' constructivism.

The Social Construction of Social Constructivism

Thomas Risse and Antje Wiener

1. INTRODUCTION[1]

This volume documents not only the arrival of social constructivism in European Union (EU) studies, but also the fact that this approach is already taken sufficiently seriously. At the same time, even the term 'social constructivism' remains deeply contested and is subject to construction and deconstruction by established scholars in the field such as Andrew Moravcsik and Steve Smith. The former smells something rotten emanating from a 'Copenhagen School' which he (mis-)constructs as the 'force of continental constructivist theories' (p. 176). The latter is more sympathetic to the constructivist enterprise, but then (de-)constructs most of us as being 'far more "rationalist" in character than "reflectivist"' (p. 190). At least, we do not smell (yet), but we are probably neither fish nor fowl. At this point, we would like to (re-)construct the pleasant aroma emanating from social constructivism against both rationalist and reflectivist critics.

We proceed in two steps. First, we argue with and against Steve Smith that social constructivism constitutes indeed the somewhat messy middle ground between the rationalist mainstream and more radical 'reflectivism' or 'postmodernism'. Second, we argue with and against Andrew Moravcsik that most theoretical claims derived from social constructivism 'compete with and should be tested against other mid-range theories' (p. 176).

2. IN DEFENCE OF THE 'MIDDLE GROUND'[2]

Let us start with meta-theory. Steve Smith claims that there is a false unity. All the chapters share is 'an opposition to the meta-theoretical assumptions of the dominant theories of European governance' (p. 189). He predicts that social constructivism is going to split into two main camps, one more rationalist, the other more reflectivist. This split is necessary, he argues, 'because the approaches adopt fundamentally different epistemological assumptions' (pp. 197–8). The Special Issue does not, however, share the 'fault line politics' that would emerge as the logical consequence of Smith's binary approach to constructivism. Quite to the contrary, it aims to chart the characteristics of a terrain that is not limited by an exclusive pole mentality.

To that end, the Special Issue assembles quite a variety of different theoretical orientations – ranging from Jeffrey Checkel's rather modest constructivism to Thomas Diez's more radical reflectivism. Collecting diverse constructivist approaches and elaborating their potential for studying European integration entail the two major goals of this book. First, it demonstrates that European integration is a profoundly social process. Socialization matters for the way that political decisions are taken, policies are developed and concepts are understood. Second, the impact of the social can be assessed by way of resorting to a variety of constructivist positions.

While drawing on Adler's metaphor of the middle ground, this book thus takes great care to identify the differences between constructivists (pp. 8–10). This perspective acknowledges the differences, yet stresses the ability of constructivists to talk beyond the middle ground with either the fish or the fowl on each pole of 'rationalism' or 'radical reflectivism'. The crucial point is stressed in the introductory chapter which emphasizes that there is indeed not one constructivist theory, but a range of constructivist positions. The issue contributes to an understanding of the different positions and of each specific contribution to understanding and explaining the 'social construction of Europe'.

In other words, while Steve Smith is right about quite serious epistemological disagreements between Checkel and Diez, he overlooks that even modest social constructivism does not share the individualist ontology of rational choice. The 'logic of consequentialism' of instrumental rationality is different from the 'logic of appropriateness' or a 'logic of argumentative rationality' (see March and Olsen 1989, 1998). The two latter modes of action are intrinsically social and focus on collective understandings and systems of meanings. The 'middle ground' which social constructivism occupies between rational choice and what Steve Smith calls reflectivism, thus, has two features: constructivism shares with rational choice an epistemological commitment to truth-seeking, and the belief that causal generalization in the form of middle range theories (cf. Moravcsik's claims) is possible. The difference concerns ontology. As to more radical reflectivism, let alone postmodernism, social constructivists share the ontological concerns about social understandings and systems of meanings. They might differ on epistemology, as Steve Smith rightly points out.

The good news is that social constructivists can engage in meaningful conversations with both meta-theoretical approaches, because of either shared ontology or epistemology. In contrast, rational choice and radical reflectivism have little to say to each other, because the common ground for a meaningful exchange of views is small. The bad news is that claiming a 'middle ground' is a somewhat uncomfortable position, because it is subject to constant (de-)construction by our friendly ontological or epistemological neighbours.

Yet, one should not overemphasize the differences. Take Steve Smith as a card-carrying member of the more reflectivist crowd. When he writes about epistemology, he emphasizes the differences between rationalism and reflectivism centring around the question of whether reasons can be causes, etc. But he praises them as showing that 'the dominance of rationalist approaches has restricted the development of the literature on European integration, and that social constructivist approaches can offer convincing (and, I would argue, deeper) explanations of European integration' (pp. 191–3). Andrew Moravcsik comes to the opposite conclusion and claims that constructivists 'have contributed far less to our empirical and theoretical understanding of European integration . . . certainly far less than existing alternatives' (p. 177). Both statements show a commitment to explanation, even though, ironically, the rationalist Moravcsik uses the language of understanding, while the reflectivist Smith employs an explanatory imagery. But both statements contain strong truth claims and, if they are not just meant as rhetoric, they imply that we need some common standards by which to judge whether a theory illuminates or darkens our understanding of the EU.

3. 'TO WHAT ISSUE WILL THIS COME?' DEBATING 'RATIONALISM'[3]

Dealing with Andrew Moravcsik's comment is both easy and difficult. It is easy, because, in principle, we share his view that 'claims derived from constructivist-inspired theories compete with and should be tested against other mid-range hypotheses' (p. 177). We are a little less certain, though, that social constructivist approaches are currently in a position to formulate such hypotheses and, moreover, that a purely deductive approach to generating hypotheses is possible from a constructivist position. But commenting on Moravcsik's comment is also difficult, because it is ultimately up to the reader of the to decide whether his indictments are correct. How shall we deal with the accusation of a 'characteristic unwillingness of constructivists to place their claims at any real risk of empirical disconfirmation' (p. 177)? Moravcsik then goes on to adjudicate that '[h]ardly a single claim in this volume is formulated or tested in such a way that it could, even in principle, be declared empirically invalid' (p. 177).

Rather than engaging in a character defence, we would like to make several points in response. First, as we understood it, was not about 'testing hypotheses'. Rather, the editors and the contributors had the more modest goal of bringing the potential of constructivist approaches for studying the social construction of Europe to the attention of scholars engaged in European studies. The aim was to point out a rich variety of research in the field of European integration, and open up a future research agenda rather than present rigorously tested empirical findings or adjudicate among rival hypotheses. The contributors intended to show how research inspired by social constructivism provides a new theoretical lens to important themes of empirical concern to most EU scholars.

They seek, for example, to facilitate a view on newly emergent institutions, concepts, and principles. As Rey Koslowski argues, 'a constructivist approach is useful because constructivist analysis is not wedded to existing legal structures or political organizations as "units of analysis" *per se*' (p. 35). It facilitates a way of assessing and understanding aspects of an emergent polity in that it seeks to identify the characteristics and meaning of new institutions. Drawing on socio-historical institutionalism, constructivists stress the role of routinized practices and the unintended and intended consequences of institution-building.[4] Koslowski's contribution thus turns to a different notion of constructivism that aims to provide a deeper understanding of European integration as a social and historical process.[5]

Second, Moravcsik misunderstands social constructivism. Take his first paragraph: he correctly points out that Alexander Wendt has presented social constructivism not as an international relations *theory*, but as an ontology. Some sentences later, however, Moravcsik treats constructivism as yet another substantive theory, next to three rationalist theories – realism, liberalism and institutionalism. He claims that the 'advent of constructivism promises to add a wider and perhaps more sophisticated range of theories concerning the causal role of ideational socialization' (p. 176). Let us reiterate here that social constructivism *per se* does not offer an alternative to substantive theories of international relations or European integration. It can, thus, not be tested against realist, liberal, institutionalist or neofunctionalist hypotheses. Social constructivism is a meta-theoretical approach offering an ontology which differs from, say, rational choice. While we can evaluate empirically substantive propositions derived from a 'rationalist' ontology, we cannot 'test' rational choice as such in any meaningful sense. The same holds true for constructivism (or reflectivism, or any other meta-theoretical approach).

Ideational socialization connotes a substantive proposition derived from a (sociological) understanding of institutions which is in turn inspired by a constructivist ontology. In this understanding, the EU consists of a system of principles, rules and procedures which might have socializing effects on actors exposed to these norms. Socialization then means the process by which actors internalize the norms which then influence how they see themselves and what they perceive as their interests. In plain English, this is what is meant when constructivists talk about the 'constitutive' effects of norms and institutions. After some further operationalization, we can test empirically whether norms indeed have these constitutive and socializing effects, whether they merely constrain the behaviour of actors, or better: under which conditions does a 'constructivist' understanding of what institutions do apply, and when can we capture their effects by a 'rationalist' understanding of institutions (on the difference, see also Checkel in this book)? In sum, we cannot 'test' rational choice against constructivism, but we can evaluate empirically the conditions under which sociological (or constructivist) institutionalism offers a better explanation of the effects of norms than rationalist institutionalism. The same holds true for liberalism, etc.

Another misunderstanding which permeates Moravcsik's comment concerns the notion that constructivism somehow deals with ideas, while 'rationalism' deals with (material) interests. It is noteworthy in this context that he uses the terms 'ideas', 'discourse', and 'identity' almost interchangeably in his comment. The problem is that there is no way that we can theorize about the role of ideas as such. Ideas are (individual or collective) states of mind which are all-pervasive in social life. Even our understanding of our material interests are only our 'ideas' about our material interests (even if these ideas are social facts and sticky over centuries). In other words, it is impossible to evaluate ideas 'against' interests in any meaningful sense, unless we specify *which* ideas we mean and *which* interests. We can then test, for example, whether actors are motivated by principled beliefs or norms of appropriate behaviour or by, say, the instrumental search for power or material resources. Or take the notion of identity. Collective identities are not simply any type of ideas, but those ideas which define social groups and how they distinguish themselves from one another. We can then evaluate empirically whether 'Europeanness' is part of that collective identity, how European integration affects various collective identities, or whether a sense of Europeanness embedded in the collective national identity of policy-makers has any impact on their actual policies toward the EU (as opposed to their understandings of economic interests; for example, Risse *et al.* 1999).

These clarifications lead us to our next point. We are rather surprised by Moravcsik's charge that hardly a single claim in this book is *formulated* (we concede the point on 'testing') in a way which could be declared empirically invalid. Checkel, for example, does precisely this (Moravcsik acknowledges this later in his comment; see p. 180). Ben Rosamond, whose claims fall under the 'in principle indeterminate' indictment, advances the proposition that globalization is not an objective reality external to the EU, but that there are several globalization discourses inside the EU ranging from an 'empty signifier' to neo-liberal conceptions (Rosamond 1999). He asks four questions to clarify the connections between globalization and European integration. His conclusions disconfirm the notion that globalization means the same to everybody and simply favours neo-liberal preferences. This runs against the conventional wisdom in about 80 per cent of the literature on globalization and can, 'in principle', be disconfirmed empirically.

Moravcsik goes on to accuse Marcussen *et al.* of committing similar sins by making indeterminate claims. He quotes two propositions about the relationship between identities and perceived interests (pp. 179–81). The first connotes a situation in which identities are rather stable and consensual ('embedded'). In such a situation, collective identities define the realm of legitimate interests in a political discourse. The second proposition connotes critical junctures in which identities are unstable and contested. We claim that perceived instrumental interests of actors determine in such a situation which identity constructions are promoted. Moravcsik overlooks the fact that the two propositions apply to different social situations which should have been apparent from the context of the paragraph. Once the various terms are specified, particularly the notion of 'critical junctures', the propositions can be easily subjected to empirical tests and disconfirmation.

This connection between a perceived crisis and complex learning (Checkel in this book) or identity change (Marcussen *et al.* in this book), argues Moravcsik, is not distinct from constructivism at all. Any instrumentally rational policy-maker should change her ideas when faced with real world events undermining confidence in these ideas. We agree with Moravcsik that a rationalist account – in this case liberal intergovernmentalism – can explain a change in ideas about strategies (preferences over strategies, to use rational choice language). But neither Checkel nor Marcussen *et al.* are concerned with changes in strategies. We claim instead that 'critical junctures' lead to changes in actors' ideas about their underlying interests and to changes in their collective identities. Rationalist accounts including liberal inter-governmentalism bracket and exogenize these interests and identities, while constructivism tries to bring them into the light of investigation. This is indeed the core of constructivist reasoning (see, for example, Kratochwil and Ruggie 1986).

The problematic rationalist tendency of bracketing interests and identities has been sufficiently demonstrated by Offe and Wiesenthal's seminal work on the 'two logics of collective action' (Offe and Wiesenthal 1979). As they show, while theoretical assumptions may assert that in liberal democracies all actors are equal in principle, empirical evidence proves that despite an institutional framework which endorses the realization of the principle of equality, sociological facts demonstrate the importance of difference. In fact, the shared experience and social structure of a society contribute to whether, and if so how, actors *know* their interests. As Offe and Wiesenthal point out, the rationale of collective actors differs crucially. The difference is, however, not simply based on given interests. Instead, it changes according to experience, i.e. position in relation to other actors and in relation to larger social structures. Depending on where actors stand, so to speak, it may appear rational to improve the rules of the game or, quite differently, not only to improve the rules of the game but change them altogether (Offe and Wiesenthal 1979: 94). Critical junctures such as the crumbling of long-time stable social structures are thus likely to cause profound changes in the perception of identity and interests.[6]

Of course, such claims about the effects of critical junctures are themselves subject to empirical evaluation and can be disconfirmed. It is here that we readily accept the limits of recent theorizing about social learning or collective identities. Why is it, for example, that the end of the Cold War led to a profound identity crisis among French political élites, while we cannot discern a similar effect among the German élites? How can the moment of critical juncture be precisely specified? For the time being, our claims are limited to stating that the impact of a juncture will be critical once certain core conditions for stable identities are destabilized. While a number of conditions can be named by drawing on recurring examples known from contingent events in history, at this stage of middle-range theory building, it is only possible to state that the particular power of a critical juncture lies in its 'unexpect-edness', i.e. critical junctures are different in varying historical contexts. We do not yet have good propositions about the conditions under which actors perceive external events as 'critical' for their collective identities. Identifying critical junc-tures and making more specific claims about their characteristic impact on politics is thus one issue on the future constructivist research agenda that provides an inter-esting challenge for further debates on the middle ground.

NOTES

1   We thank Thomas Christiansen for comments on an earlier draft. Responsibility for this version rests with the authors.
2   The 'middle ground' imagery is, of course, taken from Emmanuel Adler's article (Adler 1997b).
3   The term 'rationalism' is frequently used to connote rational choice approaches. However, rational choice only theorizes about one particular type of rationality characterized by the logic of consequentialism. Arguing and rule-guided behaviour concern different types of rationality. To use 'rationalism' exclusively for rational choice approaches is, therefore, problematic.
4   See Tilly 1975; Skocpol 1992; Thelen and Steinmo 1992; Pierson 1996; Wiener 1998a.
5   See also, albeit from a normative standpoint, the contribution by Shaw (1999).
6   Further to work by constructivists in international relations theories which has demonstrated the impact of norms in global politics (Klotz 1995; Katzenstein 1996a), European integration theorists have begun to chart ways of showing the impact of the constitutive force of norms in European integration. See, for example, Jachtenfuchs et al. (1998) who demonstrate the mutually constitutive impact of norms, identifying 'polity-ideas' as normative structures that are not only significant in the actors' perception of their own identity position during the process of European integration, but which are also (re)produced by actors.

Bibliography

Abrams, Dominic and Hogg, Michael A. (eds) (1990) *Social Identity Theory*, Brighton: Harvester Wheatsheaf.

Abu-Lughod, J.L. (1989) *Before European Hegemony: The World System AD 1250–1350*, New York: Oxford University Press.

Adler, Emmanuel (1997) 'Seizing the middle ground: constructivism in world politics', *European Journal of International Relations* 3: 319–63.

Adler, Emanuel (1997a) 'Imagined (security) communities: cognitive regions in international relations', *Millennium: Journal of International Studies* 26: 249–77.

Adler, Emanuel (1997b) 'Seizing the middle ground: constructivism in world politics', *European Journal of International Relations* 3: 319–63.

Adler, Emanuel and Barnett, Michael (1996) 'Governing anarchy: a research agenda for the study of security communities', *Ethics and International Affairs* 10: 63–98.

Adler, Emanuel and Barnett, Michael (eds) (1998) *Security Communities*, Cambridge: Cambridge University Press.

Adonis, Andrew (1991) 'Subsidiarity: theory of a new federalism?', in Preston King and Andrea Bosco (eds), *A Constitution for Europe: A Comparative Study of Federal Constitutions and Plans for the United States of Europe*, London: Lothian Foundation Press, pp. 63–73.

Agence Europe (1990) *Agence Europe Documents* 1746/1747.

Allen, David (1982) 'Political cooperation and the Euro-Arab dialogue', in David Allen, Reinhardt Rummel and Wolfgang Wessels (eds), *European Political Cooperation: Towards a Foreign Policy for Western Europe*, London: Butterworth.

Allen, David and Smith, Michael (1991) 'Western Europe's presence in the contemporary international arena', in Martin Holland (ed.), *The Future of European Political Cooperation. Essays on Theory and Practice*, London: Macmillan.

Allen, David and Wallace, William (1982) 'European political cooperation: the historical and contemporary background', in David Allen, Reinhardt Rummel and Wolfgang Wessels (eds), *European Political Cooperation: Towards a Foreign Policy for Western Europe*, London: Butterworth.

Allen, David, Rummel, Reinhardt and Wessels, Wolfgang (eds) (1982) *European Political Cooperation: Towards a Foreign Policy for Western Europe*, London: Butterworth.

Allin, Dana (1995) 'Can containment work again?', *Survival* 37(1): 53–65.

Althusius, Johannes (1964) *Politica Methodice Digesta, Atque Exemplis Sacris et Profanis Illustrata*, 3rd edn, translated in Frederick S. Carney (ed.), *The Politics of Johannes Althusius*, Boston: Beacon Press.

Amin, Ash and Thrift, Nigel (1994) 'Holding down the global', in A. Amin and N. Thrift (eds), *Globalization, Institutions and Regional Development in Europe*, Oxford: Oxford University Press.

Anderson, Benedict (1983) *Imagined Communities. Reflections on the Origin and Spread of Nationalism*, London: Verso.

Anderson, James (1996) 'The shifting stage of politics: new medieval and postmodern territorialities?', *Environment and Planning D: Society and Space* 14: 133–53.

Anderson, K. and Blackhurst, R. (eds) (1993) *Regional Integration and the Global Trading System*, New York: Harvester Wheatsheaf.

Ando, Salvo (1993) 'Preparing the ground for an Alliance peacekeeping role', *NATO Review* 41(2): 4–9.

Appadurai, A. (1990) 'Disjuncture and difference in the global cultural economy', in M. Featherstone (ed.), *Global Culture: Nationalism, Globalization and Modernity*, London: Sage.

Archer, Margaret (1982) 'Morphogenesis versus structuration: on combining structure and action', *The British Journal of Sociology* 33: 455–83.

Armingeon, Klaus (1997) 'The capacity to act: European national governments and the European Commission', in A. Landau and R. Whitman (eds), *Rethinking the European Union: Institutions, Interests and Identities*, Basingstoke: Macmillan.

Armstrong, H. (1993) 'Subsidiarity and the operation of European Community regional policy in Britain', *Regional Studies* 27: 575–606.

Armstrong, Kenneth (1998a) 'New institutionalism and European Union legal studies', in Paul Craig and Carol Harlow (eds), *Lawmaking in the European Union*, London: Kluwer Law International.

Armstrong, Kenneth (1998b) 'Legal integration: theorizing the legal dimension of European integration', *Journal of Common Market Studies* 36: 155–74.

Armstrong, Kenneth and Bulmer, Scott (1998) *The Governance of the Single European Market*, Manchester: Manchester University Press.

Armstrong, Kenneth and Shaw, Jo (1998) 'Integrating law: an introduction', *Journal of Common Market Studies* 36: 147–54.

Ashley, Richard K. (1989) 'Living on border lines: man, poststructuralism, and war', in James Der Derian and Michael J. Shapiro (eds), *International/Intertextual Relations: Postmodern Readings of World Politics*, New York, NY: Lexington Books.

Asmus, R., Kugler, R. and Larrabee, F.S. (1995) 'NATO expansion: the next steps', *Survival* 37(1): 7–33.

Aspin, Les (1994) 'New Europe, new NATO', *NATO Review* 42(1): 12–14.

Aspinwall, Mark and Schneider, Gerald (2000) 'Same menus, separate tables? The institutionalist turn in Political Science and the study of European integration', *European Journal of Political Research* 38(1), 1–36

Austin, J.L. (1962) *How to do Things with Words*, Oxford: Clarendon Press.

Austin, John L. (1975) *How to Do Things with Words: The William James Lectures Delivered at Harvard University in 1955*, edited by James O. Urmson and Marina Sbisà, London: Oxford University Press.

Avery, Graham and Cameron, Fraser (1998) *The Enlargement of the European Union*, Sheffield: Sheffield Academic Press.

Axtmann, Roland (1998) 'Globalization, Europe and the state: introductory reflections', in Roland Axtmann (ed.), *Globalization and Europe. Theoretical and Empirical Investigations*, London: Pinter.

Bailey, Richard (1983) *The European Connection: Implications of EEC Membership*, Oxford: Pergamon Press.

Bakke, E. (1995) *Towards a European Identity? (Working Paper No.10)*, Oslo: ARENA.

Banchoff, Thomas (1997) 'German policy toward the European Union: a constructivist perspective'. Paper presented at International Studies Association, Annual Meeting, March, Toronto, Canada.

Banchoff, Thomas and Smith, Mitchell (eds) (1999) *Legitimacy and the European Union: The Contested Polity*, London: Routledge.

Bańkowski, Zenon (1994) 'Comment on Weiler', in Simon Bulmer and Andrew Scott (eds), *Economic and Political Integration in Europe: Internal Dynamics and Global Context*, Oxford: Blackwell.

Bańkowski, Zenon and Christodoulidis, Emilios (1998) 'The European Union as an essentially contested project', *European Law Journal* 4: 341–54.

Bańkowski, Zenon and Scott, Andrew (1996) 'The European Union?', in Richard Bellamy (ed.), *Constitutionalism, Democracy and Sovereignty: American and European Perspectives*, Aldershot: Avebury Press.

Banting, Keith and Simeon, Richard (1985) 'Introduction: the politics of constitutional change', in Keith Banting and Richard Simeon (eds), *The Politics of Constitutional Change in Industrial Nations: Redesigning the State*, London: Macmillan.

Barav, Ami (1980) 'The judicial power of the European Economic Community', *Southern California Law Review* 53: 461–525.

Baring, Arnulf (1969) *Aussenpolitik in Adenauers Kanzlerdemokratie. Bonns Beitrag zur Europaeischen Verteidigungsgemeinschaft*, München-Wien.

Bartram, Graham (1996) 'Reconstructing the past in post-war European culture: a comparative approach', in G. Bartram, M. Slawinski and D. Steel (eds), *Reconstructing the Past*, Keele: Keele University Press.

Bates, Robert H. (1996) 'Institutions as investments', *Development Discussion Paper No. 527*, Cambridge, MA: Harvard Institute for International Development.

Baylis, John and Smith, Steve (eds) (1997) *The Globalization of World Politics*, Cambridge: Cambridge University Press.

Bédarida, François (1994) 'France and Europe – from yesterday to today', in Wolfgang J. Mommsen (ed.), *The Long Way to Europe – Historical Observations from a Contemporary View*, Chicago: Edition Q, Inc.

Behnke, Andreas (1996) 'Ten years after: the state of the art of regime theory', *Cooperation and Conflict* 30: 179–97.

Bellamy, Richard and Castiglione, Dario (1996a) *Constitutionalism in Transformation: European and Theoretical Perspectives*, Oxford: Blackwell.

Bellamy, Richard and Castiglione, Dario (1996b) 'Introduction: constitutions and politics', in Richard Bellamy and Dario Castiglione (eds), *Constitutionalism in Transformation: European and Theoretical Perspectives*, Oxford: Blackwell.

Bellamy, Richard and Castiglione, Dario (forthcoming) '"A republic, if you can keep it": the democratic deficit and the constitution of Europe', in Alain Gagnon and James Tully (eds), *Justice and Stability in Multinational Societies*, Cambridge: Cambridge University Press.

Bellamy, Richard and Warleigh, Alex (1998) 'From an ethics of integration to an ethics of participation: citizenship and the future of the European Union', *Millennium* 27: 447–70.

Bellers, Jürgen (1991) 'Sozialdemokratie und Konservatismus im Angesicht der Zukunft Europas', in Jürgen Bellers and Mechthild Winking (eds), *Europapolitik der Parteien. Konservatismus, Liberalismus und Sozialdemokratie im Ringen um die Zukunft Europas* Frankfurt a.m.: Lang.

Benavides, P. (1997) 'Globalization and the energy sector: environmental challenges and options for future action'. Speech delivered to the Fourth Environmental Northern Seas Conference.

Ben Ze'ev, Aron (1995) 'Is there a problem in explaining cognitive progress?', in Robert F. Goodman and Walter R. Fisher (eds), *Rethinking Knowledge. Reflections Across the Disciplines*, New York: SUNY Press.

Berger, Peter L. and Luckmann, Thomas (1966) *The Social Construction of Reality*, London: Penguin Press.

Bernstein, Richard J. (1976) *The Restructuring of Social and Political Theory*, Oxford: Basil Blackwell.

Beyers, Jan (1998) 'Where does supranationalism come from? The ideas floating through the Working Groups of the Council of the European Union'. Paper presented at the Third Pan-European Conference on International Relations.

Beyers, Jan and Dierickx, Guido (1997) 'Nationality and European negotiations: the working groups of the Council of Ministers', *European Journal of International Relations* 3: 435–71.

Beyers, Jan and Dierickx, Guido (1998) 'The working croups of the Council of the European Union: supranational or intergovernmental negotiations?', *Journal of Common Market Studies* 36: 289–317.

Bjøl, Erling (1966) *La France devant l'Europe*, Copenhagen: Munksgaard.

Bloed, A. (ed.) (1990) *From Helsinki to Vienna: Basic Documents of the Helsinki Process*, Dordrecht: Martinus Nijhoff.

Blumer, Herbert (1969) *Symbolic Interactionism. Perspective and Method*, Berkeley: University of California Press.

Bodin, Jean (1967) *Six Books of the Commonwealth*, translated by Jean Tooley, Oxford: Oxford University Press.

Bowie, Robert R. and Friedrich, Carl J. (eds) (1954) *Studies in Federalism*, Boulder, CO: Little, Brown & Co.

Boyer, R. (1996) 'The convergence hypothesis revisited: globalization but still the century of nations', in S. Berger and R. Dore (eds), *National Diversity and Global Capitalism*, Ithaca, NY: Cornell University Press.

Boyer, R. and Drache, D. (eds) (1996) *States Against Markets*, London: Routledge.

Bressand, A. (1990) 'Beyond interdependence: 1992 as a global challenge', *International Affairs* 66: 47–65.

Bressand, A. and Nicolaidis, K. (1990) 'Regional integration in a networked world economy', in William Wallace (ed.), *The Dynamics of European Integration*, London: Pinter/RIIA.

Bretherton, Charlotte and Vogler, Jeanette (1999) *The European Union as a Global Actor* (Routledge: London).

Breton, Raymond (1995) 'Identification in transnational political communities', in K. Knop, S. Ostry, R. Simeon and K. Swinton (eds), *Rethinking Federalism: Citizens, Markets, and Governments in a Changing World*, Vancouver: University of British Columbia Press.

Brittan, Sir Leon (1997a) 'Globalization: responding to new political and moral challenges', Address to World Economic Forum, Davos.

Brittan, Sir Leon (1997b) 'Globalization vs. sovereignty? The European response', Rede Lecture, Cambridge University.

Brittan, Sir Leon (1998) 'Speaking notes of the Rt Hon. Sir Leon Brittan QC, Vice-President of the European Commission: The challenges of the global economy for Europe', Vlerick Annual Alumni Meeting, Ghent.

Brown, M.E. (1995) 'The flawed logic of NATO expansion', *Survival* 37(1): 34–52.

Bruce, Erika (1994) 'NATO's information activities at a time of increasing demands and dwindling resources', *NATO Review* 42(4): 17–19.

Bull, Hedley (1977) *The Anarchical Society: A Study of Order in World Politics*, New York: Columbia University Press.

Bulmer, Simon J. (1989) *The Changing Agenda of West German Public Policy*, Aldershot: Dartmouth.

Bulmer, Simon (1994) 'The governance of the European Union: a new institutionalist approach', *Journal of Public Policy* 13: 351–80.

Bulmer, Simon J. (1996) 'The European Council and the Council of the European Union: shapers of a European confederation', *Publius* 26: 17–42.

Bulmer, Simon J. (1997) 'New institutionalism, the single market and EU governance', *Working Paper 97/29*, Oslo: ARENA.

Bulmer, Simon J. and Scott, Andrew (eds) (1994) *Economic and Political Integration in Europe: Internal Dynamics and Global Context*, Oxford: Blackwell.

Burgess, Michael (1989) *Federalism and European Union: Political Ideas, Influences and Strategies in the European Community, 1972–1987*, London: Routledge.

Burgess, Michael (1995) *The British Tradition of Federalism*, Madison, NJ: Fairleigh Dickinson University Press.

Burley, Anne-Marie and Mattli, Walter (1993) 'Europe before the Court: a political theory of legal integration', *International Organization* 47: 41–76.

Buzan, Barry, Wæver, Ole and de Wilde, Jaap (1998) *Security: A New Framework for Analysis*, Boulder, CO: Lynne Rienner.

Cable, V. and Henderson, D. (eds) (1994) *Trade Blocs? The Future of Regional Integration*, London: RIIA.

Campbell, David (1998) 'Epilogue: the disciplinary politics of theorizing identity', *Writing Security: United States Foreign Policy and the Politics of Identity*, Minneapolis: University of Minnesota Press.

Campbell, Tom (1998) 'Legal positivism and deliberative democracy', *Current Legal Problems* 91: 69–92.

Capelletti, Mauro, Seccombe, Monica and Weiler, Joseph (1986) *Integration through Law: Europe and the American Federal Experience*, Berlin: Walter de Gruyter.

Caporaso, James A. (1996) 'The European Union and forms of state: Westphalian, regulatory or post-modern?', *Journal of Common Market Studies* 34: 29–52.

Caporaso, James A. (1998a) 'Regional integration theory: understanding our past and anticipating our future', *Journal of European Public Policy* 5: 1–16.

Caporaso, James A. (1998b) 'Regional integration theory: understanding our past and anticipating our future', in Wayne Sandholtz and Alec Stone Sweet (eds), *European Integration and Supranational Governance*, Oxford: Oxford University Press.

Caporaso, James A. and Keeler, John T.S. (1995) 'The European Union and regional integration theory', in Carolyn Rhodes and Sonia Mazey (eds), *The State of the European Union, Vol. 3: Building a European Polity?*, Boulder, CO: Lynne Rienner, pp. 29–62.

Lord Carrington (1983) 'Lack of consistent political strategy: a case of friction', *NATO Review* 31(2): 1–4.

Castiglione, Dario (1995) 'Contracts and constitutions', in Richard Bellamy *et al.* (eds), *Democracy and Constitutional Culture in the Union of Europe*, London: Lothian Foundation Press.

Cecchini, P. (with Catinat, M. and Jacquemin, A.) (1988) *The European Challenge 1992. The Benefits of a Single Market*, Aldershot: Wildwood House.

Cederman, Lars-Erik and Daase, Christopher (1998) 'Societal constructivism in world politics'. Paper prepared for delivery at the Third Pan-European International Relations Meeting of ECPR/ISA.

Chalmers, Damian (1997) 'Judicial preferences and the Community legal order', *Modern Law Review* 60: 164–99.

Chalmers, Damian (1999) 'Accounting for Europe', *Oxford Journal of Legal Studies* 19.

Checkel, Jeffrey T. (1997a) *Ideas and International Political Change: Soviet/Russian Behavior and the End of the Cold War*, New Haven: Yale University Press.

Checkel, Jeffrey T. (1997b) 'International norms and domestic politics: bridging the rationalist–constructivist divide', *European Journal of International Relations* 3: 473–95.

Checkel, Jeffrey T. (1998) 'The constructivist turn in international relations theory', *World Politics* 50: 324–48.

Checkel, Jeffrey (1999) 'Social construction and integration', *Journal of European Public Policy* 6(4): 545–60.

Checkel, Jeffrey T. (1999a) 'International institutions and socialization'. Paper presented at the International Studies Association Annual Convention.

Checkel, Jeffrey T. (1999b) 'Norms, institutions and national identity in contemporary Europe', *International Studies Quarterly* 43: 83–114.

Checkel, Jeffrey T. (2001) 'Constructing European institutions', in Mark Aspinwall and Gerald Schneider (eds), *The Rules of Integration: The Institutionalist Approach to European Studies*, Manchester: Manchester University Press.

Christiansen, Thomas (1997) 'Reconstructing European space: from territorial politics to multilevel governance', in Knud Erik Jørgensen (ed.), *Reflective Approaches to European Governance*, Basingstoke: Macmillan, pp. 51–68.

Christiansen, Thomas (1998) 'Bringing process back in: the *longue durée* of European integration', *Journal of European Integration* 21(1): 99–121.

Christiansen, Thomas and Jørgensen, Knud Erik (1999) 'The Amsterdam process: a structurationist perspective on EU treaty reform', *European Integration online Papers (EIoP)* 3: *http://eiop.or.at/eiop/texte/1999-001a.htm*

Christiansen, Thomas, Jørgensen, Knud Erik and Wiener, Antje (1999) 'The social construction of Europe', *Journal of European Public Policy* 6(4): 528–44.

Christopher, Warren (1993) 'Towards a NATO Summit', *NATO Review* 41(4): 3–6.

Chryssochoou, Dimitris (1997) 'New challenges to the study of European integration: implications for theory-building', *Journal of Common Market Studies* 35: 521–42.

Clunan, Anne L. (2000) 'Constructing concepts of identity', in Rudra Sil and Eileen Dougherty (eds), *Beyond Boundaries*, Albany: State University of New York Press.

Cohen, Joshua and Fung, Archon (1996) 'Introduction', in Joshua Cohen and Archon Fung (eds), *Constitution, Democracy and State Power: The Institutions of Justice*, Cheltenham: Edward Elgar.

Cole, Alistair (1996) 'The French Socialists', in J. Gaffney (ed.), *Political Parties and the European Union*, London: Routledge.

Cole, Alistair (1999) 'Europeanization, social democracy and the French polity: lessons from the Jospin Government'. Paper prepared for the European Community Studies Association's Sixth Biennial International Conference, 2–5 June, Pittsburgh, PA, USA.

Collin, Finn (1997) *Social Reality*, London: Routledge.

Commission of the European Communities (1985) *Completing the Internal Market: White Paper from the Commission to the Council* COM(85) 310 final.

Commission of the European Communities (1988a) *European Economy No. 36*, May.

Commission of the European Communities (1988b) 'Annual Economic Report, 1988–89: preparing for 1992', *European Economy No. 38*, November.

Commission of the European Communities (1993) *White Paper on Growth, Competitiveness and Employment: The Challenges and the Ways Forward into the 21st Century* COM(93) 700 final.

Commission of the European Communities (1995) *An Energy Policy for the European Union* COM(95) 682.

Commission of the European Communities (1996) *Energy for the Future: Renewable Sources of Energy*, Green Paper COM(96) 576.

Commission of the European Communities (1997a) *An Overall View of Energy Policy and Actions* COM(97) 167 final.

Commission of the European Communities (1997b) *Energy for the Future – Renewable Sources of Energy*, White Paper COM(97) 599 final.

Commission of the European Communities (1997c) *European Economy: Reports and Studies* No. 3/1997.

Commission of the European Communities (1997d) *Agenda 2000 – Vol. 1 – Communication for a Stronger and Wider Union* DOC/97/6.

Commission of the European Communities (1999) 'The Commission proposes an industrial policy to encourage the competitiveness of European enterprises in the face of globalization', press release IP/99/33.

Connolly, William E. (1983) *The Terms of Political Discourse*, Princeton, NJ: Princeton University Pres.

Conzelmann, Thomas (1998) 'Europeanization of regional development policies? Linking the multi-level governance approach with theories of policy learning and policy change', *European Integration Online Papers* 2(4).

Corbett, Richard (1992) 'The intergovernmental conference on political union', *Journal of Common Market Studies* 30: 271–98.

Cotterrell, Roger (1998a) 'Why must legal ideas be interpreted sociologically?', *Journal of Law and Society* 25: 171–92.

Cotterrell, Roger (1998b) 'Law and Community: a new relationship?', *Current Legal Problems* 51: 367–91.

Coudenhove-Kalergi, Richard N. (1982) [1923] *Pan-Europa*, Wien: Pan-Europa Verlag.

Cram, Laura (1997) 'The European Commission and the "European interest": institutions, interaction and preference formation in the EU context'. Paper presented at the Fifth Biennial Conference of the European Community Studies Association, Department of Government, University of Strathclyde, mimeo.

Cresson, Edith (1999) *Knowledge-based Europe: A Competitive Asset in the Face of Globalisation*, Chambre de Commerce Française de Grande-Bretagne Ltd.

Curtin, Deirdre (1993) 'The constitutional structure of the Union: a Europe of bits and pieces', *Common Market Law Review* 30: 17–69.

Curtin, Deirdre (1997) *Postnational Democracy: The European Union in Search of a Political Philosophy*, The Hague: Kluwer Law International.

Curtin, Deirdre (forthcoming) '"Civil society" and the European Union: opening spaces for deliberative democracy?', *Collected Courses of the Academy of European Law 1996*, Oxford: Oxford University Press.

Dahl, Robert (1956) *A Preface to Democratic Theory*, Chicago: University of Chicago Press.

Dannreuther, C. and Lekhi, R. (1999) 'Globalisation and the political economy of risk', International Studies Association, Annual Convention.

Darden, Keith (2000) *Origin of Economic Interests: Economic Ideas and the Formation of Regional Institutions among the Post-Soviet States* (unpublished PhD dissertation, Department of Political Science, University of California, Berkeley).

de Búrca, Gráinne (1998) 'The principle of subsidiarity and the Court of Justice as an institutional actor', *Journal of Common Market Studies* 36: 217–35.

de Carmoy, G. (1982) 'Defence and *détente*: two complementary policies', *NATO Review* 30(2): 12–17.

Defois, G. (1984) 'The Church and deterrence', *NATO Review* 32(3): 15–20.

Dehousse, Renaud (1995) 'Constitutional reform in the European Community: are there alternatives to the majoritarian avenue?', *West European Politics* 18: 118–36.

Derrida, Jacques (1977) 'Limited inc. abc···', *Glyph* 2: 162–254.

Derrida, Jacques *et al.* (1992)*The Other Heading: Reflections on Today's Europe (Studies in Continental Thought)*, Bloomington: Indiana University Press.

Dessler, David (1989) 'What's at stake in the agent–structure debate', *International Organization* 43: 441–73.

Deutsch, Karl *et al.* (1957) *Political Community and the North Atlantic Area*, Princeton, NJ: Princeton University Press.

Diez, Thomas (1995) *Neues Europa, altes Modell: Die Konstruktion von Staatlichkeit im politischen Diskurs zur Zukunft der europäischen Gemeinschaft*, Frankfurt aM: Haag & Herchen.

Diez, Thomas (1996) 'Postmoderne und europäische Integration: Die Dominanz des Staatsmodells, die Verantwortung gegenüber dem Anderen und die Konstruktion eines alternativen Horizonts', *Zeitschrift für Internationale Beziehungen* 3: 255–81.

Diez, Thomas (1997) 'International ethics and European integration: federal state or network horizon?', *Alternatives* 22: 287–312.

Diez, Thomas (1998a) 'Discursive nodal points and the analysis of European integration policy'. Paper presented at the Third Pan-European Conference on International Relations.

Diez, Thomas (1998b) *The Economic Community Reading of Europe: Its Discursive Nodal Points and Ambiguities towards 'Westphalia'*, Copenhagen: COPRI-Working Paper 6.

Diez, Thomas (1998c) 'Perspektivenwechsel', *Zeitschrift für Internationale Beziehungen* 5: 139–48.

Diez, Thomas (1999) 'Speaking "Europe": the politics of integration discourse', *Journal of European Public Policy* 6(4): 598–613.

Diez, Thomas (1999) *Die EU lesen: Diskursive Knotenpunkte in der britischen Europadebatte*, Opladen: Leske & Budrich.

DiMaggio, Paul and Powell, Walter (eds) (1991) *The New Institutionalism in Organizational Analysis*, Chicago: University of Chicago Press.

Dobbin, Frank (1994) 'Cultural models of organization: the social construction of rational organizing principles', in Diana Crane (ed.), *The Sociology of Culture: Emerging Theoretical Perspectives*, Oxford: Blackwell.

Dogan, Rhys (1997) 'Comitology: little procedures with big implications', *West European Politics* 20: 31–60.

Doty, Roxanne (1997) 'Apioria: a critical exploration of the agent-structure problematique in international relations theory', *European Journal of International Relations* 3(3): 365–92.

d'Oliveria, Hans Ulrich Jessurun (1995) 'Union citizenship: pie in the sky?', in Allan Rosas and Esko Antola (eds), *A Citizens' Europe: In Search of a New Order*, London: Sage.

Dreyfus, Hubert and Rabinow, Paul (1982) *Michel Foucault: Beyond Structuralism and Hermeneutics*, Chicago: University of Chicago Press.

Duchacek, Ivo D. (1973) *Power Maps: Comparative Politics of Constitutions*, Santa Barbara: ABC-Clio.

Duchacek, Ivo D. (1986) *The Territorial Dimension of Politics Within, Among, and Across Nations*, Boulder, CO: Westview Press.

Duchêne, François (1995) *Jean Monnet: The First Statesman of Interdependence*, New York: Norton.

Duff, Andrew (ed.) (1993) *Subsidiarity within the European Community*, London: Federal Trust.

Duff, Andrew, Pinder, John and Pryce, Roy (eds) (1994) *Maastricht and Beyond: Building the European Union*, London: Routledge.

Duffy, G., Frederking, B. and Tucker, S.A. (1998) 'Language games: dialogical analysis of INF negotiations', *International Studies Quarterly* 42(2): 271–94.

Dworkin, Ronald (1995) 'Constitutionalism and democracy', *European Journal of Philosophy* 3: 2–11.

Elazar, Daniel J. (1987) *Exploring Federalism*, Tuscaloosa, AL: University of Alabama Press.

Elazar, Daniel J. (1993) 'International and comparative federalism', *PS: Political Science and Politics* 26: 190–5.

Elazar, Daniel J. (1998) *Constitutionalizing Globalization: The Postmodern Revival of Confederal Arrangements*, Lanham, MD: Rowman & Littlefield.

Eleftheriadis, Pavlos (1996) 'Aspects of European constitutionalism', *European Law Review* 21: 32–42.

Eleftheriadis, Pavlos (1998) 'Begging the constitutional question', *Journal of Common Market Studies* 36: 255–72.

Elster, Jon (ed.) (1986) *Rational Choice*, NY: New York University Press.

Endo, Ken (1994) 'The principle of subsidiarity: from Johannes Althusius to Jacques Delors', *Hokkaido Law Review* 44: 552–652.

Engelmann-Martin, Daniela (1998) *Arbeitsbericht für die Länderstudie Bundesrepublik Deutschland*, mimeo, Florence: European University Institute.

European Council (1998) *Conclusions of the Cardiff European Council*.

Everson, Michelle (1998a) 'Administering Europe?', *Journal of Common Market Studies* 36: 195–216.

Everson, Michelle (1998b) 'Beyond the "Bundesverfassungsgericht": on the necessary cunning of constitutional reasoning', *European Law Journal* 4: 389–410.

Falkner, Gerda (1998) 'How intergovernmental are intergovernmental conferences? Lessons from the Maastricht Social Agreement'. Paper presented at the European Consortium for Political Research 26th Joint Sessions, University of Warwick.

Falkner, Gerda and Nentwich, Michael (1999) 'The Amsterdam Treaty: the blueprint for the future institutional balance?', in Karlheinz Neunreither and Antje Wiener (eds), *European Integration After Amsterdam. Institutional Dynamics and Prospects for Democracy*, Oxford: Oxford University Press.

Favell, Adrian (1998) 'The Europeanization of immigration politics'. Paper presented at ARENA Research Seminar, Oslo: Universitetet i Oslo.

Fawcett, L. and Hurrell, Andrew (eds) (1997) *Regionalism in World Politics: Regional Organization and International Order*, Oxford: Oxford University Press.

Featherstone, Kevin (1999) 'The British Labour Party from Kinnock to Blair: Europeanism and Europeanization'. Paper prepared for the European Community Studies Association's Sixth Biennial International Conference, 2–5 June, Pittsburgh, PA, USA.

Ferguson, Yale and Mansbach, Richard (1996) 'Political space and Westphalian states in a world of "polities"', *Global Governance* 2: 261–87.

Ferrajoli, Luigi (1996) 'Beyond sovereignty and citizenship: a global constitutionalism', in Richard Bellamy (ed.), *Constitutionalism, Democracy and Sovereignty: American and European Perspectives*, Aldershot: Avebury Press.

Fierke, Karin M. (1998) *Changing Games, Changing Strategies: Critical Investigations in Security*, Manchester: Manchester University Press.

Fierke, K.M. (1999) 'Dialogues of manœuvre and entanglement: NATO, Russia and the CEECs', *Millennium*, 28(1): 27–52.

Fierke, Karin and Jørgensen, Knud Erik (2001) *Constructing International Relations: The Next Generation*, Armonk, NY: M.E. Sharpe.

Financial Times (1997) 'Enlargement may test EU's treaty: the achievements of the Amsterdam Summit cannot mask the divisions that remain', 19 June.

Finnemore, Martha (1996a) *National Interests in International Society*, Ithaca, NY: Cornell University Press.

Finnemore, Martha (1996b) 'Norms, culture and world politics: insights from sociology's institutionalism', *International Organization* 50: 325–47.

Finnemore, Martha and Sikkink, Kathryn (1998) 'International norm dynamics and political change', *International Organization* 52: 887–918.

Fiske, Susan, and Taylor, Shelley E. (1991) *Social Cognition*, New York: McGraw-Hill.

Fligstein, Neil (1998) 'Institutional entrepreneurs and cultural frames: the case of the European Union's Single Market Program'. Paper presented at the Workshop on 'Ideas, Culture and Political Analysis', Center of International Studies, Princeton University.

Fligstein, Neil and Mara-Drita, I. (1996) 'How to make a market: reflections on the attempt to create a Single Market in the European Union', *American Journal of Sociology* 102: 1–33.

Florini, Ann (1996) 'The evolution of international norms', *International Studies Quarterly* 40: 363–89.

Flynn, Gregory (ed.) (1995) *The Remaking of the Hexagon: The New France in the New Europe*, Boulder, CO: Westview Press.

Forschungsgruppe Menschenrechte (1998) 'Internationale Menschenrechtsnormen, transnationale Netzwerke und politischer Wandel in den Ländern des Südens', *Zeitschrift für Internationale Beziehungen* 5: 5–42.

Forster, Anthony and Wallace, William (1996) 'Common foreign and security policy: a new policy or just a new name?', in Helen Wallace and William Wallace (eds), *Policy-Making in the European Union*, Oxford: Oxford University Press.

Forsyth, Murray (1981) *Unions of States: The Theory and Practice of Confederation*, Leicester: Leicester University Press.

Forsyth, Murray (1996) 'The political theory of federalism: the relevance of classical approaches', in Joachim Jens Hesse and Vincent Wright (eds), *Federalizing Europe? The Costs, Benefits and Preconditions of Federal Political Systems*, Oxford: Oxford University Press.

Foucault, Michel (1984) 'The order of discourse', in Michael J. Shapiro (ed.), *Language and Politics*, Oxford and Cambridge, MA.: Blackwell.

Foucault, Michel (1991) 'Politics and the study of discourse', in Graham Burchell, Colin Gordon and Peter Miller (eds), *The Foucault Effect: Studies in Governmentality*, Hemel Hempstead: Harvester Wheatsheaf.

Frank, Manfred (1983) *Was ist Neostrukturalismus?*, Frankfurt a.M.: Suhrkamp.

Friedrich, Carl J. (1968) *Trends of Federalism in Theory and Practice*, New York: Frederick A. Praeger.

Gabel, Matthew (1998) 'The endurance of supranational governance. A consociational interpretation of the European Union', *Comparative Politics* 30: 463–75.

Gablentz, Otto von der (1979) 'Luxembourg revisited or the importance of European political cooperation', *Common Market Law Review* 16: 685–99.

Gallie, W.B. (1955–6) 'Essentially contested concepts', *Proceedings of the Aristotelian Society* 56: 167–98.

Gamble, A. and Payne, A. (eds) (1996) *Regionalism and World Order*, Basingstoke: Macmillan.

Garrett, Geoffrey and Weingast, Barry R. (1993) 'Ideas, interests, and institutions. Constructing the European Community's internal market', in J. Goldstein and R.O. Keohane (eds), *Ideas and Foreign Policy: Beliefs, Institutions and Political Change*, Ithaca, NY: Cornell University Press.

Gaunt, Jeremy (1996) 'Flexible Europe is problem for EU negotiators', *The Reuter European Community Report*, 31 May.

Gazdag, F. (1992) 'Does the West understand Central and Eastern Europe?', *NATO Review* 40(6): 14–18.

George, Stephen (1991) 'European political cooperation: a world systems perspective', in Martin Holland (ed.), *The Future of European Political Cooperation. Essays on Theory and Practice*, London: Macmillan.

George, Stephen (ed.) (1992) *Britain and the European Community. The Politics of Semi-Detachment*, Oxford: Clarendon Press.

George, Stephen (1994) *An Awkward Partner. Britain in the European Community*, Oxford: Oxford University Press.

Germany (1999) *Objectives and Priorities of the German Presidency in the Council of the European Union.*

Gialdino, Carlo Curti (1995) 'Some reflections on the *acquis communautaire*', *Common Market Law Review* 32: 1089–121.

Giddens, Anthony (1983) 'Comments on the theory of structuration', *Journal for the Theory of Social Behaviour* 13: 75–80.

Giddens, Anthony (1984) *The Constitution of Society: Outline of a Theory of Structuration*, Cambridge: Polity Press.

Gierke, Otto Friedrich von (1990) [1868] *Community in Historical Perspective:*, a translation of selections from Das deutsche Genossenschaftsrecht, Cambridge: Cambridge University Press.

Gill, Stephen (1995) 'Globalisation, market civilization and disciplinary neo-liberalism', *Millennium* 24: 399–423.

Gill, Stephen (1996) 'Structural change and global political economy: globalizing élites and the emerging world order', in Y. Sakamoto (ed.), *Global Transformation: Challenges to the State System*, Tokyo: United Nations University Press.

Ginsberg, Roy H. (1989) *Foreign Policy Actions of the European Community. The Politics of Scale*, Boulder, CO: Lynne Rienner.

Glarbo, Kenneth (1998a) 'The metatheory and the IR theories of constructivism', in Knud Erik Jørgensen (ed.), *The Aarhus–Norsminde Papers: Constructivism, International Relations and European Studies*, Århus: Department of Political Science.

Glarbo, Kenneth (1998b) 'The (re)construction of a common foreign and security policy for the European Union', MA thesis, Århus: Department of Political Science.

Glaser, C.L. (1993) 'Why NATO is still best: future security arrangements for Europe', *International Security* 18(1): 5–50.

Glatzeder, Sebastian J. (1980) *Die Deutschlandpolitik der FDP in der Aera Adenauer*, Baden-Baden: Nomos.

Goldstein, Judith (1993) *Ideas, Interests and American Trade Policy*, Ithaca, NY: Cornell University Press.

Goldstein, Judith and Keohane, Robert O. (1993) 'Ideas and foreign policy: an analytical framework', in Judith Goldstein and Robert O. Keohane (eds), *Ideas and Foreign Policy. Beliefs, Institutions and Political Change*, Ithaca, NY: Cornell University Press.

Golob, I. (1996) 'Preparing for membership: Slovenia's expanding ties to NATO', *NATO Review* 44(6): 24–5.

Gould, Harry D. (1998) 'What is at stake in the agent–structure debate?' in Vendulka Kubalkova, Nicholas Onuf and Paul Kowert (eds), *International Relations in a Constructed World*, Armonk, NY: M.E. Sharpe.

Grabbe, Heather and Hughes, Kirsty (1998) *Enlarging the EU Eastwards*, London: The Royal Institute of International Affairs.

Green, David and Shapiro, Ian (1994) *Pathologies of Rational Choice Theory*, New Haven: Yale University Press.

Greilsammer, Ilan (1976) 'Theorizing European integration in its four periods', *The Jerusalem Journal of International Relations* 2: 129–56.

Groll, Götz von (1982) 'The nine at the Conference on Security and Cooperation in Europe', in David Allen, Reinhardt Rummel and Wolfgang Wessels (eds), *European Political Cooperation: Towards a Foreign Policy for Western Europe*, London: Butterworth.

Groom, A.J.R. (1978) 'Neofunctionalism: a case of mistaken identity', *Political Science* 30: 15–28.

Guzzini, Stefano (2000) 'A reconstruction of constructivism in international relations', *European Journal of International Relations*, 6(2): 147–82.

Haas, Ernst B. (1958) *The Uniting of Europe: Political, Social, and Economic Forces 1950–57*, Stanford, CA: Stanford University Press.

Haas, Ernst B. (1964) *Beyond the Nation-State. Functionalism and International Organization*, Stanford, CA: Stanford University Press.

Haas, Ernst B. (1967) 'The uniting of Europe and the uniting of Latin America', *Journal of Common Market Studies*, pp. 315–43.

Haas, Ernst B. (1971) 'The study of regional integration', in Leon N. Lindberg and Stuart A. Scheingold (eds), *Regional Integration*, Cambridge: Harvard University Press, pp. 3–44.

Haas, Ernst B. (1975) *The Obsolescence of Regional Integration Theory*, Berkeley: University of California, Institute of International Studies, Research Series No. 25.

Haas, Ernst B. (1976) 'Turbulent fields and the study of regional integration', *International Organization* 30: 173–212.

Haas, Ernst B. (1980) 'Why collaborate?', *World Politics*, 32(3): 357–405.

Haas, Ernst B. (1990) *When Knowledge is Power*, Berkeley: University of California Press.

Haas, Ernst B. (1997) 'Nationalism, liberalism, and progress', *The Rise and Decline of Nationalism I*, Ithaca, NY: Cornell University Press.

Haas, Ernst B. and Philippe, Schmitter (1964) 'Economics and differential patterns of political integration', *International Organization*, pp. 705–37.

Haas, Peter (1990) *Saving the Mediterranean: The Politics of International Environmental Cooperation*, New York: Columbia University Press.

Haas, Peter (1992) 'Knowledge, power and international policy coordination', *International Organization* 46. Special issue.

Habermas, Jürgen (1984) *The Theory of Communicative Action, Vol. 1: Reason and the Rationalization of Society*, Boston: Beacon Press.

Habermas, Jürgen (1990) *Moral Consciousness and Communicative Action*, Cambridge: Polity Press.

Habermas, Jürgen (1992) 'Staatsbürgerschaft und nationale Identität', in Jürgen Habermas (ed.), *Faktizität und Geltung*, Frankfurt a. M.: Suhrkamp.

Habermas, Jürgen (1992a) 'Citizenship and national identity: some reflections on the future of Europe', *Praxis International* 12: 1–19.

Habermas, Jürgen (1992b) 'Staatsbürgerschaft und nationale Identität', in Jürgen Habermas,

Faktizität und Geltung: Beiträge zur Diskurstheorie des Rechts und des demokratischen Rechtsstaats, Frankfurt a.M.: Suhrkamp, pp. 632–60.

Habermas, Jürgen (1996) *Between Facts and Norms: Contributions to a Discourse Theory of Law and Democracy*, Cambridge: Polity Press.

Hacker, P.M.S. (1996) *Wittgenstein's Place in Twentieth-Century Analytic Philosophy*, Oxford: Blackwell.

Hall, Peter (1993) 'Policy paradigms, social learning and the state: the case of economic policymaking in Britain', *Comparative Politics* 25: 279–96.

Hall, Peter and Taylor, Rosemary (1996) 'Political science and the three new institutionalisms', *Political Studies* 44: 936–57.

Hanrieder, Wolfram F. (1995) *Deutschland, Europa, Amerika: Die Aussenpolitik der Bundesrepublik 1949–1994*, Paderborn: Schoeningh.

Hansard (1961) *Parliamentary Debates, House of Commons, Official Report, Fifth Series*, Vol. 645 (2–3 August): European Economic Community.

Hansen, Roger D. (1969) 'Regional integration: reflections on a decade of theoretical efforts', *World Politics* 31: 242–71.

Harden, Ian and Lewis, Norman (1986) *The Noble Lie: The British Constitution and the Rule of Law*, London: Hutchinson.

Hartley, Trevor (1999) *Constitutional Problems of the European Union*, Oxford: Hart Publishing.

Harvey, Colin (1997) 'The procedural paradigm of law and democracy', *Public Law*: 692–703.

Hattam, Victoria (1993) *Labor Visions and State Power: The Origins of Business Unionism in the United States*, Princeton: Princeton University Press.

Havel, Vaclav (1991) 'Address to the NATO Council', *NATO Review* 39(2): 31–5.

Hay, Colin and Watson, Matthew (1998) *Globalisation and the Logic of No Alternative: Rendering the Contingent Necessary in the Downsizing of New Labour's Aspirations for Government*, Department of Political Science and International Studies, University of Birmingham, mimeo.

Hayek, Friedrich A. (1945) 'The use of knowledge in society', *American Economic Review* 35: 519–30.

Hayek, Friedrich A. (1979) 'The errors of constructivism', *New Studies in Philosophy, Politics, Economics and the History of Ideas*, Chicago: University of Chicago Press.

Heater, Derek (1992) *The Idea of European Unity*, New York: St Martin's Press.

Hejl, Peter M. (1987) 'Konstruktion der sozialen Konstruktion: Grundlinien einer konstruktivistischen Sozialtheorie', in Siegfried J. Schmidt (ed.), *Der Diskurs des radikalen Konstruktivismus*, Frankfurt a.M.: Suhrkamp, pp. 303–39.

Held, David and Thompson, John B. (eds) (1989) *Social Theory of Modern Societies: Anthony Giddens and His Critics*, Cambridge: Cambridge University Press.

Helfer, Laurence and Slaughter, Anne-Marie (1997) 'Toward a theory of effective supranational adjudication', *Yale Law Journal* 107: 273–391.

Hellmann, Gunther (1996) 'Goodbye Bismarck? The foreign policy of contemporary Germany', *Mershon Review of International Studies* 40: 1–39.

Hesse, Joachim Jens and Wright, Vincent (eds) (1996) *Federalizing Europe? The Costs, Benefits and Preconditions of Federal Political Systems*, Oxford: Oxford University Press.

Higgott, Richard (1997) '*De facto* and *de jure* regionalism: the double discourse of regionalism in the Asia Pacific', *Global Society* 11: 169–89.

Higgott, Richard (1998) 'The international political economy of regionalism: the Asia-Pacific and Europe compared', in W.D. Coleman and G.R.D. Underhill (eds), *Regionalism and Global Economic Integration: Europe, Asia and the Americas*, London: Routledge.

Higgott, Richard and Reich, Simon (1998) *Globalisation and Sites of Conflict: Towards a Definition and Taxonomy*, University of Warwick, CSGR Working Paper 01/98.

Higgott, Richard and Stubbs, Richard (1995) 'Competing conceptions of economic regionalism: APEC versus EAEC in Asia', *Review of International Political Economy* 2: 516–35.

Hill, Christopher (1996a) 'United Kingdom: sharpening contradictions', in Christopher Hill (ed.), *The Actors in Europe's Foreign Policy*, London: Routledge.

Hill, Christopher (ed.) (1996b) *The Actors in Europe's Foreign Policy*, London: Routledge.

Hill, Christopher and Wallace, William (1996) 'Introduction: actors and actions', in Christopher Hill (ed.), *The Actors in Europe's Foreign Policy*, London: Routledge.

Himsworth, Chris (1996) 'In a state no longer? The end of constitutionalism', *Public Law* 1996: 639–60.

Hindess, Barry (1996) *Discourses of Power: From Hobbes to Foucault*, Oxford and Cambridge, MA.: Blackwell.

Hirschman, Albert O. (1970) *Exit, Voice and Loyalty: Responses to Decline in Firms, Organizations and States*, Cambridge, MA: Harvard University Press.

Hirst, Paul (1997) *From Statism to Pluralism: Democracy, Civil Society and Global Politics*, London: UCL Press.

Hirst, Paul and Thompson, G. (1996) *Globalization in Question*, Cambridge: Polity.

Hix, Simon (1994) 'The study of the European Community: the challenge to comparative politics', *West European Politics* 17: 1–30.

Hix, Simon (1998) 'The study of the European Union II: the 'new governance' agenda and its rival', *Journal of European Public Policy* 5: 38–65.

Hoffmann, Stanley (1966) 'Obstinate or obsolete? The fate of the nation state and the case of Western Europe', *Daedalus* 95: 862–915.

Hoffmann, Stanley (1974) 'De Gaulle's foreign policy: the stage and the play, the power and the glory', in Stanley Hoffmann (ed.), *Decline or Renewal? France since the 1930s*, New York: Viking Press, pp. 283–333.

Holland, Martin (ed.) (1991a) *The Future of European Political Cooperation. Essays on Theory and Practice*, London: Macmillan.

Holland, Martin (1991b) 'Introduction: EPC theory and empiricism', in Martin Holland (ed.), *The Future of European Political Cooperation. Essays on Theory and Practice*, London: Macmillan.

Hollis, Martin and Smith, Steve (1990) *Explaining and Understanding International Relations*, Oxford: Clarendon.

Holm, Ulla (1993) *Det Franske Europa*, Aarhus: Aarhus University Press.

Holm, Ulla (1997) 'The French garden is no longer what it used to be', in Knud Erik Jørgensen (ed.), *Reflective Approaches to European Governance*, Basingstoke: Macmillan, pp. 128–45.

Holst, J.J. (1992) 'Pursuing a durable peace in the aftermath of the Cold War', *NATO Review* 40(4): 9–13.

Honneth, Axel (1995) *The Fragmented World of the Social: Essays in Social and Political Philosophy*, Albany, NY: State University of New York Press.

Hont, Istvan (1994) 'The permanent crisis of a divided mankind: contemporary crisis of the nation-state in historical perspective', *Political Studies* 42 (special issue): 166–231.

Hooghe, Liesbet (1998) 'Euro-socialists or Euro-marketeers? EU top officials on capitalism'. Paper presented at the Workshop on 'The Rules of Integration: An Assessment of the Institutionalist Turn in European Studies', Universität Konstanz.

Hooghe, Liesbet and Marks, Gary (1996) '"Europe with the regions": channels of regional representation in the European Union', *Publius: The Journal of Federalism* 26: 73–92.

Hooghe, Liesbet and Marks, Gary (1999) 'The making of a polity', in H. Kitschelt, G. Marks, J. Stephens (eds), *Continuity and Change in Contemporary Capitalism*, New York: Cambridge University Press.

Howe, Paul (1995) 'A community of Europeans: the requisite underpinnings', *Journal of Common Market Studies* 33: 33–46.

Howe, Paul (1997) 'Insiders and outsiders in a community of Europeans: a reply to Kostakopoulou', *Journal of Common Market Studies* 37: 309–15.

Hrbek, Rudolf (1972) *Die SPD, Deutschland und Europa. Die Haltung der Sozialdemokratie zum Verhaeltnis von Deutschland-Politik und Westintegration (1945–1957)*, Bonn: Europa Union Verlag.

Hüglin, Thomas (1991) *Sozietaler Foederalismus: Die Politische Theorie des Johannes Althusius*, Berlin: Walter de Gruyter.

Hüglin, Thomas (1994) 'Federalism, subsidiarity and the European tradition: some clarifications', *Telos* 100: 37–55.

Hurley, Susan (1989) *Natural Reasons. Personality and Polity*, New York and Oxford: Oxford University Press.

Hurrell, Andrew and Menon, Anand (1996) 'Politics like any other? Comparative politics, international relations and the study of the EU', *West European Politics* 19: 386–402.

Huysmans, Jef (1998) 'Revisiting Copenhagen, or: About the "creative development" of a security studies agenda in Europe', *European Journal of International Relations* 4: 479–508.

Hyde-Pryce, Adrian (1997) 'The new pattern of international relations in Europe', in Alice Landau and Richard Whitman (eds), *Rethinking the European Union: Institutions, Interests and Identities*, Basingstoke: Macmillan.

Ifestos, P. (1987) *European Political Cooperation. Towards a Framework of Supranational Diplomacy?*, Aldershot: Avebury.

Ignatenko, A. (1994) 'American diplomacy is stepping up its activity on Russia's southern borders', *Nezavisimaya gazeta*, in *Current Digest of the Post-Soviet Press* 10.

Immergut, Ellen (1992) *Health Politics: Institutions and Interests in Western Europe*, New York: Cambridge University Press.

'The implementation of the final act of the CSCE', (1976) *NATO Review* 24(2): 19–22.

Jachtenfuchs, Markus (1995) 'Theoretical perspectives on European governance', *European Law Journal* 1: 115–33.

Jachtenfuchs, Markus (1997a) 'Conceptualizing European governance', in Knud Erik Jørgensen (ed.), *Reflective Approaches to European Governance*, Basingstoke: Macmillan.

Jachtenfuchs, Markus (1997b) 'Die Europäische Union – ein Gebilde sui generis?', in Klaus Dieter Wolf (ed.), *Projekt Europa im Übergang: Probleme, Modelle und Strategien des Regierens in der Europäischen Union*, Baden-Baden: Nomos, pp. 15–35.

Jachtenfuchs, Markus and Kohler-Koch, Beate (1996) 'Regieren im dynamischen Mehrebenensystem', in Markus Jactenfuchs and Beate Kohler-Koch (eds), *Europäische Integration*, Opladen: Leske & Budrich, pp. 15–44.

Jachtenfuchs, Markus, Diez, Thomas and Jung, Sabine (1998) 'Which Europe? Conflicting models of a legitimate European political order', *European Journal of International Relations* 4(4): 409–45.

Jacobson, John K. (1995) 'Much ado about ideas: the cognitive factor in economic policy', *World Politics* 47: 283–310.

Jacquemin, Alexis and Wright, David (eds) (1993) *The European Challenge Post-1992; Shaping Factors, Shaping Actors*, Aldershot: Edward Elgar.

Jakobsen, Peter Viggo (1997) 'The twelve and the crises in the Gulf and northern Iraq 1990–1991', in Knud Erik Jørgensen (ed.), *European Approaches to Crisis Management*, The Hague: Kluwer Law International.

Jeffery, Charlie and Savigear, Peter (eds) (1991) *German Federalism Today*, New York: St Martin's Press.

Jennings, W. Ivor (1949) *A Federation for Western Europe*, London: Routledge & Kegan Paul.

Jepperson, Ronald L., Wendt, Alexander and Katzenstein, Peter J. (1996) 'Norms, identity, and culture in national security', in Peter J. Katzenstein (ed.), *The Culture of National Security. Norms and Identity in World Politics*, New York: Columbia University Press, pp. 35–7.

Jeszenszky, G. (1992) 'Nothing quiet on the Eastern Front', *NATO Review* 40(3): 7–13.

Jetschke, Anja and Liese, Andrea (1998) 'Kultur im Aufwind. Zur Rolle von Bedeutungen, Werten und Handlungsrepertoires in den internationalen Beziehungen', *Zeitschrift für Internationale Beziehungen* 5: 149–79.

Joas, Ralf (1996) *Zwischen Nation und Europa. Die europapolitischen Vorstellungen der Gaullisten 1987–1994*, Bochum: Brockmeyer.

Joerges, Christian (1996) 'Integrating scientific expertise into regulatory decision-making', *EUI Working Paper RSC 96/10*, Florence: European University Institute.

Joerges, Christian and Neyer, Jürgen (1997a) 'From intergovernmental bargaining to deliberative political processes: the constitutionalisation of comitology', *European Law Journal* 3: 273–99.

Joerges, Christian and Neyer, Jürgen (1997b) 'Transforming strategic interaction into deliberative problem-solving: European comitology in the foodstuffs sector', *Journal of European Public Policy* 4: 609–25.

Johnson, James (1993) 'Is talk really cheap?: prompting conversation between critical theory and rational choice', *American Political Science Review* 87: 74–86.

Johnston, Alastair Iain (1998) 'Socialization in international institutions: the ASEAN regional forum and IR theory'. Paper presented at the Workshop on 'The Emerging International Relations of the Asia-Pacific Region', University of Pennsylvania (May).

Jørgensen, Knud Erik (1993) 'EC external relations as a theoretical challenge: theories, concepts and trends', in Frank R. Pfetsch (ed.), *International Relations and Pan-Europe*, Münster: LIT Verlag.

Jørgensen, Knud Erik (1995) 'The European Union as an international actor: the case of Yugoslavia', *Quaderni Forum* 4: 59–71.

Jørgensen, Knud Erik (1996) *Det udenrigspolitiske samarbejde i Den Europæiske Union*, Århus: Systime.

Jørgensen, Knud Erik (1997a) 'PoCo: the diplomatic republic of Europe', in Knud Erik Jørgensen (ed.), *Reflective Approaches to European Governance*, Basingstoke: Macmillan.

Jørgensen, Knud Erik (ed.) (1997b) *Reflective Approaches to European Governance*, Basingstoke: Macmillan.

Jørgensen, Knud Erik (1999) 'The social construction of the *acquis communautaire*: a cornerstone of the European edifice', *European Integration Online Papers* 6: 5.

Jørgensen (2001) 'Four levels and a discipline: towards a second generation of IR constructivism', in Karin M. Fierke and Knud Erik Jørgensen (eds) *Constructing International Relations: The Next Generation*, Armonk, NY: M.E. Sharpe.

Kaiser, Wolfram (1966) *Using Europe, Abusing the Europeans: Britain and European Integration, 1945–63*, London: Macmillan.

Kato, Junko (1996) 'Review article: Institutions and rationality in politics – three varieties of neo-institutionalists', *British Journal of Political Science* 26: 553–82.

Katzenstein, Peter J. (ed.) (1996a) *The Culture of National Security. Norms and Identity in World Politics*, New York: Columbia University Press.

Katzenstein, Peter J. (1996b) 'Introduction: Alternative perspectives on national security', in Peter J. Katzenstein (ed.), *The Culture of National Security: Norms and Identity in World Politics*, New York: Columbia University Press.

Katzenstein, Peter J. (ed.) (1997) *The Taming of German Power*, Ithaca, NY: Cornell University Press.

Katzenstein, Peter J., Keohane, Robert O. and Krasner, Stephen D. (1998) '*International Organization* and the study of world politics', *International Organization* 52: 645–85.

Keck, Margaret and Sikkink, Kathryn (1998) *Activists Beyond Borders: Transnational Advocacy Networks in International Politics*, Ithaca, NY: Cornell University Press.

Kelly, Michael (1996) 'Révolution, renaissance, redressement: representations of historical chance in post-war France', in G. Bartram, M. Slawinski and D. Steel (eds), *Reconstructing the Past*, Keele: Keele University Press.

Kelstrup, Morten (1998) 'Integration theories: history, competing approaches and new perspectives', in Anders Wivel (ed.), *Explaining European Integration*, Copenhagen: Copenhagen Political Studies Press, pp. 15–55.

Keohane, Robert O. (1988) 'International institutions: two approaches', *International Studies Quarterly* 32: 379–96.

Keohane, Robert O. and Hoffmann, Stanley (eds) (1991) *The New European Community*, Boulder, CO: Westview.

Keohane, Robert O. and Nye, Joseph S. (1974) 'Transgovernmental relations and international organizations', *World Politics* 27: 39–62.

Keohane, Robert O., Nye, Joseph S. and Hoffmann, Stanley (eds) (1993) *After the Cold War: International Institutions and State Strategies after the Cold War*, Cambridge, MA: Harvard University Press.

Kerremans, Bart (1996) 'Do institutions make a difference? Non-institutionalism, neo-institutionalism and the logic of common decision-making in the European Union', *Governance* 9: 215–40.

Keukeleire, Stephan (1994) 'The European Community and conflict management', in Werner Bauwens and Luc Reychler (eds), *The Art of Conflict Prevention*, London: Brassey's.

Kielmansegg, Peter Graf (1996) 'Integration und Demokratie', in Markus Jachtenfuchs and Beate Kohler-Koch (eds), *Europäische Integration*, Opladen: Leske & Budrich.

King, Preston (1982) *Federalism and Federation*, London: Croom Helm.

Klotz, Audie (1995) 'Norms reconstituting interests: global racial equality and US sanctions against South Africa', *International Organization* 49: 451–78.

Klotz, Audie (1995) *Norms in International Relations. The Struggle Against Apartheid*, Ithaca, NY: Cornell University Press.

Knopf, Hans Joachim (1998) *Ideas of European Political Order and the Construction of British Identity in the 1950s – Arbeitsbericht Great Britain*, mimeo, Florence: European University Institute.

Koelble, Thomas (1995) 'The new institutionalism in political science and sociology', *Comparative Politics* 27: 231–43.

Kofman, E. and Youngs, G. (eds) (1996) *Globalizaton: Theory and Practice*, London: Pinter.

Kohler, Beate (1982) 'Euro-American relations and European political cooperation', in David Allen, Reinhardt Rummel and Wolfgang Wessels (eds), *European Political Cooperation: Towards a Foreign Policy for Western Europe*, London: Butterworth.

Kohler-Koch, Beate (1993) 'Die Welt regieren ohne Weltregierung', in Carl Böhret and Göttrik Wewer (eds), *Regieren im 21. Jahrhundert – zwischen Globalisierung und Regionalisierung*, Opladen: Leske & Budrich, pp. 109–41.

Kohler-Koch, Beate (1996) 'Catching up with change: the transformation of governance in the European Union', *Journal of European Public Policy* 3: 359–80.

Kohler-Koch, Beate (1998) 'Die Europäisierung nationaler Demokratien: Verschleiß eines europäischen Kulturerbes?', in Michael Th. Greven (ed.), *Demokratie – eine Kultur des Westens?*, Opladen: Leske & Budrich, pp. 262–88.

Kohler-Koch, Beate (1999) 'The evolution and transformation of European governance', in Beate Kohler-Koch and Rainer Eising (eds), *The Transformation of Governance in the European Union*, London and New York, NY: Routledge, pp. 14–35.

Kohler-Koch, Beate and Knodt, Michele (1997) 'Multi-level governance: the joy of theorizing and the anguish of empirical research'. Paper presented at the European Consortium for Political Research, 25th Joint Sessions, Universität Bern.

Kolodziejczyk, Piotr (1994) 'Poland – a future NATO ally', *NATO Review* 42(5): 7–10.

Koslowski, Rey (1994) 'Intra-EU migration, citizenship, and political union', *Journal of Common Market Studies* 32: 369–402.

Koslowski, Rey (1998) 'EU migration regimes: established and emergent', in Christian Joppke (ed.), *Challenge to the Nation-State: Immigration in Western Europe and the United States*, Oxford: Oxford University Press.

Koslowski, Rey (1999) 'EU citizenship: implications for identity and legitimacy', in Thomas Banchoff and Mitchell Smith (eds), *Legitimacy and the European Union: The Contested Polity*, London: Routledge.

Koslowski, Rey and Kratochwil, Friedrich (1994) 'Understanding change in international politics: the Soviet empire's demise and the transformation of the international system', *International Organization* 48: 215–47.

Kostakopoulo, Theodora (1996) 'Towards a theory of constructive citizenship in Europe', *The Journal of Political Philosophy* 4: 337–58.

Kratochwil, Friedrich (1989) *Rules, Norms and Decisions: On the Conditions of Practical and Legal Reasoning in International Relations and Domestic Affairs*, Cambridge: Cambridge University Press.

Kratochwil, Friedrich (1993) 'Norms versus numbers: multilateralism and the rationalist and reflexivist approaches to institutions – a unilateral plea for communicative rationality', in J.G. Ruggie (ed.), *Multilateralism Matters: The Theory and Praxis of an Institutional Form*, New York: Columbia University Press, pp. 443–74.

Kratochwil, Friedrich (1994) 'Citizenship: the border of order', *Alternatives* 19: 485–506.

Kratochwil, Friedrich (2001) 'Constructivism as an approach to interdisciplinary study', in Karin M. Fierke and Knud Erik Jørgensen (eds) *Constructing International Relations: The Next Generation*, Armonk, NY: M.E. Sharpe.

Kratochwil, Friedrich and Ruggie, John Gerard (1986) 'International organization: a state of the art on an art of the state', *International Organization* 40: 753–75.

Kubalkova, Vendulka, Onuf, Nicholas and Kowert, Paul (1998) *International Relations in a Constructed World*, Armonk, NY: M.E. Sharpe.

Kühnhardt, Ludger (1992) 'Federalism and subsidiarity', *Telos* 91: 77–86.

Kymlicka, Will (1991) *Liberalism, Community and Culture*, Oxford: Clarendon Press.

Kymlicka, Will (1996) 'Three forms of group-differentiated citizenship in Canada', in Seyla Benhabib (ed.), *Democracy and Difference. Contesting the Boundaries of the Political*, Princeton, NJ: Princeton University Press.

Laclau, Ernesto and Mouffe, Chantal (1985) *Hegemony and Socialist Strategy: Towards a Radical Democratic Politics*, London: Verso.

Laffan, Brigid (1996) 'The politics of identity and political order in Europe', *Journal of Common Market Studies* 34: 81–102.

Laffan, Brigid (1998) 'The European Union: a distinctive model of internationalization', *Journal of European Public Policy* 5: 235–53.

Langlands, Rebecca (1999) 'Britishness or Englishness? The historical problem of national identity in Britain', *Nations and Nationalism* 5(1): 53–69.

Larsen, Henrik (1997a) *Foreign Policy and Discourse Analysis: France, Britain and Europe*, London: Routledge.

Larsen, Henrik (1997b) 'British discourses on Europe: sovereignty of Parliament, instrumentality and the non-mythical Europe', in Knud Erik Jørgensen (ed.), *Refelctive Approaches to European Governance*, Basingstoke: Macmillan, pp. 109–27.

Lash, Scott and Urry, John (1994) *Economies of Signs and Space*, London: Sage.

Laudan, Larry (1996) *Beyond Positivism and Relativism*, Boulder, CO: Westview.

Lenaerts, Koen (1992) 'Federalism and rights in the European Community'. Paper presented at the conference, Federalism and Rights, Center for the Study of Federalism, Temple University, Philadelphia.

Leonardy, Uwe (1996) 'The political dimension: German practice and the European experience', in Joachim Jens Hesse and Vincent Wright (eds), *Federalizing Europe? The Costs, Benefits and Preconditions of Federal Political Systems*, Oxford: Oxford University Press.

Levi, A. (1982) 'Western values and the successor generation', *NATO Review* 30(2): 2–7.

Levi, Lucio (1992) 'Alterio Spinelli, Mario Albertini and the Italian Federalist School: federalism as ideology', in Andrea Bosco (ed.), *The Federal Idea: The History of Federalism since 1945*, London: Lothian Foundation.

Levinson, Stephen (1983) *Pragmatics*, Cambridge: Cambridge University Press.

Levy, Jack (1994) 'Learning and foreign policy: sweeping a conceptual minefield', *International Organization* 48: 279–312.

Lijphart, Arend (1977) *Democracy in Plural Societies: A Comparative Exploration*, New Haven, CT: Yale University Press.

Lijphart, Arend (1984) *Democracies: Patterns of Majoritarian and Consensus Governmnet in Twenty-one Countries*, New Haven, CT: Yale University Press.

Lindberg, Leon N. and Scheingold, Stuart A. (1970) *Europe's Would-Be Polity. Patterns of Change in the European Community*, Englewood Cliffs: Prentice-Hall.

Linklater, Andrew (1998) *The Transformation of Political Community*, Cambridge: Polity Press.

Lipgens, Walter and Loth, Wilfried (eds) (1985) *Documents on the History of European Integration*, Berlin: Walter de Gruyter.

Lister, Frederick K. (1996) *The European Union, the United Nations and the Revival of Confederal Governance*, Westport, CT: Praeger.

Long, David (1997) 'Multilateralism in the CFSP', in Martin Holland (ed.), *Common Foreign and Security Policy: The Record and Reforms*, London: Pinter.

Longstreth, Frank *et al.* (eds) (1992) *Structuring Politics: Historical Institutionalism in Comparative Analysis*, New York: Cambridge University Press.

Lose, Lars Gert (2001) 'Communicative action and the social construction of diplomatic societies', in Karin Fierke and Knud Erik Jørgensen (eds), *Constructing International Relations: The Next Generation*, Armonk, NY: M.E. Sharpe.

Loughlin, John (1996) 'Europe of regions and the federalization of Europe', *Publius* 26: 141–62.

Loughlin, Martin (1992) *Public Law and Political Theory*, Oxford: Clarendon Press.

Lucarelli, Sonia (1997) 'Europe's response to the Yugoslav imbroglio', in Knud Erik Jørgensen (ed.), *European Approaches to Crisis Management*, The Hague: Kluwer Law International.

Lubkemeier, E. (1991) 'The political upheaval in Europe and the reform of NATO strategy', *NATO Review* 30(3): 16–21.

Luhmann, Niklas (1990) 'Verfassung als evolutionäre Errungenschaft', *Rechtshistorisches Journal* 9: 176–220.

Luhmann, Niklas (1993) *Recht der Gesellschaft*, Frankfurt/Main: Suhrkamp.

Lukes, Stephen (1974) *Power: A Radical View*, London: Macmillan.

Luns, Joseph (1976) 'The present state of East–West relations', *NATO Review* 24(2): 3–8.

Lynch, Peter (1996) *Minority Nationalism and European Integration*, Cardiff: University of Wales Press.

Lynch, Philip (1997) 'Großbritannien in der Europäischen Union – konstitutionelle Fragen', *Integration* 1: 13–23.

Lyon, David (1991) 'British identity cards: the unpalatable logic of European membership?', *The Political Quarterly* 62: 377–85.

MacCormick, Neil (1993a) 'Beyond the sovereign state', *Modern Law Review* 56: 1–18.

MacCormick, Neil (1993b) 'Constitutionalism and democracy', in Richard Bellamy (ed.), *Theories and Concepts of Politics: An Introduction*, Manchester: Manchester University Press.

MacCormick, Neil (1997) 'Democracy, subsidiarity, and citizenship in the "European Commonwealth"', *Law and Philosophy* 16: 331–56.

McGwire, Michael (1998) 'NATO expansion: "a policy error of historic importance"', *Review of International Studies* 24(1): 23–42.

McKay, David (1996) *Rush to Union: Understanding the European Federal Bargain*, Oxford: Clarendon Press.

Macmahon, Arthur W. (ed.) (1955) *Federalism: Mature and Emergent*, Garden City, NY: Doubleday & Co.

McNamara, Kathleen (1997) *Globalization is 'What We Make of It'? The Social Construction of Market Imperatives*, Princeton: Center of International Studies (mimeo).

Maher, Imelda (1998) 'Community law in the national legal order: a systems analysis', *Journal of Common Market Studies* 38: 237–54.

Mancini, G. Federico (1991) 'The making of a constitution for Europe', in Robert O. Keohane and Stanley Hoffmann (eds), *The New European Community*, Boulder, CO: Westview Press.

Mandelbaum, M. (1996) *The Dawn of Peace in Europe,* New York: The Twentieth Century Fund.

Mansfield, E.D. and Milner, H.V (eds) (1997) *The Political Economy of Regionalism*, New York: Columbia University Press.

March, James G. and Olsen, Johan P. (1989) *Rediscovering Institutions*, New York: The Free Press.

March, James G. and Olsen, Johan P. (1998) 'The institutional dynamics of international political orders', *International Organization* 52: 943–69.

Marcussen, Martin (1996) *The Power of Ideas in Integration Policy*. Paper prepared for the CORE Research Workshop, Krogerup, Denmark.

Marcussen, Martin (1998a) 'Ideas and élites. Danish macro-economic policy-discourse in the EMU process', Ph.D. thesis, *ISP Series*, No. 226, Aalborg University: Department for Development and Planning.

Marcussen, Martin (1998b) 'Central bankers, the ideational life-cycle and the social construction of EMU', *EUI Working Papers, RSC* No. 98/33, Florence: European University Institute.

Marcussen, Martin (1999) 'The dynamics of EMU ideas', *Co-operation and Conflict* 34(4).

Marks, Gary (1993) 'Structural policy and multilevel governance in the EC', in Alan W. Cafruny and Glenda Rosenthal (eds), *The State of the European Community: The Maastricht Debate and Beyond*, Harlow: Longman.

Marks, Gary, Hooge, Liesbet and Blank, Kermit (1996a) 'European integration since the 1980s. State-centric versus multi-level governance', *Journal of Common Market Studies* 34: 164–92.

Marks, Gary, Salk, Jane, Ray, Leonard and Nielsen, Francois (1996b) 'Competences, cracks and conflicts: regional mobilization in the European Union', in Gary Marks *et al.* (eds), *Governance in the European Union*, London: Sage.

Marti, Urs (1988) *Michel Foucault*, Munich: C.H. Beck.

Mattli, Walter and Slaughter, Anne-Marie (1998) 'Revisiting the European Court of Justice', *International Organization* 52: 177–209.

Mayes, David (1994) 'The future research agenda', in Simon Bulmer and Andrew Scott (eds), *Economic and Political Integration in Europe: Internal Dynamics and Global Context*, Oxford: Blackwell.

Mayhew, Alan (1998) *Recreating Europe: The European Union's Policy Towards Central and Eastern Europe*, Cambridge: Cambridge University Press.

Mead, George Herbert (1967) [1934] *Mind, Self, and Society: from the Standpoint of a Social Behaviorist*, edited by Charles W. Morris, Chicago: University of Chicago Press.

Meehan, Elizabeth (1993) *Citizenship and the European Community*, London: Sage Publications.

Melescanu, Teodor (1993) 'Security in Central Europe: a positive-sum game', *NATO Review* 41(5): 12–18.

Michalski, Anna and Wallace, Helen (1992) *The European Community: The Challenge of Enlargement*, London: The Royal Institute of International Affairs.

Michelmann, Hans J. and Soldatos, Panayotis (eds) (1994) *European Integration*, Lanham, MD: University Press of America.

Milner, Helen (1998) 'Regional economic co-operation, global markets and domestic politics: a comparison of NAFTA and the Maastricht Treaty', in W.D. Coleman and G.R.D. Underhill (eds), *Regionalism and Global Economic Integration: Europe, Asia and the Americas*, London: Routledge.

Milward, Alan S. (1993) *The European Rescue of the Nation-State*, London: Routledge.

Mitchell, Austin (1992) 'Nationhood: the end of the affair?', *The Political Quarterly* 63: 122–42.

Mittelman, James H. (1998) 'Coxian historicism as an alternative perspective in international studies', *Alternatives* 23: 63–92.

Mitterrand, François (1986) *Réflexions sur la politique extérieure de la France – introduction à vingt-cinq discours*, Paris: Fayard.

Moeller, Richard (1996) 'The German Social Democrats', in J. Gaffney (ed.), *Political Parties and the European Union*, London: Routledge.

Moltke, Gebhardt von (1996) 'NATO moves toward enlargement', *NATO Review* 44(1): 3–6.

Monnet, Jean (1976) *Mémoires*, Paris: Fayard.

Moravcsik, Andrew (1991) 'Negotiating the Single European Act', in Robert Keohane and Stanley Hoffmann (eds), *The New European Community*, Boulder, CO: Westview Press.

Moravcsik, Andrew (1993) 'Preferences and power in the European Community: a liberal intergovernmentalist approach', *Journal of Common Market Studies* 31: 473–524.

Moravcsik, Andrew (1997) 'Taking preferences seriously: a liberal theory of international politics', *International Organization* 51: 513–53.

Moravcsik, Andrew (1998) *The Choice for Europe: Social Purpose and State Power from Messina to Maastricht*, London: UCL Press.

Moravcsik, Andrew (2000) 'Grain and grandeur: the economic origins of de Gaulle's European policy', *Journal of Cold War History*, 2(2): 3–43.

Moravcsik, Andrew and Nicolaïdis, Kalypso (1998) 'Federal ideals and constitutional realities in the Treaty of Amsterdam', *Journal of Common Market Studies, Annual Review* 36: 13–38.

Morgan, Roger (1980) 'Integrative ideas', *Government and Opposition* 1: 107–12.

Morison, John and Livingstone, Stephen (1995) *Reshaping Public Power: Northern Ireland and the British Constitutional Crisis*, London: Sweet & Maxwell.

Müller, Harald (1992) 'German foreign policy after unification', in P.B. Stares (ed.), *The New Germany and the New Europe*, Washington, DC: Brookings Institution.

Müller, Harald (1994) 'Internationale Beziehungen als kommunikatives Handeln', *Zeitschrift für Internationale Beziehungen* 1: 15–44.

Müller, Harald (2001) 'International relations as communicative action', in Karin M. Fierke and Knud Erik Jørgensen (eds) *Constructing International Relations: The Next Generation*, Armonk, NY: M.E. Sharpe.

Nadelmann, Ethan (1990) 'Global prohibition regimes: the evolution of norms in international society', *International Organization* 44: 479–526.

Nathan, Richard (1991) 'Implications for federalism of European integration', in Norman J. Ornstein and Mark Perlman (ed.), *Political Power and Social Change: The United States Faces a United Europe*, Washington, DC: The AEI Press.

Nelsen, Brent F. and Stubb, Alexander C.-G. (eds) (1998) *The European Union*, Boulder: Lynne Rienner.

Nentwich, Michael and Weale, Albert (eds) (1998) *Political Theory and the European Union*, London: Routledge.

Neumann, Iver (1996) 'Self and other in international relations', *European Journal of International Relations* 2: 139–74.

Neumann, Iver (1998) 'European identity, EU expansion, and the integration/exclusion nexus', *Alternatives* 23: 397–416.

Neumann, Iver and Welsh, Jennifer (1991) 'The "other" in European identity: an addendum to the literature on international society', *Review of International Studies* 17: 327–45.

Neumann, Iver and Wæver, Ole (eds) (1997) *The Future of International Relations: Masters in the Making*. London and New York: Routledge, p. 165.

Neunreither, Karl-Heinz (1993) 'Subsidiarity as a guiding principle for European Community activities', *Government and Opposition* 28: 206–20.

Newhouse, John (1997) 'Europe's rising regionalism', *Foreign Affairs* 76: 67–84.

Nimetz, M. (1980) 'CSCE: looking to Madrid', *NATO Review* 29(2): 6–8.

Nuttall, Simon (1992) *European Political Co-operation*, Oxford: Clarendon Press.

Nuttall, Simon (1997) 'Two decades of EPC performance', in Elfriede Regelsberger, Philippe de Schoutheete de Tervarent and Wolfgang Wessels (eds), *Foreign Policy of the European Union. From EPC to CFSP and Beyond*, Boulder, CO: Lynne Rienner.

Oakes, Penelope J., Haslam, S. Alexander and Turner, John C. (1994) *Stereotyping and Social Reality*, Oxford: Blackwell.

Obradovic, Daniela (1997) 'Eligibility of non-state actors to participate in European Union policy formation'. Paper presented at the Workshop on 'Non-state Actors and Authority in the Global System', University of Warwick.

Offe, Claus and Wiesenthal, Helmut (1979) 'Two logics of collective action: theoretical notes on social class and organizational form', *Political Power and Social Theory* 1: 67–113.

Ohmae, Kenichi (1990) *The Borderless World*, London: Collins.

Ohmae, Kenichi (1993) 'The rise of the region state', *Foreign Affairs* 72: 78–87.

Ohmae, Kenichi (1996) *The End of the Nation State: The Rise of Regional Economies*, New York: Free Press.

Öhrgaard, Jakob (1997) 'Less than supranational, more than intergovernmental: European political cooperation and the dynamics of intergovernmental integration', *Millennium* 26: 1–29.

Ojanen, Hanna (1998) *The Plurality of Truth*, Aldershot: Ashgate.

Olsen, Johan P. (1995) 'European challenges to the nation state', *ARENA Working Paper* 95/14, Oslo.

Olsen, Johan P. (1996) 'Europeanization and nation-state dynamics', in S. Gustavsson and L. Lewin (eds), *The Future of the Nation-State*, Stockholm: Nerenius & Santérus Publishers.

Olsen, Johan P. (1998) 'The new European experiment in political organization'. Paper presented at the conference on 'Samples of the Future', SCANCOR, Stanford University.

Oman, C. (1993) 'Globalization and regionalization in the 1980s and 1990s', *Development and International Cooperation* 9: 51–69.

Onuf, Nicholas (1989) *World of Our Making: Rules and Rule in Social Theory and International Relations*, Columbia, SC: University of South Carolina Press.

Onuf, Nicholas (1998a) *The Republican Legacy in International Thought*, Cambridge: Cambridge University Press.

Onuf, Nicholas (1998b) 'Constructivism: a user's manual', in Vendulka Kubalkova, Nicholas Onuf and Paul Kowert (eds), *International Relations in a Constructed World*, Armonk, NY: M.E. Sharpe.

Onuf, Peter S. and Onuf, Nicholas (1993) *Federal Union, Modern World: The Law of Nations in an Age of Revolutions 1776–1814*, Madison, NJ: Madison House Publishers.

Owen, David (1995) *Balkan Odyssey*, London: Victor Gollancz.

Paterson, William E. (1974) *The SPD and European Integration*, Glasgow: Glasgow University Press.

Paterson, William E. (1996) 'The German Christian Democrats', in J. Gaffney (ed.), *Political Parties and the European Union*, London: Routledge.

Pedler, Robin and Schaefer, Guenther (eds) (1996) *Shaping European Law and Policy: The Role of Committees and Comitology in the Political Process*, Maastricht: EIPA.

Pentland, Charles (1973) *International Theory and European Integration*, New York: Free Press.

Peters, Guy (1996) 'Agenda-setting in the European Union', in J. Richardson (ed.), *European Union: Power and Policy*, London: Routledge.

Petersmann, Ernst-Ulrich (1995) 'Proposals for a new constitution for the European Union: building blocks for a constitutional theory and constitutional law of the EU', *Common Market Law Review* 32: 1123–75.

Peterson, John (1995) 'Decision-making in the European Union: towards a framework for analysis', *Journal of European Public Policy* 2: 69–93.

Pierson, Paul (1993) 'When effect becomes cause: policy feedback and political change', *World Politics* 45: 595–628.

Pierson, Paul (1994) *Dismantling the Welfare State? Reagan, Thatcher and the Politics of Retrenchment*, New York: Cambridge University Press.

Pierson, Paul (1996) 'The path to European integration: a historical institutionalist analysis', *Comparative Political Studies* 29: 123–63.

Pijpers, Alfred (1990) *The Vicissitudes of European Political Cooperation. Towards a Realist*

Interpretation of the EC's Collective Diplomacy, 's-Gravenhage: Gegevenes Koninklijke Bibliothekk.

Pijpers, Alfred (1991) 'European political cooperation and the realist paradigm', in Martin Holland (ed.), *The Future of European Political Cooperation. Essays on Theory and Practice*, London: Macmillan.

Pinder, John (1991) *European Community: The Building of a Union*, Oxford: Oxford University Press.

Plender, Richard (1976) 'An incipient form of European citizenship', in F. Jacobs (ed.), *European Law and the Individual*, Amsterdam: North-Holland.

Plender, Richard (1988) *International Migration Law*, Dordrecht: Martinus Nijhoff.

Poiares Maduro, Miguel (1998) *We the Court: The European Court of Justice and the European Economic Constitution*, Oxford: Hart Publishing.

Pollack, Mark (1998) 'Constructivism, social psychology and élite attitude change: lessons from an exhausted research program'. Paper presented at the 11th International Conference of Europeanists.

Potter, Jonathan (1996) *Representing Reality: Discourse, Rhetoric and Social Construction*, London: Sage.

Preston, Christopher (1997) *Enlargement and Integration in the European Union*, New York: Routledge.

Preuß, Ulrich (1995) 'Citizenship and identity: aspects of a political theory of citizenship', in Vittorio Bufacchi, Dario Castiglione and Richard Bellamy (eds), *Democracy and Constitutional Culture in the Union of Europe*, London: Lothian.

Preuß, Ulrich (1996) 'The political meaning of constitutionalism', in Richard Bellamy (ed.), *Constitutionalism, Democracy and Sovereignty: American and European Perspectives*, Aldershot: Avebury Press.

Prosser, Tony (1982) 'Towards a critical theory of public law', *Journal of Law and Society* 9: 1–20.

Prosser, Tony (1993) 'Journey without maps', *Public Law* 1993: 346–57.

Publius (1986) 'Federalism and consociationalism: a symposium', *Publius* 15: special issue.

Publius (1996) 'Federalism and the European Union', *Publius* 26: special issue.

Rack, Reinhard (1996) 'Austria: has the federation become obsolete?', in Joachim Jens Hesse and Vincent Wright (eds), *Federalizing Europe? The Costs, Benefits and Preconditions of Federal Political Systems*, Oxford: Oxford University Press.

Radaelli, Claudio (1995) 'The role of knowledge in the policy process', *Journal of European Public Policy* 2: 159–83.

Ransom, Patrick (ed.) (1990) *Studies in Federal Planning*, London: Lothian.

Rawls, John (1993) *Political Liberalism*, New York: Columbia University Press.

Regelsberger, Elfriede (1997) 'The institutional setup and functioning of EPC/CFSP', in Elfriede Regelsberger, Philippe de Schoutheete de Tervarent and Wolfgang Wessels (eds), *Foreign Policy of the European Union. From EPC to CFSP and Beyond*, Boulder, CO: Lynne Rienner Publishers.

Regelsberger, Elfriede and Wessels, Wolfgang (1996) 'The CFSP institutions and procedures: a third way for the second pillar', *European Foreign Affairs Review* 1: 29–54.

Regelsberger, Elfriede, de Schoutheete de Tervarent, Philippe and Wessels, Wolfgang (eds) (1997) *Foreign Policy of the European Union. From EPC to CFSP and Beyond*, Boulder, CO: Lynne Rienner Publishers.

Renner, Karl (1918) *Das Selbstbesimmungsrecht der Nationen in besonderer Anwendung auf Oesterreich*, Vienna.

Renzsch, Wolfgang (1989) 'German federalism in historical perspective: federalism as a substitute for a national state', *Publius* 19: 17–34.

Richmond, Cathy (1997) 'Preserving the identity crisis: autonomy, system and sovereignty in European law', *Law and Philosophy* 16: 377–420.

Riker, William H. (1964) *Federalism: Origin, Operation, Significance*, Boston, MA: Little, Brown & Co.

Risse, Thomas (1997) *'Let's Talk!' Insights from the German Debate on Communicative Behaviour and International Relations*, Robert Schuman Centre, European University Institute, mimeo.

Risse, Thomas (1998) *Ideen, Institutionen und politische Kultur: Die Europäisierung nationaler Identitäten im Ländervergleich*, mimeo. Florence: European University Institute

Risse, Thomas (1999a) *'Let's Argue!' Persuasion and Deliberation in International Relations*, mimeo, Florence: European University Institute.

Risse, Thomas (1999b) 'Identitäten und Kommunikationsprozesse in der internationalen Politik – Sozial-konstruktivistische Perspektiven zum Wandel in der Außenpolitik', in Monika Medick-Krakau (ed.), *Außenpolitischer Wandel in theoretischer und vergleichender Perspektive – Die USA und die Bundesrepublik Deutschland. Festschrift zum 70. Geburtstag von Ernst-Otto Czempiel*, Baden-Baden: Nomos.

Risse, Thomas and Sikkink, Kathryn (1999) 'The socialization of international human rights norms into domestic practices: introduction', in Thomas Risse, Stephen C. Ropp and Kathryn Sikkink (eds), *The Power of Human Rights: International Norms and Domestic Change*, Cambridge: Cambridge University Press, pp. 1–38.

Risse, Thomas, Engelmann-Martin, Daniela, Knopf, Hans Joachim and Roscher, Klaus (1999) 'To euro or not to euro. The EMU and identity politics in the European Union', *European Journal of International Relations* 5(2): 147–87.

Risse, Thomas, Ropp, Stephen C. and Sikkink, Kathryn (eds) (1999) *The Power of Human Rights: International Norms and Domestic Change*, Cambridge: Cambridge University Press.

Risse, Thomas (2000) 'A Europeanization of nation-state identities?', in Maria Green Cowles, James Caporaso and Thomas Risse (eds), *Europeanization and Domestic Change*.

Risse-Kappen, Thomas (ed.) (1995a) *Bringing Transnational Relations Back In: Non-state Actors, Domestic Structures and International Institutions*, Cambridge: Cambridge University Press.

Risse-Kappen, Thomas (1995b) 'Democratic peace – warlike democracies? A social constructivist interpretation of the liberal argument', *European Journal of International Relations* 1: 491–517.

Risse-Kappen, Thomas (1996a) 'Collective identity in a democratic community: the case of NATO', in Peter Katzenstein (ed.), *The Culture of National Security: Norms and Identity in World Politics*, New York: Columbia University Press.

Risse-Kappen, Thomas (1996b) 'Exploring the nature of the beast: international relations theory and comparative policy analysis meet the European Union', *Journal of Common Market Studies* 34: 53–80.

Rittberger, Volker (1993) 'Nach der Vereinigung – Deutschlands Stellung in der Welt', in Hans-Hermann Hartwich and Goettrik Wewer (eds), *Regieren in der Bundesrepublik*, Opladen: Leske & Budrich.

Ritzer, George (1992) *Sociological Theory*, 3rd edn, New York: McGraw-Hill.

Robbins, Lionel (1939) *The Economic Causes of War*, London: Cape.

Robertson, R. (1992) *Globalization: Social Theory and Global Culture*, London: Sage.

Robertson, R. and Haque Khondker, H. (1997) 'Discourses of globalization: preliminary considerations', *International Sociology* 13: 25–40.

Rochester, Martin J. (1986) 'The rise and fall of international organizations as a field of study', *International Organization* 40: 778–813.

Roemheld, Lutz (1990) *Integral Federalism: A Model for Europe*, Frankfurt: Peter Lang.

Rogosch, Detlef (1996) *Vorstellungen von Europa. Europabilder in der SPD und der belgischen Sozialisten 1945–1957*, Hamburg: Kraemer.

Rometsch, Dietrich and Wessels, Wolfgang (eds) (1996) *The European Union and Member States: Towards Institutional Fusion?*, Manchester: Manchester University Press.

Rorty, Richard (1979) *Philosophy and the Mirror of Nature*, Princeton, NJ: Princeton University Press.

Rosamond, Ben (1995) 'Mapping the European condition: the theory of integration and the integration of theory', *European Journal of International Relations* 1: 391–408.

Rosamond, Ben (1999) 'Discourses of globalization and the social construction of European identities', *Journal of European Public Policy* 6(4): 652–68.

Roscher, Klaus (1998) *Arbeitsbericht zur Fallstudie Frankreich*, mimeo, Florence: European University Institute.

Rose, Charlie (1994) 'Democratic control of the armed forces. A parliamentary role in partnership for peace', *NATO Review* 42(5): 13–19.

Rosenfeld, Michel (1994) 'Modern constitutionalism as interplay between identity and diversity', in Michel Rosenfeld (ed.), *Constitutionalism, Identity, Difference and Legitimacy. Theoretical Perspectives*, Durham: Duke University Press.

Ross, George (1998) 'European integration and globalization', in R. Axtmann (ed.), *Globalization and Europe. Theoretical and Empirical Investigations*, London: Pinter.

Ruggie, John Gerard (1993) 'Territoriality and beyond: problematizing modernity in international relations', *International Organization* 47: 139–74.

Ruggie, John Gerard (1998) *Constructing the World Polity: Essays on International Institutionalization*, New York: Routledge.

Rummel, Reinhardt (ed.) (1990) *The Evolution of an International Actor. Western Europe's New Assertiveness*, Boulder, CO: Westview Press.

Rummel, Reinhardt (1996) 'Germany's role in the CFSP: "Normalität" or "Sonderweg"?', in Christopher Hill (ed.), *The Actors in Europe's Foreign Policy*, London: Routledge.

Saeter, Martin (1998) *Comprehensive Neofunctionalism*, Oslo: Norwegian Institute of International Affairs.

Sand, Inge-Johanne (1998a) 'Understanding the European Union/European economic area as systems of functionally different processes: economic, political, legal, administrative and cultural', in Peter Fitzpatrick and James Bergeron (eds), *Europe's Other: European Law Between Modernity and Postmodernity*, Aldershot: Ashgate.

Sand, Inge-Johanne (1998b) 'Understanding the new forms of governance: mutually interdependent, reflexive, destabilised and competing institutions', *European Law Journal* 4: 271–93.

Sandholtz, Wayne (1998) 'The emergence of a supranational telecommunications regime', in Wayne Sandholtz and Alec Stone Sweet (eds), *European Integration and Supranational Governance*, Oxford: Oxford University Press.

Sandholtz, Wayne and Stone Sweet, Alec (1998) 'European integration and supranational governance', in Wayne Sandholtz and Alec Stone Sweet (eds), *European Integration and Supranational Governance*, Oxford: Oxford University Press.

Sandholtz, Wayne and Zysman, John (1989) '1992: Recasting the European bargain', *World Politics* 42: 99–128.

Sauter, Wolf (1997) *Competition Law and Industrial Policy in the EU*, Oxford: Clarendon Press.

Sbragia, Alberta (1992) 'Thinking about the European future: the uses of comparison', in Alberta Sbragia (ed.), *Europolitics*, Washington, DC: Brookings Institution.

Schäffner, Christina *et al.* (1996) 'Diversity and unity in European debates', in Andreas Musolff *et al.* (eds), *Conceiving of Europe: Diversity in Unity*, Aldershot: Dartmouth.

Scharpf, Fritz W. (1988) 'The joint-decision trap: lessons from German federalism and European integration, *Public Administration* 66: 239–78.

Scharpf, Fritz W. (1994) 'Community and autonomy: multi-level policy-making in the European Union', *Journal of European Public Policy* 1: 219–42.

Schauer, Hans (1996) *Europäische Identität und demokratische Tradition*, München: Olzog.

Schepel, Harm (1998) 'Legal pluralism in the European Union', in Peter Fitzpatrick and James Bergeron (eds), *Europe's Other: European Law Between Modernity and Postmodernity*, Aldershot: Ashgate.

Scheuerman, William (1997) 'Constitutionalism and difference', *University of Toronto Law Journal* 47: 263–80.

Schimmelfennig, Frank (1994) 'Internationale Sozialisation neuer Staaten. Heuristische

Überlegungen zu einem Forschungsdesiderat', *Zeitschrift für Internationale Beziehungen* 1: 335–55.

Schimmelfennig, Frank (1998) 'The eastern enlargement of the European Union. A case for sociological institutionalism', in Joint Conference of the DVPW, OEGPW and SVPW 'Europe Between Integration and Exclusion', Vienna.

Schmidt, Vivien A. (n.d.) *The European Nation State between Globalization and Integration: The Decline of National Sovereignty?*, University of Massachusetts, mimeo.

Schmidt, Vivien A. (1996) *From State to Market? The Transformation of French Business and Government*, Cambridge: Cambridge University Press.

Schmidt, Vivien A. (1997) 'A new Europe for the old?', *Daedalus* 126: 167–97.

Schmitter, Philippe (1991) *The European Community as a New and Novel Form of Political Domination, Estudio/Working Paper No. 91/28*, Madrid: Juan March Institute.

Schmitter, Philippe (1996) 'Imagining the future of the Euro-polity with the help of new concepts', in Gary Marks *et al.* (eds), *Governance in the European Union*, London: Sage.

Schmitter, Philippe (2000) 'Democracy and Constitutionalism in the European Union', *ECSA Review*, 13(2): 2–4.

Schmitz, Kurt Thomas (1978) *Deutsche Einheit und Europaeische Integration. Der sozialdemokratische Beitrag zur Aussenpolitik der BRD unter besonderer Beruecksichtigung des programmatischen Wandels einer Oppositionspartei*, Bonn-Bad Godesberg: Verlag Neue Gesellschaft.

Schmitz, Petra L. and Geserick, Rolf (1996) *Die Anderen in Europa. Nationale Selbst- und Fremdbilder im europäischen Integrationsprozeß*, Bonn: Europa-Union.

Scholte, Jan Aart (1996) 'Beyond the buzzword: towards a critical theory of globalization', in E. Kofman and G. Youngs (eds), *Globalization: Theory and Practice*, London: Pinter.

Schuman, Robert (1994) [1952] 'The Schuman declaration', in Brent F. Nelson and Alexander C.-G. Stubb (eds), *The European Union: Readings on the Theory and Practice of European Integration*, Boulder, CO: Lynne Rienner.

Schutz, Alfred (1962) *Collected Papers*, I, edited by Maurice Natanson, The Hague: Martinus Nijhoff Publishers.

Schutz, Alfred (1972) [1932] *The Phenomenology of the Social World*, London: Heinemann.

Schwartz, Hans-Peter (1966) *Vom Reich zur Bundesrepublik. Deutschland im Widerstreit der aussenpolitischen Konzeptionen in den Jahren der Besatzungsherrschaft 1945 bis 1949*, Neuwied: Luchterhand.

Scott, Joanne (1998) 'Law, legitimacy and EC governance: prospects for "Partnership"', *Journal of Common Market Studies* 36: 175–94.

Searle, J.R. (1969) *Speech Acts*, Cambridge: Cambridge University Press.

Searle, John R. (1969) *Speech Acts: An Essay in the Philosophy of Language*, Cambridge: Cambridge University Press.

Searle, John R. (1977) 'Reiterating the differences', *Glyph 1*: 198–208.

Searle, John R. (1995) *The Construction of Social Reality*, New York: The Free Press.

Sedelmeier, Ulrich (1998) 'The European Union's association policy towards the countries of central and eastern Europe: collective EU identity and policy paradigms in a composite policy', unpublished Ph.D. dissertation, University of Sussex.

Sedelmeier, Ulrich (2000) 'East of A'dam: the Amsterdam Treaty's implications for eastern enlargement', in Karlheinz Neunreither and Antje Wiener (eds), *European Integration After Amsterdam: Institutional Dynamics and Prospects for Democracy*, Oxford: Oxford University Press.

Shapiro, Martin (1980) 'Comparative law and comparative politics', *Southern California Law Review* 53: 537–42.

Shapiro, Martin and Stone, Alec (1994) 'The new constitutional politics of Europe', *Comparative Political Studies* 26: 397–420.

Shaw, Jo (1995) 'Introduction', in Jo Shaw and Gillian More (eds), *New Legal Dynamics of European Union*, Oxford: Oxford University Press.

Shaw, Jo (1996) 'European Union legal studies in crisis? Towards a new dynamic', *Oxford Journal of Legal Studies* 16: 231–53.

Shaw, Jo (1997) 'Socio-legal studies and the European Union', in Philip Thomas (ed.), *Socio-Legal Studies*, Aldershot: Dartmouth.

Shaw, Jo and More, Gillian (1995) *New Legal Dynamics of European Union*, Oxford: Oxford University Press.

Shields, James (1996) 'The French Gaullists. In political parties and the European Union', in J. Gaffney (ed.), *Political Parties and the European Union*, London: Routledge.

Sinnott, Richard (1994) *Integration Theory: Subsidiarity and the Internationalisation of Issues: The Implication for Legitimacy, EUI Working Paper RSC No. 9 4/13*, Florence: European University Institute.

Sjolander, Claire T. (1996) 'The rhetoric of globalization: what's in a wor(l)d?', *International Journal* 51: 601–16.

Skocpol, Theda (1992) *Protecting Soldiers and Mothers. The Political Origins of Social Policy in the United States*, Cambridge: Belknap Press.

Slaughter, Anne-Marie (1995) 'International law in a world of liberal states', *European Journal of International Law* 6: 503–38.

Slaughter, Anne-Marie (1997) 'The real new world order', *Foreign Affairs* 76: 183–97.

Sloan, Stanley (1994) 'Transatlantic relations in the wake of the Brussels Summit', *NATO Review* 42(2): 27–31.

Sloan, S. (1995) 'US perspectives on NATO's future', *International Affairs* 71(2): 217–46.

Smith, Anthony D. (1992) 'National identity and the idea of European unity', *International Affairs* 68: 55–76.

Smith, Anthony D. (1993) 'A Europe of nations – or the nation of Europe?', *Journal of Peace Research* 30: 129–35.

Smith, Steve (1995) 'The self-images of a discipline: a genealogy of international relations theory', in Ken Booth and Steve Smith (eds), *International Relations Theory Today*, Cambridge: Polity Press, pp. 1–37.

Smith, Steve (1996) 'Positivism and beyond', in Steve Smith, Ken Booth and Marysia Zalewski (eds), *International Theory: Positivism and Beyond*, Cambridge: Cambridge University Press, pp. 11–44.

Smith, Steve (1997) 'New approaches to international theory', in John Baylis and Steve Smith (eds), *The Globalization of World Politics*, Oxford: Oxford University Press, pp. 165–90.

Smith, Steve (1999) 'Social constructivism and European studies: a reflectivist critique', *Journal of European Public Policy* 6(4): 682–91.

Smith, Steve (2001) 'International theory and European integration', in Morten Kelstrup and Mike Williams (eds), *IR Theory and the Politics of European Integration*, London: Routledge.

Snyder, Francis (1990) *New Directions in European Community Law*, London: Weidenfeld & Nicolson.

Snyder, Francis (1998) 'Constitutional law of the European Union', in Academy of European Law (ed.), *Collected Courses of the Academy of European Law, Volume VI, Book I*, The Hague: Martinus Nijhoff.

Solesby, T. (1978) 'Helsinki to Belgrade – and beyond', *NATO Review* 26(3): 16–22.

Somsen, Han (1995) 'Subsidiarity and the enforcement of EC environmental law'. Paper prepared for the EUI Conference on 'Subsidiarity and Shared Responsibilities: New Challenges for EU Environmental Studies', Florence.

Soysal, Yasemin (1994) *Limits of Citizenship: Migrants and Postnational Membership in Europe*, Chicago: University of Chicago Press.

Spinelli, Alterio (1966) *The Eurocrats*, Baltimore: Johns Hopkins University Press.

Stankevicius, Ceslovas (1996) 'NATO enlargement and the indivisibility of security in Europe: a view from Lithuania', *NATO Review* 44(5): 21–5.

Stein, Eric (1981) 'Lawyers, judges, and the making of a transnational constitution', *American Journal of International Law* 75: 1–27.

Stein, Janice (1994) 'Political learning by doing: Gorbachev as uncommitted thinker and motivated learner', *International Organization* 48: 155–83.

Stern, David (1996) 'The availability of Wittgenstein's philosophy', in Hans Sluga and David Stern (eds), *The Cambridge Companion to Wittgenstein*, Cambridge: Cambridge University Press.

Stone Sweet, Alec and Sandholtz, Wayne (1997) 'European integration and supranational governance', *Journal of European Public Policy* 4: 297–317.

Strange, Susan (1998) 'Who are EU? Ambiguities in the concept of competitiveness', *Journal of Common Market Studies* 36: 101–14.

Stubb, Alexander C.-G. (1996) 'A categorization of differentiated integration', *Journal of Common Market Studies* 34: 283–95.

Sturua, Melor (1994) 'Every president needs a devil's advocate', *Izvestia,* 12 January. Reprinted in 'Military alliances', *Current Digest of the Post-Soviet Press* 66(2): 31.

Suchocka, Hanna (1993) 'Poland's European perspective', *NATO Review* 41(3): 3–6.

Surel, Yves (2000) 'The role of cognitive and normative frames in policy-making', *Journal of European Public Policy,* 7(4): 495–512.

Taylor, Charles (1978) 'Interpretation and the sciences of man', in Roger Beehler and Alan R. Drengson (eds), *The Philosophy of Society*, London: Methuen.

Taylor, Paul (1990) 'Consociationalism and federalism as approaches to international integration', in A.J.R. Groom and Paul Taylor (eds), *Frameworks for International Cooperation*, New York: St Martin's Press.

Taylor, Paul (1996) *The European Union in the 1990s*, Oxford: Oxford University Press.

Taylor, Trevor (1991) 'NATO and central Europe', *NATO Review* 39(5): 17–22.

TEU (1992) *Treaty on European Union*, Luxembourg: Office for the Official Publications of the European Communities.

Teubner, Gunther (1989) 'How the law thinks: toward a constructivist epistemology of law', *Law and Society Review* 23: 729–57.

Teubner, Gunther (1997a) '"Global Bukowina": legal pluralism in the world society', in Günther Teubner (ed.), *Global Law Without a State*, Aldershot: Dartmouth.

Teubner, Gunther (1997b) 'Foreword: Legal regimes of global non-state actors', in Günther Teubner (ed.), *Global Law Without a State*, Aldershot: Dartmouth.

Thatcher, Margaret (1993) 'Speech of 7 June 1993', *The Parliamentary Debates*, House of Lords, Vol. 546.

Thelen, Kathleen and Steinmo, Sven (1992) 'Historical institutionalism in comparative politics', in Kathleen Thelen, Frank Longstreth and Sven Steinmo (eds), *Structuring Politics – Historical Institutionalism in Comparative Analysis*, Cambridge: Cambridge University Press.

Thompson, Helen (1997) 'The nation-state and international capital in historical perspective', *Government and Opposition* 24: 84-113.

Thompson, John B. (1989) 'The theory of structuration', in David Held and John B. Thompson (eds), *Social Theory of Modern Societies: Anthony Giddens and His Critics*, Cambridge: Cambridge University Press.

Thurow, L. (1994) *Head to Head*, London: Nicholas Brealey.

Tilly, Charles (1975) 'Reflections on the history of European state-making', in Charles Tilly (ed.), *The Formation of National States in Western Europe*, Princeton: Princeton University Press.

Tonra, Ben (1997) 'The impact of political cooperation', in Knud Erik Jørgensen (ed.), *Reflective Approaches to European Governance*, Basingstoke: Macmillan.

Toulmin, Stephen (1972) *Human Understanding*, Princeton: Princeton University Press.

Tsoukalis, Loukas (1997) *The New European Economy Revisited*, Oxford: Oxford University Press.

Tsoukalis, Loukas and Rhodes, Martin (1997) 'Economic integration and the nation-state', in Martin Rhodes, Paul Heywood and Vincent Wright (eds), *Developments in West European Politics*, Basingstoke: Macmillan.

Tully, James (1995) *Strange Multiplicity. Constitutionalism in an Age of Diversity*, Cambridge: Cambridge University Press.

Turner, John C. (1987) *Rediscovering the Social Group. A Self-categorization Theory*, Oxford: Oxford University Press.

Ulbert, Cornelia (1997) *Die Konstruktion von Umwelt. Der Einfluss von Ideen, Institutionen und Kultur auf (inter-)nationale Klimapolitik in den USA und der Bundesrepublik*, Baden-Baden: Nomos.

Uterwedde, Henrik (1988) *Die Wirtschaftspolitik der Linken in Frankreich. Programme und Praxis 1984–87*, Frankfurt aM: Campus.

van Kersbergen, Kees and Verbeek, Bertjan (1994) 'The politics of subsidiarity in the European Union', *Journal of Common Market Studies* 32: 215–36.

Verdun, Amy (1996) *EMU – The Product of Policy Learning and Consensus Among Monetary Experts (European Public Policy Occasional Paper No. 7)*, Colchester: Human Capital and Mobility Network, University of Essex.

Verney, Douglas V. (1993) 'Are all federations federal? The United States, Canada and India'. Paper presented at the conference on 'Federalism in Diverse Societies', at the Center for the Advanced Study of India, University of Pennsylvania.

Voigt, Karsten (1996) 'NATO enlargement: sustaining the momentum', *NATO Review* 44(2): 15–19.

Voigt, Klaus (1986) 'Ideas of German exiles on the postwar order in Europe', in W. Lipgens (ed.), *Documents on the History of European Integration*, Vol. 2, Berlin: Walter de Gruyter.

von Krosigk, Friedrich (1971) 'A reconsideration of federalism in the scope of the present discussion on European integration', *Journal of Common Market Studies* 9: 197–223.

von Seydel, Max (1872) 'Der Bundesstaatsbegriff', *Tübinger Zeitschrift für die gesammte Staatswissenschaft*, reprinted in Seydel's *Staatsrechtliche und politische Abhandlungen*, 1893.

Wade, R. (1996) 'Globalization and its limits: reports of the death of the national economy are greatly exaggerated', in S. Berger and R. Dore (eds), *National Diversity and Global Capitalism*, Ithaca, NY: Cornell University Press.

Wæver, Ole (1990) 'Three competing Europes: German, French, Russian', *International Affairs* 66: 477–93.

Wæver, Ole (1994) 'Resisting the temptation of post foreign policy analysis', in Walter Carlsnaes and Steve Smith (eds), *European Foreign Policy: The EC and Changing Perspectives in Europe*, London: Sage.

Wæver, Ole (1995) 'Securitization and desecuritization', in Ronnie D. Lipschutz (ed.), *On Security*, New York: Columbia University Press, pp. 46–86.

Wæver, Ole (1996) 'European security identities', *Journal of Common Market Studies* 34: 103–32.

Wæver, Ole (1997a) 'Figures of international thought: introducing persons instead of paradigms', in Iver B. Neumann and Ole Wæver (eds), *The Future of International Relations*, London: Routledge, pp. 1–37.

Wæver, Ole (1997b) *Discourse as Foreign Policy Theory: The Case of Germany and Europe*, mimeo.

Wæver, Ole (1998) 'Explaining Europe by decoding discourses', in Anders Wivel (ed.), *Explaining European Integration*, Copenhagen: Copenhagen Political Studies Press, pp. 100–46.

Wæver, Ole and Kelstrup, Morten (1993) 'Europe and its nations: political and cultural identities', in Ole Wæver, Barry Buzan, Morten Kelstrup and Pierre Lemaitre (eds), *Identity, Migration and the New Security Agenda in Europe*, London: Pinter.

Wæver, Ole et al. (1993) *The Struggle for 'Europe': French and German Concepts of State, Nation, and European Union*, mimeo.

Waitz, Georg (1853) *Das Wesen des Bundesstaates. Allgemeine Montatsschrift für Wissenschaft und Literatur*, reprinted in Georg Waitz, *Grundzüge der Politik*, 1862.

Walker, Neil (1996) 'European constitutionalism and European integration', *Public Law* 1996: 266–90.

Walker, Neil (1998) 'Sovereignty and differentiated integration in the European Union', *European Law Journal* 4: 355–88.

Wallace, Helen (1996) 'Politics and policy in the EU: the challenge of governance', in Helen Wallace and William Wallace (eds), *Policy-making in the European Union*, Oxford: Oxford University Press.

Wallace, Helen (2000) 'Flexibility: a tool of integration or a restraint on disintegration?', in Karl-Heinz Neunreither and Antje Wiener (eds), *European Integration after Amsterdam*, Oxford: Oxford University Press.

Wallace, Helen and Wallace, William (eds) (1996) *Policy-making in the European Union*, Oxford: Oxford University Press.

Wallace, William (1982) 'Europe as a confederation: the Community and the nation-state', *Journal of Common Market Studies* 21: 57–68.

Wallace, William (1990) 'Introduction: The dynamics of European integration', in William Wallace (ed.), *The Dynamics of European Integration*, London: Pinter/RIIA.

Wallace, William (1991) 'Foreign policy and national identity in the United Kingdom', *International Affairs* 67: 65–80.

Wallace, William (1992) 'British foreign policy after the Cold War', *International Affairs* 68: 423–42.

Wallace, William (1994) 'The British approach to Europe', in W.J. Mommsen (ed.), *The Long Way to Europe – Historical Observations from a Contemporary View*, Berlin: Edition Q, Inc.

Wallace, William (1999) 'An architecture for the new Europe', *Review of International Studies* (special issue) 25.

Walt, Stephen (1998) 'International relations: one world, many theories', *Foreign Policy* 110: 29–46.

Waltz, Kenneth N. (1979) *Theory of International Politics*, New York: McGraw-Hill.

Ward, Ian (1995) 'Identity and difference: the European Union and postmodernism', in J. Shaw and G. More (eds), *New Legal Dynamics of European Union*, Oxford: Clarendon Press.

Ward, Ian (1996) *The Margins of European Law*, London: Macmillan.

Ward, Ian (1997) 'Law and the other Europeans', *Journal of Common Market Studies* 35: 79–96.

Weale, Albert and Nentwich, Michael (eds) (1998) *Political Theory and the European Union. Legitimacy, Constitutional Choice and Citizenship*, London: Routledge.

Weber, Steven (1994) 'Origins of the European Bank for Reconstruction and Development', *International Organization* 48: 1–38.

Weiler, Joseph (1986) 'Supranationalism revisited – a retroactive: the European Communities after thirty years', in Werner Maihofer (ed.), *Noi si mura*, Florence: European University Institute.

Weiler, Joseph (1991) 'The transformation of Europe', *The Yale Law Journal* 100: 2410–31.

Weiler, Joseph (1995) 'Does Europe need a constitution? Demos, telos and the German Maastricht decision', *European Law Journal* 1: 219–58.

Weiler, Joseph (1996) 'European neo-constitutionalism: in search of foundations for the European constitutional order', in Richard Bellamy and Dario Castiglione (eds), *Constitutionalism in Transformation: European and Theoretical Perspectives*, Oxford: Blackwell.

Weiler, Joseph (1997) 'The reformation of European constitutionalism', *Journal of Common Market Studies* 35: 97–131.

Weiler, Joseph (1998a) 'Bread and circus: the state of the European Union', *Columbia Journal of European Law* 4: 223–48.

Weiler, Joseph (1998b) 'Ideals and idolatry in the European construct', in Bill McSweeney (ed.), *Moral Issues in International Affairs: Problems of European Integration*, Basingstoke: Macmillan, pp. 55–82.

Weldes, Jutta (1996) 'Constructing national interests', *European Journal of International Relations* 2: 275–318.

Wendt, Alexander (1987) 'The agent-structure problem in international relations theory', *International Organization* 41: 335–70.

Wendt, Alexander (1991) 'Bridging the theory/meta-theory gap in international relations', *Review of International Studies* 17: 383–92.

Wendt, Alexander (1992) 'Anarchy is what states make of it: the social construction of power politics', *International Organization* 46: 391–407.

Wendt, Alexander (1994) 'Collective identity formation and the international state', *American Political Science Review* 88: 384–96.

Wendt, Alexander (1999) *Social Theory of International Politics*, Cambridge: CUP.

Wendt, Alexander and Duvall, Raymond (1989) 'Institutions and international order', in Ernst-Otto Czempiel and James N. Rosenau (eds), *Global Changes and Theoretical Challenges: Approaches to World Politics in the 1990s*, Lexington: Lexington Books.

Wendt, Henry (1993) *Global Embrace: Corporate Challenges in a Transnational World*, New York: Harper Business.

Wessels, Wolfgang (1982) 'European political cooperation: a new approach to European foreign policy', in David Allen, Reinhardt Rummel and Wolfgang Wessels (eds), *European Political Cooperation: Towards a Foreign Policy for Western Europe*, London: Butterworth.

Wessels, Wolfgang (1996) 'Verwaltung im EG-Mehrebenensystem: Auf dem Weg zur Megabürokratie?', in Markus Jachtenfuchs and Beate Kohler-Koch (eds), *Europäische Integration*, Opladen: Leske & Budrich, pp. 165–92.

Wessels, Wolfgang (1998) 'Comitology: fusion in action. Politico-administrative trends in the EU system', *Journal of European Public Policy* 5: 209–34.

Wheare, Kenneth C. (1964) *Federal Government*, New York: Oxford University Press.

Wiener, Antje (1997) 'Addressing the constructive potential of Union citizenship – a socio-historical perspective', *European Integration Online Papers* 1: 17.

Wiener, Antje (1998) *'European' Citizenship Practice – Building Institutions of a Non-state*. Boulder, CO: Westview Press.

Wiener, Antje (1998b) 'The embedded *acquis communautaire*. Transmission belt and prism of new governance', *European Law Journal* 4: 294–315.

Wilke, Marc and Wallace, Helen (1990) *Subsidiarity: Approaches to Power-sharing in the European Community*, London: Chatham House.

Willis, F. Roy (1968) *France, Germany, and the New Europe 1945–1967*, London: Oxford University Press.

Wincott, Daniel (1995) 'Institutional interaction and European integration: towards an everyday critique of liberal intergovernmentalism', *Journal of Common Market Studies*, 33: 597–609.

Wind, Marlene (1997) 'Rediscovering institutions: a reflectivist critique of rational institutionalism', in Knud Erik Jørgensen (ed.), *Reflective Approaches to European Governance*, Basingstoke: Macmillan, pp. 15–35.

Wind, Marlene (1998) 'Flexible integration: the European Union as a polycentric polity?'. Paper presented at the conference on 'Rethinking Constitutionalism in the European Union' (mimeo).

Wistrich, Ernest (1991) *After 1992: The United States of Europe*, London: Routledge.

Witte, Bruno de (1987) 'Building Europe's image and identity', in A. Rijksbaron *et al.* (eds), *Europe from a Cultural Perspective*, The Hague: UPR.

Wyatt-Walter, Andrew (1998) 'Globalization, corporate identity and European Union technology policy', in W.D. Coleman and G.R.D. Underhill (eds), *Regionalism and Global Economic Integration: Europe, Asia, the Americas*, London: Routledge.

Zehfuß, Maja ((1998) 'Sprachlosigkeit schränkt ein: Zur Bedeutung von Sprache in konstruktivistischen Theorien', *Zeitschrift für Internationale Beziehungen* 5: 109–37.

Zehfuß, Maja ((2001) 'Constructivisms in international relations: Wendt, Onuf and Kratochwil', in Karin M. Fierke and Knud Erik Jørgensen (eds) *Constructing International Relations: The Next Generation*, Armonk, NY: M.E. Sharpe.

Zelikow, Philip and Rice, Condoleezza (1995) *Germany Unified and Europe Transformed. A Study in Statecraft*, Cambridge, MA: Harvard University Press.

Zellentin, Gerda (1992) 'Der Funktionalismus – eine Strategie gesamteuropäischer

Integration?', in Michael Kreile (ed.), *Die Integration Europas*, Opladen: Westdeutscher Verlag, pp. 62–77.

Zimbardo, Philip and Leippe, Michael (1991) *The Psychology of Attitude Change and Social Influence*, New York: McGraw-Hill.

Zürn, Michael (1997) 'Assessing state preferences and explaining institutional choice: the case of intra-German trade', *International Studies Quarterly* 41: 295–320.

Notes on Contributors

Jeffrey T. Checkel is Research Professor of International Politics at ARENA, Advanced Research on the Europeanization of the Nation State, University of Oslo, Norway.

Thomas Christiansen is Jean Monnet Lecturer in European Studies in the Department of International Politics at the University of Wales, Aberystwyth, UK.

Thomas Diez is lecturer in the Department of Political Science and International Studies at the University of Birmingham, UK.

Daniela Engelmann-Martin is a researcher in the Department of Social and Political Sciences, European University Institute, Florence, Italy.

Karen Fierke is lecturer in the School of Politics at the Queen's University of Belfast, Belfast, UK.

Kenneth Glarbo is an official at the Danish Ministry of Research, Copenhagen, Denmark.

Ernst B. Haas is Robson Research Professor Emeritus at the University of California, Berkeley, USA.

Knud Erik Jørgensen is Associate Professor and Jean Monnet Chair in the Department of Political Science at the University of Aarhus, Denmark.

Hans Joachim Knopf is a researcher in the Department of Social and Political Sciences, European University Institute, Florence, Italy.

Rey Koslowski is Assistant Professor of International Relations at Rutgers University–Newark, New Jersey, USA.

Martin Marcussen is Assistant Professor in the Institute of Political Science, University of Copenhagen, Denmark.

Andrew Moravcsik is Professor of Government at the Center for European Studies, Harvard University, Cambridge, MA, USA.

Thomas Risse is Professor of International Relations, Department of Social and Political Sciences, European University Institute, Florence, Italy.

Ben Rosamond is a research fellow at the Centre for the Study of Globalization and Regionalization, University of Warwick, Coventry, UK.

Klaus Roscher is a researcher in the Department of Social and Political Sciences, European University Institute, Florence, Italy.

Jo Shaw is Professor of Law and Director of the Centre for the Study of Law in Europe, Department of Law, University of Leeds, UK.

Steve Smith is Professor in the Department of International Politics and Pro-Vice Chancellor of the University of Wales, Aberystwyth, UK.

Antje Wiener is Reader and Jean Monnet Chair (Politics) in the Institute of European Studies at the Queen's University of Belfast, Belfast, UK.

Index